# THE LOST ART OF THINKING

*How to Improve Emotional Intelligence and Achieve Peak Mental Performance*

*Second Printing*

*Neil Nedley, M.D.*

Nedley Publishing
info@drnedley.com
1-888-778-4445

ISBN: 978-0-9661979-2-1

**Caution:** this book does not establish a doctor-patient relationship with the reader or anyone who uses material found in this book. Persons who wish to change their lifestyle should do so under the direction of a licensed physician familiar with the effects of lifestyle change on health.

Library of Congress Catalog Number 2010936734

Nedley, Neil.

The Lost Art of Thinking: How to Improve Emotional Intelligence and Achieve Peak Mental Performance / Neil Nedley, — 1st ed.

p. em.

Includes bibliographical references and index.

ISBN: 978-0-9661979-2-1

1. Cognitive Behavioral Therapy. 2. Emotional Intelligence. 3. Cognitive Function. 4. Critical Thinking. 5. Mental Health. 6. Self-Help. 7. Psychology. 8. Nutrition 9. Health. 10. Health Promotion. 11. Self-care, health. 12. Mental Health.

I. Title

# Dedication

## *For my sons.*

All four of my boys have taught me many lessons in emotional intelligence (E.Q.) and many additional lessons in how E.Q. is best taught. As a young father, somehow I thought that since I was living a principled, self-sacrificing life, that my children would automatically see the results and choose to live this same type of life; that how-to-live would become a "no-brainer" to them. How wrong I was! It confused me when my boys would make deceptive or self-centered choices, believing that these choices would give them an advantage in overall happiness and life satisfaction.

Yes, teaching by example is important, but a violin instructor does much more than say, "Watch me play the violin." A tennis instructor does not say, "Just come and watch how I play tennis!" In a similar manner, emotional intelligence must also be taught. And even when it is taught and exemplified, there is no guarantee that a high E.Q. will be the automatic result. Like any skill, a willingness to learn and practice is needed before exceptional emotional intelligence is achieved. To the extent that my sons have demonstrated this teachable determination in their lives, they have experienced true happiness and success.

**Joel Charlton Nedley**, our firstborn son, was born almost six years after Erica and I were married, when we were just shy of turning 30. Erica learned about the effects of good music on the developing fetus and (unlike her subsequent children) consistently played classical music to Joel while still in the womb. Joel is very musically gifted and possesses perfect pitch. Although he has rarely practiced his musical instruments (violin and piano) for more than 45 minutes a day, he has still won various awards, such as the Oklahoma Music Olympics, and has released or co-released 3 music CDs. He is an instrument rated pilot with complex and high performance aircraft ratings, skier, snowboarder, and an engaging public speaker. He enjoys tennis, baseball, and working out regularly. He is in college and currently plans to become a physical therapist with an emphasis in sports medicine.

**Allen Lloyd Nedley**, was born 17 months after Joel. He carries my middle name and my father's name. In many ways, Allen owns my father's personality. He has a zest and joy for learning, particularly in science, math, and especially engineering. He loves to design anything utilizing computer assisted design software. Also, like my father, he has a broad smile that he frequently displays, and has a genuine care, compassion, and love for people.

He also enjoys the outdoors, especially backpacking in the mountains and mountain biking. He is an accomplished violist, skateboarder, snowboarder, unicyclist, and has his fixed wing private pilot license. Currently, he has a desire to become a helicopter pilot, and an orthopedic surgeon who also designs orthopedic instruments and joints.

**Nathan Eric Nedley**, at the time of this writing, is about to enter high school. Nathan has a quiet and relaxed demeanor, but is very friendly and engaging as well. He likes to spend time with people and participate in social events, and makes friends easily. In addition to being a dedicated, straight-A student, he is a fine tennis player and enjoys learning new tricks on his scooter. He is becoming an accomplished cellist, snowboarder, and unicyclist. Because of his cheerful helpfulness around the house, we are privileged to still have him at home. His desire at this time is to become a doctor or teacher, or both.

**Justin Neil Nedley** is "Justin other Nedley boy!" After having three boys, I had a strong desire for a daughter, but as it has turned out, I would not trade him, or any of my sons, for any young girl in the world. Justin has a warm, friendly, and inquisitive personality and often wears his blue-eyed smile. He relates well to people of all ages and can keep even adults spellbound for hours. Although at this writing he is only 7 years old, he cares for his younger cousins (ages 4 and 2) like an experienced baby sitter - being very protective of them, and keeping them happy and entertained. Justin is already becoming an accomplished pianist and tennis player, understands Romanian (learned from his Romanian grandparents), and wants to be a doctor when he grows up.

A word directly to my boys: This book was written not only for others, but also for you, my cherished sons. Although I could've said many more positive things about each of you (and also revealed some weaknesses) my desire is not to parade you to a curious public. My desire is for each of you to learn and practice the principles in this book to develop a higher E.Q. and attain peak mental performance. (By the way, despite what is written above, it's alright for you to change your mind on what you want to be, as long as you employ the principles of decision-making outlined in chapter 21.) Thank you for touching my life and (sometimes in challenging ways) teaching me lessons in E.Q. You've shown me that emotional intelligence is a skill that is learned, and thus can be greatly improved. You each hold a special place in my heart and I look forward to seeing how we will continue to grow as individuals and as a family. Consistently practice the principles of *The Lost Art of Thinking* throughout your life and you will be assured the highest levels of success and happiness. May you always follow after God's heart!

Dad

# Acknowledgements

## *My gratitude and thanks to:*

**Cari Haus**, who helped put my spoken concepts into written English. Cari moved to Oklahoma, with her husband David, for two years to help write the book. Cari was primarily responsible for compiling the references and assisted in the graphical layout. She helped to simplify many of the concepts in the book. Cari has been patient and helpful throughout the process of getting *The Lost Art of Thinking* to production.

**David Haus**, who assisted in compiling information for some of the figures and references. David always exhibits a quiet, friendly personality.

**Trisha Heddlesten**, who I learned about from her mother, a dear patient of mine, Patti Dean. Trisha helped to bring more clarity to the concepts contained in this book and make it more readable. Her careful, sharp, analytical mind, along with her desire to help and teach others, is a blessing.

**Daniel Pedley** for designing and graphically laying out this book. Daniel not only is a great artist, but also is very easy and enjoyable to work with.

**Eddie Ramirez, M.D.** who created the index, helped with the nutrition section, and offered his computer and network expertise.

**Don Mackintosh, R.N. M.Div.** who helped with some of the ancient spiritual concepts of peak mental performance illustrated in this book. Don is a great life and spiritual counselor with tremendous insight, although his very high I.Q. is often shrouded by his hilarious comedian-like personality.

**David DeRose, M.D.** who helped with the important research on toxins and mental performance. Dr. DeRose knows how to do a medical literature search and how to separate scientific truth from scientific fiction.

**Paula Reiter**, who is always encouraging me to disseminate useful health information to the general public. Paula is director of the *Nedley Depression Recovery Program* and has been seeking a more complete resource on emotional intelligence for the program. If it were not for her encouragement for me to provide this comprehensive resource, I might have prioritized my time differently. She was also instrumental in editing the content with an international perspective.

**Kelly Dulac**, clinical psychologist for the 10-day residential *Nedley Depression Recovery Program*, who helped with some of the important mental health principles of freedom demonstrated in this book. Kelly has an uncanny ability to identify the primary cognitive distortion impairing a person's life.

**Paula Wolfe** for once again offering her sharp eyes to be the last to proof before going to press. Paula has been a friend for many years, and is always enjoyable to be around. It is her critiques that I have appreciated most in our friendship.

**Jill Siebold**, whose keen eye for layout greatly improved the visual aspect of the book. Jill also helped compile extensive data for the figures and assisted in developing the index.

**Eddie Hernandez**, **Kerri Hitt**, **David Daum**, **Nancy Rexinger** and many others who contributed in various ways to the initiation and completion of the book.

**My patients**, who not only "put up with" my coverage while I was writing the book, but who were also on my mind as I wrote many sections of the book. Although their names do not appear in the book, they helped provide some of the true examples cited in the book. Furthermore, this book is written for any patient to read, to learn, and to apply these brain-enhancing principles towards a healthier, happier life.

**My students and lecture audiences**, who demanded the book. The book was conceived from their requests for written material to take home.

My late father and mother, **Lloyd and Orvetta Nedley**, who taught me many of the principles contained in this book, even though the scientific world had not yet validated all of them. If it were not for their respect for truth and love, I don't know where I would be today; but I know at best, my happiness and success would be a small fraction of what I have.

My four sons, **Joel, Allen, Nathan and Justin**, who willingly sacrificed time with their father, so the message of this book could reach the world. Please read more about them in the dedication.

Last, but certainly not least, my lovely wife, **Erica**, who made sure I remained focused during time dedicated to working on the book. In addition, she willingly stepped in to coordinate all aspects of producing the book. This book would still not be published if it were not for her diligence. To read more about her, see the chapter entitled, "Making Smarter Choices."

# Contents

## SECTION 2: HOW LIFESTYLE AFFECTS YOUR BRAIN



## SECTION 3: PULLING IT ALL TOGETHER



## APPENDIX

# About the Author

Neil Nedley, M.D., is a practicing physician in Internal Medicine with emphases in Gastroenterology, Mental Health, Lifestyle Medicine, and the difficult-to-diagnose patient.

He regularly provides continuing medical education courses to physicians and health professionals around the world. He also gives frequent health and mental health education seminars to general public audiences worldwide. One of his favorite hobbies is keeping up with the latest medical, nutrition and lifestyle, and mental health research.

Because Major Depression has become so commonly seen in internal medicine practices, Dr. Nedley spent considerable time in medical university libraries researching causes as well as treatments of this debilitating condition. The results of this research brought about the *Nedley Depression Recovery Program* that is highly effective in treating both depression and anxiety. He now runs a comprehensive residential treatment program for those with treatment resistant depression and/or anxiety which, to date, has produced an unprecedented 98 percent response rate in attendees. An originally unintended consequence of this program is that the average attendee comes with a below average emotional intelligence and leaves 10 days later with an emotional intelligence that is in the top 10 percentile. Not only are they likely to leave with no depression, they are likely to leave with a future happiness and success scale that is well above the potential of the average person who has never had depression.

He is author of the book, *Depression: the Way Out,* and its companion 8-part DVD Workbook Series that is used extensively in mental health education programs throughout the U.S. and other countries. He designed a test (patent pending) that helps an individual or physician determine the specific operative causes that impair mental performance. The test also determines levels of depression and/or anxiety (if present) and the level of emotional intelligence. Dr. Nedley also conducts training-the-trainer programs in mental health in various locations and online. His books have been translated into Spanish, German, Portuguese, Korean, Czech, Hungarian, Romanian and other languages.

Dr. Nedley is also author of the book *Proof Positive: How to Reliably Combat Disease and Achieve Optimal Health through Nutrition and Lifestyle.* It tackles heart disease, cancer, hypertension, diabetes, kidney failure, high cholesterol, and many other diseases, providing common sense nutritional and lifestyle therapies that can make a substantial difference in treatment and/or prevention of these common conditions.

Dr. Nedley is President of Weimar Center of Health and Education, which runs a residential lifestyle center, academy, and college in the beautiful foothills of the Sierra Mountains outside Sacramento, California. He is owner of the Nedley Clinic in Ardmore, Oklahoma, an internal medicine practice that runs a full service outpatient clinical laboratory. He is also President of Ardmore Gastroenterology Management, and President of the Southern Oklahoma Diagnostic Center that operates an MRI imaging center.

Dr. Nedley is an instrument rated pilot. He and his wife Erica have four boys. All family members enjoy flying, bicycling, mountain hiking, snow skiing, tennis, and performing or listening to good sacred or classical music.

# Preface

## A Comprehensive Approach

As a physician, I have a genuine desire to help patients recover completely from their illness. That's what led me to research a condition I see far too frequently in my practice—major clinical depression. In my observation, this debilitating illness is often only partially and inadequately treated. When I applied my exhaustive research to my patients, they experienced unprecedented improvement. In most, the depression was not only completely and permanently alleviated, but they also began to notice lasting positive changes in their mental ability. They displayed improved memory, higher levels of motivation, revitalized relationships, and a surprisingly strong ability to analyze complex decisions accurately and make correct decisions habitually. This resulted in even greater life enhancements, increased productivity, and a very happy way of life. Studies on patients who have completed the *Nedley Depression Recovery Program* (by using before and after Beck Depression Inventories and DSM-4 depression criteria) reveal that not only is the average patient no longer depressed, but they have higher emotional intelligence, and a greater overall enjoyment of life, than some who have never experienced depression at all.

Many of these patients would exclaim, "I think everyone needs this program, not just those of us who are depressed." Indeed, some of their friends and family have chosen to go through the program after observing the dramatic change in the *Nedley Depression Recovery Program* graduates. Even though they are not depressed, they want to enhance their mental performance, too. They have not been disappointed. I have seen a number of non-depressed individuals dramatically and measurably improve relationships, grades, work performance, positive influence over their loved ones, and life successes by implementing the methods taught in the program.

That's when I decided to not only put on programs for those who have a mental or physical illness, but to offer "Peak Mental Performance Programs" for people who are functioning normally. Most people could function far better than normal if they only knew and applied the tools to do so. Such a course can propel an average person, with an average I.Q. and emotional intelligence, to the top 5th percentile, thus putting them in an "elite thinker" class! Measurable, significant change can occur in as little as five days, but even greater improvements will continue month by month until a high plateau is reached six months to a year after the strategies described in this book are put into habitual practice.

The human brain is even more wonderful than I originally thought when I took on this work. You don't have to settle for an average, or even above average brain. By incorporating these simple, yet profound strategies, you can be the next thought leader in your community. Not just because your outlook on life is better and more filled with purpose, but because you will possess a superior and balanced brain that can be a source of education, motivation, and relationship-building for those around you.

***A Comprehensive Strategy***

Our modern society has been called the thoughtless generation. Objective, well-disciplined, complex thinking has almost become a thing of the past. Emotional intelligence appears to be at an all-time low. Critical thinking and emotional wellness don't have to be a lost art. By understanding and applying the principles explained in this book, the reader can use the art of thinking to achieve peak mental performance.

*The Lost Art of Thinking* is the most comprehensive book on emotional intelligence written for the general public. It is divided into three main areas that must be addressed when considering emotional and mental wellness. The first part of the book deals with our actual thoughts, specifically patterns of thinking that are a hindrance to maximizing emotional health. The second part deals with lifestyle behaviors that have a powerful influence on thinking ability. The third part discusses overarching principles that assist the brain and emotions through life changing times, such as experiencing an unexpected loss, making an important decision, or modifying lifestyle or mental habits. All three sections of the book are important. Just as a three-legged stool becomes unstable when any of the legs is removed, applying one portion of these methods without the others results in an imbalance that can lead to emotional or mental instability.

Because of the comprehensive approach of this book, many health and mental health professionals will also use the book, with its many references and how-to approaches. What sets this book apart from other volumes on the subject of emotional intelligence is that it does not ignore or marginalize the importance of the frontal lobe of the brain (sometimes called the prefrontal cortex in scientific studies). It is now conclusive that emotional health is dependent on a well-functioning frontal lobe. When the frontal lobe is compromised, true empathy is lost, and the person becomes intermittently unrestrained with occasional exhibitions of boasting, hostility, or loss of temper. Their goals become short sighted and they no longer are able to accomplish advanced planning and thinking. Their ability to analyze their own thoughts for distortions is compromised.

It is clear the frontal lobe is the seat of reasoning, spirituality, morality, and the will. Secular neurology textbooks agree that the frontal lobe is structurally and functionally the control center of the entire being.[1,2,3] I have written extensive chapters on the frontal lobe in *Proof Positive* (chapter 12) and in *Depression: the Way Out* (chapter 9). For more information on this area of the brain, I recommend reading both of those chapters. Although *The Lost Art of Thinking* does not have a chapter dedicated to the frontal lobe, it is addressed to some degree throughout the book.

There are many ways to strengthen frontal lobe function. Each chapter of this book includes principles that are designed to enhance the circulation and activity of the frontal lobe of the brain in an effort to attain a comprehensive approach to developing emotional wellness and reaching a high level of mental performance.

Since the frontal lobe is what makes us spiritual beings, it stands to reason that attending to spirituality will enhance frontal lobe function. Many mental health professionals leave out this important element that truly helps people emotionally and intellectually. Research has revealed that people with increased religiosity have better emotional health. Although mental health problems, such as major depression, can occur in religious people, the 1998 *American Journal of Psychiatry* reported that for every 10-point increase in the intrinsic religiosity assessment score, people recover from depression 70 percent sooner.

The goal of this book is to improve your emotional and general intelligence, and thus your success in life. The principles outlined in this book can help the mental health of both religious and non-religious people. Whatever your spiritual inclination, I would ask you to consider the ancient examples given in this book with an open mind. If understood and applied, they can be instrumental in optimizing your frontal lobe function.

Most of these examples are drawn from the Bible, because this ancient spiritual book is respected by Christians, Jews, Muslims, Hindus, Buddhists, and even many non-religious people. The Bible has withstood the test of time and remains a bestseller, even in today's secular society. It not only includes mind-sharpening spiritual principles, but it is also a casebook that shows both healthy and unhealthy ways of thinking and their respective consequences. One does not have to subscribe to a specific spiritual belief system in order to benefit from the truths illustrated in these stories. So please don't be put off by scriptural references from this ancient source. Although it only plays a minor role in this book (compared to current science and modern illustrations), the role it plays in obtaining comprehensive emotional and intellectual health is significant.

If you read *The Lost Art of Thinking* with a willingness to learn and an open mind, you will gain improved emotional intelligence, enhanced relationships, and greater levels of happiness and success.

## References

1. Price BH, Daffner KR, et al. The compartmental learning disabilities of early frontal lobe damage. Brain 1990 Oct;113 (Pt 5)():1383-1393
2. Stuss, DT, Benson D. The Frontal Lobes. New York: Raven Press, 1986 p. 5, 6, 204.
3. Fulton JF, editor. The Frontal Lobes. New York: Hafner Publishing Company, 1966 p. 27, 59.

# Introduction

## Understanding Emotional Intelligence

You may have seen a popular web site ad featuring two teenagers from the 70s flanked by the caption "She married him? And they have seven kids?" This ad highlights a truism that many alumni have found at their class reunions: the lives of classmates don't always turn out as expected.

In terms of intelligence, individuals with high I.Q.'s, usually viewed as most likely to succeed, don't always excel. At the same time, others who had mediocre academic performances go on to become outstanding achievers in the professional world. While I.Q. may contribute as much as 20 percent to the factors that determine life success, the remaining 80 percent or more is determined by other forces.[4] In other words, the overwhelming majority of our ultimate success in life is determined by non-I.Q. factors. A study of Harvard graduates in the fields of law, medicine, teaching, and business backs this up, finding that entrance exam scores (which would be indicative of I.Q.) had no correlation whatsoever with eventual career success.[5]

The reason behind this surprising fact is simple: success in life is much more based on E.Q. (Emotional Intelligence Quotient) than I.Q. (Intelligence Quotient). Out-of-control emotions can make even the most intelligent individuals behave in a manner that simply is not very smart. The importance of emotional intelligence in determining future success has been a hot topic in psychiatric circles in recent years, and is supported by an ever-growing body of scientific research. The concept of E.Q. is the foundation of this book, and so it must be understood before we can begin learning how to improve it.

### *Yardstick of Success*

So what exactly is the Emotional Intelligence Quotient? E.Q. is really a measure of characteristics which research has confirmed are very important to successful and enjoyable living. People with high E.Q.'s have control of their impulses and emotions. They are trustworthy, honest, conscientious, dependable, and responsible. They are flexible and able to adapt to change. They are also open to constructive criticism, innovation, novel ideas, new approaches, and information. In addition, people with high E.Q.'s are aware of limits to their abilities and have reasonable expectations.[6]

Emotional intelligence has been shown to help people think more clearly, communicate more effectively, reduce polarizing statements, and develop unity in group settings.[7] These skills are particularly critical in today's knowledge-oriented workplace, where harmonious team efforts are more critical than ever to organizational success.

### *Emotional Maturity*

What we are really talking about is emotional maturity—an openness and willingness to develop, grow, and be mature in how we handle others and ourselves. In personal relationships, an individual with a high E.Q. has the ability to step aside from their emotional reaction to an upsetting event and look logically at what really happened. Their honesty allows them to understand other points of view, as well as potential solutions to the problem. While your first job out of college will likely be directly related to your I.Q., how far you advance in that job is much more related to E.Q. Often people with a high I.Q. don't understand this. They think the reason they've been passed over for a promotion is that the rest of the world doesn't have enough intelligence to recognize their I.Q. They often feel slighted, or that life is unfair. The truth is, employers do recognize intelligence in promotion decisions. The intelligence being recognized, however, is E.Q.

Individuals with a high E.Q. understand their emotions and feelings and can express, control, and manage them. They usually have insight into the feelings and views of others, and more easily understand the dynamics of a group and their role within it. They are willing to delay gratification in favor of the greater good. Those with a high E.Q. also are more likely to motivate themselves to achieve goals and maintain a positive but realistic attitude. As a result, they often earn promotions more quickly than those with a higher I.Q. Essentially, people with a high E.Q. see the "big picture," so they are able to avoid the emotional roller coasters.

*"There are three things that are extremely hard: steel, a diamond, and to know one's self."*
—Ben Franklin

There are five basic components of emotional intelligence:

- knowing your emotions
- managing your emotions
- recognizing emotions in others
- managing relationships
- motivating ourselves to achieve goals

You may notice that the word "emotion" is a focal point in three of the five components. If you take the "e" away from the word "emotion" you get "motion," which is related to motivation (factors that activate, direct, and sustain goal-directed behavior). The close relationship between E.Q. and motivation is a prime reason why a high I.Q. doesn't automatically ensure life success. Motivation, which has everything to do with E.Q., is also a critical component to success and achievement.[8]

### *Factors Affecting E.Q.*

Genetics are more influential to I.Q. than E.Q., but heredity does play a role in E.Q. as well. Many children learn emotional intelligence—or a lack thereof—from their parents.[9] Childhood experiences also have a major impact on E.Q. Sexual abuse during childhood has an impact on the amygdala, limbic system, and prefrontal cortex areas of the brain.[10] The frontal lobe of the brain actually shrinks, while the limbic system becomes stronger. Developing a high E.Q. becomes more difficult in such situations, but not impossible. Watching entertainment television during childhood also results in a dramatically increased limbic system, which actually outweighs the frontal lobe of the brain. This is one of the reasons why many pediatric experts are now advising that no one under the age of twelve should watch theatrical television.[11] In recent years, a number of articles written by Dr. Brandon Centerwall and other researchers on the harmful effects of entertainment television on the emotional intelligence of children have been published by the American Medical Association.[12,13,14]

Your current level of emotional support will affect your E.Q.[15] Physical factors such as lack of sleep, lack of exercise, and poor nutrition also contribute to a poor E.Q., particularly in the reaction to an uncontrolled stressful event.[16]

Nutrition is emerging as a particularly important factor affecting emotional intelligence.[17] Recent studies have shown that an individual who might have reacted calmly had they been on a healthy diet, may react totally different on a junk food diet (e.g. they are much more likely to lose control and allow their emotions to spiral into rage or anger).[18] All too often, the unfortunate result is permanent harm or equally permanent regret.

***The Factor Eclipsing All Others***

While heredity, level of support, and lifestyle choices all have an important influence on E.Q., one factor eclipses all else in terms of impact. That factor, as identified by numerous emotional intelligence experts, is simply what an individual thinks. In other words, your moment by moment thoughts have a tremendous amount to do with your personal E.Q.

What you think really does affect who you are: you can change your basic values and beliefs by changing the way you think about things. When you do, you will often experience lasting improvements in mood, outlook, and productivity.[19] When I was in medical school it was commonly taught that physicians on the psychiatric ward should not tamper with anyone's values or beliefs. To do so, we were told, would be crossing an ethical barrier. In addition, our patients would likely become worse instead of better. Today we have experts saying just the opposite: that unless you change your values and beliefs, you will not experience lasting changes in mood, outlook, and productivity. Even more impressively, these experts have volumes of scientific evidence to back up their claims.[20]

Research has documented that negative, turmoil-producing thoughts nearly always contain gross distortions. While the thoughts appear valid on the surface, they are actually irrational, twisted, and wrong. Such thinking is a major cause of suffering in our world today.[21] The good news is that straightening out our thinking can improve our moods, personal relationships, and life in general—resulting in a ripple effect with the power to change the world.

### *Mind Over Mood*

So what is it that makes your mood glad or sad? The first principle of cognitive behavioral therapy (CBT) is that your moods result from your "cognitions" or thoughts. The "ABCs of Cognitive Behavioral Therapy" are frequently used to illustrate this fact. In this model, the (C) consequences are preceded by the (A) activating event. Some therapists say the "A" stands for awareness of the activating event which we see, hear, or notice, while others say it stands for adversity.[22,23]

In any case, our moods are one of the (C) *consequences* in the ABC model. When we think clearly, the (A) *activating event* should always be analyzed in light of our (B) *beliefs* before any (C) *consequences* take place.[24]

**A** *Activating Event* → **B** *Belief* → **C** *Consequences* →

A-to-C thinking, where people skip the B (belief) step in the middle, has been identified as "crooked thinking" by Dr. Albert Ellis, who many consider to be the father of CBT.[25]

If we believe that we have little or no ability to influence our feelings—that events and situations directly cause our emotions and behavior—we are also engaged in crooked thinking. The feelings resulting from A-to-C thinking may be positive, negative, or neutral. Most people understand that positive thoughts lead to positive feelings and negative thoughts lead to negative feelings. What many don't understand, however, is that neutral feelings are also possible (as a result of neutral thoughts). The word "calm" best describes a neutral feeling.[26]

### *Counseling Ourselves*

CBT is actually a form of self-counseling, something which all humans are engaged in every day of the year. Most people couldn't make it through a single day without some amount of rational self-talk. While we can get in quite a bit of trouble by not listening to our own good counsel, our self-counseling can also be irrational and unproductive.[27]

Failing to follow our self-talk from cause to effect often leads us to see good, appropriate reactions more as accidents than intentional behaviors. The "Cs" of the ABCs of CBT (consequences) are very closely tied to our own self-talk, which is why we need to carefully monitor that self-talk.

### *Truth in Your Thoughts*

Cognitive behavioral therapy is really a recognition of the all-important concept of "truth" by modern psychology. Telling ourselves and others the truth by removing cognitive distortions is a major tool in improving emotional intelligence, personal relationships, and ultimately, our success in life. CBT is largely based on removing ten "cognitive distortions" which, when it comes right down to it, are nothing more than untruths we humans are frequently tempted to think.

Many people think the best way to improve personal relationships is to get to the lowest common denominator without regard to accuracy or truth. Unity built on "putting important differences aside" is really quite superficial, however, and easily disrupted. The only unity that will stand the test of time is honesty-based, and this unity can be accomplished without compromising or sacrificing the truth.[28] The reliance of CBT on the timeless principle of truth is a major reason, no doubt, for the success of this therapy in treating a wide range of psychological conditions. CBT has proven effective in treating shyness, social anxiety, phobias, depression, low self-worth, relationship problems, obsessive-compulsive disorder, post-traumatic stress disorder, addictions, and anxiety disorders.[29,30,31] Being the greatest mental therapy to enter the psychiatric arsenal, CBT boosts emotional intelligence, is inexpensive, and (in most cases) is more effective than drugs.[32]

The core tenets of CBT are as follows:

- Thoughts precede feelings and emotions.
- You can control your thoughts (and therefore your feelings).
- Managing your emotions affects your values and behavior.
- When an individual's values line up with what is accurate (e.g. truth), he or she will often feel better and get better.

The truth-oriented principles of CBT are so pivotal to clear thinking that they are the focus of the first ten chapters of this book.

***Good News***

When we ask participants in the *Nedley Depression Recovery Program* to say why they haven't been more successful in life, they frequently mention difficulty with schoolwork as a factor in their lack of success. An initially unintended outcome of this program is that the average attendee comes with a below average emotional intelligence quotient and leaves 10 days later with an E.Q. that is in the top 10 percentile. Not only are they likely to leave with no depression, they are likely to leave with a future happiness and success scale that is well above the potential of the average person who has never had depression.

Participants are relieved to learn that, although they can't easily improve their I.Q., emotional intelligence can be vastly improved. This is in contrast to I.Q., which doesn't tend to change much once you reach adulthood and is largely affected by heredity and environment.

Like I.Q., E.Q. can be measured through testing. An assessment offered on my website (www.drnedley.com) is a helpful tool in this regard. It measures E.Q. as well as level of depression and anxiety, sources of depression, and factors that inhibit a high level of emotional intelligence.

*"The world is what we think it is. If we can change our thoughts, we can change the world."*
—H. L. Tomlinson

*"Anyone who stops learning is old, whether at twenty or eighty. Anyone who keeps learning stays young. The greatest thing in life is to keep your mind young."*
—Henry Ford

***Strategies For Success***

Most of us learned through a childhood proverb that "sticks and stones may break my bones but words can never hurt me." The truth is, however, that words do affect our psyche. They also affect the way we are perceived by others.

To begin improving your E.Q. and achieve lasting change, you will have to consider both the words you are using and the thoughts you are thinking. New expectations and beliefs will have to replace old ones while new cognitions replace automatic negative thoughts. You'll need to train yourself to recognize unhealthy thinking for what it is—a bad habit that leads to poor self-worth and an even worse mood.

The goal is to systematically challenge and dispute your thoughts, discover if they are valid, and question their accuracy. By analyzing and reflecting on what you are thinking, you will be able to see if you are playing old, dysfunctional messages in your brain. In order to evaluate your thinking, you must learn to listen to yourself and others, watching carefully how you categorize events in your life.

You'll want to keep an eye on your memories as well, for they can be easily skewed. Some life experiences naturally make more of an impression than others. Stressful moments and upsetting events can be much more memorable than the mundane. In many cases, the stronger the emotional response, the more vivid the memory. It is up to us to put our memories, no matter how unforgettable, into perspective while challenging distorted patterns of thinking.

The key to controlling your thoughts is realizing that you are the cinema manager. If a mental movie creates problems, you can switch to another film. The following chapters provide valuable tools for intercepting the internal self-talk or internal "running commentary" that frequently causes trouble. To get started, however, I would encourage you to begin "thinking about your thoughts."

Is your mind always in overdrive, expecting the worst? Do others generally consider you to be a pessimist? Do you tend to talk using absolute words such as all, always, completely, no one, must, none, never, everything, totally, or nothing? Have you caught the highly contagious virus of I-can't-stand-it-itis, or is your dialect composed of the HTAs (Horrible-Terrible-Awfuls)? You'll learn much more about these detrimental habits in the chapters that follow, but for now, give the above questions some thought.

***Change Requires Effort***

When we do, think, or feel something that's the opposite of what we are used to, we sometimes experience a strange emotion referred to as "cognitive-emotive dissonance."[33]

Like a left-handed person trying to write with the opposite hand, things just "feel wrong." As you read new ideas in this book, you may experience a sense of discord yourself. Cognitive-emotive dissonance is unavoidable in life. No matter how hard we try, we will experience or be exposed to things that seem unusual or wrong. Changes we make in life—even good changes—often result in an out-of-sync feeling.

When we start feeling happy after years of depression, or someone treats us well after years of abuse, cognitive-dissonance is likely to rise. Marrying after years of singlehood, becoming wealthy after decades of poverty, or getting promoted from the factory line to top management are also good changes that can be sources of serious cognitive dissonance.

Stopping the cycle of unhealthy recurring thought patterns will take patience and, quite possibly, hard work. Taking an honest look at your thoughts and evaluating them for accuracy and truth will require diligence. In addition, the process of positive change can be painful.

The good news is that cognitive techniques can help you to cope with the anger, frustration, fear, and depression triggered by various life events—whether real or imaginary. You can improve your E.Q., and with it, your prospect for personal happiness. Despite whatever effort may be involved, the success, happiness, and improved relationships you'll enjoy because of your heightened E.Q. will make the time spent in this valuable pursuit well worth your investment in effort.

## References


4. Riggs NR, Greenberg MT, Kusche CA, Pentz MA. "The Mediational Role of Neurocognition in the Behavioral Outcomes of a Social-Emotional Prevention Program in Elementary School Students: Effects of the PATHS Curriculum." *Prevention Science*. March 30, 2006.
5. Akers MD, Porter GL. "Your EQ Skills: Got What It Takes?" *Journal of Accountancy* (2003). 11 Jan. 2008 <http://www.aicpa.org/pubs/jofa/mar2003/akers.htm>.
6. Goleman D. *Emotional Intelligence: Why it can matter more than I.Q.* New York, NY: Bantam Books. 1995. 42-45.
7. Goleman D. *Emotional Intelligence: Why it can matter more than I.Q.* New York, NY: Bantam Books. 1995. 161-163.
8. Goleman D. *Emotional Intelligence: Why it can matter more than I.Q.* New York, NY: Bantam Books, 1995. 80.
9. Hooven C, Katz L, Gottman J. "The Family as a Meta-emotion Culture." *Cognition and Emotion* (Spring 1994).
10. Spates CR, Samaraweera N, Plaiser B, Souza T, Otsui K. "Psychological Impact of Trauma on Developing Children and Youth." *Primary Care: Clinics in Office Practice*. June 2007 Vol. 34, Issue 2, Pages 387-405.
11. Wheeler J. *Remote Controlled: How TV Affects You and Your Family*. Hagerstown, MD: Review and Herald, 1993. 140, 141.
12. Centerwall BS. Television and violence. "The scale of the problem and where to go from here." *JAMA* 267.22 (1992): 3059+.
13. Landhuis CE, et al. "Does Childhood Television viewing Lead to Attention Problems in Adolescence? Results from a Prospective Longitudinal Study." *Pediatrics* 120.3 (2007).
14. Wheeler J. *Remote Controlled: How TV Affects You and Your Family*. Hagerstown, MD: Review and Herald, 1993. 121, 122.
15. Freeman P, Rees T. "How does perceived support lead to better performance? An examination of potential mechanisms." *Journal of Applied Sport Psychology*, April, 2009.
16. Killgore WD, Killgore DB, Day LM, Li C, Kamimori GH, Balkin TJ. "The effects of 53 hours of sleep deprivation on moral judgment." *Sleep* 2007;30(3):345-52.

17. Schmidt MA. *Brain-building Nutrition: How Dietary Fats and Oils Affect Mental, Physical, and Emotional Intelligence.* 3rd ed. Berkeley, CA: Frog Books, 2006. XVI.
18. *Impact of Fresh, Healthy Foods on Learning and Behavior: 5-year Study* (as featured on the DVD *Super-size Me*), Natural Press, 2004.
19. Burns DD. *Feeling Good: The New Mood Therapy*. rev. and updated. New York: Avon, 1999. xix. 12.
20. Burns DD. *Feeling Good: The New Mood Therapy*. rev. and updated. New York: Avon, 1999. xix. xix.
21. Burns DD. *Feeling Good: The New Mood Therapy*. rev. and updated. New York: Avon, 1999. xix. 13.
22. Pucci AR. *The Client's Guide to Cognitive-Behaivioral Therapy*. Lincoln, NE: iUniverse, 2006. 23.
23. Ellis A. *Overcoming Destructive Beliefs, Feelings, and Behaviors: New Directions for Rational Emotive Behavior Therapy*. Amherst, NY: Prometheus Books, 2001. 19.
24. Clark, Lynn. "Achieving Contentment and Our Goals." *SOS Help for Emotions: Managing Anxiety, Anger, and Depression*. 2nd ed. Bowling Green, KY: Parents Press, 2001. 21.
25. Ellis A. *Overcoming Destructive Beliefs, Feelings, and Behaviors: New Directions for Rational Emotive Behavior Therapy*. Amherst, NY: Prometheus Books, 2001. 19.
26. Pucci AR. *The Client's Guide to Cognitive-Behaivioral Therapy*. Lincoln, NE: iUniverse, 2006. 23-24.
27. Pucci AR. *The Client's Guide to Cognitive-Behaivioral Therapy*. Lincoln, NE: iUniverse, 2006. xi.
28. Clark L. Achieving Contentment and Our Goals. *SOS Help for Emotions: Managing Anxiety, Anger, and Depression*. 2nd ed. Bowling Green, KY: Parents Press, 2001. 10-15.
29. Ito LM, Roso MC, Tiwari S, Kendall PC, Asbahr FR. "Cognitive-behavioral therapy in social phobia." *Revista brasileira de psiquiatria* (Sao Paulo, Brazil : 1999).
30. Borkovec TD, Costello E. "Efficacy of applied relaxation and cognitive-behavioral therapy in the treatment of generalized anxiety disorder." *Journal of Consulting and Clinical Psychology*, 1993. 61, 611-619.
31. Fava GA, Ruini C, Rafanelli C, Finos L, Conti S, Grandi S. "Six-year outcome of cognitive behavior therapy for prevention of recurrent depression." *Am J Psychiatry* 2004. 161:1872–1876.
32. Rush AJ, Beck AT, Kovacs M, Hollon S. "Comparative Efficacy of Cognitive Therapy and Pharmacotherapy in the Treatment of Depressed Outpatients." *Cognitive Therapy and Research*, Vol. 1, No. I, March 1977. 17-38.
33. Pucci AR. *The Client's Guide to Cognitive-Behaivioral Therapy*. Lincoln, NE: iUniverse, 2006. 9.

# THE LOST ART OF THINKING

*How to Improve Emotional Intelligence and Achieve Peak Mental Performance*

## Section 1:

# *HOW THINKING CHANGES BRAIN CHEMISTRY*

Chapter 1

THERE IS NO IN-BETWEEN FOR ALL-OR-NOTHING THINKERS.

# Live Between the Lines

## *Why all-or-nothing thinking can be necessary in some situations, harmful in others, and how to tell the difference.*

Fred sifted through a bucket of junk in his garage, stumbling repeatedly over what could only be called "stuff" as he looked for one of his favorite fishing lures.

"I've got to clean out this garage some day if it's the last thing I do," Fred mumbled, tripping over the same overturned bucket for the third time that morning as he tried to make his escape.

"Such a big project," Fred sighed, taking one last guilty look at the accumulation of ten years before slamming the garage door back to its job of hiding the ugly mess. "I hate to get started until I've really got time, and that day never seems to come."

Jennifer stared intently at the root beer floats, 14-inch pizzas, and array of hors d'oeuvres on the sumptuous table before her. The room hummed with the sound of familiar voices, but there was only one voice Jennifer heard; one that played over and over again in her head: "To eat, or not to eat? That is the question."

This was Jennifer's 25-year class reunion, a weekend she had looked forward to for months. Wanting to look good, she had lost 35 pounds (16 kg) with an evening such as this in mind. She'd even sworn off pizza, her favorite food. But now the smell of melted cheese wafted enticingly through the air, refusing to go away. "I've blown it now," Jennifer murmured as she loaded one, then two, then three pieces of pizza next to the growing pile of hors d'oeuvres on her plate. "Guess if I'm going to do it, I might as well do it up right..."

What do Fred and Jennifer have in common? Both engaged in a form of negative self-talk known as "all-or-nothing" thinking. Fred refused to get started unless he could clean the whole garage. The "Big Cleaning Day" never came, so the mess, and Fred's irritation, grew. He could have set aside 15 minutes each day to work on a corner of his garage. In time the whole job would have seemed more manageable. Jennifer told herself that she had failed, and started a cycle of negative thinking that easily spiraled into a broken diet and regained weight. She could've given herself permission to eat a slice of pizza or a few other treats without going overboard. Both Fred and Jennifer could have improved their mental performance with a more balanced view of their situations.

## ALL-OR-NOTHING THINKERS

All-or-nothing thinkers like to simplify the world by putting everything into extremes or absolutes like black and white, good and bad, or up and down.[34] Psychologists also know it as polarization or dichotomous thinking.[35] They also tend to speak in sweeping terms such as "I'm right and she's wrong about this," or "my project was totally ruined by that mistake."[36]

To the person struggling with all-or-nothing thinking, there are only two choices, "magnificent" or "awful."[37] Caught in a cycle of rigid thinking, they cheat themselves out of a great deal of happiness by failing to see the vast gray area in which most of life takes place.[38] Common characteristics of the all-or-nothing mentality are listed in **Figure 1.1**.

## A VERY EXPENSIVE BOWL OF SOUP

One of the worst business deals in ancient history was actually a result of distorted all-or-nothing thinking.

The Bible says that Esau was a great hunter. Any would-be target of his was doomed when within range of his bow. But even Esau had some bad hunting days.

One day when Esau returned from a frustratingly fruitless hunting expedition, he found himself totally famished. Perhaps he was so focused on chasing elk that he forgot to nibble on some berries along the way. At the end of the day he was left with nothing but a painfully empty stomach.

With his blood sugar dropping, Esau had one thing in mind. He wanted food, and he wanted it fast. Unfortunately for Esau, the closest thing to fast food in that day happened to be the outdoor "kitchen" of his twin brother, Jacob.

**ALL-OR-NOTHING THINKERS HAVE:**

- difficulty accepting anything less than the best.
- unrealistically high expectations of themselves and other people.
- trouble acknowledging that we all make mistakes and that many things in life are actually learned through a series of small mistakes.
- the belief that they or others must be either a total success or a total failure.

***Figure 1.1***

To fully understand this story, you have to know that Jacob and Esau were the ultimate sibling rivals, so much so that they started a wrestling match right in their mother's womb. The issue at stake then was who would come out first. Esau won that initial battle, but the Bible records that Jacob came out with his hand on Esau's heel.[39]

It mattered a great deal which twin came out first, because their father Isaac was a very rich man and the firstborn would receive the very coveted birthright. The son with the birthright would be the next leader of the home and receive a double portion of his father's inheritance as well as an additional spiritual blessing.

And now back to our story...where we find Jacob, a forward thinker who had been plotting to wrest the birthright from his brother for years, and Esau, a spontaneous sort who only seemed to care about the present.

Esau was on his way home when he passed his brother's fire, where Jacob has just cooked up a steaming pot of soup. Esau collapsed in front of the fire, literally begging for food. Jacob saw his big chance in this moment, and offered to sell Esau one heaping serving of lentil soup in exchange for the birthright. Although the inheritance was vastly more valuable than the dinner, Esau didn't flinch for a moment. He probably didn't have the energy to flinch, and besides, he was totally overcome by his bout of all-or-nothing thinking.

"What good will this stupid birthright do me if I'm dead anyway?" In his cognitively distorted state, Esau saw things only in black-and-white, lentils or death. Though he would not have died from hunger for weeks, he convinced himself he would, and that was what mattered. In the absence of a notary public, Jacob made Esau raise his right hand and commit to

**ALL-OR-NOTHING THINKING LEADS TO:**

- low self-worth
- procrastination
- incomplete projects
- exaggeration
- suicidal thoughts
- discouragement
- pessimism
- frustration

***Figure 1.2***

a solemn oath before handing over the beans.[40] Thus was completed the hardest deal ever driven—the equivalent of one bean burrito for the complete holdings of Bill Gates—all due to distorted, all-or-nothing thinking. **Figure 1.2** documents some of the negative effects of this common thinking error.

## THINGS HAVE TO BE "PERFECT"

All-or-nothing thinkers are also very often perfectionists.[41] If they can't do something well, they'd rather not do it at all; if a situation doesn't go perfectly, they feel like an abject failure.

Even the goals that such thinkers set for themselves are measured in absolute terms. Perfectionism is really a distortion of the challenge to "do your best" in the person who believes his or her best must always mean perfect. The individual becomes fearful of making mistakes and may experience stress, anxiety disorders, and depression as a result.[42]

According to Dr. David Burns, perfectionists are motivated by a fear of failure, sense of duty, need to control, or a drive to be "number one." Healthier motivations would be enthusiasm for a project, enjoyment of a sense of accomplishment, or working with other people. In the healthy pursuit of excellence, people are not driven by a need for love or success. While failure is never pleasant, such individuals understand that failure can actually be a positive learning process. As a result, they are not afraid to fail.[43]

There is nothing wrong with pursuing perfection. We must be reasonable in our expectations, however. While we should always strive for, hope for, and desire the best, it is unrealistic to believe that we and everything we do will be met with smashing success.

The reality is that much of life happens in that messy gray area between black and white. Most things in life have a middle ground. Life is really much more like a light with a dimmer switch than one limited to "on" and "off" options. The light may be on, but there are degrees of brightness.[44] Some people pride themselves on being all-or-nothing thinkers. To them, the very idea implies strength and certainty. The fact is, there are many levels of success in life.

## THE ULTIMATE ALL-OR-NOTHING THOUGHT

Thoughts about suicide are the most extreme and dangerous example of all-or-nothing thinking.[45] Often a suicide attempt is really a call for help, made by persons who have convinced themselves that if they can't have what they consider "all," they would be better off to have "nothing."[46]

Individuals often become suicidal when they fail to cope with depression. They may be overcome by pain or fear, or suffering from extreme pressure or a mental disorder. Suicide takes more than a million lives per year worldwide (30,000 of those suicides take place in the United States), and more than 60 percent of individuals who die by suicide are suffering from major depression.[47,48]

Unhealthy all-or-nothing thinking, which contributes to a number of depressed thinking habits, may also lead to anxiety, panic, depression, guilt, feelings of inferiority, hopelessness, perfectionism, and anger.[49]

Since all-or-nothing thinkers tend to apply polarized thinking to themselves, others, and the world around them, the distortion can be quite expansive. An example would be the common expression, believed by some Americans within the past 150-200 years, that "the only good Indian is a dead Indian." How much better our country could have been—and could still be—if we would put aside all-or-nothing racial stereotypes.

Throughout history, there have been heroes willing to stand up to corporate all-or-nothing thinking. Hotel manager Paul Susesabagina was just such a hero. As a Rwandan Hutu during the genocide that took the lives of 800,000 of his countrymen in 100 days, Paul was handed a gun and ordered to join in killing "the cockroaches." Refusing to succumb to the all-or-nothing characterization of the Tutsis, Paul paid a ransom to save them instead. Then, using the skills he had polished as the manager of the four-star hotel in the Rwandan capital of Kigali, Paul reasoned, bartered and outright bribed his way into saving the lives of 1,268 fellow citizens who took refuge behind his doors while the civil war raged outside. Paul, whose story was told in the Golden Globe film nominee *Hotel Rwanda*, never considered himself a hero. "I was just doing my job," he said.

**At any stage of development, our lives may be perfect, but there will always be room for growth and advancement.**

## THERE IS A PLACE FOR POLARIZED THINKING

Some psychologists have mistakenly labeled any "all-or-nothing" thinking as bad, distorted, and inappropriate. However, there are times when all-or-nothing thinking is appropriate. If all-or-nothing thoughts are accurate, they can be powerful motivators. This is especially true for those battling addiction. Many recovering alcoholics realize that to take even one drink would be the first step down the slippery slope. The same principle is true for many other dangerous addictions. A successful ex-smoker, ex-pornography addict, or ex-gambler knows that one cigarette, one soft-porn video, or one night at the casino (respectively), will begin that slide toward a yawning chasm that will swallow him or her up, plummeting him or her back into ruin.

### APPROPRIATE ALL-OR-NOTHING THOUGHTS

"If I drink just one beer, my lifelong habit of binging, which caused my cirrhosis of the liver, will start all over again. It will change the person I am; I will lose my job, my family, and ultimately, my health. I am one drink away from death."

"If I forget my spare oxygen tank, I'll run out of air at the top of the mountain. I must not forget that tank."

"If I give up my baby for adoption, she will have a much better home—but I'll never be a part of her life. I will either have all of the responsibility of raising her, or none."

"If I swerve onto this exit, I may avoid that oncoming semi-truck. Otherwise, it will be the end for me."

***Figure 1.3***

In these areas goal-setting really must be rigid, because what is really needed is a clean break. It is only by recognizing the reality of the danger involved that a former addict's complete and lifelong victory is assured.

Another good example of all-or-nothing thinking is found in the wedding ceremony. The vow to "forsake all others...as long as life shall last" is central to a strong, secure, committed marriage. Those who choose to cohabitate without taking this vow feel less secure, are less happy, less productive in their relationship, lead less enjoyable sexual lives, and are less likely to keep this exclusive relationship for life.[50]

A climber who has lost the rope clings to the edge of a crumbling rock near the top of a towering precipice. There are 2,000 feet of sheer drop-off below him, and only a tiny toe hold to grasp. For him at that moment, everything is accurately all-or-nothing, life or death, tragedy or triumph. Before writing off our all-or-nothing thoughts, then, we should analyze each thought or statement to see if it is true. Some examples of undistorted all-or-nothing thoughts are given in **Figure 1.3**.

### STRATEGIES FOR SUCCESS

At the close of the introduction, I asked you to become more aware of the thoughts you are thinking. Now I'm going to ask you to take that mindfulness one step further, by starting to write things down. Begin by making a list on a 3 x 5" card of all-or-nothing words you frequently find yourself saying. Write the following words on your card: always, never, must, everything, nothing, useless, horrible, terrible, awful, totally, and completely. If you think of similar words that are in your regular vocabulary, add them to the list. Then for a period of several days, keep track of how often you say those words.

Another useful exercise for all-or-nothing thinkers, as suggested by Dr. David Burns, is "thinking in shades of gray." To implement this strategy, try evaluating things on a scale ranging from 0 to 100. If something doesn't turn out as you had hoped, try thinking of it as a partial success instead of a total failure. More often than not, there is something you can learn from the situation. Any experience that you have learned something valuable from, no matter how difficult, should not be ranked as an abject failure. Award yourself a diploma from the "School of Hard Knocks." If nothing can be done to "undo" the situation, learn what you can and move on. **Figure 1.4** lists additional strategies effective in combating the habit of all-or-nothing thinking.

## STRATEGIES FOR SUCCESS

- Watch for all-or-nothing phrases that are not really true.
- Adhere to truthful all-or-nothing statements.
- Avoid negative thought patterns.
- Evaluate for distortions.
- Journal your thoughts.

***Figure 1.4***

## ACCEPTING OUR IMPERFECTION

An important key to overcoming distorted all-or-nothing thinking is to forgive yourself for minor lapses in behavior, learn from your mistakes, and allow for human weakness. The Christian worldview recognizes that people make mistakes, even providing a way for confession and forgiveness of wrongs committed. **Figure 1.5** offers possible internal responses and corrections to unforgiving all-or-nothing thoughts.

In addition to adopting less condemning thoughts regarding your mistakes, it is also important to avoid making absolute promises that place you one step away from failure. Unbalanced goals or rigid schedules ("I will never be late again in my entire life.") tend to trigger binge reactions to any "slip." You can avoid those reactions by ensuring that goals you set are reasonable and attainable. In many life situations, the rational way to set goals is to allow for gradual progress and change and to make goals more flexible.

| COGNITIVE DISTORTIONS AND CORRECTIONS | |
|---|---|
| "I really can't deal with rejection." | "I don't like rejection, but I will get through it." |
| "Now that I've eaten a cookie and blown my diet, I might as well eat the whole bag." | "I'm sure glad I can stop at one cookie, since I can do that without gaining weight." |
| "Good things never happen to me." | "I have to admit some good things have happened." |
| "I'm a total failure." | "I really am reasonably good at some things." |
| "I'm too out of shape for this exercise program; guess I'll give up." | "I can work up to this exercise routine, and just trying will have a positive impact." |
| "My husband doesn't agree with me, so he's being non-supportive." | "We can agree to disagree without jeopardizing our relationship." |

*Figure 1.5*

You'll also want to apply some careful analysis to your personal relationships. If there are people in your life who you have ranked as perfect or evil, it would be wise to rethink that stance. While it is certainly hard to find any redeeming characteristics in some hardened criminals, chances are good that the vast majority of your acquaintances fall somewhere between perfect and perfectly evil on the all-or-nothing scale. Adopting a realistic attitude that recognizes both the strengths and weaknesses of those in our lives can do much to strengthen struggling relationships, and is particularly helpful where romance is involved.

While your initial efforts in a less polarizing direction may seem like pretty hard work, the payoff will come quickly enough in terms of less conflict, better relationships, more stable emotions, and a higher E.Q.

## References


34. Pucci AR. *The Client's Guide to Cognitive-Behavioral Therapy.* Lincoln, NE: iUniverse, 2006. 49.
35. Watkins A. *Mind-body Medicine: A Clinician's Guide to Psychoneuroimmunology.* New York: Churchill Livingstone, 1997. 196.
36. Burns DD. *Feeling Good: The New Mood Therapy.* New York: Avon-HarperCollins, 1999. 32.
37. Beck AT., et al. *Cognitive Therapy of Depression.* New York: Guilford Press, 1979. 3.
38. Pucci AR. *The Client's Guide to Cognitive-Behavioral Therapy.* Lincoln, NE: iUniverse, 2006. 49.
39. Genesis 25:22-26. *The Holy Bible.* New King James Version.
40. Genesis 25:31-33. *The Holy Bible.* Authorized King James Version.
41. Burns DD. *Feeling Good: The New Mood Therapy.* New York: Avon-HarperCollins, 1999. 32.
42. Burns DD. *Feeling Good: The New Mood Therapy.* New York: Avon-HarperCollins, 1999. 359, 372.
43. Burns DD. *The Feeling Good Handbook.* New York: Penguin Group, 1999. 176.
44. Pucci AR. *The Client's Guide to Cognitive-Behavioral Therapy.* Lincoln, NE: iUniverse, 2006. 49.
45. American Psychiatric Association. *American Psychiatric Association Practice Guidelines for the Treatment of Psychiatric Disorders.* American Psychiatric Pub. 2006. 1432.
46. Harvard Medical School, Komaroff AL. *Harvard Medical School Family Health Guide.* Free Press. 2004. 397.
47. Suicide Prevention [SUPRE]. World Health Organization. <http://www.who.int/mental_health/prevention/suicide/supresuicideprevent/en/>.
48. *Facts and Figures: National Statistics.* American Foundation for Suicide Prevention. <http://www.afsp.org/index.cfm?fuseaction=home.viewpage&page_id=050FEA9F-B064-4092-B1135C3A70DE1FDA>.
49. Burns DD. *The Feeling Good Handbook.* New York: Penguin Group, 1999. 104.
50. Brown S, Booth, A. "Cohabitation versus marriage: A comparison of relationship quality." *Journal of Marriage and The Family* 58: 668+.

Chapter 2

"AS A MAN THINKETH IN HIS HEART, SO IS HE." —*PROVERBS 23:7*

# Generalize with Care

## *Making generalizations can be helpful and healthy, but overgeneralizing is risky.*

Taylor sighed deeply as Professor Mack made the rounds in the classroom, passing out graded mid-term exams. She had a sinking feeling in the pit of her stomach, a feeling that told her she hadn't done well. Her worst fears were realized when Professor Mack finally did drop the exam, complete with more "red graffiti" than she'd ever hoped to see, on her desk.

"I'm not sure what happened here," Professor Mack looked concerned. "You've been to class faithfully every day. You do well on the homework, and take lots of notes."

"I couldn't pass a test if my life depended on it!" Taylor burst into tears, and, snatching up her books, rushed from the room. "I'm horrible at taking exams, always have been, always will be."

Justin snapped on his helmet and took one last glance at the game clock. This was it, the pressure-packed crunch time he'd dreamed of for years. Here he was, quarterback for his high school team, playing for the state championship. It had all come down to this, a final drive during the final minute in the last game of his high-school career. Breaking from the huddle, Justin started picking apart the opponents' defense in a way that few quarterbacks could. He worked the clock, and the sidelines, until his team was on the five-yard line—poised to drive in for the win.

There would be no time left for the opponent to score, they had no more time outs, and the clock would run down anyway.

Justin took the snap, checking his options quickly. Then he saw his favorite target, a sure-handed, burly receiver all by himself in the end zone.

"This is it!" Justin let the football fly as the clock ticked down to zero. But somehow the football sailed over the receiver's outstretched arms, out of the end zone entirely, into the waiting hands of a nearby fan. Justin was devastated as the opposing team celebrated wildly on the field, shouting, "We won! We won! We won!"

Justin had a different kind of message pounding through his head—"I'm a loser! I'm a loser! All I ever do is lose, lose, lose."

*"All that a man achieves and all that he fails to achieve is the direct result of his own thoughts."*
—James Allen

What do Taylor and Justin both have in common? Both are engaged in a form of unintentional exaggeration known as "overgeneralization." People who overgeneralize tend to oversimplify reality, choosing to take one or two negative events as a "pattern of life."

Taylor should not have taken one low test score as an omen of doom in her schoolwork. By telling herself repeatedly that she couldn't pass an exam if her life depended on it, Taylor had actually created a self-fulfilling prophecy. Her confidence was eroded because of her own negative self-talk. What she needed to say to herself was "I did poorly on one test, but I can do better on the next." Taylor had scored well on some previous exams and could have built her confidence by dwelling on that and her other successes in life.

Justin had lost sight of the fact that, while victory would have been sweet, winning wasn't everything. The important thing wasn't whether or not his team won the final game, but that he had done his best. It would have been a shame to let a very successful high school career be eclipsed by one loss on the field.

"Nobody can win them all," Justin could have told himself. "This loss stings pretty badly, but I'm not going to let one bad pass color my entire life."

By taking one incident and assuming the outcome will be the same in similar situations, they formed untrue stereotypes that affected their success.

## PROFILE OF AN OVERGENERALIZER

Overgeneralizers tend to conclude that since something bad happened to them once, it will happen repeatedly for the rest of their lives.[51] In other words, a single negative event will automatically translate into an endless pattern of defeat.

If a bird leaves a present on the windshield of their car, they remark "that always happens to me," when in reality it has happened two times in twenty-five years of driving. If one person turns down their date invitation, they assume that they will be lonely forever, when it is likely that the declined invite had nothing to do with the person's opinion of them. This cognitive error is based on the wrong assumption that if something is true in one case, it is true in all similar cases.[52] The words "always" and "never" are also hallmarks of this distortion.[53] Some common overgeneralizations are featured in **Figure 2.1**.

## A PROPHET LOSES PERSPECTIVE

The ancient story of the prophet Elijah provides a good example of overgeneralization. Elijah lived in the days of wicked Queen Jezebel, a woman so renowned for her cantankerous character that belligerent cows and unpredictable vehicles are still nicknamed after her today. Although Elijah tried to stand for right against Jezebel and her errant husband, King Ahab, sometimes it seemed to the prophet that he was thigh-high in an unstoppable mud slide of distorted thinking and behavior.

Elijah complained about it to God one day, making a somewhat sweeping generalization as he registered his complaint.

"I have been very zealous for the Lord God of hosts," he said, detailing the sins of Israel before wrapping it up with the self-pitying statement of

### COMMON OVERGENERALIZATIONS

- "I've had two panic attacks in the store now. Guess I can count on having one every time I go shopping..."
- "Every time I drive, my heart starts to race. I'm going to die from a heart attack behind the wheel, just like my mom."
- "My boss is sure to fire me now because I made a typo on that letter."
- "If I work hard, I can't help but be successful."
- "Bad things don't happen to good people."
- "You never wash the dishes."
- "I'm going to fail the final exam, then I'll never get a good job and my life will be ruined."
- "I can't ask her for a date. I'll be so nervous my hands will shake, and she'll see what a loser I am."
- "Nobody likes me."

**Figure 2.1**

"I alone am left, and they seek to take my life." Seeing that Elijah's mental state was not good, God put him through a mini *Depression Recovery Program* involving nutritious food, physical exercise, light therapy (by getting him out of the cave) and treatments outside the arsenal of cognitive behavioral therapists today (hail, whirlwinds, and fire).

God concluded with the cognitive correction that "I have reserved seven thousand in Israel all whose knee has not bowed to Baal and every mouth that has not kissed him."[54] In other words, "You are not alone, Elijah. You're statement about being the only one left is a vast overgeneralization. I have seven thousand faithful followers in Israel." Elijah was not the last historical figure to engage in overgeneralization, as illustrated in **Figure 2.2**.

## PATTERNS THAT DON'T EXIST

**Overgeneralization is a form of "lazy thinking" where we try to avoid having to think things through.**

A number of serious problems can arise from the practice of overgeneralization. People are often so good at generalization that they see patterns that don't exist. While generalization can make people very smart, it can also lead to some very unhealthy thinking patterns.[55]

In reality, overgeneralizations turn the scientific method for reaching a conclusion upside down. Instead of observing all available data, formulating a law that explains the data and then testing the law, overgeneralizers take one fact or event, construct a general rule based upon it, but never test the rule.[56]

Sweeping generalizations about any person or group of people tend to exaggerate, ignore important details, or oversimplify reality. Prejudice, stereotyping, and judgmental attitudes are all forms of overgeneralization.

People struggling with depression, who tend to focus on overblown negative generalizations, are especially prone to this harmful cognitive distortion.[57] A depressed person will remember the two days it rained during their vacation at the beach, rather than the five days of sunshine. If anything goes wrong, the depressed person evaluates the entire event as a failure or negative life experience. As a result, a depressed individual's memories are almost always negative. This is reflective of unrealistic expectations. Very few things in life ever work out just as we want. If we expect perfection, we will almost always be disappointed.

The thinking error of overgeneralization is also frequently found in suicidal individuals (together with catastrophization, self-denigration, and all-or-nothing thinking).[58] For example, the researchers Prezant and Neimeyer (1988) found that overgeneralization emerged as a predictor of suicidal thoughts among moderately depressed patients. They concluded that the combination of overgeneralization with depressive symptoms was better as a predictor of suicidality than self-reported depression alone.[59]

## THE SNOWBALL EFFECT

If we are not careful, one overgeneralization can lead to a series of wrong conclusions. Imagine, for example, that you played professional baseball in the seventh game of a World Series. You went to bat with the bases loaded and two outs in the bottom of the ninth inning, and your team was down by three runs. The weary pitcher served a juicy fastball right down the middle of the plate, and you cranked it over the stadium roof for an incredible, last-minute, come-from-behind win. You could draw several correct generalizations from this wish-it-had-happened story. You must be a pretty good baseball player or you wouldn't be playing professional ball. The fact that your team made it to the World Series, and thought enough of your talents to allow you to hit with the final game on the line, actually says that you are a very excellent, top-notch, and highly paid baseball player.

If the victory went to your head, however, and you started to say things like "I am the best baseball player in the world" or "I should have the highest salary in sports," you have crossed the line between rational thinking and overgeneralization.

There are some rather striking examples of such overgeneralizations in college and professional sports. To their great harm, some athletes have followed this line of crooked thinking. Because they are very good in their respective sports, coddled by boosters and benefactors from their alma mater, handed perks, provided an easy ride through college, and given a multi-million dollar pro contract, they develop an excessively high opinion of themselves. The worship of adoring fans only encourages this "god-mentality."

### HISTORIC OVERGENERALIZATIONS

- *"Stocks have reached what looks like a permanently high plateau."* — Economist Irving Fisher on October 16, 1929 (two weeks before the stock market crash that started the Great Depression)
- *"Whatever happens, the U.S. Navy is not going to be caught napping."* — Frank Knox, U.S. Secretary of the Navy, on December 4, 1941 (three days before the Japanese bombed Pearl Harbor.)
- *"With over 50 foreign cars already on sale here, the Japanese auto industry isn't likely to carve out a big slice of the U.S. market"* — *Business Week*, 1958
- *"Airplanes are interesting toys, but they have no military value."* —Marshall Foch, 1911

**Figure 2.2**

Such athletes convince themselves that they are the greatest, and sadly, at some point some of them decide that they are above the law. It is not until it is too late—they have ruined their careers through addiction, murder, DUI car wrecks, or even dog-fighting—that they finally come to their senses. And this whole rocky road—this slippery slope—started with one right conclusion (they were good) that mushroomed into a cloud of overgeneralizations.

"Well, I'm not a professional athlete," you may be saying, "or a rock star, or anything close to it." While this may be true, chances are that you are good—and perhaps very good—at something. You may be a very good cook, business person, sales woman, or writer. While there is nothing wrong with being good, there is plenty wrong with snowballing wrong conclusions. Some negative side effects of this cognitive distortion are detailed in **Figure 2.3**.

**NEGATIVE EFFECTS OF OVERGENERALIZING**

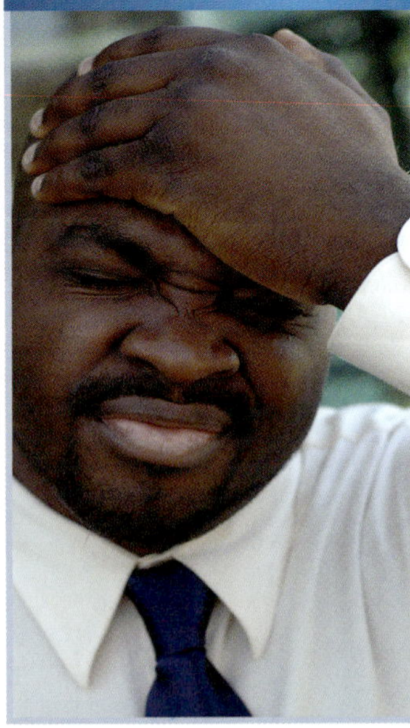

- demoralization
- fear of rejection
- fear of trying new things
- unnecessary suffering
- anger
- depression
- despair
- hopelessness
- failure
- doubt
- anxiety
- worry
- tension

*Figure 2.3*

## AN APPROPRIATE TOOL IN SOME CIRCUMSTANCES

While the previous examples demonstrate the results of overgeneralization, generalizing is not always bad. The ability to find patterns or reason from cause to effect actually helps us to make intelligent decisions in our lives. For example, we may notice that we are cranky after missing too much sleep, nervous before a test, or bloated after eating pizza.

Accurate generalizations have played an extremely useful role in medical history. Before doctors really understood much about the causes of disease, a man named Paracelsus generalized that many miners seemed to die of the same disease, which was later called "Miner's Disease." Despite opposition from the local authorities, Paracelsus' generalization happened to be not only accurate, but extremely helpful in combating the disease.[60]

**Healthy thinkers recognize that information is often incomplete or biased, so they make tentative conclusions and state them with care.**

Ignaz Semmelweis noticed—and generalized—that new mothers were more likely to contract childbed fever if the doctor delivering their baby had performed a dissection just prior to the delivery. Semmelweis' generalization helped pave the way for the practice of using antiseptics in surgery.[61]

One of the greatest historical examples of healthy generalization, together with a refusal to overgeneralize, would have to be the story of Thomas Edison. Edison was the most successful—and the most unsuccessful—inventor of all time. When he died, he held 1,093 U.S. patents.[62]

In a tribute to the greatest inventor in our history, the electric lights throughout the United States were dimmed for one minute on October 21, 1931, a few days after his death.[63]

Yes, Edison was an amazing success as an inventor, although the fact that he applied for an average of 400 patents per year was also a reminder of the many failures he had. Edison did not see these "extra experiments" as failures.

"I have not failed," he once said, "I've just found 10,000 ways that won't work."[64] "I am not discouraged," he was also quoted as saying, "because every wrong attempt discarded is another step forward."[65] Despite the many experiments he tried that did not work, Edison never overgeneralized by calling himself a "failure." Perhaps the avoidance of unhealthy generalizations was something he learned from his mother. When Mrs. Edison learned that young Thomas' teacher had labeled her son as "addled," she promptly pulled him from the school and taught him herself.[66] It seems safe to say that most, if not all, of Edison's inventions were based on scientifically accurate generalizations. These generalizations, and the inventions that resulted from them (for example the phonograph, mimeograph, alkaline storage battery, dictating machine, motion picture camera and projectors), literally changed the world. Edison persistently used generalizations in the right way to develop his inventions.

Another wise man with regard to generalizations was Andrew Carnegie, the steel magnate. He was the richest man in the world at one time, and commissioned a book to record the factors behind the success of the rich and famous so that people wouldn't have to learn them by trial and error. In doing this, he was involved in making positive accurate generalizations.

Carnegie also asked Napoleon Hill to record secrets of success. Hill interviewed more than 500 of the most successful people of his day, including Thomas Edison, Henry Ford, William Wrigley, Jr., and George Eastman.

He found out how they succeeded and shared his findings in his books. In the process, Hill became famous and well-respected himself, serving as an advisor to Presidents Woodrow Wilson and Franklin D. Roosevelt.

A key point that Hill hammered home in his books is that failure is only temporary defeat. Hill understood that setbacks are not permanent, and that jumping to conclusions about failure stops action, kills motivation, and destroys dreams.

Hill might not have realized it, but his book was actually a collection of positive and mostly accurate generalizations.[67]

## SURVIVAL OF THE ACCURATE

One common denominator in people who survive life-threatening situations is that when things seemed darkest for them, they did not overgeneralize about their situation. Despite whatever odds were against them, they refused to give in to the two most deadly assumptions that could be made about a setback: permanence ("there's no way out of this") and pervasiveness ("my life is over").

The 33 Chilean miners who spent 69 days trapped underground after a sudden collapse of the mine were certainly in a life-or-death scenario. Rather than succumb to their extreme circumstances, they relied on positive morale and ingenuity to survive. They refused to give up while there was still a glimmer of hope by overgeneralizing about their situation.

## WHEN OTHERS OVERGENERALIZE

As you become more aware of the cognitive distortions, you will catch *others* making overgeneralizations *about you*. When this happens, it's important to realize that there is often truth to be found, even in overgeneralizations. There usually isn't much to be gained by pointing out that others are wrong or that their thoughts are distorted. The best strategy (before moving on) is simply to mention that you are aware of the problem and are presently working on it.

**Overgeneralization tends to cause arguments, since others are quick to point out exceptions to the overgeneralization.**

For example, if your spouse meets you at the door with the accusation "you're always late," your immediate response could likely determine the level of tranquility for the evening. If you do struggle with tardiness, you could respond truthfully by saying, "I realize that I am frequently late, and I am working to improve that."

Such a response will assure your spouse that you care about their concerns and realize they have a point. In contrast, a defensive retort of "I am not always late" is likely to trigger a heated discussion, setting an unhappy tone for what's left of the day.

## STRATEGIES FOR SUCCESS

Whether you are trying to defeat all-or-nothing thinking, overgeneralization, or one of the other cognitive distortions, many of the techniques are the same. The key is to recognize automatic thoughts, identify thinking errors (or cognitive distortions), and modify your thoughts accordingly.

## THE OBSTINACY CONNECTION

Obstinacy is actually a close relative of overgeneralization. Stubborn people aren't easily convinced of anything they can't see or don't agree with. They stick to their own plans and opinions, no matter how wrong they are. They make bold statements, as if they know everything, and hold their ideas as the only good ones. Obstinacy is a form of selfishness. Such individuals overgeneralize to support their own way of thinking and refuse to change their mind under any condition. This practice of obstinacy eventually becomes a habit, and sadly, part of a person's character.

As you seek to recognize distortions, it's important to realize that two primary mistakes turn generalizations into overgeneralizations:

**1. Holding the generalization as fact rather than a hypothesis.** In the end, generalizations are nothing more than educated guesses. When you have more certainty about your generalization than the facts can justify, it is an overgeneralization. You've gone too far.

**2. Generalizing from too few instances.** The fact that something has happened two or three times in succession doesn't mean that a pattern can be predicted from those incidents. For example, a person who has had two bad relationships in a row should not conclude that all members of the opposite sex are worthless bums!

You'll also want to continue watching for, and altering (if necessary), your self-talk or automatic thoughts. Such thoughts are rapid, knee-jerk thoughts that directly influence our emotions. They are repetitive, habitual, silent, and can be very detrimental.

If your automatic thoughts are accurate and positive, you have nothing to worry about. Trouble arises, however, when a continual stream of distortions run through the mind. Regardless of the thinking trends of your past, it doesn't have to be your future. As with the other cognitive distortions, the key is to recognize the problem, analyze your thinking, and take steps to make sure the generalizations you make are accurate, positive, and helpful.

## References

51. Burns DD. *Feeling Good: The New Mood Therapy*. rev. and updated. New York: Avon, 1999. xix. 33.
52. Beck AT, Rush AJ, Shaw BF, Emery G. *Cognitive Therapy of Depression*. New York: The Guilford Press, 1979. 262.
53. Pucci AR. *The Client's Guide to Cognitive-Behaivioral Therapy*. Lincoln, NE: iUniverse, 2006. 51.
54. 1 Kings 19:10,18. *The Holy Bible*. New King James Version.
55. Ellis A. *Overcoming Destructive Beliefs, Feelings, and Behaviors: New Directions for Rational Emotive Behavior Therapy*. Amherst, N.Y.: Prometheus Books, 2001. 224,225.
56. McKay M. Fanning P. *Self-Esteem*. St. Martin's Paperbacks. 1987. 78.
57. Beck AT, Rush AJ, Shaw BF, Emery G. *Cognitive Therapy of Depression*. New York: The Guilford Press, 1979. 39.
58. Shea SC, *The Practical Art of Suicide Assessment: A Guide for Mental Health Professionals and Substance Abuse Counselors.* John Wiley. 1999. 42.
59. Salkovskis PM, Rachman S. *Frontiers of Cognitive Therapy*. The Guilford Press. 1997. 232.
60. Shackelford J. *A Philosophical Path for Paracelsian Medicine*. Museum Tuscalanum Press. 2004. 12.
61. Wilson WC, Grande CM, Hoyt DB. Trauma: *Emergency resuscitation, perioperative anesthesia, surgical management.* Informa Healthcare USA. 2007. 15.
62. Cregan ER. *Thomas Alva Edison: and the Developers of Electromagnetism.* Compass Point Books. 2009. 17.
63. Woodside M. *Thomas A. Edison: The Man Who Lit Up the World.* Sterling Publishing Co. 2007. 119.
64. Shaw R. *Great Inventors and Inventions*. Wizard Ideas. 2002. 25.
65. Shaw R. *Great Inventors and Inventions*. Wizard Ideas. 2002. 25.
66. Guthridge S. *Thomas Edison: Young Inventor.* Simon and Schuster. 1986. 93.
67. Hill N, Sartwell M. *Napoleon Hill's Keys to Success: The 17 Principles of Personal Achievement.* Penguin Group. 1997. vii.

# Chapter 3

"IT'S NOT WHAT WE DON'T KNOW THAT HURTS US SO MUCH, IT'S WHAT WE KNOW FOR SURE THAT JUST AIN'T SO." —*WILL ROGERS*

## Spring Clean Your Filters

***When we focus on minor aspects of a situation to the exclusion of others, we look through "mental filters." Here's how to be sure yours are clean.***

Bethany spun around, making one last inspection in her bedroom mirror before leaving for a pivotal meeting. This was it—her chance to impress both the powers-that-be and her peers with a well-planned, fascinating presentation.

Bethany had bought a sporty new suit for the occasion that made her feel confident and professional. Bethany's presentation was nothing short of a smashing success.

Congratulations flowed from the higher-ups and colleagues alike, and Bethany was literally walking on air—that is, until she arrived back at her condo and took one last look in the bedroom mirror.

That's when she noticed it—the large price tag still attached to her new wool skirt. Bethany was devastated. She had worked so hard to look and be perfect, and now the whole day was wrecked!

"Oh, how could this happen to me?" Bethany threw herself on the bed and dissolved into tears. "I wanted everything to be so perfect, and thought it was, until I noticed this embarrassing tag on my skirt."

"I bet every person there was focused on this tag instead of my presentation, secretly snickering under their breath!"

"Troy, I was truly impressed with your trumpet audition!" The words fell like music on Troy's ears as the high school band director pulled up a chair to talk. "You did a great job. You memorized your part flawlessly and played with feeling and precision. You have a great future in music here at Valley View High!"

"Did I get first chair then?" Troy's eyes sparkled with anticipation.

"Well, not exactly." There was an awkward silence as the teacher searched for just the right words. "You've surely got the talent to play difficult music, and I know you would do a good job. But I need one of the older students to take the lead in this section of the band."

**When we look through a mental filter, we see any sign of trouble as a disaster in the making.**

Troy was so devastated he didn't hear a word more of the teacher's explanation. From his point of view there was only one thing that mattered—he didn't get first chair.

"I'm no good at playing the trumpet," Troy complained to his mother later when she asked him how tryouts had gone. "I'm never going to get my hopes up again about winning first chair."

Mary peered over the steering wheel of her Ford Expedition, looking for some way to nose into rush-hour traffic.

"This place really needs a stop light," she grumbled to herself. After what seemed like an eternity, a kind gentleman slowed his car to a crawl and waved Mary into the lane.

"Thank you!" Mary heaved a visible sigh of relief, waved at the man and pulled into the lane ahead of him.

A few blocks back, a reckless motorcyclist dodged in and out of lanes, cutting between cars with abandon as horns blared behind him. Before Mary even saw him coming, the Harley roared by her front fender with less than a foot to spare. Mary added her horn to the honking chorus of unhappy drivers behind her, thinking, "This road is full of rude people."

What do Bethany, Troy, and Mary all have in common? They are all seeing life through a mental filter, focusing exclusively on certain negative or upsetting events while ignoring the positive. For Bethany, all the positive feedback she received about her successful presentation was overshadowed by the tag on her skirt. Troy was so focused on not getting first chair that he ignored the very complimentary comments made by his band teacher.

When the Harley nearly clipped Mary's bumper, she forgot all about the nice gentleman who gave her the right of way just moments before. Mary allowed one annoying driver to color her perception of all other drivers on that particular road. Like many of us today, Bethany, Troy, and Mary were all looking through unclear mental filters. Other examples of unhealthy mental filters are shown in **Figure 3.1**.

## EXAMPLES OF UNHEALTHY MENTAL FILTERS

- Your boss praises your report but wants a few changes. All you can do is dwell on the criticism.
- You ran out of time when taking a test, and are now preoccupied with the time limit on every exam you take. You look at the clock every five minutes, have trouble concentrating, and can't stop thinking, "I'm going to run out of time."
- You feel so bad about yourself that you think that compliments directed your way are given out of pity.

***Figure 3.1***

## WHEN A FILTER IS OUT OF KILTER

When looking through a mental filter, the tendency is to single out one aspect of a situation to the exclusion of others that should be considered. A mental filter is actually a perceptual sieve through which events pass as they are encountered. This gives all of those events social meaning and context based on prior experiences. The filter through which one views life could also be compared to looking through binoculars. If our binoculars are flipped around, smudged, or broken, the view of life will be skewed.

Each of us has developed a set of expectations based on schematic mental structures which exist in our minds and strongly affect the way we process sensory experiences.[68] It is common to develop strong cognitive commitments to these schematic structures, to the point where we try to make our perceptions fit into our preconceived schemes instead of the other way around.[69] As a result, the things that we see, hear, and experience are affected by our particular cognitive orientation before the actual act of perceiving.

The opinion of a piece of music may be impacted, for example, by whether or not it is revealed that the composer is Mozart.[70] Individuals who are struggling with depressed thoughts are likely to look at events through a negative mental filter.[71]

Since our tendency is to filter new data through old perceptions and models, mental filters can cause even the most objective of data to not be received in a totally accurate way. In cases of poor decision-making, it is the filters, rather than valid information sources, providing the data.[72] Even in scientific circles, perceptions are affected by mental filters. Despite the lofty goal of simply observing the world as it is, how researchers perceive what they see is affected by their cognitive orientation prior to the act of observation.[73] A prime example of this would be scientists during the time of Galileo, who had difficulty accepting his assertion that the earth orbits around the sun instead of vice versa. Looking through the mental filters of traditional scientific thought, the scholars of Galileo's day believed in the geocentric view that the Earth remained motionless at the center of the universe. Galileo, who made original contributions to the science of motion through an innovative combination of experiment and mathematics, had observed otherwise. Today Galileo has been called the "Father of Modern Science," but during his lifetime he paid a price for looking outside the established mental filters of his day. Forced to stand trial before the Inquisition and later to recant his views, he spent the last years of his life under house arrest for publishing, among other scientific facts, that the earth did indeed revolve around the sun!

**Clean mental filters promote healthy, free-flowing decisions.**

## ANCIENT MENTAL FILTERS

Eve was looking through a mental filter—or some might say blinders—when she saw and heard the message of doubt from the serpent in the Garden of Eden.[74] When Noah preached about the flood, the vast majority of people who heard him looked through their mental filters and saw a demented old man.[75] Samson was also looking through a mental filter when he couldn't "find" an attractive woman among his own people and instructed his father to get him a certain Philistine woman.[76]

Nathaniel was looking through a mental filter when his brother called him to come and meet Jesus of Nazareth. "Can there any good thing come out of Nazareth?" he wanted to know.[77] Evidently Jesus' hometown had such a bad reputation that it was hard for Nathaniel and probably others to envision anything positive emerging from it.

## FILTER FALLOUTS

There are a number of unhappy outcomes, or "filter fallouts," associated with seeing life through a smudged or distorted mental filter. Though remorse for past failures can be a positive motivating force, people who focus on previous negative experiences will almost always be disappointed with their performance. Relying on distorted or negative assumptions can also make us afraid to formulate, much less utter, a truly novel idea. In a very practical sense, creativity involves escaping from assumptions and beliefs which block us from an otherwise obvious solution. In order to be creative, we must move from old to new habits of thinking.

The longer we have been immersed in an inaccurate way of thinking, the more likely we are to form distorted mental filters about what is possible or true. In order to be creative problem-solvers, we must relax these negative mental filters.[78] Negative thought patterns also contribute to poor decisions by weighing us down with emotional baggage. When our mental plumbing is clogged, the nimble mindset needed to make free-flowing decisions and live life to its fullest is missing. In contrast, when the mental filters are clear, our emotional operating system is also clear of concerns, prejudices, negative memories, and cloudy personal beliefs. Free from judgmental clutter, we can now observe the world about us with clarity, confidence, and unfiltered perceptions.

## DAMAGED PERSONAL RELATIONSHIPS

Distorted mental filters can also have a damaging effect on personal relationships, as detailed in **Figure 3.2**. When a student becomes a teacher's pet, or a worker becomes the bosses' favorite, the perception is he can do no wrong. The teacher or boss is filtering out the bad and focusing on the good at the expense of other relationships. On the opposite end of the spectrum, a scapegoat is faulted for everything that goes wrong. Divorcees commonly complain that their ex-spouse "can't do anything right."

**Unhealthy mental filters create emotional baggage.**

Mental filters are especially prevalent and dangerous around romantic relationships. Many couples tend to see only the good until they are married. After the initial infatuation wears off, they start seeing more of the bad, until in some cases they see only the bad.

If the marriage crumbles, the man who once was a prince somehow becomes a mean ogre, bully, or jerk while the darling princess becomes a nag, witch, or hag. In many cases it is the perception—not the person—who changed.

Communication between couples is hampered by the fact that each spouse looks through his or her own mental filter. As a result, the two of them may interpret the same message in totally different ways. When sociocultural, ethnic, and educational differences are added to the mix, it's easy to see how misunderstandings occur.[79] Emotions also play a role in relationship-related mental filters. Most humans, at some point, bring distress from home to the workplace and vice versa. These mental filters then influence the home or work setting in negative or nonproductive ways.

### DISTORTED MENTAL FILTERS ARE BAD FOR RELATIONSHIPS

- "Teachers' pets" or "bosses' favorites" are seen as infallible and resented by others.
- "Scapegoats" are never given the benefit of the doubt and are unfairly blamed.
- Filters are especially prevalent and dangerous around romantic relationships.
- Perceptions are more likely to change than people themselves.

*Figure 3.2*

**THE HIGH COST OF PESSIMISM**

- greater risk of depression
- impaired immune system
- increased risk of premature death
- increased risk of fatal accidents
- more likely to contract heart disease, the flu, and other health challenges
- more likely to seek medical and mental health care services
- more frequent doctor visits
- more likely to be inactive
- a reduction in overall physical and mental health

*Figure 3.3*

## DANGER AROUND EVERY CORNER

When properly used, mental filters are actually part of our brain's innate survival instinct. Each of us has been given a drive for self-preservation, which includes looking at the world in which we live for possible dangers. But while healthy mental filters are designed to keep us safe, they can also trigger our fight-or-flight response whenever our minds interpret something as unusual or alarming. This "red alert" stage, which results in a sudden epinephrine (adrenaline) rush to the body, has one function—to enable your muscles to work hard and fast in case you need to escape or do battle.

Since your muscles are fueled by oxygen and glucose, your entire physiology changes to enable the speedy transportation of these bodily fuels. Heart rate and blood pressure leap, while anything else going on in the body (such as digestion) slows down or stops altogether. It's kind of like a fire alarm going off in a building. As the emergency is dealt with, everything else is ignored. Not until the alarm is over do things return back to normal.[80]

Problems arise in the body when mental filters (combined with a fast-paced, high-stress existence) cause our "fire alarms" to go off dozens of times every day. In such cases, the body never has a chance to calm itself or regain its natural equilibrium. This level of mental stress eventually takes a toll, resulting in high blood pressure, compromised immune systems, or difficult digestion.

## WELLNESS CONCERNS

Researchers have found that pessimists (people who seem determined to view life through a negative mental filter) really do have something to worry about. A study by researchers in the Netherlands found that people who are temperamentally pessimistic are more likely to die of heart disease and other causes than those who are by nature optimistic.[81] Subjects with the highest level of optimism were 45 percent less likely than those with the highest level of pessimism to die of all causes during the study.[82] As documented in **Figure 3.3**, more than a few scientific studies have shown the danger that pessimism poses to a person's health.[83]

## AN OPTIMISTIC BALANCE

While much has been made of the power of positive thinking, there is also danger involved in unbridled optimism, or positive thinking just for the sake of positive thinking. Rather than looking through the mental filter of a pessimist or pure optimist, the goal should be "realistic optimism" where we always expect the best but prepare for the worst. (Some benefits of being a realistic optimist are detailed in **Figure 3.4**). A pessimist who contracts the flu thinks it will surely progress into pneumonia, and may actually create a self-fulfilling prophecy by conveying the wrong message to her body and mind. In contrast, a purely optimistic person might ignore the symptoms, subjecting her body to overwork at a time when it needs to rest. A realistic optimist would recognize that she has a history of respiratory complications, and while expecting the best, take adequate precautions to prevent progression into pneumonia.

A pessimist with a flight to catch might say to himself, "there's no way I can make the gate on time." He might as well put lead in his shoes; since he doesn't believe he can make the gate, he almost certainly won't. A purely optimistic person will progress glibly to the airport, sure that the plane will be waiting for him 10 minutes after the scheduled departure time.

### REALISTIC OPTIMISTS CAN:

- roll out of bed each morning and face the day with their mental and emotional operating systems completely clear of prejudices, negative memories, or other mental errors.
- avoid judgmental clutter and acquired "soot" when analyzing information received each day.
- make life's decisions with crystal-clear perception.
- plan their days with clarity and confidence.
- look at people close to them not as they are, but as what they could become.

*Figure 3.4*

In contrast, a realistic optimist will say "I know it's going to be close, but the flight could be late or even if the door is closed, they might let me in." While understanding and preparing for the potential consequence of a missed flight, the realistic optimist is also best positioned to calmly turn on the afterburners and get to the gate on time.

Realistic optimists believe Murphy's Law that whatever can go wrong will, but they also act as if they're bound to succeed. Accurate in their estimations, they anticipate hurdles but also believe in their capacity to overcome. Motivated by the taste of success, they achieve it more often than their less accurate counterparts.

Realistic optimism has also been strongly associated with better stress management and the tendency to seek social support, both of which contribute to health and longevity.[84] Perhaps realistic optimists fare better because they are better able to cope with adversity or tend to engage in more health-promoting behaviors.[85]

While a cheery, optimistic spirit is certainly something worth striving for, researchers have correlated a positive impact for individuals who simply try to avoid negative thinking.[86] So if becoming a sunshiny optimist seems like too much of a stretch at the moment, you may improve your health by simply cutting off negative thoughts. Over the years, a 14-day plan to eliminate negative thoughts has been extremely helpful to many of my patients. Details of exactly how to try this plan in your own life can be found in **Figure 3.5**. The story of Leslie, one of the many persons whose life was literally transformed by shifting to more positive thoughts, is documented at the end of this chapter, in **Figure 3.7**.

## THE POWER OF POSITIVE FILTERS

Mental filters are not, of themselves, always a negative thing. Our senses are exposed to more than a trillion bits of information every second, so the process of automatically filtering what is unimportant or already known is a normal part of everyday life. Through our mental filters, we are able to sort through mountains of minutia, allowing only the most important information into our consciousness.

As we live each moment, events that make up our lives pass through the mental filter of our beliefs, values, and expectations, creating our daily reality. Every time we make a decision in life, we have to wiggle through this gamut of established belief systems and thought associations created by a lifetime of feelings and experiences. If our mental filter only lets in negative things, life will be truly depressing. In contrast, if our filters are set up to look for more positive things, life takes on a happier hue. Some of the greatest biblical examples of realistically positive mental filters are demonstrated by God, who is an expert at looking at what people may become instead of what they are and even more expert at leading them to a better way of life.

## 14-DAY PLAN TO IMPROVE THOUGHTS

The topics of our conversation really can have a negative or positive influence on our health. Following is an exercise that many of my patients, and individuals attending my seminars have found to be of great benefit. If you dedicate yourself to succeeding at this, it can certainly help you, too.

- For two weeks (14 consecutive days) decide to say nothing critical or negative about anything or any person.
- Not one critical word is allowed to be spoken to others (not even "constructive" criticism).
- Speak to others using positive or neutral words or speak nothing at all (use the same rule for thoughts).
- If you slip up on any day during the two weeks, you begin counting again until you achieve all 14 consecutive days.
- Don't get discouraged if you have to start over; things will get easier as you become more aware of your thoughts.
- After completing 14 consecutive days, constructive criticism is allowed and you will be a far better judge of what that really means.

This exercise may seem impossible for those raising children or leading in a business environment. It is possible, however, to communicate expectations and enforce consequences without critical words.

***Figure 3.5***

### ANCIENT POWER OF POSITIVE FILTERS

A good ancient example of a positive mental filter is found in the story of Joseph. Joseph's life actually started out very well. Born into a wealthy household, treasured son of the favorite wife, he had much to look forward to early on. The first big blow came when Joseph's beautiful mother, Rachel, died. He was only four years old at the time.[87] At age seventeen he was sold into slavery by his hateful brothers. Joseph's own hard work, combined with the blessing of God, led him to be promoted until he was chief of his master's house. His life crumbled around him again, however, when he was falsely accused by his master's wife and thrown into prison for doing what was right. From the depths of the dungeon, Joseph worked his way up the ranks once more until he was basically in charge of the prison. But even then, after helping a soon-to-be-released fellow prisoner who would have some clout with the king, he seemed a forgotten man. The prisoner Joseph helped agreed to say a good word for his friend, but somehow it slipped his mind.[88]

If any man ever had a reason to have negative mental filters, it was Joseph. Motherless at a young age, hated and betrayed by his brothers, sold as a slave, falsely accused, thrown into prison—Joseph had every reason to lapse into a "poor me" mentality—but he didn't. When Joseph's fortunes finally turned and his betraying brothers knelt at his feet to see if they could buy bread, he even excused their earlier foolish actions.

"You meant what you did for evil," he told them, "but God meant it for good."[89] Early on in his life, Joseph chose to look through the mental filter of God's big, overall plan allowing him to view any situation in a positive light. In the words of the apostle Paul, "All things work together for good to them that love God."[90]

**Behind every dark cloud is a silver lining...**

## SINGING IN THE DUNGEON

Positive mental filters, combined with faith in the providence of God, are the reasons why Paul and Silas could amaze their captors by maintaining a cheerful attitude in a dingy, rat-infested dungeon, singing hymns while locked in the stocks.[91] This is how martyrs through the centuries have sung, sought to cheer up others, or even smiled while knowingly en route to a painful, public demise. This is how Jesus Himself, "who for the joy that was set before Him endured the cross, despising the shame," went peacefully to His death.[92]

Because of His study of and love for the Scripture, Jesus had a Scriptural world view. He looked through the mental filter of the Bible, frequently saying "it is written."[93] Even when falsely accused, slapped, scourged, and unjustly convicted, Jesus could pray for His persecutors. His example of love under the cruelest of circumstances, of noble and patient suffering, is what gave His story such power to change people's lives. And all this was possible because of His realistically positive mental filter—a filter in harmony with Scripture and God's will for His life.

The exciting thing about all of this is that such a positive, healthy mental filter is available to each one of us today. Even though many bad things may have happened in our past, defeat does not have to be ours. There is a positive plan for this universe, and for each of our lives. While you can't control every circumstance that happens in your life, you can control your response.

Bad things do happen to good people, but they will always be easier to endure when put in proper perspective. If you have not considered the circumstances of your life from a realistically positive, balanced, and healthy

***Figure 3.6***

mental filter such as is portrayed in the biographies of Scripture, now would be a good time to give it a try. There is much to be gained from such a perspective, and in the final analysis, nothing at all to lose.

## STRATEGIES FOR SUCCESS

Even if your mental filters have become sooty or clogged, they don't have to stay that way. With a strong dose of discipline and a well-thought-out plan, the smudges and dust can be cleared away. Some of the best advice for seeing things clearly is found in Philippians 4:8, which details seven positive mental filters (as listed in **Figure 3.6**).

In addition, ask yourself if you are taking the entire picture into consideration, if there is a positive side to this situation that you are overlooking, or if you are engaging in too many activities that dwell on the negative.

When you catch yourself with a negative "mental filter", replace the unhealthy thoughts with ones that balance the story. There really is a silver lining behind every cloud. There are "hidden positives" in just about every situation. If you look hard enough, you will find them. Train yourself to recognize unhealthy thoughts right away for what they are—a type of thinking that leads to poor self-worth and an even worse mood.

When you think more balanced thoughts, your brain will release neurotransmitters that make you feel better. You may not realize what is happening, but your mood will lighten. That lighter mood is a by-product of telling yourself a better, more realistic story. A balanced view, or clearer thinking, in turn soothes the mind, and as the mind is soothed, you will be able to enjoy what is good about life. Yes, you can have a mental and emotional operating system that is clean, healthy, and running at maximum capacity, even in the midst of great trials. Why not get started today?

## HOW THE "14-DAY CURE" CHANGED A LIFE

I didn't know I was depressed. My husband thought my hormones had gone haywire and pleaded with me for years to see a doctor, which I did without any positive results.

I was very unhappy in my marriage and so filled with anger that I was being eaten alive by negative thoughts. My thoughts were very fearful, and I picked on my husband incessantly. I really didn't like most everyone, but he was the one who got the brunt of my pent-up anger and frustration. My thoughts were extremely fanatical, and I felt very much alone.

One day my husband heard of tryptophan on TV and suggested I try it. After just a few weeks, I was feeling considerably better. I was still angry and still had mood swings, but not so severe. I took tryptophan for about three years, but every 8 months or so, I would try to stop taking it. Each time I would announce, "I'm cured! I'm getting off the tryptophan!" My children would plead, "Mom, please take a vacation while you do that!"

In reality, I would have loved to take a vacation and get away from them all. I needed lots of time without someone trying my patience (easy to do). I stuffed all my emotions inside, and I was a mess.

My husband was still telling me that my hormones were messed up. I got a book on hormones and started taking them. That helped a bit in some areas, but I still didn't have peace real deep in my heart.

I began to realize my life was out of control. I had had stomach problems for years, and continual thoughts of running away. It was frightening at times.

Then I got your book ***Depression: the Way Out***, and read that tryptophan supplements can have side effects. Upon hearing this, I nearly had an anxiety attack! How could I live without tryptophan? I began trying other things, such as light therapy, a vegan diet, walnuts and flax seed—but still I had not "arrived."

Then I learned about your 14-day exercise involving the avoidance of any critical words. It seemed impossible, but I was fresh out of solutions.

***Figure 3.7***

I posted little sticky notes with "14" all over the house to remind me of my countdown. One week later, I had walls dotted with "14s." I was feeling a bit discouraged. Was I really that wretched? After about a week or two, I really let my husband have it. He said I needed to get professional help and stop trying to self-treat. Within the next day or two a TREMENDOUS light went on. I have not been the same since.

I am free. I feel like a new person. My walk with God is sweeter than ever. My marriage is delightful, and so is my husband. I think he's a new man! But honestly, he hasn't changed, it is my heart that has changed. My children are more affectionate, and my daughter says I'm so easy to get along with. The judgmental, fearful, hateful thoughts are 98% gone, and when I feel tensions arise, I think, "this is a strange thought!" Then, through knowledge or prayer, I expel it as quickly as it came.

What seemed like extreme therapeutic efforts are, in reality, not that hard after all and worth every minute I put in. How I feel cannot be explained, it must be experienced to be believed. I'm down to one tryptophan a day, and confident I will be totally off it very soon.

The last six weeks have been the best in 20 years. I hadn't had six consecutive good days in 20 years, or hardly six consecutive hours of peaceful thoughts. I am completely serious. Praise God for His power to heal, and I thank you, Dr. Nedley, for your work. I also thank God for my patient family that has loved me all these years.

I can now look forward to the next 20 years of marriage to the wonderful man God has given me, my beautiful children, and the precious church we are blessed to be part of. I need to sign off before I cry for complete joy. My heart is full.

Blessings to you, Dr. Nedley. May the Lord grant you strength and wisdom to order your steps and continue to point people in the way of healing.

"He brought me up also out of a horrible pit, out of the miry clay, and set my feet upon a rock, and established my goings. And he hath put a new song in my mouth, even praise unto our God." (Psalms 40:2-3)

***Leslie***

## References

68. Johnson-Laird PN, Wason PC (eds.), *Thinking: Readings in Cognitive Science* (Cambridge: Cambridge University Press, 1977), pp. 421-432.
69. Anderson RC, Spiro RJ, Montague WE (eds.), *Schooling and the Acquisition of Knowledge* (Hillsdale, N.J.: Lawrence Erlbaum, 1977), p. 112.
70. Cahn SM, Griffel LM. "The Strange Case of John Shmarb: An Aesthetic Puzzle," *Journal of Aesthetics and Art Criticism* 34 (1975): 21-22.
71. Burns DD. *Feeling Good: The New Mood Therapy*. New York: HarperCollins, 1999. 34.
72. Suhr J. *The Choosing by Advantages Decisionmaking System,* Quorum Books. 1999. 175.
73. Fleck L, et. al. *Genesis and Development of a Scientific Fact*. University of Chicago Press. 1979.
74. Genesis 3:1-6. *The Holy Bible*. Authorized King James Version.
75. Hebrews 11:7. *The Holy Bible*. Authorized King James Version.
76. Judges 14:3. *The Holy Bible*. Authorized King James Version.
77. John 1:44-46. *The Holy Bible*. Authorized King James Version.
78. Tudor R, *Creativity and Problem Solving at Work*. Ashgate Publishign. 1997. 10-11.
79. Yoder-Wise PS. *Leading and Managing in Nursing*. Mosby. 2002. 330.
80. Guyton AC. *Textbook of Medical Physiology*. Arthur C. Guyton, John E. Hall. 11th ed. Elsevier Saunders. 2006. 758.
81. Friedman RA. "Yet Another Worry for Those Who Believe the Glass is Half-empty." *The New York Times* 9 Jan. 2007.
82. Friedman RA. "Yet Another Worry for Those Who Believe the Glass is Half-empty." *The New York Times* 9 Jan. 2007.
83. Maruta T, et al. "Optimism-pessimism Assessed in the 1960s and Self-reported Health Status 30 Years Later." *Mayo Clinic Proceedings* 77 (2002): 748+.
84. Friedman RA. "Yet Another Worry for Those Who Believe the Glass is Half-empty." *The New York Times* 9 Jan. 2007.
85. Friedman RA. "Yet Another Worry for Those Who Believe the Glass is Half-empty." *The New York Times* 9 Jan. 2007.
86. Robinson-Whelen S. "Distinguishing optimism from pessimism in older adults: Is it more important to be optimistic or not to be pessimistic?" *Journal of Personality and Social Psychology* 73.6 (1997): 1345+.
87. Genesis 35:16-18. *The Holy Bible*. Authorized King James Version.
88. Genesis 39-40. *The Holy Bible*. Authorized King James Version.
89. Genesis 50:20. *The Holy Bible*. Authorized King James Version.
90. Romans 8:28. *The Holy Bible*. Authorized King James Version.
91. Acts 16:22-25. *The Holy Bible*. Authorized King James Version.
92. Hebrews 12:2. *The Holy Bible*. Authorized King James Version.
93. Luke 4:4,8,10. *The Holy Bible*. Authorized King James Version.

Chapter 4

"MAN LOOKS ON THE OUTWARD APPEARANCE, BUT THE LORD LOOKS ON THE HEART." *—1 SAMUEL 16:7*

# Cross-check Your Conclusions

***Most of our mind-reading efforts are less accurate than we think—and the results can be truly disastrous.***

Jackie sank into the cushy living room couch and buried her face in a pillow.

"Just another trying day in the classroom," she sighed. Things wouldn't have been nearly so bad if it weren't for Steve, a challenging 12-year-old with a penchant for punching others.

Steve seemed to specialize in picking on other children. Lately the target of his harassment, and fists, had been little Billy. Despite Jackie's best efforts, Steve pummelled Billy both verbally and physically whenever he got the chance.

The principal had stepped in and parents had been contacted, but thus far, all efforts to curb Steve's bad behavior seemed to fall on deaf ears.

"They just think bad thoughts about me," Steve would complain about his classmates. Even when the other children tried to be kind to Steve, he would say things like, "You can't fool me," and "I know you're trying to trick me." Steve was sure he knew what everyone else was thinking—and no one could convince him otherwise.

It was a hazy, lazy summer afternoon that found Ryan and Noah window shopping on the main street of Little Town, Minnesota.

"Would you look at that!" Noah was just admiring an expensive baseball mitt in the display of a sporting goods store when Ryan noticed a young man across the street.

"Hey, it's Brett," Ryan nudged Noah. Brett was the star hitter for the high school baseball team, which both Ryan and Noah were hoping to make in the fall.

"He talked to me the other day at the beach," Ryan whispered.

"Naaww—a big shot like him wouldn't talk to a small fry like you, Noah was quick to set his friend straight.

"Watch this," Ryan walked over the to edge of the curb.

"Howdy, Brett!" he yelled across the street, waving his Little Town Lions baseball cap. But Brett didn't even turn his head.

"Hey Brett!" Ryan tried again.

"I can't believe it," Ryan slapped his baseball cap back on and stormed down the street. "He was real nice to me the other day, but he sure is stuck up now."

"Told you," Noah snickered.

"Well, I'll get even," Ryan muttered. "I'll start by winning his spot on the team. Then he'll be sitting on the bench, and I won't say 'Hi' to him!"

What do Steve and Ryan have in common? Both are engaging in the cognitive distortion known as "mind reading." Psychologists define "mind reading" as the attribution of mental states to others from their behavior and the use of that assumption to guide our actions and predict those of others. In CBT, you are mind reading when you assume that people are reacting negatively to you when there's no definite evidence to support that view.[94] Some examples of mind-reading statements are found in **Figure 4.1**.

Steve thought he could read the minds of his classmates, but the truth was, unless the other children expressed their opinions, he couldn't really know what they thought.

## EXAMPLES OF MIND READING

- "If he really cared, he'd know that I'm too tired to go out tonight."
- "I know what you're thinking…"
- "You're only saying that because…"
- "You know what I mean…"
- "You would never do that unless…"
- "I just know they are talking about me right now…"

***Figure 4.1***

Ryan automatically assumed that Brett was stuck up when he didn't return Ryan's greeting. Brett could have been absorbed in his thoughts or looking in a different direction. He most likely never saw or heard Ryan call him from across the street. When Ryan assumed that Brett was stuck up, he was really trying to read Brett's mind.

There are few tasks as important in life as distinguishing between what we know for certain and what we merely believe. Yet many of us have acquired a habit of mind reading that limits our ability to make this important distinction. In many cases, this habit is so pervasive we don't even see it.

*"I know what you're thinking!"*

## MIND READING ISN'T ALWAYS USEFUL

Reading the intentions of others is actually a valuable social skill. Having some intuition about what others are thinking can help us build stronger relationships, make better decisions, and improve our perceptions of people and events. However, there are certain risks involved (see **Figure 4.2**).

While there are benefits associated with the ability to understand what others are thinking, there are also pitfalls to be avoided. Most people think they are better at reading minds than they actually are. For example, many individuals think they really do know a liar when they see one. A lot of experimental data suggests otherwise, however. Even law enforcement professionals such as policemen and judges can distinguish truth tellers from liars at a rate no better than chance.[95]

### RISKY MIND READING IN BUSINESS

"Our customers aren't requesting that feature, but let's include it — we know what's best for them."

"The labor union would never agree to a pay cut, so we'll just have to move our manufacturing to China."

"They're estimating $5 million for that project, but they always pad estimates — I'll cut it 25%."

"They always cut our estimates, so let's pad them by 25%."

"I'll bet that narrow-minded zoning board is anti-progress. We'll never get this shopping center project approved."

***Figure 4.2***

Despite the fact that most of us really are not very good at reading the minds of others, the point that matters is that we think we are. It is so easy to jump to conclusions about what another is thinking without stopping to verify what they really do think.

While it is often cumbersome to try and figure out what other people are really thinking, having the ability to read the minds of others would take a lot of the fun and surprise out of life, not to mention the ethical issue of intruding on the privacy of others.

## MEASURING MIND-READING PROWESS

Dr. William Ickes, professor of psychology at the University of Texas and author of the book, *Everyday Mind Reading: Understanding What Other People Think and Feel,* has been studying the mind-reading behavior of people for fifteen years. Ickes and his colleagues developed a procedure for measuring how well people can discern the thoughts of others.

Ickes' research strategy involved unobtrusively videotaping pairs of people engaged in spontaneous conversation, then having each person review the tape twice: once to label his or her own thoughts and feelings at precise points and again to identify those of his or her partner. By comparing their responses, he was able to measure the accuracy with which research subjects empathetically read each other's minds. If the person really was thinking what the other person thought he or she was thinking, the raters categorized those thoughts at that particular time as "essentially the same." When one person came close to guessing the other's thoughts, but wasn't quite on, the raters categorized those thoughts as "similar but not the same." Lastly, when the "guesser" was pretty much off in terms of what he or she thought the other was thinking, the raters classified those thoughts as "essentially different."

The raters, usually three or four per study, typically agreed on nearly 9 out of 10 of their rankings for the same item. A computer software program then calculated a score denoting each volunteer's average empathic accuracy during the experimental session.

Results from Ickes' studies and others suggested that while individuals often become fairly good at knowing what friends, lovers, and even strangers may be thinking, they are still wrong a significant number of times. The studies also seem to show that men and women read the thoughts and feelings of others about equally well, despite the superiority usually assigned to "women's intuition."[96,97] More of Ickes results are documented in **Figure 4.3**. Ickes findings would agree with a fundamental principle of CBT, namely, that overvaluing one's ability to read the minds of others is a cognitive error which can lead to many frustrations. In attempting to correct the challenges of "crooked thinking," one of the bad habits we must overcome is attempting to read the minds of others.

## MIND-READING RESEARCH FINDINGS

- When dealing with strangers, only about one in four mind-reading assumptions is correct.
- The ratio of mind-reading accuracy shoots up considerably in close, long-term relationships, to as much as 4 out of 5 chances of being correct.
- Some people are better at mind reading than others, but nearly everyone overestimates his or her talent at mind reading.
- With good feedback, people can improve mind reading ability.
- Even people who were highly skilled in social "mind reading" still encountered situations where, in an attempt to keep an alliance afloat, they totally misread a romantic partner.

***Figure 4.3***

### ANCIENT EXAMPLES OF CORRECT MIND READING

In ancient times, two women came to King Solomon for judgment one day. They brought two infant sons with them, but tragically, one of the babies was dead.

"Her son died in the night," the one mother accused. "She switched babies with me and gave me the one who had died."

"Not so," retorted the other. "The living baby is mine."

And so the argument continued vehemently until King Solomon intervened.

"Cut the live baby in half," King Solomon ordered. "Give half to each woman. That should settle it." While one of the mothers seemed to think that the judgment was fair, the second came completely unglued.

"Give the baby to her," she said. "Only please, do not kill it."

King Solomon then knew who the real mother was—the one who was willing to give up her child if that would mean sparing his life. Reading the minds of the mothers, he knew that the one who really loved the child was the true mother.[98]

The parable of the ten talents furnishes another ancient example of mind reading. In this story told by Jesus, a businessman went on an extended trip, leaving three servants in charge of his assets or "talents of silver". The businessman, who understood the capabilities of his various servants, gave five talents to one, two to another, and only one talent to the third. When the businessman returned from his journey, he found that two of the servants had faithfully discharged their duty. The man who had been given five talents turned in ten to his master, while the man who had two turned in four. Unfortunately, the man who had been entrusted with only one talent presented a speech—instead of a summary of earnings—to his master.

"I knew that you were a hard man," said the unprofitable servant, reminding the master that he sometimes reaped where he himself had not sown. "So I buried the talent and kept it for you, and now here it is. I am giving you back exactly what you gave me."[99]

The servant, who met with an unhappy fate in the parable, inaccurately mind read his master. He shirked his duty because he expected to be treated badly, and in the end got what he expected—not because his assumptions were true—but because he deserved what he got. The unprofitable servant not only tried to mind read his master, he was looking through a negative mental filter at his master as well.

**Overestimating our mind-reading prowess can lead to a great deal of trouble.**

This should be a warning to us today. If through inaccurate mind reading we expect someone to be rude or unfair and treat them as such, they may recognize our assumptions and treat us as we expect—even if this is not their normal way of doing things. If we are not careful, inaccurate mind reading can lead to negative self-fulfilling prophecies.

## SHOULD WE JUDGE OTHERS?

The topic of whether and how to judge others is a confusing one to many people. On the one hand, we want to be forgiving, loving, and nonjudgmental. At the same time, we must carefully and wisely judge situations in order to draw wise conclusions.

A man named Bishop Potter once set sail from America to Europe on one of the great transatlantic ocean liners. When Mr. Potter boarded the ship, he found he would have to share a cabin with another passenger. After visiting his accommodations, Mr. Potter made a visit to the purser's deck and asked if he could leave his gold watch and other valuables in the ship's safe.

"I wouldn't normally ask for this," he explained, "but judging from the appearance of my cabin-mate, I was afraid he might not be a trustworthy man."

"The gentleman you are rooming with was just here," the purser remarked as he stored the valuables away. "He wanted me to store his for the very same reason!"[100]

Judging others by their appearance is generally not a good idea. We are also likely to make wrong assumptions when we judge a situation before we know all the details. John Wesley, who was one of great leaders of the Protestant Reformation, once told of a man he had little respect for because the man appeared to be miserly and covetous. One day when the man made only a small gift to a worthy charity, Wesley criticized him openly. After the incident the man went to Wesley privately.

"I've been living on nothing but parsnips and water for the past several weeks," the man informed the preacher. "By skimping on everything and buying nothing for myself, I am able to pay off my creditors one by one. Christ has made me an honest man," the parishioner told Wesley. "I must settle up with my worldly neighbors and show them what the grace of God can do in the heart of a man who was once dishonest." Wesley, who was understandably embarrassed by his unfair judgment of the man, quickly apologized and asked for forgiveness.[101]

As demonstrated in these two stories, it is easy to misinterpret another person's motives. Someone who flies past at 90 mph (145 km/hr) on the freeway may be a reckless driver who is high on drugs, but they could just as easily be a loving parent trying to get a child who is choking to the emergency room. While we can definitely judge the appearance of what is taking place, it would be unfair to judge the motives of the driver.

The natural human tendency is to judge others more harshly than we judge ourselves. It's easy to look at others and make quick decisions based on what is taking place, but we tend to cut ourselves some rather generous slack. We often judge others on their behavior, while judging ourselves on intentions.

Humans cannot see the intentions and motives of others, however. We can only see outward appearances. And there is often a very wide chasm between outward behavior and inner motives. This is why, in trying to explain themselves, people so often say, "What I meant was…" Their only hope of explaining certain actions is in telling the motive behind the action.

So, should we judge others? While the ancient injunction to "judge not that ye be not judged" is frequently quoted, some want to stay so far away from anything remotely resembling judgment that they err in the opposite direction.[102] The Bible does clearly state that we are not to judge others' motives. However, we can judge their actions. For example, a man who is judging the actions of another could accurately say, "You stole my car; that was bad." However, when he says, "You stole my car; you are bad," he crosses the line from judging actions to judging the man. God alone can judge the motives and intentions of the people around you.

It is imprudent to try to judge someone else's motives.

## STRATEGIES FOR SUCCESS

A good test to determine whether you are mind reading is to ask, "How do I know that?" If the answer doesn't involve a direct report from the owner of the mind in question, chances are good that you are mind reading. Following are some useful strategies for overcoming the mind-reading habit:

### 1. Avoid putting words in the mouths of others.

Even if you have a pretty good idea what another person is going to say, do not say it for them. This is especially important when the other individual is upset. Listen carefully to what they are saying, and let them tell you

**Is this driver speeding recklessly—or trying to get a woman who is about to deliver her baby to the hospital in time? Unless you're a mind reader—how can you really know?**

how they feel. It's also important for you to state your message as clearly, honestly, and constructively as possible. This means avoiding destructive or unnecessary criticism and being sensitive to what the other person really is trying to say. Watch out for the key phrases that tend towards judging the motives of others. Stop such thoughts immediately and ask the person you are conversing with what they are really thinking. You may also find yourself in situations where someone appears to be trying to read your mind. If you lack sufficient evidence, however, watch out! You may be the one who is mind reading!

### 2. Play the *Mind Compatibility* Game.

If you can find a copy, try playing the *Mind Compatibility* board game. This game is a fun reminder of the human mind reading "deficit." Playing it can also strengthen the frontal lobe of your brain. The game is out of print, but you might be able to get a copy on eBay™. Another useful exercise to test your mind-reading ability involves taking 3 x 5" cards and writing down, at 15-minutes intervals, what you think a person you are talking with might be thinking about just then. Each person involved in the game should write down what they are thinking at given intervals of time, as well as what they themselves were thinking.

After an hour or two of this, gather up the cards and grade your mind reading ability. Chances are excellent that you are not quite as good at knowing what even your spouse or long-term friends are thinking as you assume. This should be a warning to all of us to avoid jumping to conclusions by engaging in the detrimental practice of trying to read each other's minds.

### 3. Listen to others and do not assume.

People who share daily living as families can easily slip into the habit of assuming they know each other too well. Couples who have been married ten, twenty, or even fifty years often come to believe they know how their partner feels and thinks. They are so comfortable with each other, they may even feel little need for verbalization.

Unfortunately, a breakdown in communication can result in hurt, disappointment, frustration, resentment, alienation, and loneliness. While it is true that individuals who have shared life for a number of years become very well acquainted with the thoughts and feelings of their beloved, nothing should ever be taken for granted.

The story is told of one elderly couple from Birmingham, Alabama, who had been married for 65 years when the wife served her husband some grapefruit juice.

"I don't like grapefruit juice," he said.

"You do like grapefruit juice!" she shot back.

The argument proceeded for quite some time, with both parties sure that after more than six decades of marriage, they certainly had it right! The truth was, he liked grapefruit, but not grapefruit juice. She hadn't served him grapefruit juice often, and the few times she did, he had never complained. But he really did not like it, and finally got around to making his point—much to her shock and amazement—after all those years!

The moral of the story: even after many years of friendship or marriage, you still may not know what another person is thinking. You may make educated guesses with much more accuracy than others who are not acquainted with this person, but there will still be surprises which help to make life much more interesting!

Communication—which involves both good listening and expression of emotions—is the key to avoiding the mind-reading trap.

### 4. Practice your skills.

In the studies mentioned earlier in this chapter, Dr. Ickes found that people who were coached could improve their mind-reading ability. You don't have to be involved in Dr. Ickes study to improve this ability, however. Simply make a mental note of what you think someone is thinking at any given moment, then ask them what they *really* were thinking.

Given time and a little practice, you are likely to learn that sometimes, no matter how good you think you are at reading other people's minds, you are just flat out wrong about what they really do think. This should give us all pause in making assumptions about others—if in doubt, the very best policy usually is to ask.

## References

94. Burns DD. *Feeling Good: The New Mood Therapy*. New York: HarperCollins, 1999. 42.
95. Adelson R. "Detecting deception." *Monitor On Psychology* 35.7 (July/August 2004). 6 Dec. 2007 <http://www.apa.org/monitor/julaug04/detecting.html>.
96. Ickes W. *Everyday Mind Reading: Understanding What Other People Think and Feel.* Amherst, N.Y.: Prometheus Books, 2003.
97. Ickes W. *Everyday Mind Reading: Understanding What Other People Think and Feel.* Amherst, N.Y.: Prometheus Books, 2003.
98. 1 Kings 3:16-28. *The Holy Bible*. Authorized King James Version.
99. Matthew 25:14-30. *The Holy Bible*. Authorized King James Version.
100. "Folly of Judging Others." Ed. *Our Daily Bread.* NETBibleOu. 11 Dec. 2007 <http://net.bible.org/illustration.php?topic=843>.
101. "Only God Knows." Ed. *Our Daily Bread.* 20 July 1992. NETBibleOu. 11 Dec. 2007 <http://net.bible.org/illustration.php?topic=843>.
102. Matthew 7:1. *The Holy Bible*. Authorized King James Version.

Chapter 5

FORTUNE TELLERS THINK THEY KNOW FOR SURE HOW SITUATIONS WILL TURN OUT.

# Steer Clear of Fortune Telling

***We humans aren't very good at foretelling the future — so why do we keep on trying?***

Kate buried her face in her hands, her body wracked with sobs. She had been through a lot in her life, but this latest round of events seemed like more than even she could handle. First there had been the unfaithfulness of, and finally abandonment by, her husband Ken. Ken had left her with two small children, making it clear that he wanted no part in their lives. Now one of the children had been diagnosed with a serious illness which would require several major surgeries over the next ten years.

To make matters worse, Kate's employer was facing difficult economic times and had just laid Kate off. Without a job or husband, she was faced with mounting medical and other bills, plus the prospect of raising her children alone. Kate couldn't afford the house payments anymore, and didn't want to go live with her parents, although they had offered.

"I'll never be able to repair the shambles of my life," Kate wept. "My children would be better off without me. My parents wouldn't be able to tolerate me for long if I were living at their house, and no one will want to marry into a ready-made family like I have. Yet I don't see how I can make it alone…"

Kate felt like this was the end for her, that she should simply give up and not try any more.

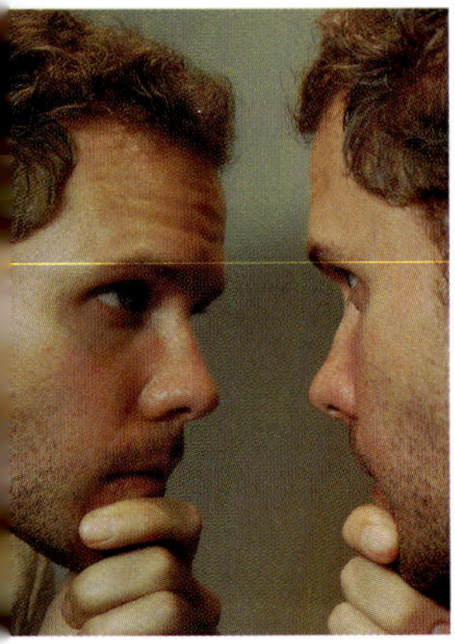

*"We have met the enemy and he is us."*

—Pogo

Larry leaned against the living room window, searching anxiously for any sign of headlights coming down the lane.

"Oh, where are those kids?" he worried. "They said they'd be in by midnight, and here it is 2 a.m. They must have been in a tragic accident..." At the very thought, Larry's mind whirled into overdrive. He imagined the tense hospital phone call and the wild ride to the emergency room. His heart was crushed at the idea of arriving too late to say "good-bye." When he got into the "identifying bodies" segment of the sordid scenario, he started to sweat profusely.

Kate and Larry are engaged in "fortune-teller error," a cognitive distortion in which a person concludes that his or her predictions are 100% accurate regardless of the probability that they might actually occur. People who commit fortune-teller error anticipate that things will turn out badly and feel convinced that their prediction is an already-established fact.[103] Fortune-teller error brings with it a number of dangerous and detrimental side effects, as documented in **Figure 5.1**.

Kate was drawing a lot of very wrong conclusions. Her parents did care for her, her children would not have been better off without her, and she had no way of predicting if another man would want to commit to her family or not.

**NEGATIVE EFFECTS OF FORTUNE TELLING**

- doom and gloom mentality
- pessimistic outlook on life
- negative self-fulfilling prophecies
- anxiety, excessive worry, and/or panic attacks
- suicidal tendencies
- jumping to conclusions
- strain on personal relationships
- tendency towards obsessive-compulsive behavior
- leads to an "end justifies the means" rationale
- counteracts altruistic thinking
- contributes to addictive behavior
- financial loss
- failed businesses
- divorce
- disease

***Figure 5.1***

**CALAMITOUS THOUGHTS**

- "This project will turn out horribly!"
- "My life is over!"
- "My career is finished!"
- "I'll never recover!"
- "I'll never find anyone to love me."

***Figure 5.2***

There was plenty of room for hope in her life, despite how defeated she felt. She believed in God, who had promised to be a faithful guide. There were family and friends who would step in to help. Together, she and her children could rebuild their lives. Instead of giving up she could say, "I can and will work my way through this."

Larry also allowed his thoughts to run freely, working himself into a sweat over a catastrophe that wasn't likely to happen. There were many reasons (besides an accident) that could have resulted in the late arrival of Larry's children. Perhaps their vehicle broke down, and they couldn't get a cell phone signal. If they were adult children coming home for a vacation, perhaps there had been a mix-up about what day they would come. Teenage children might have partied at a friend's house, then fallen asleep without thinking to call their father. While such behavior would have been irresponsible, it would not have resulted in the dire consequences that filled Larry's heart with dread.

### IMAGINING THE WORST

When you arbitrarily predict dire endings even when the evidence doesn't support catastrophic thinking, you bring about unnecessary fear and anxiety. A person who regularly entertains the possibility of a worst-case scenario may mentally develop detailed disaster scenes which become more alarming by the hour as they work themselves into a frenzy of worried expectation. The constant replaying of stressful mental movies can result in depression, dejection, and the total absence of hope.

Perhaps you've heard the story of "Chicken Little," the infamous bird who, because something fell on her head, assumed that the sky was falling and all in the world were doomed. Doomsday thinking is an easy trap to fall into, and one that causes many to shed tears over events that don't even happen. In his Julius Caesar classic, Shakespeare wrote that "cowards die many times before their deaths".[104] The same might be said about those who imagine the worst possible outcomes of their circumstances. Some examples of calamitous thoughts are shown in **Figure 5.2**.

**One way to combat the devastating effect of panic attacks is to steer clear of exaggerated interpretations of body sensations.**

## PRELUDE TO PANIC

Some calamitous thinkers can turn their worry into full-blown panic attacks. A person prone to panic attacks may notice a small physical sensation and anticipate a dire prognosis when they don't really know what is causing the symptom. For example, they might note a subtle heart rate change, tell themselves that something is wrong, and quickly escalate the fear-inducing self-talk until their thinking becomes irrational. In reality short-term heart palpitations can occur for a number of non-life-threatening reasons. The negative train of thinking often increases the physical symptoms, leading to an all-out panic attack. Some symptoms of panic attacks are listed in **Figure 5.3.**[105]

## WHEN THOUGHTS BECOME OBSESSIONS

Mindy couldn't seem to wash her hands often enough; she imagined millions of dangerous germs on every surface. This compulsion was especially trying for her, since she was the mother of two preschool boys who seemed to revel in dirt. From sand castles to mud pies to digging up worms, they were always into something grimy or slimy. Mindy washed the children meticulously and often, many more times than was necessary for ordinary health concerns. They had to take baths in the morning, in the evening, and quite frequently in between. Yet still they were never quite clean enough, long enough, to stay in the good graces of their mother.

Unbeknownst to her, Mindy was struggling with Obsessive-Compulsive Disorder (OCD), a form of fortune-teller error aimed at preventing some dread situation. When obsessions (disturbing and frequently recurring thoughts or images) are combined with compulsions (the rituals that a person uses to try and get rid of them), the result is known as obsessive-compulsive disorder. Individuals suffering from OCD may experience extremely persistent thoughts and images of undesirable conditions, and engage in repetitive behaviors (such as hand washing, hoarding, placing things in order, or checking things off) in a compulsive and rigid manner.[106] OCD sufferers come to rely on compulsive rituals to relieve their anxiety. When

### SYMPTOMS OF A PANIC ATTACK

- sudden, overwhelming anxiety
- rapid heartbeat
- dizziness
- shortness of breath
- tingling sensations
- hot flashes
- chills
- abject terror

***Figure 5.3***

## OBSESSIVE-COMPULSIVE DISORDER (OCD)

- obsessions about germs or dirt, resulting in exorbitant and repetitious washing rituals
- fear, doubt, and the need to "check things" repeatedly
- frequent thoughts of violence
- fear of harming someone else
- repetitious touching or counting
- fixation on order or symmetry
- the preoccupation with sexual acts which are repulsive to the person dealing with the obsession, or thoughts that oppose your religious beliefs

***Figure 5.4***

the ritual is not performed, the anxiety level becomes overwhelming, resulting in a panic attack. In order to avoid the anxiety reactions, the individual then becomes a slave to their rituals and compulsions.

Fortune telling can actually be part of a ritual for some people. Caught in a cycle of dire predictions, they may also engage in the rituals listed in **Figure 5.4**.[107] Obsessive-compulsive behaviors, which are clearly excessive, are not directly related to the fear they are meant to neutralize. In other words, they don't solve anything. OCD is a time-consuming preoccupation which can dramatically interfere with a person's normal routine, job, scholastic endeavors, or personal relationships.

**Excessive hand washing is a common obsessive-compulsive disorder (OCD).**

Brain PET scans of individuals suffering from OCD have demonstrated some patterns of abnormality, namely a trend towards right-side predominance in the frontal lobe and limbic systems of the brain.[108] In some studies, these areas of abnormality have normalized following successful treatment with SSRIs or Cognitive Behavioral Therapy (CBT).[109]

### SUICIDAL REGRETS

The Golden Gate Bridge in San Francisco is a popular attraction for tourists because of its tremendous towers, sweeping cables, and great span. Sadly, it has become a popular location for those attempting to end their life as well. Over the years, a number of people have committed suicide by jumping off the 25-story structure. Amazingly, some individuals have actually survived this jump.

Dr. David Rosen, professor of psychiatry at Texas A&M University, interviewed six of them and published the results in the *Western Journal of Medicine*. Those surviving had all suffered severely as a result

## THE SUICIDE CONNECTION

Suicide is the ultimate fortune-teller error. In great psychological distress, suicidal individuals come to believe that:

- they would be better off dead, and/or
- the world would be better off without them.

People who contemplate or commit suicide often don't really want to die. They simply feel that they have more pain than they can cope with.

When we start thinking things like "I can't stand it" or "this pain is unbearable" we can actually set ourselves up for suicidal thoughts.

***Figure 5.5***

of the jump. All had broken bones, many with compression fractures, etc. Virtually every survivor said that the moment they stepped off into space, they had second thoughts. They wished they hadn't taken the plunge. They wanted to live.[110] Just before jumping, these individuals inaccurately predicted that the world would be better without them. Dr. Rosen's study illustrates how impulsive and short-sighted suicide attempts often are. Some important facts about the fortune telling and suicide connection are documented in **Figure 5.5**[111].

### ANTIDOTES FOR CATASTROPHIZING

If you catch yourself in the act of fortune telling or catastrophic thinking, it's important to step back and ask "what is really the worst thing that could happen?" It's important to recognize that when you worry about future events, there are really only two possible outcomes, as outlined in **Figure 5.6**. If you find yourself imagining the worst about situations that could really be minor, it might be helpful to compare them to the physical injury scale provided on **Figure 5.7**. When compared with items at the top of the scale, the importance of a gash requiring stitches or even a broken nose fades in comparison. The key is to keep everything in perspective.

You are especially in danger of catastrophic thinking during times of duress. Each person has different thresholds of tolerance for stress and anxiety, but when the brain's chemistry is altered by a significant level of sensory overload, the result can be the complete abandonment of sense. During a difficult time in your life, it is even more important to avoid calamitous

**REMEMBER, THERE ARE ONLY TWO POSSIBLE OUTCOMES:**

**A.** The feared thing doesn't come true, in which case undue worry has created misery over something that did not come to pass.

**or**

**B.** The worst scenario does come true, in which case undue worry has caused you to suffer the catastrophic experience multiple times in your mind, rather than just once.

***Figure 5.6***

thoughts, because increased stress will hinder your ability to face the crisis at hand. Not only will you have to deal with the circumstantial concerns, but you'll have to face it with a brain that has been clogged by chemical compounds created by your negative thoughts. You are much better prepared to overcome life's hardships when you learn to dispute your irrational thoughts with pure logic, stifling any tendency to predict disaster. Three solutions for fortune teller error are summarized at the end of this chapter.

### FOOLING YOURSELF

While many people have pessimistic ideas about what will happen, some fortune tellers make unrealistic optimistic predictions that are also errors in foretelling the future. Former New York governor Eliot Spitzer,

**THE PHYSICAL INJURY SCALE**

100 — death
90 — paralyzed from waist down
80 — dominant arm cut off
70 — 1 hand cut off
60 — 2 fingers cut off
50 — 3 broken limbs
40 — dominant arm broken
30 — broken nose
20 — gash requiring stitches
10 — bruise
0 — nothing

***Figure 5.7***

*"Sow an act, and you reap a habit; sow a habit, and you reap a character; sow a character, and you reap a destiny."*
—Charles Reade and others

who built a career as a "Mr. Clean" bent on halting corruption, ironically believed that his own depravity would not be discovered. However, he was caught red-handed while patronizing a prostitution service. The fallout from this mistaken presumption dropped him from the zenith of his career to a disgrace in a few short days.[112]

When alcoholics and other addicts convince themselves that things will turn out all right even as they engage in habits that inevitably lead to great harm, they are engaged in fortune telling. Individuals who engage in gambling maintain an unwarranted expectation of winning, even though the odds are stacked against them. The truth is, if you gamble very much you will lose more money than you take in.[113] In the words of one sage, "gambling is a tax on people who aren't very good at math."

Whether you foretell undesirable situations or favorable outcomes, the error is in believing that you can know what will happen in the future. This can be dangerous when applied to significant areas in your life, such as relationships and finances. Many people think they know exactly what will make them happy, and behave as if they are certainly destined for that result in their romantic and business ventures.

## HAPPILY EVER AFTER?

One of the worst fortune-telling errors perpetrated today involves the expectation that newlywed couples will live "happily ever after." One need look no further than the divorce statistics to recognize that wedded bliss eludes a high percentage of couples. Nevertheless, many young people continue to dream of a magical wedding, complete with a handsome prince and a charmed life after the altar.

While hormones (such as pheromones) may tempt you to foretell a fairy tale ending in your intimate relationships, it is up to you to think clearly, analyzing the relationship in light of the principles for success. Inaccurate fortune telling is the reason why many marriages fail. If the expectations were accurate and realistic, some couples might choose not to get married in the first place, and therefore avoid an eventual divorce.

A second serious fortune-teller error is committed by married couples who feel their personal happiness will increase if they divorce. Researchers from the University of Chicago, who studied 5,232 unhappily married adults, found no evidence that those who divorced were any happier down the road than those who stayed married. Furthermore, the study showed that two-thirds of the unhappily married spouses who stayed married reported that their marriages were happy five years later. Surprisingly, the unhappiest marriages reported the most dramatic turnarounds. In summary, the researchers found that couples in the process of divorce who expect that their lives will be happier or better after the split are quite likely making a false prediction.

## MONEY DOESN'T BUY HAPPINESS

Despite the popular belief to the contrary, money doesn't buy happiness. Research suggests that once a family's annual income reaches a certain base "comfort level" of about $50,000 per year, where food, shelter, and clothing are secure, more money does not translate into happiness.[114] This flies in the face of the prediction of many people—that "if I could just win the lottery, all my troubles would be over." Researchers who have followed the lives of lottery winners have found that years after the lottery is won, these "lucky" people are not generally very content.[115]

Other researchers have found that the United States, which is one of the richest nations in the world, ranks lower in percentage of happy people than much poorer countries such as Nigeria or Mexico.[116] Some have even suggested the implementation of a Gross National Happiness (GNH) index to compare right along with our Gross Domestic Product (GDP). It seems ironic that a country with such a high GDP, and one whose citizens consume such large quantities of goods, could be ranked so low on an index of aggregate happiness.[117]

These unpleasant statistics should give you pause if you are tempted to wish for more money. The fact that so many think money would make them happier, when statistics speak so eloquently to the contrary, is simply more evidence that fortune-teller error is alive and well in modern culture.

## HOW TO AVOID CHASING AN ILLUSION

In his book *Stumbling On Happiness*, Harvard Professor Daniel Gilbert presents scientific evidence to demonstrate that we humans really aren't very adept at predicting what will make us happy in the end.[118] Weaving together facts and theories from psychology, cognitive neuroscience, philosophy, and behavioral economics, Gilbert shows how we make regular and systematic mistakes when we try to imagine our personal futures. When you try to look forward, your imagination often plays tricks on you. Apparently human foresight doesn't extend much farther than eyesight. As Gilbert so aptly points out, most of us spend our lives steering ourselves towards the best of all possible futures only to find that tomorrow rarely turns out as we had presumed.[119]

*"The best thing about the future is that it comes only one day at a time."*
—Abraham Lincoln

It is possible to escape the disheartening cycle of continually reaching for unlikely dreams in hopes of attaining happiness. To do this, you must evaluate your ventures based on established principles and proven methods. If you apply guiding precepts to your romantic relationships, your expectation of a happy marriage is much more realistic. When you employ tested formulas to your business ventures, the probability of a profitable result goes up significantly. Also, remember that in every situation there are factors you cannot control. Take those things into account when you appraise how something will turn out, and you will prevent disappointment when unpredictable things happen.

## THE END: DOES IT JUSTIFY THE MEANS?

In addition to happiness-related fortune-teller errors, many people fool themselves in the matter of ethics. They base their unscrupulous actions on mistaken predictions of moral and virtuous effects. For example, a politician may excuse funding her campaign with illegally-obtained money because of her intentions to accomplish a tremendous amount of good if elected. Developed countries often believe that humanitarian purposes override sovereignty issues when it comes to less developed countries. This is commonly described as the idea that "the end justifies the means." Proponents of this philosophy believe that a good outcome excuses whatever wrongs were committed to attain it. The problem with this type of thinking is that it assumes the individual involved knows what the outcome will be. This in itself is a fortune-teller error.

Some Christians, who view the glory of God and the fulfillment of His wishes as the greatest value, inaccurately feel that persecuting people who "get in the way" is justified. Some young Muslim men, who see martyrdom and participation in a "holy war" as the ultimate honor and believe they will have numerous virgins at their beck and call in some beautiful land hereafter, somehow convince themselves that horrific acts of terrorism on innocent people is justified.

People who believe that any action is acceptable as long as it contributes to "the greater good," assume that they can not only see the future, but that they know what is best for everyone involved. If you lie to protect someone's feelings or prevent yourself from falling into trouble, you have no way of being certain that those involved are better off with the deception rather than the truth. People who lie rarely foresee the consequences of their dishonesty. When confronted with situations where dishonesty might seem advantageous or even "the right thing to do," we would do well to remember that "whatsoever a man soweth, that shall he also reap."[117]

## COUNTERING "THE GREATER GOOD" JUSTIFICATIONS

To resist deceiving yourself with this fortune-telling error, let decisions be driven by principled behavior rather than hoped-for outcomes. Individuals who are focused on destinations tend to cut corners, take shortcuts in matters of integrity, or do "whatever it takes" (even if unethical) to reach their intended goal. In contrast, individuals who maintain high standards in their thoughts and actions are much more likely to accomplish their stated tasks than will those who perform solely in pursuit of rewards.

The best approach is to consider whether an action is right or wrong, in and of itself. From this point of view, lying is always wrong, regardless of any potential "good" that might result. The end does not justify the means, and we would all do well to avoid the error of thinking that it does.

## NOT ALL VISIONS ARE FORTUNE-TELLING ERRORS

Looking expectantly toward the future isn't automatically a negative thing. Indeed, there are many instances in life where making accurate predictions about certain behaviors and their probable outcome can save us a tremendous amount of trouble.

A good example of this would be our decisions with regard to health-related lifestyle choices. Scientific research resoundingly confirms that a diet high in sugar, sodium, saturated fats, or refined foods will adversely impact your health sooner or later. When you admonish yourself to cut down on sugar or fat in the diet or else, you are engaging in a "fortune-teller truth," not error. Understanding the good consequences of certain actions, and the grievous results of others, can be a powerful motivational factor.

Similarly, if a child hears messages from the day they were born that they are special, will do great things, or are destined to have a successful career, the child is more likely to hold these goals as valuable and feel that he or she can achieve them. Imagining and expecting the best from your offspring is good fortune telling which will encourage them to set high goals for themselves and strive to achieve those goals. Preparing for the future is different from predicting the future. Being prepared can help lessen the anxiety in your life and propel you toward success, while speculation only drives you to worry or miss opportunities to prosper. Sensible preparations are things like familiarizing yourself with emergency procedures and basic first aid, observing the rules of safety, and preparing thoroughly for a performance or presentation.

Use fortune telling to recognize negative consequences to your actions and change your behavior, get ready for things to come, or aim for an admirable dream and take practical steps to attain it—but never to assume that you know for certain the outcome.

SERENITY PRAYER

*"God grant me the serenity to accept the things I cannot change; courage to change the things I can; and wisdom to know the difference."*

—Reinhold Niebuhr

## STRATEGIES FOR SUCCESS

As you work to overcome fortune-teller error, remind yourself often that you don't really know what is going to happen. While you cannot predict the future, it is true that living by (or discarding) certain life principles will increase the likelihood of certain predictable endings.

You may find that you are worrying about a lot of things that never even happen. If so, recognize those cognitions as the fortune-telling thoughts they are. Then, when you feel tempted to start the cycle of worry again, remind yourself of the outcome of past worries. Most people who worry excessively have failed to take valuable lessons from their earlier experiences. For example, if we expect something bad and it fails to materialize, we heave a sigh of relief and go on. The next time the threat of trouble arises, however, we forget about our previous "escape" and worry all over again. When trouble fails to materialize a second time, we feel relieved once more and repeat the cycle of forgetting good outcomes all over again.

If you think you might have a tendency to predict improbable outcomes, good or bad, try keeping track of how many times you are right—or wrong—about the future. When you catch yourself thinking fortune-telling thoughts, work to re-wire your thinking. An example of how to "rewire your thoughts" to avoid fortune-teller error is provided in **Figure 5.8**.

## RE-WIRING YOUR THOUGHTS: AN EXAMPLE

| **Fortune-telling Thoughts:** | **More Accurate Thinking:** |
|---|---|
| *"Oh no, someone is knocking on my door at 5 a.m.! Why would they wake me at this hour? Something terrible must've happened. Maybe it's the police coming to tell me someone has died. I can't take it! Maybe if I ignore it, they'll go away. I'm starting to feel sick."* | *"It seems odd that someone would knock on my door this early in the morning. Maybe one of the neighbors is in trouble and needs my help. Or perhaps my horse got out of the pasture. It could be my fiancé inviting me to come watch the sunrise with him. Whatever it is, I can handle it. Guess I'd better go answer the door!"* |

***Figure 5.8***

When obsessive thoughts come, distract yourself by doing some work (such as washing dishes), listening to music, going outside for a run, etc. In time the thoughts, if not responded to, will become less frequent and more manageable.

Measure your forecast against the realistic probability of it occurring, taking into account logical factors that affect the situation. Remind yourself that there is no such thing as "magical worry." There comes a time where the risk is not appreciably altered by thinking thoughts or performing an activity just to relieve our stress. Write down some true thoughts to replace the obsessions with, then allow only emotional reactions or behaviors that are completely true.

You can also improve brain chemistry through diet, exercise, and light therapy (see the subsequent chapters that tell how to do this).

It's possible to eradicate fortune telling, imagining the worst, and blindly optimistic thoughts from your life by viewing every situation from a rational perspective, carefully examining the validity of any dramatic suppositions. Do this, and you are likely to enjoy the predictable results of increased happiness, lowered stress levels, and improved relationships.

## References

103. Pucci AR. *The Client's Guide to Cognitive-Behaivioral Therapy.* Lincoln, NE: iUniverse, 2006. 57.
104. Shakespeare W. *The plays of William Shakespeare: With the corrections and illustrations of various commentators.* Volume 14, page 50. Published by C. and A. Conrad, 1809.
105. Anxiety. Ed. American Psychological Association. 2008. APA Online. 21 Mar. 2008 <http://www.apa.org/topics/anxietyqanda.html>.
106. Clark DA. *Cognitive-behavioral therapy for OCD.* Guilford Press. 2006. 4.
107. De Silva P, Rachman S. *Obsessive-compulsive disorder: the facts.* Oxford University Press. 17.
108. Friedman HS. *Encyclopedia of Mental Health*, Volume 3. Academic Press. 1998. 25.
109. Clark DA. *Cognitive-behavioral therapy for OCD.* Guilford Press. 2006. 270.
110. Glenn WM. "The Magnet and the Veil." *MD Canada* (May/June 2003).
111. Beck AT, et al. *Cognitive Therapy of Depression.* New York, N.Y.: Guilford Press, 1979. 12, 210-211.
112. Elkind P. *Rough Justice: The Rise and Fall of Eliot Spitzer.* Portfolio Hardcover. 2010.
113. Grinols EL. *Gambling in America: Costs and Benefits.* Cambridge University Press. 19.
114. Revkin AC. "A New Measure of Well-being From a Happy Little Kingdom." New York Times 4 Oct 2005. 11 Dec. 2007 <http://www.nytimes.com/2005/10/04/science/04happ.html>.
115. "Does Money Make You Happy? [...Or, Everything You Wanted to Know About Unhappy Lottery Winners]." Ed. Wesley. 26 Apr. 2007. *LifeTwo.* 12 Dec. 2007 <http://lifetwo.com/production/node/20070425-does-money-make-you-happy-lottery-winners-not-happy>.
116. "Feeling of Happiness." Ed. *The Values Surveys.* 1999, 2000. World Values Surveys. 11 Dec. 2007 <http://www.worldvaluessurvey.org/>.
117. Revkin AC. "A New Measure of Well-being From a Happy Little Kingdom." *New York Times* 4 Oct 2005. 11 Dec. 2007 <http://www.nytimes.com/2005/10/04/science/04happ.html>.
118. Gilbert D. "Journey to Elsewhere." *Stumbling On Happiness.* New York: Vintage, 2005. 26, 27.
119. Gilbert D. "Journey to Elsewhere." *Stumbling On Happiness.* New York: Vintage, 2005. 26, 27.

Chapter 6

WHEN WE TREAT LOSING A GAME AS A MAJOR CATASTROPHE, WE ARE INVOLVED IN MAGNIFICATION.

# Balance Your View

***Blow things out of proportion—or shrink them below their size—either way you're in trouble. Here's how to avoid both.***

"What is he, blind?" Alan growled under his breath as the umpire called yet another strike on 9-year-old Alan Jr.

"Now Alan, it's just a game," Joann patted him on the knee.

"It is NOT just a game," Alan shot back. "Junior's team has a shot at the Little League World Series, and this incompetent, belligerent ump is going to ruin their chances.

"That was a horrible call!" Alan roared when Junior struck out.

"Could you simmer down, sir?" some nearby spectators were becoming annoyed with Alan Senior's booming pronouncements and unsportsmanlike antics.

"It's a free world, isn't it?" Alan glowered at the people nearby while Joann patted his knee again in an effort to calm him down. Junior's team was losing so badly that Senior soon began "sideline coaching" as well as deriding the umpire.

"Should have thrown it to home…"

"Why didn't he cut them off at the plate?"

"Can't they do anything right?"

With Junior's team down by nine runs in the top of the 5th inning, Alan Sr. had reached his limit. "I can't take this anymore," he angrily whipped his hat off and threw it on the ground. "I can't stand losing and I especially can't stand it when the ump throws the game." With that, he stormed off to his truck, pulling Joann behind him.

"Hey John, you're late again," the foreman shouted over the hum of machinery on the factory floor.

"Yeah, sorry, boss," John flashed his infectious grin. "Just a little hung over from the weekend, I guess."

"Well, let's not make a habit of it," the foreman looked stern. "We've got production quotas to meet and a big order to get out."

"Sure thing!" John donned his safety hat and headed to his position on the factory floor.

"What was the foreman chiding you for?" one of John's coworkers whispered later, during the morning break.

"Aw, it was nothing," John laughed. "He's just a grump, I guess. Too old to understand how hard it is to get up on a Monday morning after an active weekend."

"I wouldn't take it too lightly," the co-worker warned. "I've seen them let people go around here for a lot less than being late."

"Fire me?" John threw back his head and roared with laughter. "They'd never do that! I'm the only one who knows how to run that new router they got. They need me!"

"Just be careful, John," another worker chimed in. "That charming smile might have gotten you through some things, but it may not work around here."

But John wasn't careful. While he liked and valued his job, in his heart he felt his employer just couldn't function without him. So he was regularly late on Monday mornings and occasionally at other times. The foreman's comments grew sterner and more severe, but John wasn't paying attention. That is until one day when the foreman's boss called John into his office. "John," the man began, "You've been a good worker in so many ways. But in spite of repeated warnings from the factory foreman, you've been late too many times."

"Aw, I know," John shuffled his feet a little. He was just getting ready to flash his winning smile when the manager cut him off.

"You're fired, John," he said. "I'm sorry, but that's how it is."

"But sir!" John really was worried now, but somehow still thought he could save the dire situation.

"There's nothing to discuss!" the manager opened the door and motioned for John to go out. "You've had plenty of chances. We just can't give you any more." Dazed and stunned, John was ushered to his locker to pick up his things. "If I ever thought things would come to this," he mumbled to himself, "I would have showed up on time!"

Though their stories may seem quite different, Alan and John were actually involved in variations of the same type of cognitive error – a mental distortion that inappropriately alters the size of one's circumstances, events, or comments. Alan was involved in "magnification" when he turned Little League fun into more than just a game. John was engaging in "minimization" when he blew off the warnings from his supervisor. Both were engaged in significant levels of inaccurate thinking.

## THE TELESCOPE FLIP

Magnification involves inappropriately exaggerating the way people or situations truly are, as if viewing them through a telescope. Often the negative characteristics of other people are exaggerated (magnified), while the positive characteristics are understated (minimized).[120]

Minimization, which is the opposite of magnification, is like flipping the telescope around and looking through the wrong end so that everything appears much smaller than it actually is. A minimizer inappropriately shrinks the importance of various people, things, or events, diminishing the value of things they don't want to acknowledge. They may overlook important red flags in romantic relationships, business opportunities, or major life decisions. Another type of minimizing involves down playing good things that happen.[121]

When we engage in the cognitive error of magnification or minimization, we are actually "majoring in minors and minoring in majors." Some of the adverse effects of these twin cognitive errors are listed in **Figure 6.1**.[122]

## MAKING MOUNTAINS OUT OF MOLEHILLS

A form of magnification is known as catastrophizing. People involved in this thinking error frequently lapse into the lingo of the "Horrible-Terrible-Awfuls." They may describe situations to be agonizing, when in reality they are simply uncomfortable, or they might depict problems or adversity

### ADVERSE EFFECTS OF MAGNIFICATION & MINIMIZATION

| Magnification | Minimization |
|---|---|
| • lack of patience | • ignoring red flags |
| • pride | • poor social relationships |
| • stress and anxiety | • undervaluing others |
| • can lead to depression | • risk of financial failure |
| • obsessive-compulsive disorder | • pessimism |

***Figure 6.1***

as "huge" when they are actually quite small. Using this inappropriate language to describe circumstances only increases negative emotions and often exacerbates the situation by distracting from a sensible solution.

There are a number of ancient examples of magnification and minimization. King Saul's pride would not have been so severely wounded had he not allowed it to grow so exponentially. He required music therapy and cognitive behavioral therapy, but unfortunately refused to consistently believe the undistorted truth. With his enemies closing in, his sad life ended in suicide.[123]

King Nebuchadnezzar of Babylonian times was magnifying when he exclaimed "is not this great Babylon which I have built?" Nebuchadnezzar's pride was so problematic it required a 7-year program for complete correction. That program included exercise, the eating of raw green vegetables, correction of circadian rhythms, light therapy, hydrotherapy, and cognitive behavioral therapy.[124]

In the parable of the ten virgins told by Jesus, five of the virgins minimized the importance of having abundant oil in their lamps and were not ready when their bridegrom arrived.[125] Minimization and magnification have always had significant consequences, since ancient times.

## LOW FRUSTRATION TOLERANCE

*"I can't stand it!"*

People with magnification problems also invariably have low frustration tolerance.[126] LFT occurs when individuals feel entitled to a life that is fair, easy, well-ordered, comfortable, exciting, pleasurable, interesting, or hassle-free. They don't feel they can stand discomfort, anxiety, anger, or depression—or be happy at all if they have to endure those feelings.

When life doesn't conform to their demands, they are more likely to panic than persist, and quickly denounce the circumstances as unbearable (I-can't-stand-it-itis). The frustration of such individuals results from their habit of comparing reality with an unattainable ideal. When reality doesn't live up to their expectations, they condemn reality. Although their anger is self-defeating, they unleash it anyway to let others know how frustrated they really are. It never occurs to them that they might change their expectations instead. Unfortunately, their frustration adds to a sense of futility, increasing their urge to retaliate against the unfairness of it all, or simply give up, or wish punishment and ruin on others. Sometimes, though not always, individuals with LFT express their frustration through profanity.

One very familiar curse word, a form of "damnation," is frequently used in reaction to events that aren't anywhere near the magnitude of the everlasting hellfire it calls for. Other undesirable words which refer, for example, to an individual's parentage in a derogatory way, are overreactions where we try to put a person in their place by insulting their culture or circumstances of birth. Even when someone has committed a grievous error against us, there is nothing to be gained (and often much to be lost) by such attacks.

"Anti-magnification" is one of the major cornerstones of Cognitive Behavioral Therapy, so relying on profanity (e.g. off-the-charts magnification) to make a point is counter-productive to CBT. My own father aptly taught me during my youth that curse words are a sign of a person's limited vocabulary. In other words, using these words displays an inability to describe persons or things in accurate words.

## DOWNGRADE YOUR DESCRIPTIONS

People with magnification (whether it involves catastrophizing or low frustration tolerance) are notorious for phrases such as "I can't stand this" or "this is horrible!" Such "I can't stand it" statements can be real emotion shapers, stoking the fires of our discontent.

By rephrasing the way we describe things, we take an important step in controlling both our thoughts and emotions. Instead of saying "I can't stand this," we might say "I can stand this, but it is a nuisance." Phrases such as "that's totally awful" can also be transposed into something a little less catastrophic, such as "that sure is unpleasant!"

There is a big difference between a nuisance and a total catastrophe. Often the simple action of changing the way we describe an event can alter negative emotions, leaving us with a more positive feeling toward life. Some replacement terms for the "Horrible-Terrible-Awfuls," or HTAs as some like to call them, are provided in **Figure 6.2**. [127]

## THE POWER OF RE-WORDING

One way to stop minimizing or magnifying is to re-phrase some of the things you say—both to yourself and to others. It may seem like a simple tactic, but words are really a very powerful thing. Dr. Lynn Clark, in the book *S.O.S. Help for Emotions*, describes how negative self-talk leads to unhealthy, unpleasant feelings.[128] According to Dr. Clark, irrational self-talk starts with three major "musts" (which are essentially preferential "shoulds"). These major "musts" are then connected to anxiety, anger,

**REPLACING THE HTA WORDS**

| HTAs: | Replace with: |
|---|---|
| Horrible | Bad or Inconvenient |
| Terrible | Hassle |
| Awful | Unpleasant |

***Figure 6.2***

depression, and other unhealthy emotions by "hot links," as illustrated in **Figure 6.3.** The words and phrases we choose to utilize can truly make a difference in how we think. **Figure 6.4** offers helpful alternatives to negative self-talk. The maximizing choice of words leads to escalating emotions, anxiety, and possibly confrontation. The rerephrased option states how you feel in a manner conducive to calm nerves and inner peace. The phrases on the right are a good remedy for "I-can't-stand-it-itis."

My sons were engaged in a game of baseball with friends when a perceived injustice occurred on the field. Tempers flared. Half of the boys felt they couldn't tolerate the incident, while the other half "couldn't stand" the reaction of the other boys. Efforts to smooth things over did not cool the tempers, thus the game was called to a sudden halt. It could've continued if they had taken to heart the words to a little song I had them each sing before leaving the field that day. The song, featured in **Figure 6.5**, might be helpful to you as you run into life's inevitable frustrations. Did the travel agent make an error on your reservations? Did the mechanic accidentally scratch your car door when pulling it into the garage? Did someone say something unkind? You may not like what happened, but you'll handle the frustration better by telling yourself "It's OK" and "I really can stand this!"

| THE "MUSTS" THAT TRIGGER NEGATIVE EMOTIONS | |
|---|---|
| **Three Major "Musts"** | **1.** *"I must..."*<br>**2.** *"You-he-she must..."*<br>**3.** *"The world and the conditions in which I live must..."* |
| **"Hot links" or Connectors** | • condemnation and damnation<br>• I-can't-stand-it-itis<br>• awfulizing<br>• feelings of worthlessness<br>• "always" and "never" |
| **Resulting Emotions** | • anxiety<br>• anger<br>• depression<br>• frustration |

***Figure 6.3***

## REPHRASE MAXIMIZING WORDS

| INSTEAD OF: | REPLACE WITH: |
|---|---|
| I must... | I would like to... |
| I mustn't... | I would prefer not to... |
| I should... | I wish I could... |
| I shouldn't... | I would rather not... |
| I can't stand it. | This is difficult. |
| This is unbearable. | This is very difficult. |
| I am worthless. | I am worthwhile. |
| This is absolutely crazy. | I don't understand this at all. |
| You always do this. | It seems like you always do this. |
| You never do that. | It seems like you never do that. |

***Figure 6.4***

### SHOULD YOU SAY "SHOULD?"

At times it is tempting to use the word "should" to refer to things that are actually personal preferences. For example, thinking "I should get more respect for the work I do." When you magnify your preferences into imperatives, you are bound to be dissatisfied when the world does not deliver

## A SONG TO REMEMBER (TO THE TUNE OF *FRÈRE JACQUES*)

*I don't like it, I don't like it.*
*It's OK, It's OK.*
*I can stand it anyway.*
*I can stand it anyway.*
*I'm all right.*
*I'm all right.*

***Figure 6.5***

according to your ideal. Conversely, when you minimize the importance of absolute "shoulds" – the moral code of behavior - you are inviting trouble into your life. The solution is to distinguish between these preferential and absolute "shoulds" so that you do not fall in to the trap of maximizing or minimizing.

A number of these absolutes are found in the biblical Ten Commandments and their moral counterparts in other cultures, such as the "Moral Code of the Builder of Communism" in the atheistic Soviet Union. Across the globe you will find the same tenets ("thou shalt not kill") repeated.[129] The Islamic Quran includes ten verses which are substantially similar to the biblical decalogue.[130] Moral injunctions not to kill, steal, lie, or commit adultery are not negotiable, and regardless of religious persuasion, we run into danger when we choose not to honor them.

*"When trials arise that seem unexplainable, we should not allow our peace to be spoiled. However unjustly we may be treated, let not passion arise. By indulging a spirit of retaliation we injure ourselves."*

—Ellen G. White

Preferential "shoulds" are things we would like but are not absolutely required.[131] Some people set unattainable goals that they "should" be able to reach, then mourn when they don't achieve them. Others develop a definite opinion of how others "should" act or how the world "should" function, and are frustrated when everyone doesn't conform to their standards. Failure should be defined not as what happens when we fail to reach a high mark, but in terms of the effort and dedication expended in trying to achieve a task. Did you spend three hours making a soufflé, only to find it burned in the oven after racing out the door for a family emergency? You have not failed. You did your best, kept your priorities straight, and focused on what actually matters.

There is a time to use the word "should" and a time to reject it. If you employ it to describe preferred conditions, you will maximize the significance of minor shortfalls and set yourself up for disappointment. If you fail to apply it to the absolute essentials, you will minimize important values and lead yourself into trouble. It can be a powerful word, so use it wisely.

## YOU HAVE A CHOICE

Drew was an excellent basketball player. Extremely intelligent and well-coordinated, he had the ability to literally take over a game when his teammates were doing poorly. Though his team often played larger, more dominant schools, Drew was known to score 40-50 points anyway.

Unfortunately, in addition to his basketball skill, Drew was well-known for another highly-developed trait: he was very good at losing his temper. Drew could draw a technical from refs who were not known for doling them out. His mannerisms after a loss were particularly challenging. Clenching his fists, he would find the nearest gym mat and start in—working himself into a frenzy until his teammates stopped him for fear he would hurt himself. In a world where road rage has become common, Drew had his own variation of the tantrum—basketball rage.

Another player on the team, Joe, stood out in stark contrast to Drew.

Like Drew, Joe was an exceptional basketball player. But Joe was good at something Drew never quite conquered: he was a good sport. Joe always gave other players the benefit of the doubt. In a game filled with trash talk, he frequently helped opponents who had fallen, back to their feet. He respectfully raised his hand when called for a foul, and was even heard to compliment opponents on a "good shot."

What was the difference between these two players? One motivated himself with rage, as his anger surged in and out of control. The other, even when recipient of a flagrant foul, took a more charitable line of thought. You, too, have a choice when presented with possibly offensive circumstances: you can choose to nurse outrage at any perceived injustice, like Drew, or you can have a generous attitude, like Joe, and say, "That guy didn't really mean to hurt me."

## ANGER DANGER

Often when we have magnified a flaw in some situation, or fallen into trouble because we have minimized an important detail, we become more than irritated – it can seem infuriating. This emotion is fueled by our thoughts, both psychologically and physically. If we feel insulted, threatened, or ashamed, it sets off a limbic surge in the brain, releasing catecholamines in response to the stress. These "fight or flight" hormones generate a rush of energy that lasts for several minutes.[132]

Meanwhile, another wave of hormones swells from the lower emotional portion of the brain (the amygdala) through a branch of the neuroendocrine system, preparing the brain for physical action.[133] This second stage, which keeps the brain in a state of readiness, lasts much longer than the first (for hours or even days). This heightened state enables subsequent reactions to be built with particular quickness. This hair-trigger condition explains why people who have already been provoked or slightly irritated are so much more prone to an outburst.

In one study, psychologist Dolf Zillman (of the University of Alabama) had one individual make provocative remarks to some volunteers. Later some of the volunteers watched a film that was upsetting, while others watched one that was pleasant. In the last phase of the study, Zillman asked the volunteers to evaluate the individual who had levied the snide remarks and state whether they would hire them for a job or not. Zillman found a direct correlation between the retaliation of the volunteers and the degree to which they were upset over the film.[134]

In other words, the more disturbed the volunteers were by what they had watched, the harder they were on the person who had annoyed them before they watched the film.

Stress of any sort can create adrenocortical arousal, lowering the threshold for what provokes anger. There is usually a series of provocations before people become enraged. Each aggravation sets off another surge of amygdala-driven fight-or-flight catecholamines before the preceding wave has a chance to subside. This builds hormonal momentum until the body is in an escalated state of edgy arousal. At this point, a relatively small event can set off a storm of unreasonable rage, and quite possibly violence.[135]

When this volatile cycle is set into motion, the thoughts of the angered individual are beyond reason. Focused on revenge rather than reconciliation, they completely disregard the consequences of their irate actions. It is vital to stop this escalation of anger in its tracks, a task that CBT is ideally equipped to do.[136] The earlier in the anger cycle you curb it, the better the chance of short-circuiting the intensification.

## TAMING THE BEAST

Of all the moods people want to escape, anger seems to be the most seductive, stubborn, and hard to control. Propelled by a self-righteous monologue, it fills the mind with the most convincing arguments until we feel compelled to vent our rage. While sadness can drag you down, anger can be energizing, even somewhat exhilarating.[137] The persuasive power of anger is no doubt one reason why so many view it as uncontrollable or even "healthy." Some feel that even if anger can be controlled, it should not be. Arguing that "you need to get it out of your system," they promote venting as some sort of catharsis.

On the opposite end of the spectrum lies an equally deadly deception: the belief that anger can and must be suppressed at all cost. Though some psychologists teach that unvented anger can cause physical and psychological problems, the free expression of anger can be both unpleasant and dangerous. Psychologists who have studied release as an anger management tool have found that although venting may feel satisfying, it does not dispel our anger.[138] Rather than offer relief, the free expression of anger tends to reinforce and increase our fury by pumping up the brain's arousal system.[139] While there may be some instances where angry communication appears therapeutic, venting anger is one of the worst ways to cool down.

When tempted to become angry, the best strategy is almost always to keep quiet about the momentary irritations, take time to think, and re-evaluate the situation. By controlling your anger in these ways you are also less likely to provoke the person you are angry with into further retaliation. Feelings of anger will happen to all of us at times, but those feelings need to be elevated to our consciousness where any distortion can be analyzed and then corrected. "Let not the sun go down upon your wrath."[140] Methods for diffusing anger are described in the following sections.

## THE TIME OUT

An effective strategy for rage reduction is simply to take a "time out." In other words, quickly remove yourself to a place where the adrenal surge can subside in an atmosphere where there are not likely to be further triggers for rage. That means getting away from the person or situation that is making you angry.

The story of Cheri, who was playing co-ed volleyball with a church group, furnishes a good example of anger management. Cheri found one of the men playing the game to be particularly obnoxious. Loud and boisterous, Robert delighted in leaping high above the net and slamming the ball down with what seemed like extreme force for a friendly volleyball game. Robert was basically a nice guy, just extremely competitive.

One particular evening Cheri had the unhappy fate of being just across the net from Robert when he performed one of his ferocious spikes. There was no time to react as the ball hit her squarely in the chest, taking her breath away. Cheri was torn between wanting to cry out in pain and feeling furious with Robert.

Quickly, Cheri realized that she was about to say—or rather shout—something she would later regret. This little episode was the latest example of Robert taking the game too far, and she was about to lose it with him. In a split second reaction, she decided to exit the game. Before anyone could even ask how she was, Cheri zipped out the door and into the safety of her car, which she quickly drove home.

In the hours and days that followed, Cheri began to analyze the event and the subsequent thoughts that led to her anger. She thought that Robert should behave in a more courteous manner, and if not, he must be blamed and punished. She also combined this thought with the related thought that if Robert acted in such a manner, she personally could not tolerate it. Then she realized that Robert was not as emotionally mature as most of the volleyball "regulars." Although it was just a game, he was playing to win (as many sport enthusiasts do), and most likely not trying to hurt her at all. And even if Robert personally magnified the importance of winning a point, she could, in reality, stand it. She realized that she was in control of her own emotions, not Robert, and determined to remain cool when he behaved in a way that she did not prefer. Though she felt very angry about the violence with which he played, her feelings had simmered since the game.

Meanwhile, Robert had time to think about his actions. He realized that winning a point or a game is not everything, and that human relationships are far more important than game outcomes. As a result of Cheri's obvious "injury," he felt guilty and desired to ask her forgiveness. Robert determined that he could stand losing, and realized the importance of behaving kindly under all "game" circumstances.

At the next game, much to Cheri's surprise, Robert made a special point to apologize for what had happened the week before. Robert then played the game in a much more gentlemanly manner than he had in the past, a practice which he continued for as long as the two were acquainted. In retrospect, Cheri was always thankful that she managed not to tell Robert off "at the scene of the crime." Robert was not the type to back down, and

*"Nothing gives one so much advantage over another than to remain calm and unruffled under all circumstances."*

—Thomas Jefferson

things could have easily escalated. Instead, with both parties having time to think through what had happened, the story had a positive ending.

This strategy of taking time out, which is not new, was described in detail by a subject of one of the first scientific studies of anger back in 1899. He states, "Once when I was about 13, in an angry fit, I walked out of the house vowing I would never return. It was a beautiful summer day, and I walked far along lovely lanes, till gradually the stillness and beauty calmed and soothed me, and after some hours I returned repentant and almost melted. Since then when I am angry, I do this if I can, and find it is the best cure."[141] Exercise, cleaning, deep breathing, reading, and playing the piano are just a few of the distractions that can effectively de-escalate anger. Going for a long drive, which some seem to prefer as a cool-down method, may not be the safest alternative. (Do you want to meet a man who is furious with his wife while he is driving down the road?)

*"Let nothing be done through strife or vainglory; but in lowliness of mind let each esteem other better than themselves."*
— Philippians 2:3

Though a cool-down period can be highly effective, it only works if it halts the angry train of emotions. A cool-down works best by correcting the distorted thoughts of magnification that led to the anger. Activities such as shopping or eating, where the mind can continue in an unreflecting angry vein, are not as effective as those that divert our minds from the cause of our fury so that we can later thoughtfully correct the distorted thoughts and reconstruct our thinking correctly.

## THE PERSPECTIVE CHECK

The key to defusing anger is to interrupt the train of angry thoughts that are stoking it. Extended ruminations about grudges fuel the flames, as the mind relives the circumstances that provoked the anger. In contrast, calmly re-thinking and re-framing a situation is one of the best ways to put anger to rest. A better understanding of the situation involved can be quite helpful. When we follow the Indian prayer to "help me never to judge another until I have walked in his moccasins," we tend to be more patient with the foibles of others. For example, someone who understands that another individual is under a great deal of stress is less likely to retaliate against that person, and more likely to show compassion. The opportunity to defuse anger is much greater early on. Once a high level of rage sets in the window of opportunity for de-escalation has largely passed. Furious individuals, who can no longer "think straight," quickly dismiss information that might otherwise have mitigated their anger. Where some level of confrontation is needed, it usually works much better to take time to think. After taking time to think things through, a more constructive conversation can take place.

## ANOTHER FORM OF MAGNIFICATION

One often overlooked form of magnification is egotism or an inflated sense of pride. Those who develop too much self-esteem may feel great, but major problems are fast approaching. Feelings of worthlessness are often preceded by an inflated sense of pride. Such feelings would have never developed without the cognitive distortion of magnification of self. William Backus, a clinical psychologist who utilized cognitive behavioral therapy, was also a Lutheran minister. He wrote a book, *What your Counselor Never Told You: The Seven Sins that Lead to Mental Illness*. The first sin discussed is pride. The book also provides a test that can help determine if you need to deal with this issue. An adapted list of the symptoms of pride are listed in **Figure 6.6.**[142]

## VIEW OF SELF: A PRIMER

While many instances of magnification or minimization stem from an unbalanced view of others or the world around us, there are times when we hold a skewed view of ourselves. Self-esteem, a much-touted concept in this country, is actually a rather unhealthy form of pride. Following are some definitions to help clarify these terms:

**Self-worth:** the inherent worth of every human being.

**Self-respect:** the degree to which an individual likes himself—even when encountering the inevitable failures in life. A healthy self-respect does not ebb and flow based on how a person feels they measure up to others.

### INDICATORS OF INFLATED PRIDE

- trying to be noticed
- craving attention
- itching for compliments
- needing to be important
- detesting the idea of being submissive
- loathing the idea of admitting to wrong-doing
- being strongly opinionated
- being argumentative
- demanding your way
- wanting control over others
- flaunting your individual rights
- refusing advice
- being critical, yet resenting criticism
- thinking you have excellences you don't have

*Figure 6.6*

**Self-esteem:** pride in oneself, or a measure of a person's belief in how worthy, lovable, and capable we are, especially when compared to others. (Some studies on self-esteem refer to "self-worth" as being somewhat synonymous with self-esteem, making the results somewhat confusing.)

While we all need a healthy sense of self-worth, an unbalanced level of self-esteem leads to bad behavior more often than not. Although modern culture has attributed many of the problems in our society to "low self-esteem," several commonly held beliefs about self-esteem are nothing more than myths. Studies by Nicholas Emler, social psychologist, have shown that people with a high opinion of themselves pose a far greater threat to others than those with low self-esteem.[143]

Studies have also shown that people with high self-esteem are more likely than others to hold racist views, reject social pressures from adults and peers, and engage in physically risky pursuits such as drinking and driving or driving too fast. Apparently, people who think too well of themselves are more likely to damage other people by being reckless or downright unkind.

Proponents of building self-esteem often cite low self-esteem as a causative factor in many of society's ills. Research has demonstrated, however, that low self-esteem is not a risk factor for delinquency, violence, drug use, alcohol abuse, educational under-attainment, or racism. However, a low sense of self-worth is a risk factor for depression, teenage pregnancy, eating disorders, and being victimized by bullies.[144]

Despite the questionable value of increasing self-esteem, the widespread belief in the cure-all value of raising self-esteem has created a huge market for flawed self-help manuals and educational programs. The state of California in particular has spent significant public funds in trying to raise the self-esteem of its citizens. Unfortunately, all such efforts at raising self-esteem are nothing more than the psychotherapeutic equivalent of snake oil.[145]

## MINIMIZING YOUR SELF-WORTH

Some people are harder on themselves than anyone else in their lives. We have a tendency to judge ourselves based on our personal identity, family relationships, academic accomplishments, social successes, sense of security, and even our body images. While some may be their own worst critics, an attitude of self-disgust is seldom, if ever, useful. As explained in **Figure 6.7**, if you can do anything positive for anyone, you are not worthless!

People who hate themselves find it easy to also hate others, particularly those who have deflated their pride. As erring humans, we're all capable of actions which cause guilt or shame. While some acts deserve this response, others do not. The problem for most is distinguishing between the two.

While guilt can often be useful, it is only a helpful tool when it leads to change. Shame that pounds away on our psyches, with no possibility of release, is worse than totally useless. Some people have absorbed a sense of

## I AM NOT WORTHLESS BECAUSE:

- I have something to contribute to the well-being of others.
- what I do can have a positive effect.
- my being alive makes a difference to at least one person (and that person can be me).
- giving love, understanding, companionship, encouragement, sociability, counsel, or solace mean something.
- I can respect my opinions and my intelligence. (If others also respect me, that is a bonus.)
- I have self-respect and dignity.
- I can help contribute to the livelihood of my employees' families.
- I do my best to help my customers and vendors through my productivity and creativity.
- my presence in this milieu does make a difference to others.

***Figure 6.7***

shame from an early age. They have a mind-set that they are worthless and deserving of punishment. Such guilt can even defeat our ability to lead a reasonable life. Through the forgiveness offered at the cross, Christianity offers a highly effective and viable solution to the challenges of guilt and low self-worth. The tremendous sacrifice made at the cross provides confirmation of the intrinsic value of every human being.

Those who accept this gift need not put others down or even compare themselves with others to build their own self-esteem. The intrinsic infinite value of each human being assures them of their own self-worth, leaving them free to heed the time-honored injunction to "esteem others better than themselves" without fear of losing their stature in life.[146]

When you accept the fact that you are of infinite value and make it part of your thinking, that realization will have a positive impact on your sense of self-worth. And the understanding that all other humans are also of infinite value levels the playing field. This is why the term self-esteem, which implies that you are intrinsically more valuable than other humans, is off base. Infinity (your value) simply cannot be greater than infinity (the value of someone else).

### STRATEGIES FOR SUCCESS

Downgrading your descriptions, rewording, deliberately choosing a calm reaction, and taming your anger are all effective approaches to finding success over an unbalanced view of circumstances in the outside world. When it comes to magnification or minimization of your own self-worth, it is equally important to avoid feelings of worthlessness and self-denigration (e.g. minimization of your personal value) as it is to avoid the other side of the ditch (magnification of self-esteem). Only by developing a healthy sense of self-worth, coupled with consideration and respect for the value of others, will you truly be able to "balance your view of you and the world."

## References


120. Beck JS, Beck AT. *Cognitive therapy: basics and beyond.* The Guilford Press. 1995. 119.
121. Burns DD. *Feeling Good: The New Mood Therapy.* New York: HarperCollins, 1999. 42.
122. Burns DD. *Feeling Good: The New Mood Therapy.* New York: HarperCollins, 1999. 37-38, 158.
123. 2 Samuel 1:1-4. *The Holy Bible.* Authorized King James Version.
124. Daniel 4:30-37. *The Holy Bible.* Authorized King James Version.
125. Matthew 25:1-13. *The Holy Bible.* Authorized King James Version.
126. Ellis A, Tafrate RC. *How to Control Your Anger Before It Controls You.* Citadel. 2000. 127.
127. Clark L. *SOS Help for Emotions: Managing Anxiety, Anger and Depression.* 2nd ed. Bowling Green: SOS Parents and Programs Press, 2002. 172.
128. Clark L. *SOS Help for Emotions: Managing Anxiety, Anger and Depression.* 2nd ed. Bowling Green: SOS Parents and Programs Press, 2002. 40.
129. Lane C. *The rites of rulers: ritual in industrial society: the Soviet case.* Cambridge University Press. 1981. *258.*
130. Rosen L. *Varieties of Muslim experience: encounters with Arab political and cultural life.* University of Chicago Press. 2008. 116.
131. Zeig J. *The evolution of psychotherapy: the third conference. "Response by Dr. Ellis."* Routledge. 1996. 82.
132. Goleman D. *Emotional Intelligence.* Bantam. 2006. 205.
133. Goleman D. *Social intelligence: the new science of human relationships.* Bantam. 2006. 14.
134. Zillman D. "Television Viewing and Physiological Arousal." In J. Bryant & D. Zillman (Eds.), *Responding to the Screen: Reception and Reaction Processes.* 1991. 103-133.
135. Goleman D. *Emotional Intelligence.* Bantam. 2006. 60-62.
136. Ellis A, Tafrate R. *How to Control Your Anger Before It Controls You.* Citadel. 2000. 27-28.
137. Wicks RJ, Parsons RD, Capps D. *Clinical handbook of pastoral counseling, Volume 1.* Integration Books. 1985. 489.
138. Goleman D. *Emotional Intelligence.* Bantam. 2006. 64.
139. Ellis A, Tafrate RC. *How to Control Your Anger Before It Controls You.* Citadel. 2000. 20.
140. Ephesians 4:26. *The Holy Bible.* Authorized King James Version.
141. Dallenbach KM, Bentley M, Garrigues E, Boring M, Washburn F. "A Study of Anger." *The American journal of psychology,* Volume 10. 537.
142. Backus W. "Pride-The Root of the Root Sins." *What Your Counselor Never Told You.* Minneapolis: Bethany House, 2000. 73.
143. Dent D. "Bursting The Self-Esteem Bubble." *Psychology Today* (Mar/April 2002). 13 Dec. 2007 <http://psychologytoday.com/articles/pto-20020301-000005.html>.
144. Emler N. *Self-Esteem: The Costs and Causes of Low Self-Worth.* Layerthorpe: York Publishing Services Ltd, 2001. 58.
145. Baumeister RF, Campbell JD, Druger J, Vohs KD. "Exploding the Self-esteem Myth." *Scientific American* (2004). 14 Dec. 2007. <http://www.sciam.com/article.cfm?id=000CB565-F330-11BE-AD0683414B7F0000&print=true>.
146. Philippians 2:3. *The Holy Bible.* Authorized King James Version.

Chapter 7

"THERE IS LUXURY IN SELF-REPROACH. WHEN WE BLAME OURSELVES, WE FEEL NO ONE ELSE HAS A RIGHT TO BLAME US." —*OSCAR WILDE*

# Don't Take It Personally

## *How the personalization and blame game can hurt others and ourselves, and how to avoid it.*

"I'm never going to drive again," Anthony slouched against the side of the carport, eyeing his once-beloved pick-up truck.

"Oh, come on, Anthony," Darcy patted him on the arm. It had been 5 weeks since little Jacob darted out in front of Anthony's truck. There had been no time to stop, swerve, or slow down in any way. Just a sickening sound—followed by tragedy, shock, and a very painful funeral. It had been weeks since the accident, and Anthony's truck had just come back from the shop—but he just couldn't get the accident out of his mind, right down to the minutest detail.

"If only I had stayed later at work… If only I hadn't gone to the store …If only I had seen him sooner…" Anthony ruminated on those thoughts over and over again, blaming himself for the pain Jacob's family felt and the fact that Jacob was not alive.

"Some of you have not worked very hard at learning this material," Mrs. Bender looked sternly over her reading glasses and down her nose at the 24 students seated before her. "I'm not going to mention names, but you know who you are."

"She means me," Sophia thought to herself as she slumped down into her chair.

"Same old, same old," she complained to her mother later that night. "I work my head off to do the assignments, study for the quizzes, and be ready for the tests. And what does she do? Point me out to the entire class. Just another mean teacher—dumping on me again."

What do Anthony and Sophia have in common? Both are involved in the cognitive distortion of personalization. With this type of "crooked thinking," we blame ourselves for things we couldn't have avoided or aren't primarily responsible for.[147]

Anthony was not at fault in little Jacob's death. He had been driving responsibly and within the speed limit. There was no way he could have anticipated a bicycle zinging in front of his truck at a high rate of speed. Yet Anthony just couldn't stop blaming himself for the accident. He sold his truck and took public transportation, sank into a deep depression, and eventually lost his job. While the accident was truly tragic and Anthony was the person driving the vehicle that hit Jacob, he personalized the blame to the detriment of his health, job, and family.

Sophia had been working hard in Mrs. Bender's class. If Sophia had been goofing off, she might have benefitted from taking the teacher's stern words to heart. Because Sophia was not an "A" student, she assumed Mrs. Bender was talking about her. By personalizing the teacher's comments, she made herself resentful and quickly developed a bad attitude towards the class, thinking there was no point in trying if she was going to be criticized in this way. As a result, Sophia became hurt, angry, and disgusted. Her "B" average eventually turned into an "F." Because she failed to

### BLAME GONE BAD

When playing the "blame game," people may:

- blame themselves for things they couldn't have avoided or aren't entirely responsible for.
- blame others for things they are partly responsible for.
- interpret the comments, questions, and behavior of others as attacks on their own esteem.
- reject constructive criticism that was important for them to hear.
- make assumptions about what other people think.

***Figure 7.1***

screen out criticism that wasn't directed at her, Sophia suffered a wound from a shot that wasn't even fired her way! Even if the criticism were aimed at her, Sophia would be better off not to take it personally.

## PLAYING THE BLAME GAME

Personalization is blaming yourself 100% for bad outcomes because you might have had some small role to play in it. For example, what if you blamed yourself for the Great Depression in 1929 because you voted for the president who won the election in 1928. The catastrophe did not occur entirely because you were not wise enough to see the picture and voted for the "wrong guy." There was a multitude of contributing factors.

***"I praise loudly, I blame softly."***

—Catherine the Great

At times personalization can become so extreme that the prevalence of negative thoughts distracts from a person's goals and responsibilities. These "nonsense arguments" may or may not be accurate, but they are irrelevant once you have learned from past events. When you dwell on past events and are consumed with "if only" statements, you cannot move forward and focus on more important things. Anthony allowed nonsensical arguments and self-blaming thoughts to negatively affect his life even though there was nothing he could change about the past. His energy would have been much better spent on current concerns and his present situation. The only good reason to dwell on the past is to learn from it.

Personalization also involves interpreting the comments, questions, and behavior of others as attacks on your own self esteem.[148] When you take even well-meaning comments wrong, you become prickly and defensive. For example, if someone asks where you got your tennis racquet, totally different responses are possible: either "I bought it at MC Sports," or "What do you think I did—steal it?" One answer is a non-threatened, simple reply to an innocent question. The other is a defensive, blame-casting response that could quickly escalate into an argument if the other party to the conversation responds in an equally defensive way.

A person may also become so self-protective that they reject constructive criticism that really was important to hear.[148] While a certain level of personalization may be healthy in receiving constructive criticism, when gone astray it causes undue difficulty and defeat. Some common pitfalls that blame-game players fall into are documented in **Figure 7.1**.

## AN EQUAL OPPORTUNITY ERROR

The blame game can affect anyone. It's perfectly possible for a sensible person to be objective about some things and maddeningly subjective about others. While some might assume women are more prone to personalization than men, a tendency towards blame plagues both genders. It seems no one is immune to assigning blame to themselves or others.

In this often challenging world, we learn to be on the alert for rivals and enemies so we can defend ourselves against them. Yet some individuals can also be very hard on themselves. Whether admitted or not, many people monitor personal acceptance, performance, and approval rating from others as carefully as any politician. See some interesting quotes from famous politicians on blame, see **Figure 7.2**)[149,150,151]

## ESCALATED FEELINGS

Playing the blame game can be particularly damaging to family relationships. Parents who are not thinking clearly sometimes actually see their child as an "enemy," when the child is really just being a child.

This happens when the parent takes their child's rebellious behavior, which is most likely typical for their emotional maturity, as a personal rejection. In extreme cases, the end result can be child abuse. More than a few parents, when convicted of abuse, have tried to excuse themselves for hurting their child by saying "she hurt me first" or "he didn't love me." The child never intended to make a personal attack aimed against the parent, but it was perceived and reacted to as such.

Personalization can also be a major problem in marriage relations. Perhaps one spouse had a really bad day at the office and comes home in a grumpy mood. When she stomps through the door, her hyper-sensitive

### THE POLITICS OF BLAME

*"Let us not seek the Republican answer or the Democratic answer, but the right answer. Let us not seek to fix the blame for the past. Let us accept our own responsibility for the future."*
—John Fitzgerald Kennedy

*"...to err is human. To blame it on someone else is politics."*
—Hubert H. Humphrey

*"We must remember not to judge any public servant by any one act, and especially should we beware of attacking the men who are merely the occasions and not the cause of disaster."* —Theodore Roosevelt

***Figure 7.2***

husband, who quickly assumes she is angry with him, snaps at her. She returns the favor, and an evening of cold shoulders and snide remarks leads to one party sleeping on the couch.

Another common instance of personalization takes place when somebody is cut off in traffic and acts as though they've been personally attacked. Road rage can lead to stress, serious injury, and even death - all because of a traffic offense that may or may not have been intentional. Having an overactive personalization radar that detects insults, rejection, and criticism at every turn can lead to unnecessary hurt feelings and cause all kinds of distress.

*"If your girlfriend laughs at your tie, don't take it personally. Find another tie or find another girlfriend."*

—Marilyn vos Savant

## HOT HEADS IN HISTORY

The disciples James and John were ready to take their personalization to a new level when they asked Jesus if they should call down fire from heaven to consume a village that refused to welcome them.[152] Haman, a high official of the Persian King Ahasuerus, spitefully tried (and failed) to destroy all Jews within the kingdom because of his rage over Mordecai's refusal to bow down to him.[153] When personalization goes unchecked, the reaction can be extreme.

In another Biblical example, the prophet Samuel took it personally when the people of Israel called for a change. Samuel was a widely recognized judge and military leader in his country. At that time, the nation was ruled by judges who settled disputes, not kings. But the people demanded to have a king like other nations. Samuel knew this was caused partly because of the corruption of his sons, whom he had appointed to office, and blamed himself. God reassured Samuel that it was not Samuel they rejected, but the Kingship of God.[154] God told Samuel to give the people what they wanted and anoint Saul as king.

## WHEN IT RAINS, IT POURS

Even the calmest, most rational of thinkers might start taking things personally when multiple unfortunate events pile up. If enough negative circumstances occur at the same time, people who are not normally prone to personalization may fall into the habit rather quickly.

Somehow our brains have an uncanny knack for grouping things that shouldn't necessarily be together. For example, a man's teenage son trips in a basketball game and tears his ACL. One week later, the man falls off a ladder on the job and breaks his leg. Two days later the previously trusty engine in his car throws a rod. "Why me?" the man wants to know. He is starting to feel like the ancient character Job, to whom trouble came by the truckload.[155]

Why is this man's reaction to his unlucky chain of events so important? If he starts to feel like life is ganging up on him, considering himself a loser, he'll be less likely to manage the stress he faces. If, however, he recognizes that there really is no connection between the recent adversity that has come his way, he will not feel marked as a "loser."

He will no doubt feel unhappy about his lack of good fortune, but will also be able to reason his way through and deal with it all, while actually improving his life in the long run.

## WHEN GUILT IS INAPPROPRIATE

*"The best years of your life are the ones in which you decide your problems are your own. You do not blame them on your mother, the ecology, or the president."*
—Albert Ellis

Having feelings of guilt when you are not actually at fault is another indicator of the cognitive distortion of personalization. It's critical to understand that in many cases it is tempting to claim responsibility for unfortunate circumstances surrounding you, when in reality you actually do not have control over the situation. For example, if your child returns home from school with a report card that shows several low grades, despite your grand efforts to support good study habits, you cannot automatically assume that it is your failure that resulted in the poor scores. It is unreasonable to discount the role of the student in earning those grades.

As a parent, you can do many things to encourage and promote excellent academic performance by your children, but ultimately it is their responsibility to execute the schoolwork. You have influence, but not control. Your child has his or her own frontal lobe which governs their thoughts and actions. Fostering inappropriate guilt is consequential to not only you but anyone else involved in the situation. Since there is nothing you can do to take charge of someone else's thoughts or actions, a defeated attitude can only affect your life negatively.

On the other hand, guilt does serve a beneficial purpose when it is warranted. Appropriate guilt can be a powerful agent of change for the good. When admitting your error and avoiding passing the blame to someone or something else, you can then acknowledge areas of weakness and work toward improving your character and behavior. Also, admitting guilt is the first step in asking for forgiveness and moving toward emotional and spiritual healing. This is important to the health of your brain and your body. There are significant adverse health and relational consequences to not acknowledging appropriate guilt and asking for forgiveness.

The important thing is to remember that even if you are at fault in the situation, your wrong actions do not define you as a person. When you make the dangerous mistake of equating yourself with your actions, this can only lead to two undesirable kinds of thinking: you will either accept fault and consider yourself worthless and inadequate, or deny fault and refuse to change your ways. Both schools of thought are an overreaction to the false conclusion that a person's actions determine that person's worth.

When you recognize that the blame should be assigned to the wrong act and not to self-worth, you can accept responsibility for your role in the transgression and work toward avoiding a similar offense in the future. When you identify an area of weakness and confess that you need help in that area, God promises to provide His almighty strength to support you in your weakness.[156] You can then focus on the relatively simple act of correcting your behavior and making amends, because you're not preoccupied either with punishing yourself or with denying the wrongdoing altogether. **Figure 7.3** provides guidance on how to identify inappropriate guilt.

## HOW TO APOLOGIZE

If you find yourself in a situation where you are truly in the wrong and need to make amends with another person, you want to make sure that your apology is the kind that will set you both free from guilt and resentment. No matter how severe your violation, you are still alive and free to sincerely ask for forgiveness.

Saying you're sorry is difficult for many people, especially when they harbor the cognitive distortion of magnification (inflated pride). When self is magnified, the relationship with the person is proportionally minimized. It is usually easier to make an apology when you think of it as a commitment to a relationship, rather than a sign of weakness. The purpose of an apology should be to say you are sorry for things you are responsible for. Apologizing for things you didn't do just to make an unpleasant situation go away is never a beneficial approach.

Sometimes the incident you need to apologize for will require an immediate response. At other times, you will have time to reflect about what happened and why you are sorry. You may find it helpful to write

### IDENTIFYING INAPPROPRIATE GUILT

If you can honestly answer "no" to the questions below, then you are experiencing inappropriate guilt.

- Was I negligent in important details that caused this bad situation?
- Did I know what the negative consequences of my actions would be prior to the incident?
- Do other people consider me at fault for these circumstances?
- If my best friend were in this situation, would I consider him guilty?
- Were there any key factors that I had no control over, such as other's actions or unpredictable natural events?
- Can I do anything to correct any damage?

***Figure 7.3***

out your apology in advance. This can help organize your thoughts, not to mention calm your nerves. If a personal apology is more than you feel you can handle, the apology might even be given in writing.

Depending on the seriousness of the situation and intensity of the feelings of the person(s) you are apologizing to, you may also benefit from practicing what you plan to say in advance.

## 4 STEPS TO FORGIVENESS

There is a right way to ask for forgiveness. A good apology includes the following statements, or some variation thereof, in order:

**1. "I want to ask your forgiveness for something."**

Don't say "I'm sorry" – this simply means "I feel bad," and they probably feel bad too. You're going beyond that by asking for forgiveness.

**2. "I manifested…"**

- a rebellious spirit.
- a prideful spirit.
- a selfish attitude.
- a condemnatory spirit.

Identify the spirit or action that offended rather than just the action. The spirit is more offensive than the action.

**3. "I know how much this must have hurt you."**

To say this with sincerity, place yourself in their position and visualize yourself as the recipient of the action, spirit, or attitude.

**4. "It would mean a lot to me if you would forgive me. Will you forgive me?"**

You're seeking release for the offended (from bitterness and resentment), as well as for yourself. Ask, "Will you forgive me?" and wait for a response.

(Adapted from Bill Gothard's *Basic Youth Conflict Seminar)*

***Figure 7.4***

When the time comes for the actual apology, state clearly what you are sorry for doing. Acknowledge your actions and share your feelings about what happened without making excuses, blaming, exaggerating, or becoming verbose. If the situation calls for it, offer to make amends. Then listen to the other individual's response without becoming defensive.

From the start, it's important to remember that the individual you hurt may or may not choose to accept your apology. Though you cannot control their response, you can make sure your apology, request for forgiveness, and offer to make things right are sincere and without excuses. The other person involved may need time to sort out their feelings, so don't be discouraged if you aren't completely forgiven as soon as you apologize.

Once the apology is made, try to put the incident behind you. There is nothing to be gained from bringing up the same situation over and over again. Whether the other person forgives you or not, it is important to forgive yourself, recognize that you have learned from your mistake, set up barriers to prevent it from happening again, and move on. You have done the honorable thing by taking responsibility for your actions, apologizing for them, and where appropriate, making amends. Some helpful steps to follow in seeking forgiveness are detailed in **Figure 7.4.**[157]

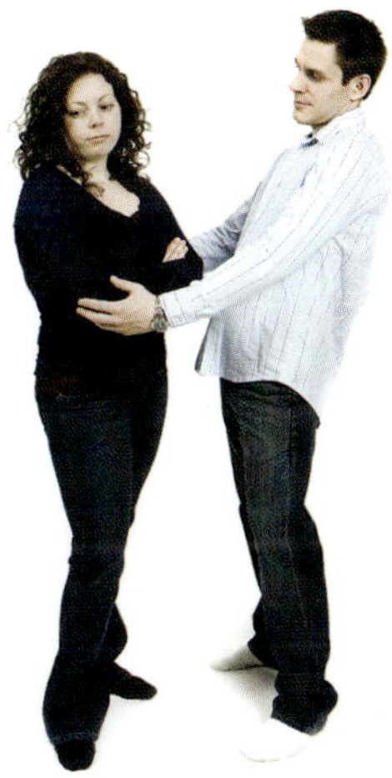

It's easier to say "Sorry" when apologizing is viewed not as a sign of weakness—but a commitment to a relationship.

## GRANTING FORGIVENESS

Forgiveness is one of the hardest tasks we may face in life. It is well worth the effort, however, as corroborated by the research of psychologist Dick Tibbits.[158]

Dr. Tibbits, who struggled with anger issues himself at one point, designed a study to show that forgiveness can mitigate the toxic effects of anger. Fifty Florida Hospital patients, who were divided into two equal groups, participated in the study. The first group did nothing but monitor their blood pressure. The second group went through an eight-week course where Tibbits taught them how to add forgiveness to their "grievance stories," or the past events that stirred anger within them. Participants in the second group who made other positive lifestyle changes during the study (such as starting to exercise) were excluded from the final findings.

At the end of the eight-week study, Tibbits found that the control group had no blood pressure change and the group that underwent forgiveness training had slight but measurable blood pressure improvements. The results were much more dramatic for the angriest people who took the forgiveness training, however. The participants with the six highest anger scores all went from diagnosed stage one hypertension to normal blood pressure in eight weeks.[159]

According to Tibbits, it is chronic anger (rather than temporary emotional elevations such as road rage) that is most in need of repair. Many people frequently deny this type of anger, keeping it well hidden below

## QUESTIONS TO ASK BEFORE PERSONALIZING

*"Is he really picking on me, or is there another explanation?"*

*"Is so-and-so really my personal blood enemy, or is she, for whatever reason, simply behaving badly at this particular time in her life?"*

Consider any other plausible explanation for what is going on before assuming it is a personal attack.

***Figure 7.5***

the surface. Tibbits believes that anger is simply a reaction to hurt. Each time we retell our "grievance stories" the hormone cortisol is released in the body, causing the blood pressure to rise and the immune system to weaken.[160] Repeating the same story over and over keeps you trapped in it, but true forgiveness (which is more than simply forgetting) can set you free.[161] Forgiveness, when accompanied by repentance, is also about letting yourself off the hook when appropriate.

While most people try to forgive the offender and forget the pain, the pain is still there. The key is to reframe the issue, widening it until you can view the object of your anger, not with a mental filter but as a person with both positive and negative characteristics. This can be done by thinking about what has happened to that person (or yourself) to get to this point. Tibbits compares forgiveness to a journey, a process, and a muscle in need of exercise. Feelings of self-righteousness don't help. The key is to empathize with the person or persons in question.

The risks associated with unforgiveness are high. High blood pressure, emotional despair, broken relationships, and serious health risks are just a few of the negative side effects of a failure to forgive.[162] A chronic burden of guilt can also hamper our ability to live a full and active life, hurting not only ourselves, but those we love in the process.

## STRATEGIES FOR SUCCESS

When you analyze your thoughts to identify personalization, you'll be less likely to be hurt and more likely to give other people the benefit of the doubt. Bigotry and prejudice do exist in this world. There are times that you'll feel you've been insulted, and sometimes it may actually be true. At such times, take a break to think things through. What will be accomplished by responding to the insult? You may be perfectly justified in your hurt feelings, yet you must ask yourself what will be gained through a confrontation. When you are slow to anger, you can more easily deal with the stresses life throws your way. **Figure 7.5** suggests some questions to ask before taking something personally.

Analysis of your thoughts is also important when you are tempted to personalize negative events and circumstances surrounding you. The key is to determine rationally whether the guilt you're feeling is appropriate or inappropriate. If you're truly not to blame for the situation, then it's crucial that we allow ourselves to release the guilt and move away from "nonsense arguments" that plague your thoughts. On the other hand, if your actions actually played a role in the unfortunate outcome, then it's valuable to accept responsibility, apologize, and use the difficult conditions to grow and improve. If you apply lessons from our mistakes toward a positive change, then misfortune can result in gain instead of loss.

*"Sir, my greatest concern is not whether God is on our side; my greatest concern is to be on God's side, for God is always right."*
—Abraham Lincoln

## References


147. Leahy RH. *Cognitive therapy techniques: a practitioner's guide.* The Guilford Press. 2003. 298.
148. Ellis A, Abrams M, Abrams LD. *Personality Theories: Critical Perspectives.* Sage Publications. 2008. 463.
149. Barnes JA. *John F. Kennedy on Leadership: The Lessons and Legacy of a Presidentt.* Amacom. 2007. 93.
150. Luce HR. *Time,* Volume 132, Issues 19-26. 1988. 28.
151. Roosevelt T. *The strenuous life: essays and addresses.* The Century Co. New York, New York. 1906.
152. Luke 9:54. *The Holy Bible.* New King James Version.
153. Esther 3:5-6. *The Holy Bible.* New King James Version.
154. 1 Samuel 8:7. *The Holy Bible.* New King James Version.
155. Job 13:1-22. *The Holy Bible.* Authorized King James Version.
156. 2 Corinthains 12:9. *The Holy Bible.* New King James Version.
157. Adapted from Bill Gothard's Basic Youth Conflict Seminar.
158. Gothard B. *Institute in Basic Youth Conflicts: Research in Principles of Life.* 1976.
159. Tibbits D. *Forgive to Live: God's Way—Spiritual Guidance on Forgiveness that could Save Your Life.* Florida Hospital Publishing. 2009. 98-100.
160. Tibbits D. *Forgive to Live: God's Way—Spiritual Guidance on Forgiveness that could Save Your Life.* Florida Hospital Publishing. 2009. 51.
161. Tibbits D. *Forgive to Live: God's Way—Spiritual Guidance on Forgiveness that could Save Your Life.* Florida Hospital Publishing. 2009. 48-56.
162. Simon HB. *The Harvard Medical School Guide to Men's Health: Lessons from the Harvard.* Free Press. 2004. 218.

Chapter 8

EMOTIONAL REASONERS TELL THEMSELVES "I FEEL LIKE IT, THEREFORE IT MUST BE TRUE."

# Let Your *Head* Do the Thinking

## *It's ok to feel with your heart, but thinking with your heart (emotional reasoning) can lead to trouble.*

Tom and Sherrie's marriage was clearly on the rocks. Despite both of their intentions to the contrary, they seemed destined for divorce after three years of marriage. In a last-ditch effort, the couple visited a counselor to try and save their union.

It didn't take long for Sherrie to reveal how upset she was that Tom went fishing with his buddies every weekend. To her way of thinking, he hardly remembered he had a wife.

Tom countered that he really did want to spend more time with Sherrie. When the weekend rolled around, however, he simply felt like fishing.

"I'd be a hypocrite to stay and do things with Sherrie when I really want to be with the guys," he reasoned.

Fortunately, the counselor helped Tom to see that acting on his feelings wasn't in the best interest of his marriage. As a result, Tom determined to spend more of his weekends at home with Sherrie.

The first few weekends Tom stayed home, he felt moody and deprived. But he knew he had made a good decision when, a few months after prioritizing time with Sherrie, new life came into their relationship. Their marriage was saved, and home had become a pleasant place again.

Weekends were hard for Bruce. While weekdays were a whirl of activity, on the weekends he just couldn't seem to get himself out of bed, much less organized. It wasn't that there was a shortage of things to do. Bruce had a rather long list staring him in the face at any given time. But he never quite seemed to get to it.

"I just don't feel like doing that today," he would tell himself, or "That task is really difficult; I'm not in the mood to tackle it."

His usual habit was to lie in bed until noon on the weekends, then settle in as a major couch potato during the seemingly endless round of sporting events. He didn't usually bother to shower on those days, and stopped watching TV only long enough to check the refrigerator or order a pizza. Bruce wasn't happy with the way he was spending his weekends. In fact, he was very unhappy about it. But no matter how much he chastised himself for being lethargic, he seemed to fall into the same sleepy routine every Saturday morning…

What do Tom and Bruce have in common? Each are engaged in a common cognitive distortion known as "emotional reasoning." Individuals engaged in emotional reasoning take their emotions as evidence that whatever they feel is really the way things are.[163]

**Saying to yourself, "I really don't feel like getting up today, so I guess I won't," is reasoning with your emotions.**

Tom felt like fishing every weekend, so he convinced himself that he would be a hypocrite if he reserved his weekends to spend with his wife. Bruce was not in the mood to tackle his mounting weekend to-do list, so he "solved" the problem by staying in bed. The trouble is, emotions are not a very reliable barometer for drawing conclusions about yourself, others, or life in general. The fact that you feel inadequate doesn't mean that you are inadequate. Just because I am angry and upset at you does not prove that you have mistreated me at all. When I feel overwhelmed it does not automatically mean that my problems are impossible to solve. Accepting your current emotions as fact or truth can cause you to make poor decisions.

## FEELINGS CAN LIE

The primary problem with emotional reasoning is the fact that feelings can be misleading. Unhappy, disappointed, or distressed feelings do not undoubtedly indicate that your circumstances are hopeless. If you don't yet agree with this concept, think of it in the reverse. Does the fact that you are in a fantastic mood prove that you are especially great or worthy? Or does it simply mean that you are having a good day, week, or month?

Your personal characteristics and worth are not determined by feelings. You are who you are, regardless of how you feel. Your feelings never determine your worth as a person, only your relative state of comfort. If you are temporarily sad, that really means only one thing: you are feeling

## EMOTIONAL THOUGHT PROCESS

Emotional reasoners conclude that because they feel:

- like a loser, they must be a failure.
- guilty, they must have done something bad.
- inadequate, they must be a worthless person.
- overwhelmed and hopeless, their problems must be impossible to solve.
- lazy, they might as well stay in bed.

*Figure 8.1*

low at the moment. Not surprisingly, emotional reasoning plays a role in nearly all cases of depression.[164] When life in general seems very negative, people start to assume that they themselves are negative. It doesn't often occur to them to challenge their perceptions or the negative thoughts and feelings that fuel the depression. Individuals who are prone to addiction also have a great problem with emotional reasoning. Examples of other thought processes common to emotional reasoners is documented in **Figure 8.1**.[165]

### WHEN TO LISTEN TO FEELINGS

Feelings can also sometimes be accurate reflections of truth, and if so, can motivate us into appropriate action.

Consider the case of Morgan, who gets a call from an old friend at 11 p.m. on Sunday night inviting her to go to the nearest all-night casino.

"They're running a double or nothing," Morgan's friend urges. In response to the invitation, Morgan may go out for a night of gambling. Alternatively, since she is recovering from a gambling addiction, she may have feelings of disgust rise within her. Morgan's disgusted feelings can actually be a positive thing—if she elevates them to her rational thought, concludes that they are accurate, and acts upon those feelings by saying "no" to the unwise activity.

*"Do not bite at the bait of pleasure till you know there is no hook beneath it."*
—Thomas Jefferson

The following morning, Morgan feels far better than she would have had she spent the night gambling. Instead of being irritable for the next two days, missing work, or at the very minimum being late, Morgan feels refreshed and ready to have a productive day on the job. When a different friend calls asking Morgan to volunteer at the soup kitchen for the homeless that night, Morgan does not really "feel like" going. By elevating her feelings to rational thought, however, Morgan remembers that acts of altruism are associated with increased happiness and life satisfaction.

She also remembers that she doesn't have any plans for that evening and volunteers with her friend.

The following day, Morgan feels better about herself—much better than she would have had she stayed home and watched a movie. The next time she is asked to help people in need, Morgan actually feels like volunteering. Once again she elevates her feelings to rational thought, agrees that they are accurate reflections of truth, and volunteers, having even more fun in the process of helping others than she did before. Morgan is feeling and doing well, not because she does not have emotions, but because she is no longer using emotional reasoning to make her decisions.

All of us have tendencies to emotional reasoning. A good way to analyze that tendency is to say to yourself, "Would I think this, if I did not feel this way?" If the true answer is no, then identify the distorted thought as emotional reasoning. I learned a song at age 12 that is helpful in combating emotional reasoning. It goes to the tune of "Yankee Doodle," and the words are in **Figure 8.2**.

## ANCIENT EXAMPLES OF EMOTIONAL REASONING

Moses, who led the children of Israel out of slavery and to the brink of the Promised Land, provides several fascinating examples of emotional reasoning. While still crown prince of Egypt, Moses came across an Egyptian taskmaster brutally beating a Hebrew slave. Though trained by the Egyptians and a favorite in the palace, Moses had not forgotten his Hebrew roots and secretly sided with the suffering slave. Overcome by his anger (emotional reasoning), he ignored the disastrous outcome of his contemplated action, quickly killed the Egyptian, and hid his body in the sand. Exiled from Egypt because of his crime, Moses repented from his action and spent 40 years herding sheep. Those years as a shepherd were a real growth experience for Moses. In killing the Egyptian, he had displayed an impetuous take-no-prisoners spirit. Now he was a humble man.[166, 167, 168]

The ancient story of Job, or rather Job's wife, provides another powerful example of emotional reasoning. Job's story was the classic "rags to riches" tale, only told backward. Having tragically lost whole herds of livestock, a large number of servants, his ten children, and finally his health all in a very short period of time, Job still clung to his faith in God. Despite the temptation from his wife to turn from God, Job refused to do so, reacting with a studied calm to the string of calamities.[169] His wife, however, engaged in a fit of emotional reasoning, urging her husband to just "curse God and die."[170]

In the wilderness of temptation, Satan tried to get Jesus to engage in emotional reasoning. Having fasted for forty days and forty nights, Jesus' entire body—not to mention emotions—must have cried out for food. Satan asked Jesus to do a seemingly very simple thing in providing food

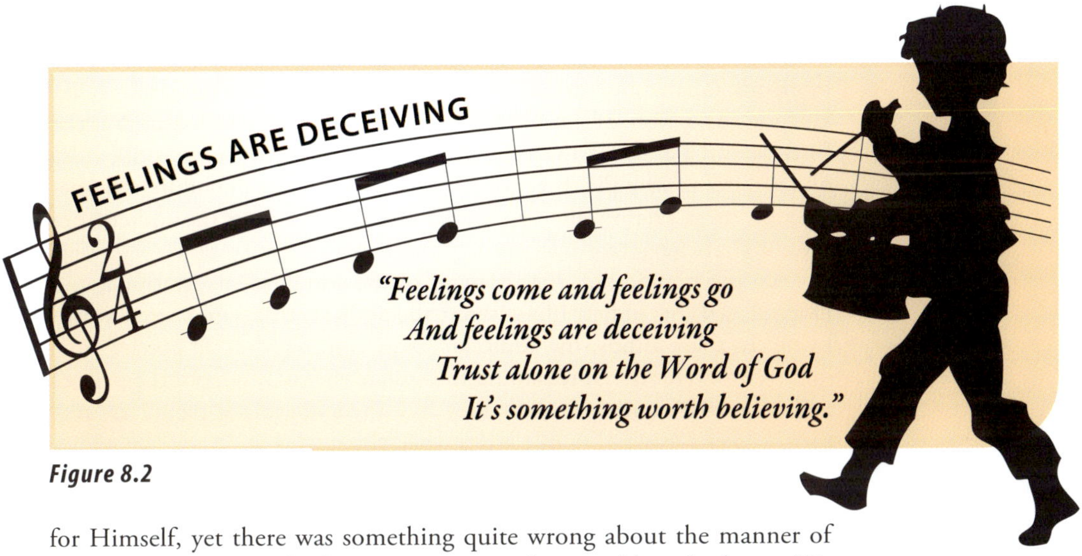


*Figure 8.2*

for Himself, yet there was something quite wrong about the manner of the request. Fortunately, Jesus, as our example, was able to look past His own emotions, engage His frontal lobe, and act out of reason.[171]

Jesus loved the people He came to save. How easy it would have been for Him to want to leap off a tower as Satan invited Him to do, make a dramatic showing, and win the homage of the people. But showmanship is not God's way. By utilizing reason rather than emotion, Jesus once again saw through the temptation of emotional reasoning.

This is not to say that Jesus had no emotion. He was filled with compassion for the people, wept over Jerusalem, and cried at the tomb of Lazarus. The night before He went to the cross, He literally sweat "great drops of blood" in the Garden of Gethsemane.[172] This was a very emotional experience for Christ, though He did not succumb to emotional reasoning. The mob that shouted "crucify Him, crucify Him" was the ultimate example of emotional reasoning. Many of the same people who had "heard Him gladly," who responded to Him throughout His ministry and were even attached to Him, now wanted to end His life. Humans engaged in emotional reasoning all the way to the cross, including everyone from Peter and Judas to the raging mob.

Through it all, Jesus kept His emotions under the guidance of a holy calm. He felt the betrayal, rejection, and physical pain. Even as the nails were driven through His hands, He prayed, "Father forgive them."[173] He had plenty of excuses to yield to emotional reasoning—but He did not.

## EMOTIONAL REASONING AND POOR LIFESTYLE CHOICES

Emotional reasoning is a primary explanation for why many individuals remain trapped in destructive lifestyle habits, seemingly unable to change. It is a major component in the epidemic of obesity, addiction, and other lifestyle-related diseases.[174]

"I feel like eating a Twinkie, therefore I will," is the mantra followed by many. Chain smokers, alcoholics, drug users, and other addicts also fall prey to a rash of emotional reasoning, locked in a harmful cycle. Friends and family of those caught in addictions often have difficulty understanding why the threat of job loss, divorce, loss of children, homelessness, incarceration, illness, or even death, don't deter the addict from the chosen behaviors.

To the non-addict, the behavior of the addict seems irrational and illogical. To the addict, life without the addiction does not seem worth living. In their minds, the addiction must continue—at all costs.[175] Addicts rely on emotional reasoning to insulate themselves from the pain of addiction. By focusing on how they feel, the addict finds plenty of "reasons" to keep using. Trouble arises when those who care about an addict wish to show empathy, but engage in emotional reasoning themselves. When we join an addict in their negative feelings or accept their skewed perceptions, we are engaging in the same cognitive distortions that entrap them in addiction.

## THE TWIN BROTHER OF EMOTIONAL REASONING

Procrastination is one of the banes of our culture today. It is also closely related to the cognitive distortion of emotional reasoning.[176] Notice the common thread in the statements above: "I don't feel like studying right now, so I'll just wait until tomorrow." "I don't feel like repairing the fence today, so I'll just do it this weekend." "I don't feel like visiting my sick grandmother, but I'll do it soon."

**Procrastination is a form of emotional reasoning.**

Procrastination allows feelings to determine what should, should not, or will be done. Individuals struggling with depression find procrastination to be especially tempting. Someone who is depressed often doesn't feel like doing much. Feeling overwhelmed, unmotivated, and lacking in willpower leads to an unproductive lifestyle, which in turn amplifies the feelings of apathy and hopelessness. When things get started in this vein, they can quickly spiral into a vicious cycle. Lack of productivity fuels a sense of self-hatred, resulting in further isolation, incapacitation, and even less productivity. With all this in mind, it is no wonder that procrastination is one of the hallmarks of clinical depression.

When you procrastinate, you convince yourself that it's easier to put off life's difficulties than it is to face them. It is common for a procrastinator to tell himself that a particular task is awful, he simply can't handle the frustration of dealing with the situation, and this is a hassle that he shouldn't have to face.

People procrastinate on many tasks, such as income tax returns, writing a term paper, or doing chores. Unfortunately, the very act of procrastination often leads to additional problems with past-due deadlines or worsening conditions. In combating procrastination, we need to tell ourselves that dealing with responsibilities, chores, and hassles is simply an integral part of life. While taking care of problems in their early state is certainly inconvenient, you feel much better when the job is completed.

## PERILS OF "DO-NOTHINGISM"

In his best-selling book *Feeling Good, the New Mood Therapy*, psychiatrist David Burns devotes some significant time to a condition closely related to procrastination, which he calls "do nothingism." According to Dr. Burns, "do nothingism" is one of the great paradoxes of human nature.[177] Sufferers of this affliction always hang back, defeating themselves at almost every turn. You would be tempted to think they were involved in a plot against themselves. This is in stark contrast to other individuals who throw themselves into life with great zest, which leads Dr. Burns to ask the question, "Why do we humans frequently behave in ways that are really not in our self-interest?"[178] This is a perplexing question, and one which has been answered by many popular, but incorrect, theories. Some choose to believe that they are basically lazy, because it's their nature. Others think it's normal to enjoy suffering, to want to hurt themselves, or to want to hurt others. Some have been accused of enjoying the attention that comes with being depressed.

While there could be a grain of truth in some of these theories, most who have fallen into the trap of procrastination are engaging in a self-feeding cycle of lethargy. The cycle begins with self-defeating thoughts, such as "I'm not in the mood, I'll probably fail if I try" or "Things are just too difficult." The next step in the cycle is self-defeating emotions of boredom, discouragement, worthlessness, or overwhelming fatigue. These emotions are followed by self-defeating actions, such as avoiding people, staying in bed, and refraining from activities that could've been fulfilling. These actions are quickly followed by more feelings of inadequacy, unproductiveness, and misery, starting the unhealthy cycle all over again. Instead of all this, tell yourself the truthful messages in **Figure 8.3**.

***"I can stand dealing with problems as they occur."***

***"Taking care of responsibilities as they arise will actually make life easier."***

***"I can get started on a task even if I don't feel like it."***

*Figure 8.3*

## EAT THAT FROG!

**Unpleasant tasks are like "frogs" we must eat.**

The motivational speaker Brian Tracy offers some great advice on how to "get moving" in his book, *Eat that Frog*. If eating a frog seems like a distasteful task, that is precisely the point of the book. Tracy compares unpleasant tasks to frogs which must be "eaten."[179] If the very idea of eating frogs is so distasteful to you that it destroys the whole concept here, think of something else you'd rather not eat.

One elderly woman, who had just been introduced to this concept and thought she would put it into practice, had a "senior moment" and proclaimed, as she set off to tackle her task, "Well, I'm off to swallow my turtle!"

If you have tasks you have put off due to emotional reasoning, give yourself a push to get them done. You are likely to find that such tasks were not as bad as you thought they might be. The accomplishment of such tasks can be really quite gratifying, lessening your stress level tremendously. So "eat that frog!"

## A STRESS-FREE LIFE IS NOT THE GOAL

Many people long for reduced stress or a stress-free life where they might sleep in every morning, have few, if any, responsibilities, or lounge on the beach for extended vacations. They don't realize that challenge and moderate stress can actually help them feel better, improve their overall health, and lead to a more rewarding life! A study by Dr. Joseph A. Bosch of Ohio State University revealed that certain types of stress can actually be good for you!

Dr. Bosch studied two types of stress: passive and active. Passive stress results from engaging in activities that we watch but can't participate in, such as watching a scary movie. In contrast, active stress involves an event or situation that a person can actually respond to (such as meeting a deadline).

In Dr. Bosch's study, 30 volunteers aged 18 to 34 were exposed to both an active and passive stressful event. In the active stressful event, volunteers were asked to memorize information and take a 12-minute test. In the passive stressful event, they watched a 12-minute video of "gruesome" surgical procedures. During the experiments, each person gave saliva samples that were analyzed for immune system components known as secretory proteins. These proteins help protect the lining of organs such as the lungs and stomach, guarding against the invasion of bacteria and viruses while possibly fighting cancer cells. Dr. Bosch found that levels of secretory proteins increased during active stress.

"Stress is not the big bad thing everybody is thinking it is—in fact, most acute stressors boost the immune system," remarked Dr. Bosch. "Only when the stress is unusually prolonged or repetitive does it become a potential threat to health."[180]

An exception would be the body's reaction to acute stressors to which there is no way of responding except to passively endure. In his study, Dr. Bosch found that passive stress had a rapid and strong suppressive effect on some aspects of immune function. In other words, passive stressors such as those caused by violent television programs can actually lower immune system function.

Eliminating or avoiding life's stresses, then, is not the goal to pursue. Confronting challenges, even when we don't "feel like it," is healthy! The key, of course, is to seek the right kind of stress (active, immune-boosting stress instead of the passive variety). In terms of active stressors, it is also possible to get too much of an otherwise beneficial thing. Piling on active stressors so that sleep, exercise, or the devotional life suffers is not good and will eventually impair the immune system.

## WHAT TO DO WHEN EMOTIONS WELL UP

No doubt each of us will have moments of great emotion in our lives. This is to be expected. But whether it is joy at the birth of a child, grief at the loss of a loved one, or anger over a traffic citation, our emotions must be guided by a God-inspired frontal lobe. There is only one true way to get this inspiration, weigh our emotions, and ensure they are lined up with truth rather than a cognitive distortion: as with all of our thoughts and actions, our emotions must be held up to the light of accuracy.

*"Be sure to put your feet in the right place, then stand firm."*
— Abraham Lincoln

When emotions begin to rise up, practice impulse control. Stop and ask yourself, "What is the truth here, and what is the evidence for that truth?"[181] The goal should be to elevate feelings to an analytical level and replace emotional reasoning with true, powerful thoughts that bring peace in the midst of a storm.[182]

"Because I feel like it" or "because I don't feel like it" should never be a reason for behavior. A well-thought out, accurate reason should always form the basis for all thoughts and actions.[183] Emotion and passion have their place, but the cognitive error of emotional reasoning is why many people get stuck in negative life ruts. A move away from emotional reasoning to a more practical manner of thinking will provide proper motivation to tackle problems and implement lifestyle changes.

## PRACTICAL VERSUS EMOTIONAL

One of the best steps to take towards more rational (as opposed to emotional) thinking involves recognizing the difference between practical and emotional problems. Practical problems are difficulties with other people or the world. Losing a job, a teenage pregnancy, or a car in need of repair—these are practical problems. Emotional problems, on the other hand, are the unpleasant feelings experienced due to practical problems. For example, you may feel guilty about losing your job, shame that your daughter is expecting a baby out of wedlock, or stressed out about the car

Practical problem

breaking down. Because the emotional response to practical problems can be so intense, it's important to deal with emotional hurdles before solving the practical end when possible. In order to do this, you must first identify the type of problem you are facing. Then you can "divide and conquer," so to speak.

An example of this is the way you would handle being first to arrive on the scene of a terrible accident. Two challenges would immediately present themselves: the need to manage the rush of emotions (such as fear, grief, or anger) that the accident has triggered either in yourself or others, and the need to assist any injured persons as quickly and effectively as possible.

Emotional problem

If you are to effectively help the injured, you must first gain control of and manage your own emotions. It is important to take a few deep breaths and remain calm in order to see clearly what needs to be done. The same principle holds true in many of life's less tragic moments. If you have lost your job, there is the practical problem of paying the mortgage and putting food on the table. There is also the emotional challenge of feeling unwanted, unlucky, or simply unproductive. If you come to grips with the emotional side of the challenge first, managing to keep your feelings firmly in check, you will be much better able to face the financial challenges ahead. It's true that practical problems will exist regardless of the emotional reaction involved. Though it is natural to express emotions, you can leave yourself with the practical dilemma as the only major problem by eliminating emotional reasoning.

## STRATEGIES FOR SUCCESS

Whether you struggle with emotional reasoning or are trying to help someone who does, the key is to identify and verify any assumptions being made, then consider the evidence for or against those assumptions before allowing emotions to well up inside..[183] Your goal should be to be informed, rather than compelled, by emotion. Then you can consciously choose the action that is most consistent with reason, purpose, and intended results.

Both reason and emotion are necessary in the human experience. In the absence of feeling or emotion, people and decisions become highly impersonal and lack motivation. It is passion that stokes the fire of initiative, igniting those involved in a project. However, if decisions are made based solely on feelings, then impulsive and short-sighted actions will follow. The solution is to find a balance between emotional reasoning and rational thought by looking past the feelings of the moment and into the future. What is the ultimate outcome of the immediate decision? Employ analytical thinking in your decision making, and you will be able to break free from the emotional thought process that holds you in an undesirable lifestyle.

## References

163. Leahy RH. *Cognitive therapy techniques: a practitioner's guide.* The Guilford Press. 2003. 173.
164. Pucci AR. *The Client's Guide to Cognitive-Behaivioral Therapy.* Lincoln, NE: iUniverse, 2006. 59.
165. Burns DD. *Feeling Good: The New Mood Therapy.* Rev. and updated. New York: Avon, 1999.
166. Exodus 2:11-25. *The Holy Bible.* Authorized King James Version.
167. Exodus 32:15-19. *The Holy Bible.* Authorized King James Version.
168. Exodus 34:1-5, 28, Hebrews 9:1-5, and Revelation 11:19. *The Holy Bible.* Authorized King James Version.
169. Job 1:13-22. *The Holy Bible.* Authorized King James Version.
170. Job 2:9 . *The Holy Bible.* Authorized King James Version.
171. Matthew 27:12-14. *The Holy Bible.* Authorized King James Version.
172. Luke 22:44. *The Holy Bible.* Authorized King James Version.
173. Luke 23:34. *The Holy Bible.* Authorized King James Version.
174. Dayton T. *Trauma and addiction: ending the cycle of pain through emotional literacy.* HCI. 2000. 18.
175. Herrington RE, Jacobsen GR, Benzer DG. *Alcohol and drug abuse handbook.* W. H. Green. 1987. 82.
176. Burns DD. *Feeling Good: The New Mood Therapy.* Rev. and updated. New York: Avon, 1999. 38.
177. Burns DD. "Do-Nothingism: How to Beat It." *Feeling Good: The New Mood Therapy.* New York: Avon-HarperCollins, 1999. 82, 83.
178. Burns DD. "Do-Nothingism: How to Beat It." *Feeling Good: The New Mood Therapy.* New York: Avon-HarperCollins, 1999.
179. Tracy B. *Eat That Frog.* 2nd ed. San Francisco: Berrett-Koehler, 2002. 2.
180. Bosch, JA. *Psychophysiology* 2001;38:836-846, Ohio State University.
181. Backus W. *Telling Yourself the Truth.* Bethany House Publishers. 2000. 59.
182. Halpern J. "From detached concern to empathy: humanizing medical practice." Oxford University Press, 2001.
183. Evans AN, Rooney BJ. *Methods in psychological research.* Sage Publications. 2007. 8.

Chapter 9

WE HURT OURSELVES WHEN WE ALLOW NEGATIVE LABELS APPLIED BY OTHERS TO BECOME OUR OWN.

# Learn to Label Correctly

***There are times when we need to call things as we see them. Mislabeling, however, can be very detrimental. Learn how to know the difference.***

"Idiot!" the words of her father rang in Margaret's ears.

"Why can't he ever call me by my name?" Margaret fumed to herself. "If it's not 'idiot,' it's 'fool,' 'stupid,' or some similar name." In her heart, Margaret knew all of the reasons.

She was the last of four daughters. By the time she came along, her father desperately wanted a son—but it was not to be. Margaret's mother suffered all kinds of complications with the pregnancy, which ended with a premature delivery and emergency hysterectomy. As the result of her difficult birth, Margaret was left with lifelong learning disabilities and a bitter father.

Although Margaret's mother loved her little girl and was very kind, the angry words of her father wedged their way into her heart. With the deck stacked against her from the start, Margaret had one round of failure after another at school.

"It figures, I sure am stupid," Margaret scolded herself over and over again. The negative labels her father had so unkindly applied to her as a child had become her own.

Angie stormed into her office cubicle and slammed the door, delcaring that her boss, Bruce, is a major jerk.

"What makes you say that?" Angie's office mate, Sarah, asked.

"He watches everything I do with an eagle eye. He ordered new computer monitors for everyone in the office but me. When major clients come by, he doesn't even introduce me. And I'm supposed to be the sales-manager-in-training. Need I say more?"

Across the hall, Bruce was equally angry.

"We should never have hired Angie," he fumed. "She's a PMS-driven, insensitive queen bee if ever I saw one."

"Oh dear," Bruce's secretary was understandably worried. "She seemed so engaging and sweet when you first brought her in."

"Well, it was all a façade. She actually accused me of watching her with an eagle eye this morning, but it doesn't take eagle eyes to see what's wrong with her. Steer clear, she's a witch!" With that kind of rhetoric under their breaths, what had been a skirmish between Bruce and Angie quickly escalated into an all-out war. Each had a collection of less-than-complimentary names for each other, which they used quite freely whenever the other stepped out of the room. Bruce couldn't see anything good in Angie, nor she in him. In a short time, a sense of vengeful unhappiness pervaded the entire office.

## THE TROUBLE WITH LABELING

"Your life is a complex and ever-changing flow of thoughts, emotions and actions. To put it another way, you are more like a river than a statue. Stop trying to define yourself with labels—they are overly simplistic and wrong. Would you think of yourself exclusively as a "breather" just because you breathe? This is nonsense, but such nonsense becomes painful when you label yourself out of a sense of your own inadequacies." —***David Burns, MD***

***Figure 9.1***

What do Margaret, Bruce, and Angie all have in common? All are engaged in the highly detrimental habit of mislabeling.

Mislabeling is describing oneself or others with words that are heavily loaded emotionally and not completely true. Mislabeling involves the use of inaccurate, inflammatory descriptions to label oneself or another person.[184]

When a food factory slaps a label on a can of beans, the ingredient list describes what's inside the can—and it doesn't change. Labeling yourself has about the same effect, which is precisely what makes mislabeling so very dangerous to your psyche. When you call yourself names based on things that have happened, you identify with your shortcomings, making it all too easy to think things can never change. Soon you are stuck in a rut. Instead of saying "I made a mistake," you reinforce a negative sense of self-worth by telling yourself that you're a born loser, failure, rotten parent, bore, or even a creep.

*"How many legs does a dog have if you call the tail a leg? Four. Calling a tail a leg doesn't make it a leg."*
—Abraham Lincoln

Mislabeling is based on the philosophy that "the measure of a man is the mistakes he makes."[185] If you find yourself saying "I'm a blankety-blank-blank" whenever you make a mistake, you are involved in mislabeling. If you hold unrealistic expectations of others, it can be tempting to mislabel someone as selfish or uncaring if they do not devote all their attention to you.

The problem with mislabeling is that, in addition to being self-defeating, it is quite irrational. Who you are simply cannot be equated with any one thing you do.[186] Dr. David Burns makes this point abundantly clear in the quote featured in **Figure 9.1**.[187]

## RELATED COGNITIVE DISORDERS

A rigid, perfectionistic definition of success might lead you to label yourself as a failure in response to the smallest mistake. This error is closely related to all-or-nothing thinking, where the fact that there are degrees of success in life is ignored. People also engage in the cognitive distortion of mislabeling when they are angry. When you become so angry with someone that you call them ugly names, you "monsterize" them.[188] Writing people off in this way is really a form of overgeneralization. It is then easy to look at them through a negative mental filter as you discount the positive.[189]

As anger grows, so does the level of distorted thinking and the strength of mislabeling others. Soon the mislabeler feels both indignant and superior. Destructive as it is, they build up themselves by tearing others down, a form of magnification and minimization. Perhaps someone has insulted, disagreed with, criticized, or simply failed to like you. Whatever the case, there is a tendency to personalize the comment. Therefore, mislabeling is closely related to six of the ten cognitive distortions.

## POSSIBLE OUTCOMES OF MISLABELING

- escalation of angry, upset feelings
- polarized relationships
- verbal and physical hostility
- political and military conflicts
- reduced hope for change
- a damaged sense of self-worth

***Figure 9.2***

### RESULTS OF MISLABELING

When we habitually define ourselves or others in terms of a negative label, we are likely to stay angry and upset.[190] Worse yet, we reduce our hope for change in ourselves or in others.[191] It then becomes all too easy to resign ourselves or others to the social role implied by the mislabel.[192]

Children whose parents constantly scold and insult them often come to believe their parents' descriptions of them are true. Such children develop a low sense of self-worth, lose hope that they can change, and because of their discouragement, put little effort into self-improvement.[193]

While children seem particularly adept at applying mislabels to each other, parents and other adults are not immune. You may pat yourself on the back for acting maturely by refraining from such mislabels as "nerd" or "moron." Yet, other terms that are frequently used by adults to describe the behavior of children, can be equally damaging. Some examples would be "babyish," "silly," "selfish," "rude," "lazy," and so on.

While mislabeling may seem like a grammatical gray area, there is a difference between applying a label to an individual's behavior and applying it to the individual.[194] It's true that sometimes we have to call error by its right name when instructing others. If a child indeed misbehaves, there is nothing wrong with saying "your choice in behavior was not very good today." In contrast, to say "you are a juvenile delinquent" has quite a different implication. The child might assume that delinquency is an ingrained part of their personality, and therefore not subject to change.

In my work with psychiatric patients, I have often seen the unfortunate results of people being mislabeled during childhood or later. Sadly, adults who have been subjected to insulting mislabels throughout their childhood often come to feel less adequate, less competent, and less loveable than they would have otherwise.[195] These feelings of being damaged, worthless, useless, bad, or defective can start at an early age, influencing the child to act in ways that are consistent with their own self-image.

Assigning a wrong label to someone is really a very powerful thing. Whether mislabels are levied by parents, siblings, peers or even oneself, the results can be crippling. Through mislabeling, people often create self-fulfilling prophecies where the very condition they predict comes true.[196]

Continued mislabeling and belittling of others often triggers a thirst for retaliation, intensifying the conflict, and bringing out similar distorted attitudes in the person you are furious with. Thus hostility is generated. For example, if you see a co-worker as an "uncooperative pig," you will likely jump at every chance to criticize him or her. Your co-worker will sense this, and likely coin a few less-than-complimentary names for you. As a result you and your co-worker will focus on each other's faults and complain about each other at every opportunity.

Soon you are engaged in a name-calling duel of honor from which there is no easy retreat. Yet by lowering yourself to name-calling, you damage your own self-respect. A good number of verbal wars, and quite possibly military conflicts, have started when one party mislabeled another. A list of frequent results of labeling is shown in **Figure 9.2.**[197]

## AS HE SEES US

An admirable goal is to look for the good in others. Despite their failings and weaknesses, seek to see them as they can be—in a positively changed, improved way. Always expect success for them and, if you do apply labels, apply them according to the worth that God has assigned. In people, ruined as they may be, Jesus sees precious pearls. Jesus looks at humans not as vile and worthless, but as what they might become. "For they shall be as the stones of a crown, lifted up as an ensign upon His land."[198] "They shall be Mine, saith the Lord of hosts, in that day when I make up My jewels."[199]

Also, always treat yourself with respect by refusing to engage in the hurtful habit of mislabeling yourself as well as others. Your life may be scarred, your heart a battleground in what seems like a losing conflict, yet you are more precious to Jesus than angels who never sinned. He gave everything for you, because you are His "pearl of great price." If you are a mislabeler, one of the best pieces of advice you can take from this book is to refrain from applying negative labels and to encourage others to do the same. Some common mislabels, together with suggested phrase replacements, are suggested in **Figure 9.3** on the following page.

> *"Christ looks upon...souls, not as they are in themselves, but as they may be if they will surrender themselves to him in sincerity, as did the thief on the cross."*
> — Ellen White

## ACCURATE NAME-CALLING

One of the first commandments of polite society is to never call people names. As a general rule, name-calling is considered uncivilized evidence of bad taste.

While some forms of name-calling are definitely hurtful, many names denote a certain type of kinship and can be helpful. Accurate labeling

## PHRASE REPLACEMENT THERAPY

| Replace: | With: |
|---|---|
| "You're such a messy person." | "It's important to keep your room clean and tidy." |
| "You must be the World's Most Disorganized Person." | "You could save a lot of time if you improved your organizational skills." |
| "You are so selfish!" | "Generosity is a trait to be cultivated." |
| "You klutz!" | "Could you please be a little more careful?" |
| "You're such a big baby." | "I'll be glad when you act more maturely." |
| "Jerk!" | "Your consideration for others could use a little improvement." |

***Figure 9.3***

(a positive form of name-calling) is an important way in which communities identify and understand the one being referred to, and is often the first step in the establishment of a relationship. Name-calling actually involves a generalization descriptive of an approximate place on a spectrum (as opposed to a single point of reference).[200]

To label accurately means to acknowledge similarities and differences between people. In turn, this process enables us to function as communities, with a growing understanding of those who exist around us. As such, descriptive name-calling is a great social blessing. For example, calling yourself a member of a specific political party indicates a set of beliefs and understandings distinctive from other worldviews. Such labeling stereotypes can be the start of a good conversation, leading to dialogue where the "labeled" individual clarifies his or her position.

While some decry all labeling as uncivil and unhealthy, labeling should not be avoided simply because we are lacking in courage. When properly utilized, accurate labeling is a helpful generalization, in addition to being a healthy prerequisite to true dialogue and growth.

## AN ANCIENT EXAMPLE OF LABELING CORRECTLY

God is not afraid to call errors by their right names, and that often involves using labels. Significant mistakes are called "sin." False churches are labeled as Babylon and the devil is labeled as the "Father of Lies." These labels, which had relevant parallels, were helpful to people who wanted to rise above the prevailing deception.[201] But while God uses instructional, accurate labels, He is also in the business of correcting inaccurate labels.

The woman caught in adultery and dragged to Jesus for judgment had been labeled a sinner, worthy of death, by the people who surrounded her that day. Jesus knew she was a sinner, but He also knew that in her heart of hearts she really wanted to do better. He knew she had been enticed into sin and then dragged into public humiliation by the very same ones who framed her in the first place. Though Jesus did label her activity as sin, He spared her from the full consequences by accurately labeling her accuser's similar sinful activities.[202]

Months later, Jesus would take a humiliating walk through the Kidron valley and up to the Mount of Olives. Another King (this time innocent and undeserving) would be the victim of name-calling, scourging, spitting, slaps, and abuse. He became sin for us—taking our "sinners" label—so that we could have life in Him and receive the label of adopted sons and daughters of God, children of the heavenly kingdom. He labels us as His family members, and is "not ashamed to call us brethren."[203]

A positive example of labeling can be found in the story of the Garden of Eden, when God asked Adam to "label" or name all of the animals.[204] Another would be when Christians were labeled as such because they acted, or wanted to act, like Christ. Throughout history, He has taken people with negative labels (such as Rahab the Harlot) and given them new life, hope, and meaning. Some of them He labeled with new names (like Jacob/Israel, Abram/Abraham, or Simon/Peter), but most will have to wait, like the rest of us, until we reach the New Jerusalem to receive a new and accurate label. "To him that overcometh will I give to eat of the hidden manna, and will give him a white stone, and in the stone a new name written, which no man knoweth saving he that receiveth it."[205] Now that is a label to look forward to!

The practice of labeling itself is not always wrong. Both positive and negative labels are used in the Bible. Correct labeling can be a good practice, if the label is accurate, helpful, and instructional.

## STRATEGIES FOR SUCCESS

If you, your family, your friends, or your co-workers have been caught in a cycle of negative labeling, the five tips on the following pages can help you break free of the trap.

### Tip #1: Cultivate an atmosphere of respect.

While it is important for children to respect their parents, it is also critical for parents to avoid talking to their children in a manner that degrades them as individuals. A good rule to adopt as a family unit would be "I do not give verbal abuse." When an entire family accepts the standard of respectful courtesy as their rule of life, the foundation for true family love will be laid and members will feel more emotionally safe. Home really can be a haven of rest and peace.

As you develop an atmosphere of respect towards others, don't forget that it's also very important to respect yourself. Many people talk to themselves in degrading ways they might never use on other people. This is detrimental to a true sense of self-worth. If you wish to be respected by others, you must also respect yourself and demonstrate that respect in your own self-talk.

### Tip #2: Be a model of respectful behavior.

People who were raised in a name-calling environment will find it especially tempting to slide into that rut. Some parents aren't sure how to describe the poor behavior of a child without using negative labels.

There is an easy solution, however. The key is to replace a negative label with a positive word instead. This does not mean to praise bad behavior. Rather, it means to correct bad behavior in more positive terms.

For example, if your son is mouthing off, telling him that "you need to be polite when speaking to me" is a better choice of words than calling him "rude." When you put positive word choices into practice, others hear the "target words" or desired labels rather than the offensive ones. Over the course of time, the repetition of those positive target words can help others remember your goal of uplifting talk. So if you want your children to be smart, considerate, prompt, honest, helpful, kind, or creative, use those words consistently when directing behavior.

### Tip #3: Explain to others why name-calling is harmful.

Teaching a topic is often the best way to learn it. If you are in an authority or leadership role where opportunity is provided to share your wisdom with others (e.g. parenting, teaching, coaching, or giving a talk at your church), take an opportunity to explain what you have learned about mislabeling.

Many people lose sight of the fact that there are ways to express annoyance and frustration without resorting to insults. It's fine to say "I disagree" or "I don't like what you did." It's also fine to say "I am very unhappy with my actions of this morning." Given time and practice, you can learn to rephrase your language and self-talk to avoid the use of over-the-top, insulting terms.

### Tip #4: Avoid name-calling as entertainment.

Name-calling is such an integral part of some entertainment options that it's practically impossible to watch them without falling into a similar habit. Although there are many suitable examples, a good case in point would be the Disney movie *Toy Story*. In the words of one reviewer, the movie includes impudent and hateful material, such as "Potato Head (voice of Don Rickles) taking his lips off and kissing his own posterior with them to express his opinion of another, lots of name-calling, arguing, brat tactics, adolescent meanness, and one veiled foul word."[206]Although *Toy Story* has faded into Disney history, it would be difficult to convince children of the evils of name-calling, either as applied to themselves or to others, after they have seen it so effectively modeled in this and so many other films. If you really wish to stop calling name-calling, you would do well to avoid entertainment choices that portray hurtful name-calling as humorous.

### Tip #5: Correct or walk away.

The key is to determine whether the label is inaccurate and needs to be gently corrected, or if it is the behavior that needs correction because the label is accurate. Some questions are listed in **Figure 9.4** that will help you decide if you should correct or simply walk away.

When others mislabel in your presence, tactfully try to deter them. Asking a question such as "are you sure that is entirely accurate?" will often slow down a mislabeler long enough to consider the truth of their assertions, together with any consequences that might be attached. Highly colored or emotionally charged language often sets the stage for mislabeling, but mentioning some positive points about the individual being mislabeled can help to offset or stall the inaccuracies from reaching wider circulation.

If someone mislabels you, take the high road and do not defend yourself. Realize you are responsible for your own emotions. If the label is accurate in any way, learn from your mistake and possibly let the name-caller know you are seriously working on changing.

**QUESTIONS TO ASK BEFORE APPLYING A LABEL**

- Is the label true and completely accurate?
- If the label is accurate, is there anything to be gained from using it?
- Are you labeling an error (this is safe), or a person (passing judgment)?
- Is this label truly instructional, and does it allow for positive change?

***Figure 9.4***

Your goal should be to defend others, though not yourself, from mislabeling. A good historical example in that regard is that of Jesus. During His trial and persecution, He chose not to respond to the cruel comments directed His way (other than to pray for His enemies).

If you have lapsed into the habit of mislabeling or name-calling confrontations with friends, family, or foes, think ahead and have a plan in place for handling the next potential mislabeling situation. The fact that you have determined not to use inaccurate or hurtful names doesn't mean that others share your resolve. As a result, you'll need to prepare to roll with the verbal punches or walk away at the first chance. Reaction is what the mislabelers are generally after, so if you show no reaction or the opposite reaction from the one desired by the name-caller, they are more likely to become frustrated, analyze their own behavior, or eventually move on. It will take self-control on your part, especially if someone is on the attack. The results of such a strategy can be extremely rewarding, however.

### Tip #6: Keep Track of Your Progress

If mislabeling is a major problem for you, write down your slip-ups and victories. Keeping track is really the only way to know you are making progress as you seek to reframe your thinking.

Like the other cognitive distortions, overcoming the mislabeling habit comes down to being truthful and accurate in all that you say.[207] Following the tips listed here (summarized in **Figure 9.5**) will help you avoid mislabeling in your own words and tactfully correct it in the words of those around you. It's always beneficial to stop and ask yourself, "Is what I just said accurate, or is it a mislabel?"

## TIPS TO AVOID MISLABELING

1. Cultivate an attitude of respect in your home.
2. Be a model of respectful behavior yourself.
3. Explain to your children and others why name-calling is harmful.
4. Avoid entertainment that encourages the use of name-calling.
5. Tactfully offer correction, or walk away from situations where mislabeling is taking place.
6. Keep track of your progress.

*Figure 9.5*

## References

184. Pucci A. *The Client's Guide to Cognitive-Behavioral Therapy: How to Live a Healthy, Happy Life...No Matter What!* iUniverse. 2006. 60.
185. Burns DD. *Feeling Good: The New Mood Therapy.* New York: Avon-HarperCollins, 1999. 39.
186. Pucci A. *Feel the Way You Want to Feel, No Matter What!* iUniverse. 2010. 64-67.
187. Beck AT. *Cognitive therapy of depression.* The Guilford Press. 1987. 63-64.
188. Burns DD. *Feeling Good: The New Mood Therapy.* New York: Avon-HarperCollins, 1999. 157.
189. Burns DD. *Feeling Good: The New Mood Therapy.* New York: Avon-HarperCollins, 1999. 139.
190. Burns DD. *Feeling Good: The New Mood Therapy.* New York: Avon-HarperCollins, 1999. 157.
191. Wilson R, Branch R. *Cognitive Behavioral Therapy for Dummies.* For Dummies. 2006. 30.
192. Clark L. *SOS Help for Emotions: Managing Anxiety, Anger and Depression.* 2nd ed. Bowling Green: SOS Parents and Programs Press, 2002. 202.
193. "How to Avoid Giving Your Children Labels." Ed. Amanda Kowal. Mofamweb@missouri.edu. 20 Dec. 2007 <http://missourifamilies.org/features/parentingarticles/parenting38.htm>.
194. Pucci A. *The Client's Guide to Cognitive-Behavioral Therapy: How to Live a Healthy, Happy Life...No Matter What!* iUniverse. 2006. 60.
195. Pucci A. *The Client's Guide to Cognitive-Behavioral Therapy: How to Live a Healthy, Happy Life...No Matter What!* iUniverse. 2006. 59.
196. Pucci A. *Feel the Way You Want to Feel, No Matter What!* iUniverse. 2010. 64.
197. Burns DD. *Feeling Good: The New Mood Therapy.* New York: Avon-HarperCollins, 1999. 157.
198. Zechariah 9:16. *The Holy Bible.* Authorized King James Version.
199. Malachi 3:17. *The Holy Bible.* Authorized King James Version.
200. Pucci A. *The Client's Guide to Cognitive-Behavioral Therapy: How to Live a Healthy, Happy Life...No Matter What!* iUniverse. 2006. 59.
201. Revelation 17:3-5, John 8:44, Matthew 3:7, and Matthew 23:27. *The Holy Bible.* Authorized King James Version.
202. John 8:3-11. *The Holy Bible.* Authorized King James Version.
203. Hebrews 2:11. *The Holy Bible.* Authorized King James Version.
204. Genesis 2:20. *The Holy Bible.* Authorized King James Version.
205. Revelation 2:17. *The Holy Bible.* Authorized King James Version.
206. Entertainment Media Analysis Report. Ed. ChildCare Action Project: (CAP Ministry). 10 Jan. 2006. CAP Ministry. <http://www.capalert.com/capreports/toystory1995.htm>.
207. Beck AT, Alford BA. *Depression: Causes and Treatment.* University of Pennsylvania Press. 2009. 205.

Chapter 10

ENCOURAGE OTHERS TO RECOGNIZE THE POSITIVE ATTRIBUTES IN THEIR LIVES IN EVERY SITUATION. SEEING ONLY THE NEGATIVE IS ONE-SIDED.

# Count the Positive

***Tempted to write off positive experiences? Wait until you read this first.***

"How could I have possibly gotten a pink slip?" Melody was flabbergasted. "For five years I've heard nothing but positive feedback about my work!"

At the age of 23, Melody had enjoyed the affirmation and security from her high-paying job. Now it was gone, and there didn't seem to be a light at the end of the tunnel. Plunging into despair, Melody quickly showed signs of deep depression - sleeping until noon, losing interest in friends and hobbies, and a dampening of her usually sunny disposition.

"Cheer up, Melody." A middle-aged neighbor, Marie, had noticed the young woman's despondency. "You've got to go on with your life."

"What life?" Melody moaned. "I'll have the black mark of being fired on my record forever. There's no future for me. Before long I'll lose my apartment and be out on the street."

Brock leaned into the weight machine, straining to lift the last rep. With a final push he made it, then let the weights clatter back into place.

"Hey, dude, those biceps are getting hard as a rock," Brock's trainer gave him a playful punch on the shoulder before handing him a towel.

"Aw, they're nothin' to write home about," Brock winced. "I could win a gold medal for the world's spindliest legs, my torso muscles are

**RESULTS OF DISCOUNTING THE POSITIVES**

- drags down self-worth
- takes the joy out of living
- decreases motivation
- decreases accomplishments
- leads to depression
- leads to action that brings on more negativity

***Figure 10.1***

practically non-existent, and my six-pack looks more like a keg."

What do Melody and Brock have in common? Both are engaging in a negative thinking pattern known as discounting the positive, which can lead to the negative effects documented in **Figure 10.1**.[208]

Melody completely disregarded the fact that she had gained valuable experience for five years at her job that she could carry into her next professional position. She also didn't count the advantage of her youth in building her career. Brock failed to acknowledge the impressive features of his physique because he was entirely focused on the areas he wished we better.

At first glance, this cognitive distortion might seem identical to the distortion of looking through a negative mental filter. There is a difference, however. People who view circumstances through a negative mental filter only see negative aspects. In contrast, those who "discount the positives" see and acknowledge the positive aspects, but insist "that doesn't count because..."[209]

Those who discount the positive may initially seem more objective because they acknowledge both the good and bad. But that is misleading, because those who recognize positive experiences and personal achievements, and then proceed to discount them, can sometimes be worse off than those who use a negative mental filter and ignore the good altogether. Unlike a mental filter, discounting the positive gives the false impression of objectivity. **Figure 10.2** lists some common habits of those who disqualify the positive.

## ANCIENT EXAMPLES OF DISCOUNTING THE POSITIVES

The story of the children of Israel in the wilderness, under the leadership of Moses, provides a notable example of discounting the positives. Acknowledging but discounting the many evidences of God's leading, they pointed to any trouble they had along the way as proof that Moses had brought them into the wilderness to die. The fact that God had parted the Red Sea to save them from the Egyptians, sent water gushing out of a rock, rained down fresh food daily, shaded them by day, illuminated the camp by night, fought their battles, and even extended the life of their clothing was all discounted by whatever crisis they were experiencing at the moment.[210] The result was anxiety, depression, and panic—the opposite of productive calm that would have produced a far better outcome.

In another ancient example, King Saul was rather adept at discounting the positives of his future successor. Although just a young shepherd when he first entered the courts of Saul, the Bible says that David behaved himself wisely in all that he did. David was a loyal and faithful servant to King Saul, and also proved himself to be very valuable as a military leader. Saul discounted all these positives, however, focusing on his jealousy over the fact that the people were enamored with David. The song the women of Israel sang when David came back from battle, "Saul hath slain his thousands and David his ten thousands," further inflamed Saul. Though David had done nothing wrong and was even Saul's son-in-law by that time, the king acknowledged but discounted all the good and thus focused on a desire to kill David.[211] The result was depression, obsessions, and incapacitation.

When Elijah was hiding from Ahab and Jezebel during the 3½ year drought, God had his servant stay with a woman known as the "Widow of Zarephath." This woman owed her very life to the presence of Elijah, since God sent enough food for his servant and the widow during that time of great famine. Yet when the widow's son suddenly became ill and died, she quickly discounted all the positive things that had resulted from Elijah's presence, and blamed the prophet for the death of her son.[212]

No doubt the ultimate example of discounting the positives would be the crowd heckling Jesus as he went to the cross. All of the positive things

**HABITS OF DISCOUNTERS**

- marginalizing positive experiences and personal achievements by insisting "they don't count"
- turning good things into negative experiences
- acknowledging the good but believing it is of no value

**Figure 10.2**

Jesus had done for His people—the healings, the love, the food, the sound spiritual counsel, even raising people from the dead—were discounted in those climactic moments when the crowd clamored for the crucifixion of Christ. Pilate himself saw no fault in Jesus, and even received a special message intended to help him make the right decision, yet to please the people he discounted the positives about Christ and handed him over to be crucified.[213]

## DISCOUNTING THE POSITIVE COMMANDS OF GOD

While the previous historic examples focused on the unhealthy practice of discounting the positives in other people, there are other snares to watch out for as well. Some people are experts at discounting the positive instructions given by leaders, yet evidence reveals that following these instructions will lead to a healthier, happier existence.

Some discount the positives of God's guidelines by downgrading the importance of the Ten Commandments. Thus they remove the sound and healthy way of living that has been put in place for their own good. After all, the Ten Commandments teach us how to love God and each other—and learning how to love is never negative. We are not wise when we discount the positives as defined by God.

### BODY IMAGE: THE STAGGERING STATS IN FEMALES

- 85% of college girls think they are overweight.
- Underweight women are just as dissatisfied with their bodies as normal and overweight women.
- Girls as young as six desire to be thin.
- The desire of women to be thinner does not diminish with age.
- Body image for girls becomes progressively worse during adolescence (in contrast to boys, whose body image improves).
- Only 3-5% of women even have a chance of achieving the current "ideal" (6' tall, 130 lbs or 183 cm, 59 kg).
- Girls who distort their body image are at special risk for eating disorders. About 1% of teenage girls will become anorexic, and 10% of the ones who do may die as a result of the disorder.

*Figure 10.3*

## DISCOUNTING TURNED DEADLY: BODY IMAGE DISORDER

People tend to be hard on themselves is in the area of body image. Society values certain physical attributes, and many people fall into the trap of feeling inadequate because they don't measure up to society's impossible expectations. This challenge, which has been called "Body Image Disorder," has become so prevalent that psychiatrists are actually describing it as a "normative discontent" in women.[214] In other words, a woman who is satisfied with her body could actually be considered abnormal!

Body image can be defined as the attitude toward one's body, particularly it's shape, size and aesthetics.[215] Body image distortion occurs when a person's view of their body is different from reality.[216] The prevalence of this condition is documented in (see **Figure 10.3**).[217,218,219,220,221,222,223,224]

For example, some women always see themselves as overweight and view women of normal weight as fat. The logic seems to work just the opposite for men, where normal weight men are often considered scrawny and the buffest bodybuilders are considered to be ideal.[225] Boys and men who succumb to these social pressures are more likely to engage in dangerous behaviors such as taking creatine, or even worse, steroid use.[226]

### RELATED UNHEALTHY BEHAVIORS

- a poor sense of self-worth
- excessive unhealthy dieting
- cycles of binging and purging
- Social Anxiety Disorder
- anorexia nervosa
- bulimia
- fear of change
- extreme efforts to transform into an impossible image

***Figure 10.4***

At first, Body Image Disorder seems harmless enough - most people know of something they wish they could change about their appearance. Problems arise, however, when the perception of one's appearance is out of touch with reality, or the wish becomes a fixation. This is most likely to occur when the individual discounts the positive aspects of their appearance. **Figure 10.4** documents the unhealthy behaviors and conditions associated with this disorder.[231]

There are a number of cultural reasons for the skyrocketing incidence of Body Image Disorder in our culture today. Recent studies have provided convincing evidence that media images play a significant role in how women feel about their bodies. Unfortunately, the current standard for beauty emphasizes characteristics that are impossible for most people to achieve. Research has shown that women in particular feel more guilty, anxious, and depressed after viewing thin models in the media.[227] During the past 30 years, the ideal feminine shape presented in the media has become thinner and thinner, while the average woman has actually gotten heavier.

Consider Barbie, a doll owned by about 90% of girls ages 3-11. Fewer than 1 in 100,000 women are likely to have proportions similar to Barbie's.[228] If Barbie were life-size, she would stand 5'9" and weigh 110 pounds (about 76% of the healthy weight for her height). Today's GI Joe is just as unrealistic and unattainable for boys. The GI Joe of 1964 would have had a 32-inch waist, 44-inch chest, and 12-inch biceps (if he were 5 feet, 10 inches tall). In contrast, GI Joe's 1998 counterpart would have a 55-inch chest, 27-inch biceps, and 36-inch waist. GI Joe's biceps would be bigger than that of the greatest body builders of all time![229] Such unrealistic body ideals are reinforced every day on TV shows, movies, magazine covers, and even video games.

It's important to acknowledge your positive physical attributes and capabilities and put them into perspective as far greater in value than traits you dislike. This can help you highlight your strong features and use your abilities to a greater advantage. It can also lead to a spirit of gratitude that can bring healing. Remember, true success and happiness in life is much more dependent on emotional intelligence than perceived physical beauty. Using this book to improve your emotional intelligence will bring about far greater dividends than undergoing a series of the most expensive cosmetic surgeries in the world.

## LACK OF MOTIVATION

Discounting the positive can also lead to serious lack of motivation in achieving attainable goals.[230] Realistic goals can be worthwhile and can lead to a great sense of satisfaction. However, to someone who displays the cognitive distortion of discounting the positive, often the beneficial outcomes of reaching a goal are downplayed. This results in diminished incentive to attempt a worthy endeavor. Thus, the obstacles to achieving this goal seem larger than life, and the goal goes by the wayside. For instance, a goal of healthfully losing 30 pounds in six months can be attainable for a truly overweight person, but is often not seriously attempted simply because the person discounts the positives of achieving this goal. The benefits of healthy weight loss are not only an improved appearance, but also improved energy, mood, brain chemistry, memory, physical endurance, blood pressure, blood cholesterol, blood sugar control, and triglycerides in the blood, just to mention a few.[231] Although these benefits are well documented and true, a person who discounts their importance will be unlikely to achieve this goal. The goal of attaining weight loss seems insurmountable to them because they are focused on obstacles, which, as Hannah Moore says, "are those frightening things you see when you take your eyes off your goal."[232] Motivation to strive for worthwhile achievements depends on a healthy mental view that accounts for both the positive and negative facets of each situation.

## STRATEGIES FOR CHANGE

Pop psychology emphasizes the importance of positive thinking, and there is some truth in this approach. While positive thoughts by themselves may accomplish some good, their power is limited. The best weapon against discounting the positives is not pop psychology. It is believing the truth.[233] True beliefs can be positive thoughts that take root and spring into action. In His sermons, Jesus talked a lot about faith and belief, but never about positive thinking. No doubt He understood what many have learned since His time: that true belief is more powerful than fantasy positive thinking could ever be. If we would achieve our goals, we must truly believe that we can. In the words of Thomas Fuller, "He does not believe who does not live according to his belief."[234] A few other statements that can help in avoiding discounting the positive are mentioned in **Figure 10.5**.[235,236,237]

Thus examine your attainable goals, research possible true positive consequences, keep these positive consequences in mind by not discounting them, and experience one of the hallmarks of improved emotional intelligence—motivation to achieve your goals.

### HELPFUL POSITIVE STATEMENTS

*"I don't think of all the misery but of the beauty that still remains."* –Anne Frank

*"When it gets dark enough you can see the stars."* –Lee Salk

*"Determine that the thing can and shall be done, and then we shall find the way."* –Abraham Lincoln

***Figure 10.5***

## References

208. Burns DD. *Feeling Good: The New Mood Therapy*. New York: Avon-HarperCollins, 1999. 34, 35.
209. Pucci A. *Feel the Way You Want to Feel, No Matter What!* iUniverse. 2010. 58-59.
210. Exodus 13:21, 22, 14 and Deuteronomy 8. *The Holy Bible*. Authorized King James Version.
211. 1 Samuel 16:18, 19 and 18:1-16. *The Holy Bible*. Authorized King James Version.
212. 1 Kings 17:1-7. *The Holy Bible*. Authorized King James Version.
213. Matthew 27:19-26. *The Holy Bible*. Authorized King James Version.
214. Rodin J, Silberstein L, Striegel-Moore R. "Women and weight: A normative discontent." Nebraska Symposium on Motivation. Vol 32,1984, 267-307.
215. Cash TF, Pruzinsky T. *Body Image: A Handbook of Theory, Research, and Clinical Practice.* The Guilford Press. 2004. 269.
216. Blood SK. *Body work: the social construction of women's body image.* Routledge. 2005. 7.
217. Waltz GR, Yep R. "Body Image Among Female College Students." VISTAS: Perspectives on Counseling 2004. Alexandria, VA and Greensboro, NC: ACA and Caps Prss., 2004. 155-60. <http://www.counselingoutfitters.com/vistas/vistas_2004_Title.htm>.
218. Cash TF, Henry PE. (1995). "Women's body images: The results of a national survey in the U.S.A. *Sex Roles*, 33, 19-29.
219. Cash TF, Pruzinsky T. *Body Image: A Handbook of Theory, Research, and Clinical Practice.* The Guilford Press. 2004. 66.
220. Allaz AF, Bernstein M, Rouget P, Archinard M, Morabia A. (1998). "Body weight preoccupation in middle-age and ageing women: A general population survey." *International Journal of Eating Disorders*, 23, 287-294.
221. Weinshenker N. "Adolescents and Body Image: What's Typical and What's Not." Child Study Center Letter 6.4 (March/April 2002).
222. Waltz GR, Yep R. "Body Image Among Female College Students." VISTAS: Perspectives on Counseling 2004. Alexandria, VA and Greensboro, NC: ACA and Caps Prss., 2004. 155-60. <http://www.counselingoutfitters.com/vistas/vistas_2004_Title.htm>.
223. Thompson JK, Smolak L. *Body Image, Eating Disorders, and Obesity in Youth: Assessment, Prevention, and Treatment.* American Psychological Association. 2001. 5.
224. Weinshenker N. "Adolescents and Body Image: What's Typical and What's Not." Child Study Center Letter 6.4 (March/April 2002).
225. Pope HG, Phillips KA, Olivardia R. *The Adonis Complex: How to Identify, Treat and Prevent Body Obsession in Men and Boys.* Free Press. 2002. 1-2.
226. Weinshenker N. "Adolescents and Body Image: What's Typical and What's Not." Child Study Center Letter 6.4 (March/April 2002).
227. Wykes M, Gunter B. *The Media and Body Image: If Looks Could Kill.* Sage Publications Ltd. 2005. 174-175.
228. Cash TF, Pruzinsky T. *Body Image: A Handbook of Theory, Research, and Clinical Practice.* The Guilford Press. 2004. 71.
229. Cash TF, Pruzinsky T. *Body Image: A Handbook of Theory, Research, and Clinical Practice.* The Guilford Press. 2004. 193,211.
230. Pucci A. *The Client's Guide to Cognitive-Behavioral Therapy: How to Live a Healthy, Happy Life...No Matter What!* iUniverse. 2006. viii.
231. World Health Organization. *Obesity: Preventing and Managing the Global Epidemic.* WHO Technical Report Series. 2009. 69-73.
232. McLellan V. *Wise Words & Quotes*. Tyndale House Publishers. 111.
233. Backus W. *Telling Yourself the Truth.* Bethany House. 2000. 171.
234. Cook J, Gibson LA. *The Book of Positive Quotations*. Fairview Press. 2007. 168.
235. Frank A, Frank OH, Pressler M. *The Diary of a Young Girl: The Definitive Edition.* Doubleday. 2001. 211.
236. *Reader's Digest*, Volume 126, Issues 753-758. 120.
237. Lincoln A, Fornieri JR. *The language of liberty: the political speeches and writings of Abraham Lincoln.* Gateway Editions. 2004. 101.

THE LOST ART OF

# THINKING

*How to Improve Emotional Intelligence and Achieve Peak Mental Performance*

## Section 2:

# *HOW LIFESTYLE AFFECTS YOUR BRAIN*

Chapter 11

**WE WOULDN'T PUT SLUDGE INTO THE GAS TANK OF OUR VEHICLES; WHY THEN FEED ANYTHING LESS THAN THE BEST TO THE BRAIN?**

# Nourish Your Brain

***Proper diet, together with necessary supplements, can be a powerful tool to enhance cognitive function.***

Over a decade ago, Terry Moreland, a Bakersfield, California businessman, was in charge of a number of California state prisons. Moreland was aware of some of the research presented in this chapter, and decided to have each prison inmate interviewed by a nutritionist upon admission to the prison. Prisoners had a choice: either to opt for a diet that would improve their emotional intelligence, or select the old-fashioned, typical American prison diet. Some prisoners, who thought it was punishment enough to be in prison, felt that consuming a plant-based diet was cruel and unusual punishment. Accordingly, they chose the typical American prison food. Other prisoners concluded that since they had to spend time in a correctional facility anyway, they might as well try a diet that might actually help "correct" them. Thus they chose the plant-based diet.

Stressful events would frequently happen in both sections of the prison. However, those on the plant-based diet noticed that they were able to calmly deal with the very stressful conditions. Previously the same conditions would have tempted them to seriously injure either the perpetrator of a perceived injustice or a prison guard. Though they still attempted to intervene when such situations arose, they now did so in a calm and effective manner. These prisoners stated how their control amazed even themselves.

After repeated demonstrations, some stated that they thought if they had consumed this improved diet on the "outside," they likely would have never ended up in prison. To their surprise, they also found, as a bonus, that the plant-based diet was not only great tasting, but satisfying.

## AN OFTEN OVERLOOKED FACTOR

Over the past 20 years, much research on nutrition and its relationship to mental performance has been published. Though frequently overlooked, nutrition is an important factor in achieving peak mental performance. I'm always amazed that many patients, who are hospitalized in behavioral medicine units or treated by preeminent mental health professionals, have never been questioned about what they are eating. "You're the first one to ask me about diet," are words I've heard over and over again. The fact that what they put into their bodies actually helps or hinders the brain's neuronal function is a new concept to many, but one that deserves much more attention than it currently receives.

In many cases of major depression, sub-optimal nutrition is a significant causative factor. Junk food, red meat, and excessive refined foods are prime offenders in this regard, as they inhibit optimal brain function.[238,239] Sugar-laden foods also impede peak mental performance. While a morning donut does help the carbohydrate addict feel better for a short while by increasing serotonin, the spike is temporary, followed by a nadir (low point). The unhealthy dietary habit must be repeated over and over again with greater intensity to achieve the same result.[240]

Chocolate is another comfort food that transiently raises the serotonin and dopamine levels but is followed by a nadir associated with a negative impact on thinking ability.[241]

## THE MIND-BODY CONNECTION

While people frequently turn to caffeinated, sugar-laden, or other mind-manipulating foods as a form of self-medication, many physicians are also seeking to alter brain function through nutrition. By monitoring dietary nutrients, a doctor can help optimize certain chemical levels in the brain, which in turn can adjust how well different kinds of messages are transmitted. The net effect is a change in how you feel and think.

Scientists have identified more than 50 kinds of neurotransmitters, all of which have some impact on mental health. Every anti-depressant on the market is trying to control depression by manipulating one or more of three important neurotransmitters which facilitate communication between the neurons or cells of the brain: serotonin, dopamine, or norepinephrine.[242,243] **Figure 11.1** illustrates the interrelationship between these three highly significant chemicals and the impact they can have on our anxiety levels, mood, and motivation.

## NEUROTRANSMITTERS 101

Neurotransmitters are chemicals released in the brain that act as messengers, delivering signals from a neuron to a target nerve cell. Each neurotransmitter can directly or indirectly influence neurons in a specific portion of the brain, thereby affecting behavior.

**Serotonin** in the brain helps maintain a "happy feeling" and keeps our moods under control by calming anxiety, promoting sound sleep, and relieving depression.

**Dopamine**, a chemical messenger that is a relative to adrenaline, affects brain processes that control movement, emotional response, and the capacity to feel pleasure and pain. Dopamine moves into the frontal lobe of the brain, regulating information flowing in from other areas of the brain. It is vital for performing balanced and controlled movements. A dopamine shortage or impediment to dopamine flow can result in irrational thinking, impaired memory, or paranoia. In contrast, an increase of dopamine in the frontal lobe can relieve pain and boost feelings of pleasure.

**Norepinephrine** is another relative to adrenaline. Norepinephrine and serotonin have been directly linked to controlling feelings of anxiety and depression. In fact, they are the target neurotransmitters of many drugs and alternative therapies designed to mitigate anxiety, insomnia,

### THE MOOD MAKERS

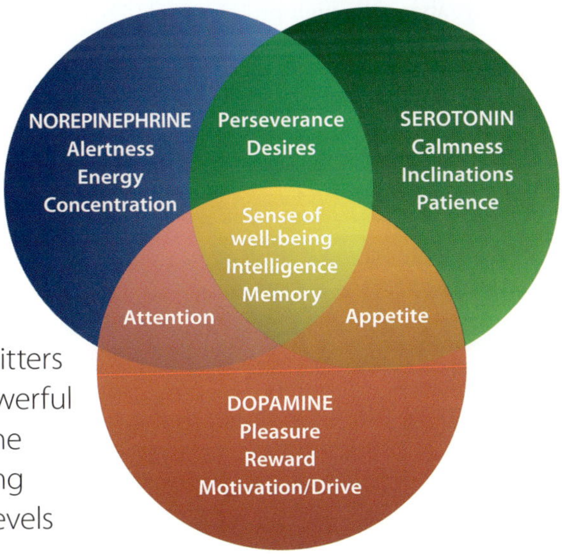


Neurotransmitters react in a powerful way within the brain, affecting our anxiety levels and moods.

***Figure 11.1***

stress, and depression.[244] (Norepinephrine can not be supplemented directly because it doesn't cross the blood-brain barrier). When combined with dopamine and phenylethalimine, norepinephrine can also create feelings of infatuation. Adequate levels of norepinephrine can increase energy levels. However, higher levels of norepinephrine can cause hostile or aggressive behavior.

## BOOSTING YOUR NEUROTRANSMITTERS

One of the best ways to create serotonin in the brain is to increase the intake of tryptophan, an amino acid which facilitates serotonin production.[245] Tyrosine is another amino acid with the ability to boost neurotransmitter (brain messenger) levels. Higher levels of brain tyrosine can result in increased brain production of dopamine and norepinephrine. This is especially important as improvements in tyrosine metabolism have been linked to improved tolerance for physically and mentally stressful situations.[246,247,248,249]

Animal-based foods tend to be high in tryptophan and tyrosine. However, the carbohydrate-rich plant sources of nutrition are best at promoting the important raw materials needed to increase the levels of these neurotransmitters in the brain. A recent study at the Massachusetts Institute of Technology, where researchers compared high carbohydrate meals to high protein meals, explains why lower protein plant-based amino acid sources are superior. The high-carb meals resulted in significantly better tryptophan and tyrosine ratios in the brain, averaging 54% and 28%, respectively, above the high protein meals.[250]

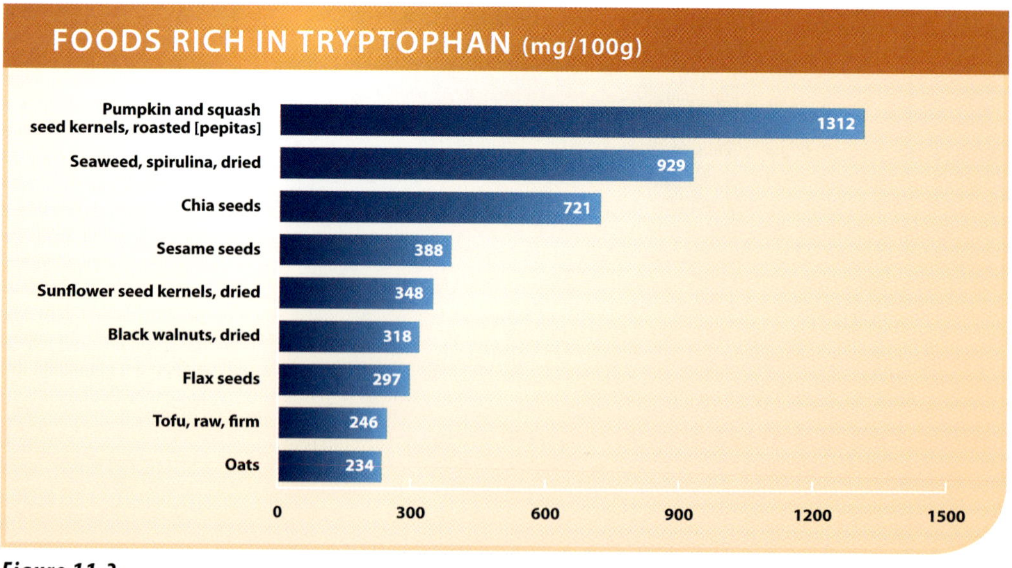


*Figure 11.2*

Meat is deficient in carbohydrates. In addition, it increases the body's resistance to insulin. Insulin production helps facilitate the movement of tyrosine and tryptophan into the brain. This "double whammy" delivered by meat consumption decreases the brain concentration of these raw materials. In contrast, foods containing tyrosine or tryptophan that are higher in carbohydrates promote elevated brain levels of these raw materials, thus supporting the production of serotonin, dopamine, and norepinephrine.

This is why, in a study of 48 stress-prone individuals, a high complex carbohydrate, lower protein diet prevented a deterioration of mood and performance under uncontrollable laboratory stress conditions. Even though this diet was lower in tryptophan and tyrosine than the high protein diet, more tryptophan and tyrosine were taken up by the brain. The study's authors stated that a higher carbohydrate and lower protein diet "increased personal control" in their study participants.[251] This means that their emotional intelligence improved just by changing their diet to a lower protein, plant-based diet.

While milk is commonly promoted as a good source of tryptophan, there are many richer sources of this vital amino acid. As shown in **Figure 11.2**, roasted pumpkin seeds, almonds, walnuts, and black-eyed peas are all excellent plant-based sources of tryptophan.[252]

Plant-based foods which are rich in tyrosine can actually have a stimulating effect, resulting in higher energy levels and increased alertness. In **Figure 11.3**, lentils are shown as one of the highest sources of tyrosine. Tofu, wheat germ, peaches, and watermelon are also significant sources of tyrosine.

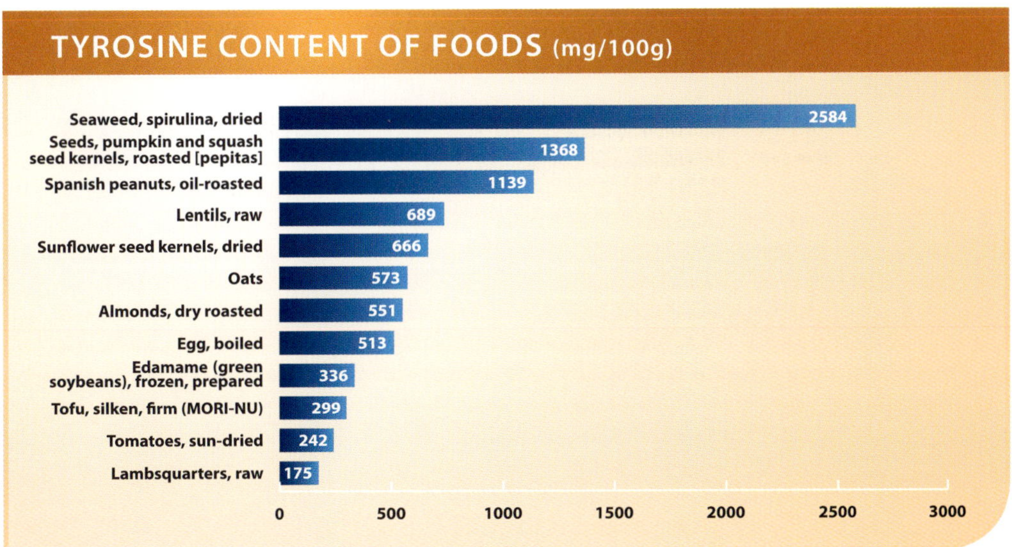


*Figure 11.3*

## INCREASED AMINO ABSORPTION

As well as eating foods rich in carbohydrates, other factors influence the ability of tryptophan and tyrosine to pass from the bloodstream into the brain.

Researchers have discovered a fairly complex relationship between tryptophan or tyrosine and other amino acids known as large neutral amino acids (LNAAs). Each of the LNAAs rely on the same transport carrier to cross the blood-brain barrier. Because they compete with each other for brain access, the more LNAAs that are present in the blood stream, the less tryptophan or tyrosine will get into the brain. This provides an additional reason why eating an abundance of protein-laden tryptophan-rich foods does not result in higher uptake by the brain. Foods that contain high amounts of the competing amino acids actually reduce the flow of tryptophan and tyrosine to the brain.[253] Thus, if your diet is adequate in tryptophan and tyrosine, but high in the other amino acids, you may still develop deficiencies in the frontal lobe of the brain.

The amount of the desired amino acid compared to the amount of the LNAAs is the critical yardstick. As shown in **Figure 11.4**, chia seeds, and grapes have high amounts of tryptophan relative to the other amino acids.[254] As such, they are excellent sources of tryptophan in the diet. Incorporating these foods, or others on the list, into your diet will increase your absorption of available tryptophan. In contrast, a beef steak has a low amount of tryptophan compared to the other amino acids, making it a less effective brain tryptophan source.

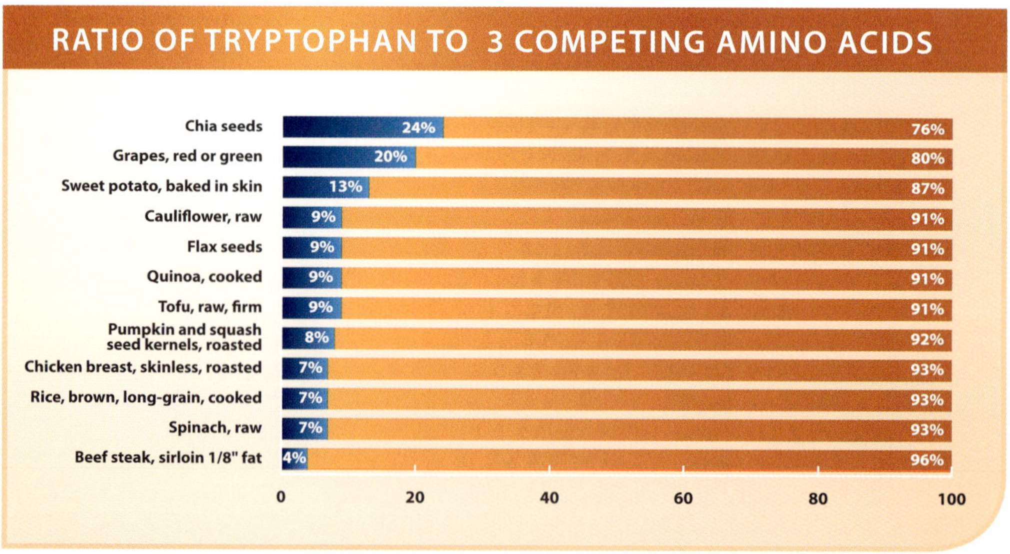


*Figure 11.4*

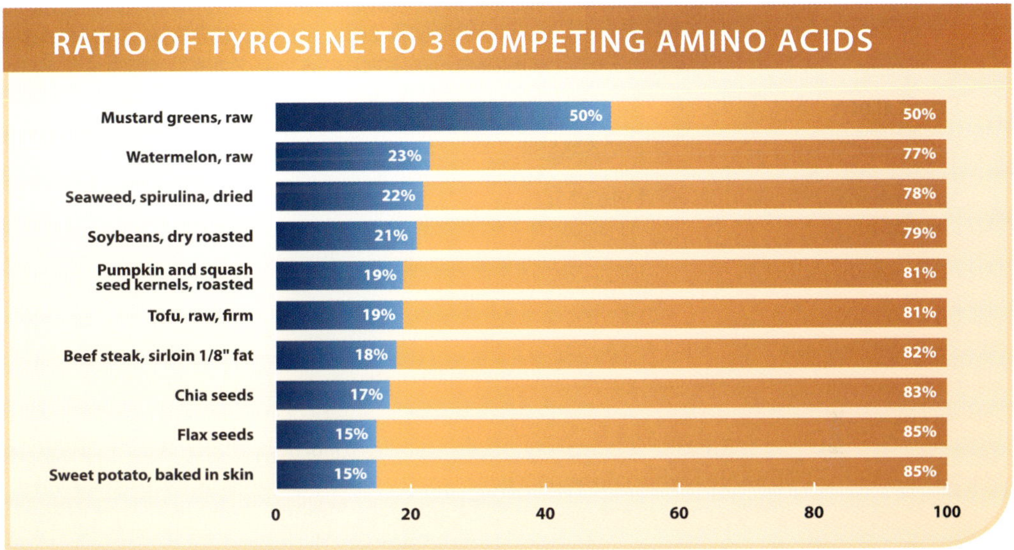


***Figure 11.5***

The same theory applies to food sources of tyrosine. **Figure 11.5** shows that mustard greens, soybeans, and spirulina (a sea vegetable) have the highest amounts of tyrosine relative to the other amino acids.[255] Watermelon, which also has a high tyrosine to amino acid competitor ratio, can be particularly effective in giving a boost of energy by contributing to higher brain dopamine and norepinephrine levels.

**The tyrosine to LNAA ratio in watermelon gives it a somewhat stimulating effect.**

## OMEGA-3 FATS: THE SMARTEST CHOICE FOR YOUR BRAIN

Omega-3 fats have emerged as an extremely important nutritional element in brain science. In fact, a deficiency in omega-3 is one of the most common contributing factors for individuals facing mental health issues.

Current research has identified omega-3, a fatty acid that is highly concentrated in the brain, as an effective memory booster.[256] Omega-3 is particularly important for efficient cognitive performance.[257] Symptoms of omega-3 fatty acid deficiency include extreme tiredness (fatigue), poor memory, dry skin, heart problems, mood swings or depression, mania or anxiety, and poor circulation.[258,259,260,261,262,263] Omega-3 supplements have been shown to help in both major depression and bipolar disorders.[264]

Omega-3 fats can help deter neurodegenerative diseases, such as Alzheimer's disease, as well. These devastating illnesses are associated with decreased brain blood flow, which has been shown in animal studies to contribute to dementia.[265] In such cases, omega-3 fats can be particularly helpful in preventing blood vessel changes and improving brain circulation. Researchers in the United Kingdom found that 70% of depressed individuals who did not respond to any medication responded to omega-3 supplementation.[266]

| COMPARISON OF OMEGA-6 TO OMEGA-3 FATTY ACIDS (mg) | | | | |
|---|---|---|---|---|
| **Food Item** | **Serving** | **Omega-6** | **Omega-3** | **Ratio** |
| Salmon, canned | 1 oz/28g | 28 | 356 | 1:12 |
| Spinach (Fresh) | 1 cup/30g | 8 | 41 | 1:5 |
| Flaxseed Oil | 1 Tbs/14g | 1715 | 7196 | 1:4 |
| Chia seeds, dried | 1 oz/28g | 1620 | 4915 | 1:3 |
| Blueberries | 1 cup/148g | 130 | 86 | 2:1 |
| Walnuts, English | 1 oz/28g | 10666 | 2542 | 4:1 |

***Figure 11.6***

Another fascinating study related to omega-3 involved Greenland Eskimos who consumed generous amounts of cholesterol in their diets. Despite their high cholesterol intake, the Eskimos had lower rates of heart disease than would normally be expected. Their results weren't as good as those of the vegetarian population, but they were much better than the average American eating that much cholesterol. One reason cited for the lower disease rate among these Eskimos was their improved circulation to the heart and brain, which was most likely enhanced by their high consumption of food with omega-3 fatty acids (fish).[267]

Animal models reveal that omega-3 supplementation favorably influences the function of twenty-three genes in a brain region known as the hippocampus.[268] The hippocampus, which is located in the side of the brain just above the ear, has to do with learning, attentiveness, verbal, and declarative memory. Research has shown that omega-3 supplementation results in a 10-fold rise in the production of transthyretin (TTR), which is vital to the long-term health of the brain. TTR appears to scavenge, or round up, a compound called amyloid beta protein. This compound accumulates and tangles in the brains of patients with Alzheimer's disease. By gathering up abnormal proteins, TTR is believed to prevent the damaging amyloid tangles, thus potentially staving off dementia.[269] Researchers in animal studies have been able to reverse Alzheimer's disease to some extent by boosting the TTR.

## OMEGA-3 FATS: THE RIGHT RATIO

There are actually two essential fatty acids in the human diet, omega-3 and omega-6. "Essential" means these nutrients are needed and your body is unable to make them. You have to acquire them from your diet. Although omega-6 fatty acids are also vital to health, omega-6 is far more plentiful in the average person's diet than omega-3 fats. Unless the person is severely calorie deprived (starving) or getting all of their fat from coconut, tropical oils, or animal fat, the person is likely getting enough omega-6. The more common problem is consuming too much omega-6 as compared to omega-3. This imbalance has been well proven to increase inflammation, which increases the risk of blood clots, dementia, depression, mania, arthritis, autoimmune disease, some skin conditions, and possibly even some forms of cancer. A lower ratio of omega-6 to omega-3 fatty acids is more desirable in reducing the risk of many chronic diseases.[270] The average American's diet contains a ratio of 20:1; I recommend a ratio of 4:1 or lower for optimal health benefits. An improved omega-6 to omega-3 ratio can improve mental performance as well as preserve brain function with aging. A list of foods with favorable omega-6 to omega-3 ratios is provided in **Figure 11.6.**[271]

## OMEGA-3 FATS: THE FISH DILEMMA

Most people get omega-3 from fish, which obtain it by eating seaweed or phytoplankton. Not all fish are good sources of omega-3. The richest fish sources, like Atlantic salmon, tend to come from cold water oceans simply because that's where the sea plants are the highest in omega-3. The fish that are particularly high in this fatty acid are listed in **Figure 11.7.** Interestingly enough, fish that are highest in omega-3 all have fins and scales, qualifying them for the ancient classification of "clean fish."[272]

Up until several generations ago, fish was still a very healthy food. There are problems with fish consumption today, however, as demonstrated by a study in Clear Lake, California. Many years prior to the study, the lake had been exposed to a pesticide called DDD (similar to DDT). Researchers studied the effect of biomagnification (increased contamination levels as you move up the food chain) by measuring the levels of the pesticide in the lake water in comparison to levels of the pesticide found in the fish living in the lake.[273]

### FISH THAT ARE HIGH IN OMEGA-3

| Fish Type | Serving Size | Omega-3 (mg) |
|---|---|---|
| Atlantic Salmon | ½ fillet/178g | 4023 |
| Atlantic Herring | 1 fillet/143g | 3171 |
| Rainbow Trout | 1 fillet/143g | 1680 |
| Freshwater Drum Fish | 1 fillet/154g | 1531 |
| Atlantic Mackerel | 1 fillet/88g | 1251 |
| Atlantic/Pacific Halibut | ½ fillet/159g | 1064 |
| White Tuna, canned in water | 3oz/85g | 808 |
| Freshwater Bass | 1 fillet/62g | 628 |

***Figure 11.7***

## BIOMAGNIFICATION OF CONTAMINATION

| Sample Site | DDD, ppm *in parts per million* |
|---|---|
| Clear Lake, CA (water itself) | 0.02 |
| Phytoplankton (living in DDD-contaminated water) | 5.00 |
| Herbivorous fish (which eat the phytoplankton) | 40-300 |
| Carnivorous fish (which eat the herbivorous fish) | up to 2,5000 |

***Figure 11.8***

The lake water had low amounts of DDD - a level considered safe by the EPA. You could drink that water and have no appreciable damage from the DDD. The researchers found, however, that the phytoplankton and fish in that water had DDD levels that were much higher. The herbivorous fish that dined on phytoplankton had a large amount of DDD, while the carnivorous fish that consumed the herbivorous fish had huge amounts of DDD. The results of the study are found in **Figure 11.8**.

That's a very unsafe level, high enough to significantly increase risk not only of cancer, but of mental health problems. Such a concentrated presence of insecticides and other pesticides can also result in significant adverse effects to the neurochemistry of the brain. Over the years, many people have asked me about the quality of water they are drinking. While this is an important questions, there is a question which is a thousand times more important: what is the quality of the water where the fish you eat come from? Whatever toxins are present in the water in small amounts will be found a thousand to a million-fold in the fat of the fish.

The increased mercury level in fish today poses a particularly delicate difficulty for children. Mercury poisoning is severely detrimental to the developing brains of the young. Many fetal brain problems, and even lower I.Q., result from elevated mercury levels.[274] Yet omega-3 fatty acids are absolutely vital to brain development in a fetus and infant. Babies who don't get enough omega-3 as a fetus or as a developing infant will have lower I.Q.s.

Studies show that breast-fed babies have I.Q.s that are 9 to 10 points higher than babies who are not breast-fed, most likely due to the fact that breast milk contains omega-3, while most infant formulas do not.[275] So, while it's necessary to guard against mercury in the diet of the young, it is also critical to ensure sufficient omega-3 is obtained. The sad facts are that fish is often the primary dietary source of omega-3, and only recently has a formula been released that contains omega-3 from plant sources.

Obviously, omega-3 is a necessary component of a healthy diet. Problems arise, however, when mercury is obtained along with the omega-3 as a result of fish consumption. In such cases, the mercury may actually be worse than the benefit derived through omega-3. More information on how exposure to harmful toxins in your environment and diet effects your health can be found in the next chapter, "Protect Against Toxins."

## OMEGA-3 FATS: CLEAN SOURCES

There is an easy way around the fish and mercury dilemma: get your omega-3 nutrients from plant-based sources. You don't have to eat fish to receive the benefits of seaweed. To decrease your toxin intake, it is often better to eat the seaweed yourself. Because people are starting to become aware that seaweed is high in omega-3, an increasing number of menu options based on seaweed are now available.

A list of other plant-based sources of omega-3 is provided in **Figure 11.9.**[277] Plant foods such as spinach, green soybeans, soybean oil made from green soybeans, and wheat germ are also good sources of omega-3.

**PLANT-BASED OMEGA-3 SOURCES**

| Food Item | Serving | Omega-3 (mg) |
|---|---|---|
| Flaxseed, ground | 1 oz/28g | 6388 |
| Chia seeds, dried | 1 oz/28 | 4915 |
| Walnuts, English | 1 oz/28 | 2524 |
| Canola oil | 1 Tbs/14g | 1031 |
| Wheat germ oil | 1 Tbs/14g | 932 |
| Green soybeans | 1 cup/155g | 569 |
| Pecans | 1 oz/28g | 276 |
| Avocado | 1 whole/136g | 221 |
| Sweet Red Pepper | 1 oz/28g | 217 |
| Blueberries, fresh | 1 cup/148g | 86 |
| Oregano, ground | 1 tsp/2g | 73 |

***Figure 11.9***

Black walnuts, English walnuts, and flaxseed are even richer in this valuable nutrient. Another rich source, chia seeds. have been growing in popularity lately. Chia seeds are also a very good source of iron, fiber, and other nutrients.

At the Nedley Clinic we recommend some simple recipes that are high in omega-3. The one shown in **Figure 11.10** includes flaxseed, ground into flax meal, which is a very good source of tryptophan as well as omega-3. This recipe, which can be sprinkled over fruit, toast, or cereal, has 9,000 milligrams of omega-3.

I typically recommend a 9,000 milligram dose of omega-3 for bipolar disorder, and 3,000 milligrams for major depression. You don't have to be bipolar or depressed to benefit from this recipe, and many of my patients have improved their mental health through the use of this simple food.

**FLAX-NUT SPRINKLE (HIGH IN OMEGA-3)**

¼ cup ground walnuts
¼ cup flax meal
1 Tbs brown sugar
1/8 tsp salt

Mix and sprinkle
over fruit, toast, or cereal.

***Figure 11.10***

## OMEGA-3 FATS: THREE TYPES

Most of the studies that have been done on omega-3 involve eicosapentaenoic acid, or EPA. The second most studied omega-3 fat is docosahexaenoic acid, or DHA, while the least studied omega-3 fat is the type that is present in land plants, a-linolenic acid, or ALA. While the importance of EPA and DHA is emphasized by health researchers, ALA is the exclusive omega-3 fat consumed for vegetarians who don't eat fish.

A book was recently published on the areas of the world that have the longest-living people (called the blue zones). This book highlighted the only blue zone where longevity continues to improve: the vegetarian non-fish-eating Seventh-day Adventists in Southern California.[276] Although more studies are being done on this particular group, such vegetarians actually live longer and have lower rates of heart disease than their fish-eating counterparts.[277]

The question that arises is, if EPA and DHA are so important, why does this group do so well without eating a dietary source of such? First, it is important to recognize that the human body can make EPA and

DHA from ALA.[278] This conversion (ALA to EPA and DHA) is not very efficient in most people. However, preliminary evidence reveals that this reaction works far better in vegetarians. Thus, vegetarians who have never consumed fish or phytoplankton can have very healthy quantities of EPA and DHA circulating in their bloodstream.[279,280]

Thus, vegetarians just need to be sure to get enough ALA in their food, and don't need to worry about supplementing EPA or DHA unless they know their blood levels are too low or they are suffering from the conditions listed below. Also, ALA likely has benefits apart from EPA and DHA, though more research is needed.

**Many plant foods provide rich sources of omega-6, but omega-3 is much more abundant in seaweed and other plants that grow in the water.**

## OMEGA-3 FATS: RECENT STUDIES ON EPA AND DHA

There is no doubt that EPA and DHA are helpful to humans in preventing and treating many diseases. Most of the studies on treating disease mentioned in this section involve EPA and/or DHA supplementation.

The highest dose used in supplementation is around 3000 mg total of EPA and DHA. Some studies use as little as 600 mg of combined EPA and DHA. Most of the studies on preventing various illnesses involve consuming EPA and DHA as food. High doses of EPA/DHA supplementation has been shown to stabilize and halt the progression of mild to moderate Alzheimer's disease over a six-month period.[281]

Youth with bipolar disorder experienced dramatic improvement with EPA/DHA supplements.[282] Youth with major depression also experience significant improvement with supplementation.[283] Women with psychological distress with or without concurrent major depression also improved with only moderate EPA/DHA supplementation.[289]

High doses of EPA with low doses of DHA have also been shown to be helpful in anger management.[284] Some people with strong aggressive tendencies were helped by these supplements.[285] EPA supplementation alone has been shown to be helpful in early psychosis.[286]

For those with epilepsy, EPA/DHA supplementation decreased the frequency of subsequent seizures by 50 percent.[287,288] People with major depression associated with Parkinson's disease had significant improvement in their depression with EPA/DHA supplementation.[289] Multiple sclerosis patients put on a low fat diet along with EPA/DHA supplementation experienced significant improvement in their symptoms.[290,291]

Supplementation in pregnancy can improve the mood of the mother and the I.Q. of the children.[292,293] It lowers the risk that the child born will develop ADHD as well.[294] And kids with ADHD experience some improvement with EPA/DHA supplementation.[295] Children who consumed even low amounts of supplementation or foods higher in omega-3 experience improved learning, memory, and an improved attention span when learning.[296,297] Additionally, adolescents who eat foods higher in omega-3 get better grades.[298]

Those with inflammatory conditions, like rheumatoid arthritis, ankylosing spondylitis, back pain, or simply inflammation noted on blood tests, all improved with EPA/DHA supplementation.[299,300,301,302] DHA supplementation helped those with macular degeneration, the leading cause of blindness in the U.S., stabilize their disease over a five-year period of supplementation.[303] Those who eat foods higher in omega-3 have significantly lower rates of non-Hodgkin's lymphoma, colon cancer, and skin cancer.[304,305,306,307,308] When combined with an exercise program, EPA/DHA can decrease abdominal obesity.[280]

Much of the EPA/DHA research has been done on the heart and circulation in humans. It has been shown to reduce the risk of heart attack, decrease triglycerides, and improve circulation, by increasing blood vessel elasticity.[309,310,311,312,313]

It's clear that if EPA and or DHA were a chemical manufactured by a pharmaceutical company, it would be by far the highest-selling drug on the planet. Side effects are almost zero in the doses studied, and the benefits are far-reaching and profound. It certainly would be the best-selling antidepressant on the market. Of course, if a pharmaceutical company tries to patent it, the government will send them back a short letter saying, "no chance, prior art." In other words, "this molecule has been in nature for thousands of years; you were not the first to make it, so no patent for you."

One innovative drug company went at it from a different angle. They patented a process used to purify and refine the fat obtained from the fish and put it into capsules.

The process gets rid of, as much as possible, cholesterol, oxidized fatty acids, and mercury. Although this process does not guarantee complete removal of these problems, it does greatly reduce them. Before processing, the crude fish oil contains less than 10 percent quantity of omega-3, but by the end of the process it is 90 percent omega-3 with each capsule containing 465 mg of EPA, 375 mg of DHA, and 80 mg of ALA.[314] Because of the patent and dose recommended for lowering triglycerides, the product is available by prescription only and is quite expensive.

A far cheaper and safer alternative is to get EPA/DHA from the plants of the waters themselves, or supplements that get their EPA and DHA directly from these plants. (Plant EPA/DHA supplements can be found at www.drnedley.com) Because of biomagnification (as discussed above), plant-based sources of omega-3 are safer and lower in toxins than fish, even after a mercury-removal process has been performed on fish oil. In addition, many new supplement studies have been conducted on plant DHA.

The only DHA-fortified infant milk formula that the U.S. Food and Drug Administration allows on the market is a plant-based source of DHA. This is simply because the fish source of DHA will always contain some toxins, including small amounts of mercury. Even the lowest level of mercury in a tiny infant's body can be devastating. It is safest to get DHA exclusively from plant sources.

## OTHER BENEFICIAL NUTRIENTS

In addition to tryptophan, tyrosine, and omega-3, there are many other nutrients that are fundamental in achieving peak mental health. These vitamins, minerals, and phytonutrients, which can be obtained through the diet or conscientious supplementation, greatly benefit mental functioning. An overview of some of the most important nutrients for brain health, along with the best dietary sources, follows.

## VITAMIN $B_1$ (THIAMINE)

Thiamine is necessary for optimal brain and nervous system function. Common symptoms of thiamine deficiency include irritability, fatigue, staggering, painful neuropathy (a form of nerve dysfunction), eye movement, paralysis, confusion, memory loss, and depression.[315] In addition to brain and nervous system effects, thiamine deficiency has been linked to muscle cramps and EKG (heart) changes.[316]

Deficiencies of this important B vitamin are more common in developing nations that rely on polished white rice as a staple food.[318] In Western nations, you shouldn't have to worry about your intake of thiamin if you eat a balanced diet. **Figure 11.11** illustrates the thiamine content of a variety of foods.

The best advice I can give with respect to getting adequate thiamine is to avoid excessive use of alcoholic beverages. Active transport of thiamine into enterocytes is disturbed during acute alcohol exposure, resulting in decreased uptake of thiamine from the GI tract. If you have a family history of alcohol-related problems, you are at increased risk for alcohol abuse.

**THIAMINE CONTENT OF SELECT FOODS** — ***RDA is 1.2 mg/day**

| Food Item | Serving | Thiamine (mg) |
|---|---|---|
| Rice bran | 1 cup/118g | 3.2 |
| Wheat germ | 1 cup/115g | 2.2 |
| Macadamia Nuts | 1 cup/134g | 1.6 |
| Flaxseed | ½ cup/84g | 1.4 |
| Oats | 1 cup/156g | 1.2 |
| Oat bran, raw | 1 cup/94g | 1.1 |
| Pistachio nuts, dry roasted | 1 cup/123g | 1.0 |
| Sunflower seed kernels, dry | 1 cup/46g | 0.7 |

*Figure 11.11*

The best course of action, especially in such cases, is removing any potential for addiction by total abstinence.

There are some indications that thiamine may also have a role in the treatment and prevention of Alzheimer's disease. Researchers have found that thiamine deficiency causes adverse changes in brain blood vessels that allow increased accumulation of compounds like iron in the brain. The resulting abnormal concentrations of such substances foster inflammation and oxidative stress—two processes that are operative in Alzheimer's disease.[317,318]

While these theories are compelling, at present they are still relegated to the realm of educated speculation, since current human studies are inconclusive as to whether or not thiamine does indeed confer such benefits.[319] Nonetheless, the data suggests prioritizing thiamine intake may have benefits beyond those conventionally recognized.

## VITAMIN $B_6$ (PYRIDOXINE)

Vitamin $B_6$ (pyridoxine) is one of several nutrients needed to keep blood levels of homocysteine in an optimal range.[320] Without adequate amounts of vitamin $B_6$, homocysteine levels climb—a situation that appears to dramatically increase one's risk of depression as well as neurodegenerative diseases such as Parkinson's and Alzheimer's.[321]

Vitamin $B_6$ is an important contributor to the health of the nervous system and is necessary for the production of neurotransmitters such as GABA and serotonin.[322] Seizures, behavioral changes, and motor function abnormalities have been reported in vitamin $B_6$ deficient humans and animals.[323,324]

When consuming a plant-based diet, it is not difficult to get adequate amounts of this essential nutrient. However, an animal-based diet may cause a need for supplemental vitamin $B_6$.[325] Some vitamin $B_6$-rich foods

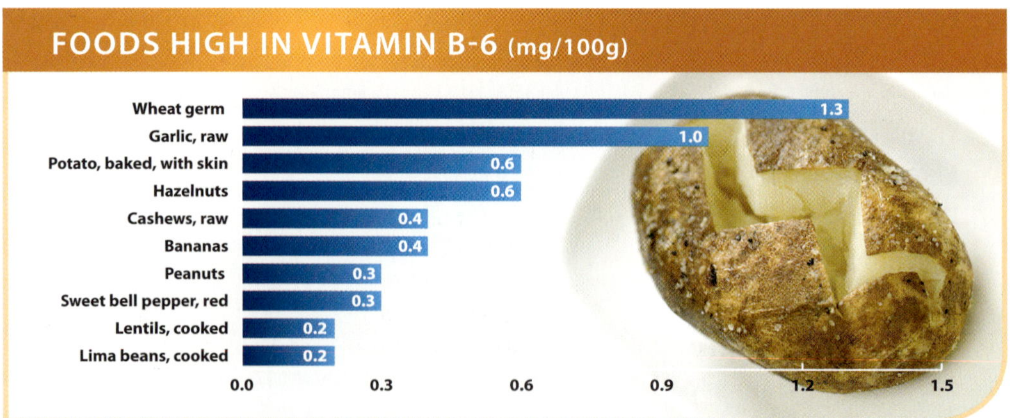


*Figure 11.12*

are found in **Figure 11.12**. The recommended daily allowance of vitamin $B_6$ is 1.5 mg per day. For people with high blood homocysteine levels, I recommend a supplement of 25-50 mg a day. Many people think that because B vitamins are water-soluble, they can't get too much of them. However, studies have shown that vitamin $B_6$ in large amounts can worsen Parkinson's disease and cause other nerve problems.[326]

## VITAMIN $B_9$ (FOLATE)

In the past few decades, vitamin $B_9$ (also known as folate or folic acid) has emerged as a vital nutrient for efficient brain function. Folate is necessary for the production of certain neurotransmitters, which in turn play an important role in making the body "feel good."

Cognitive decline and some forms of dementia, including Alzheimer's disease, have been associated with lower folate levels.[327] In addition, individuals with major depression and lower folate levels have been shown to be less responsive to antidepressants. Studies have demonstrated the value of folate in treating depression and other psychiatric illnesses.[328] Researchers in one clinical trial also confirmed that folate supplementation improved memory and cognitive function.[329]

The U.S. government has targeted folate as being undersupplied in the average American's diet. While humans require a minimum of 400 µg of folate per day for optimal physical health, I recommend a minimum of 1000 µg per day for optimal brain health. A double serving of steak has only 16 µg. It would take a lot of steak to supply the dietary recommendation for folate! Plant foods are better sources of this important B vitamin (see **Figure 11.13** for some of the richest folate sources).[330]

### DIETARY SOURCES OF FOLATE

| Food Item | Serving | Folate (mcg) |
|---|---|---|
| Black-eyed peas, cooked | 1 cup/172g | 358 |
| Lentils, cooked | 1 cup/198g | 358 |
| Pinto beans, cooked | 1 cup/171g | 294 |
| Black beans, cooked | 1 cup/172g | 256 |
| Asparagus, boiled | 1 cup/180g | 243 |
| Mustard greens, raw | 1 cup/56g | 105 |
| Spinach, raw | 1 cup/30g | 58 |
| Napa Cabbage, cooked | 1 cup/109g | 47 |
| Arugula, raw | 1 cup/20g | 20 |

*Figure 11.13*

## VITAMIN $B_{12}$ (COBALAMIN)

Vitamin $B_{12}$ is another nutrient that plays a vital role in optimal brain and nervous system function, including avoidance of a depressed mood.[331] A deficiency of this important vitamin can result in anemia, numbness or tingling in the arms or legs, weakness, fatigue, or a loss of balance.[332] A number of people with $B_{12}$ deficiency have been mistakenly diagnosed with Alzheimer's disease.[333] Despite its importance to the human diet, vitamin $B_{12}$ is needed only in tiny amounts. Less than one hundredth of an ounce is more than enough $B_{12}$ to last a lifetime (provided you took it in small increments throughout your life). Despite our very meager need for this vitamin, a total lack of it can trigger health challenges such as anemia and nerve problems.

Since it does not naturally occur in a plant-based diet, $B_{12}$ has been a source of perplexity for vegetarians.[334] The only plant-based sources of $B_{12}$ are fortified sources or foods grown in soils and fertilizers that are very rich in $B_{12}$.[335] For vegetarians, I recommend the fortified plant sources of $B_{12}$ as a good way to obtain this vital nutrient.[336] For overall health reasons I advocate adhering as closely to a plant-based vegetarian diet as possible and taking a vitamin $B_{12}$ supplement daily. Food sources of $B_{12}$ are listed in **Figure 11.14**.

As the body ages, the intestine does not absorb $B_{12}$ as well. As a result, individuals not using $B_{12}$ supplements by the age of 80 run a greater than 20% chance of developing at least a subtle $B_{12}$ deficiency. Even with no obvious health problems, it may be necessary to take as much as 1000 µg (micrograms) of vitamin $B_{12}$ daily once you reach your 60s or 70s.

### DIETARY SOURCES OF $B_{12}$

| Food Item | Serving | $B_{12}$(mcg) |
|---|---|---|
| Nutritional Yeast Flakes | 16g/1.5 Tbsp | 7.8 |
| Big Franks (Loma Linda) | 1 link/51g | 6.7 |
| Whole Grain Total, dry cereal | .75 cup/30g | 6.0 |
| All-Bran Wheat Flakes, dry cereal | .75 cup/30g | 6.0 |
| Silk soymilk, unsweetened | 1 cup/243g | 3.0 |
| Beef Steak, sirloin | 3 oz/85g | 1.4 |
| Whole milk, 3.25% fat | 1 cup | 1.1 |
| Egg, large | 1 ea | 0.6 |
| Chicken breast, cooked | 1 cup/140g | 0.4 |
| Fruits, vegetables, nuts, grains | | 0 |

***Figure 11.14***

A daily dosage of 5-10 µg of vitamin $B_{12}$ is generally adequate for healthy individuals age 30 or less with no history of digestive problems or other conditions affecting vitamin status (e.g. HIV infection, parasitic diseases, use of acid-blocking drugs, etc.) The best $B_{12}$ supplement available is hydroxocobalamin that has no cyanide molecule and is a detoxifying $B_{12}$. It is best chewed or taken under the tongue. (If you have difficulty finding a source for hydroxocobalamin, try www.drnedley.com).

Individuals over age 30 should have periodic blood tests (every five years at a minimum) to evaluate the presence of heart disease risk factors (such as cholesterol, triglycerides, and homocysteine). $B_{12}$ and folic acids should also be checked. If homocysteine is running above 8 µmol/L, I generally advise my patients to increase their intake of vitamin $B_{12}$, folate, and $B_6$.

One of the reasons why vitamin $B_{12}$ and folate are so important in achieving optimal mental performance is that they both help the body to produce SAMe, or S-adenosylmethionine.[337] SAMe (which can also be taken as a dietary supplement) provides the final step in converting tryptophan and tyrosine into serotonin, dopamine, and norepinephrine. This is why some people feel so much better and have more energy after taking a $B_{12}$ shot or after taking SAMe. Most of these people could get the same benefit by simply taking a hydroxycobalamin supplement and chewing it daily.

## VITAMIN $B_p$ (CHOLINE)

In addition to being necessary for peak mental performance, choline plays an important role in key metabolic processes throughout the body. In one of these critical roles, choline serves as the raw material for the important brain messenger (neurotransmitter) known as acetylcholine (ACh). Increasing the amount of choline in the diet allows the brain to make more ACh when stimulated.[338]

Current research indicates that pregnant women should be conscious of their choline status. Prenatally, choline deficiency has adverse effects on brain development in a number of animal models.[339,340] Another fascinating insight from animal research is that mothers with excellent choline status during pregnancy provide lasting protection to the brains of their in utero offspring.[341] Even in adult life, those offspring have a measure of protection from toxic insults.[342]

Promising data suggests that choline compounds may help improve memory in older individuals without dementia. Cytidine 5-diphosphocholine (commonly known as citicoline or CDP-choline) is one such compound that has proved helpful.[343] A small study from Spain looked at 24 elderly individuals with memory deficits.[344] Compared to placebo, those who received between 300 and 1000 mg of citicoline daily showed significant improvements in three different memory assessments.

## CHOLINE CONTENT (mg/100g)

| Food Item | Choline | Betaine | Sum of both |
|---|---|---|---|
| Quinoa, uncooked | 70 | 630 | 700 |
| Spinach, raw | 18 | 550 | 568 |
| Lambsquarters, raw | 20 | 332 | 352 |
| Eggs (2 large) | 251 | 1 | 252 |
| Egg noodles, enriched | 79 | 132 | 211 |
| Soy Flour | 192 | 3 | 195 |
| Amaranth, uncooked | 70 | 68 | 138 |
| Beets, raw | 6 | 129 | 135 |
| Soybeans, raw | 116 | 2 | 118 |
| Whole grain wheat flour | 31 | 73 | 104 |
| Barley flour or meal | 38 | 66 | 104 |
| Flaxseed | 79 | 3 | 82 |

*recommended daily amounts of choline range from 1000-1500mg

***Figure 11.15***

Researchers at the Massachusetts Institute of Technology conducted a larger study involving nearly 100 subjects (47 women and 48 men) between 50 and 85 years old.[345] Those with measurable memory problems showed significant improvements with citicoline. The best results occurred with 2000 mg per day.

Citicoline has also been shown to be extremely beneficial following brain injury in both animal and human studies.[346,347] A synthesis of human citicoline studies involving over 1600 patients is particularly illuminating. Compared to those who did not get citicoline, those who received 2000 mg of this choline-containing compound within 24 hours of a moderate to severe stroke were 38% more likely to have full recovery three months later.[348] Unfortunately, current data suggests we cannot obtain this significant amount of citicoline (CDP-choline) from an unsupplemented diet.[349] Fortunately, CDP-choline is available as a dietary supplement.

Choline's roles extend far beyond mental health issues. This compound is necessary for optimal liver health. In fact, severe deficiency results in liver abnormalities.[350] Choline is also a vital nutrient when it comes to homocysteine metabolism, since elevated homocysteine levels contribute to circulatory problems and may play a role in the development of dementia. Choline, like folate, is able to lower blood levels of this hazardous amino acid.[351] However, our bodies have to convert choline into betaine to obtain this homocysteine-lowering benefit.

One interesting feature of betaine is that although our bodies can make it from choline, it cannot be converted back into choline.[352] We can therefore lower our homocysteine with betaine or any other choline-related compound—but betaine cannot be used to make neurotransmitters like acetylcholine. Nevertheless, eating plenty of betaine theoretically leaves you with more choline for brain-related functions. When trying to identify the best choline sources, it seems prudent to look at all choline-related compounds in foods—including betaine. **Figure 11.15** shows some foods with the highest choline content.[350,351]

## VITAMIN C

Vitamin C, which is found in abundance in fruits and vegetables (see **Figure 11.16**), is critical to the conversion of certain substances into neurotransmitters such as dopamine, norepinephrine, and serotonin.[360] Without adequate intake of vitamin C, tryptophan cannot be converted to serotonin.[361] Vitamin C also assists in converting the amino acid L-Tyrosine to dopamine, which is then converted to norepinephrine with the assistance of vitamin $B_6$ cofactors.[362]

Research links long-term higher blood levels of vitamin C and beta carotene to better performance on tests of memory during old age. A study involving 442 men and women tested their antioxidant levels in 1971 and again in 1993. When the second set of tests were run, the ages of the study participants ranged from 65 to 94 years old. In addition to testing blood

**FOODS RICH IN VITAMIN C (mg/100g)** *RDA is 2000 mcg

| Food Item | Vit C (mg) |
|---|---|
| Acerola cherry | 1677 |
| Guavas, common | 228 |
| Sweet red bell peppers, raw | 128 |
| Kale, raw | 120 |
| Broccoli, raw | 89 |
| Cauliflower, green, raw | 89 |
| Brussels sprouts, raw | 85 |
| Kiwifruit, raw | 75 |
| Oranges, raw, with peel | 71 |
| Strawberries, raw | 59 |

*Figure 11.16*

levels of vitamin C and beta carotene, researchers assessed participants on the free recall of words, picture naming, recognition, recall of picture images flashed on a computer screen, and word definitions.

Higher scores on these memory tests were associated with increased blood levels of vitamin C and beta carotene. These findings held up statistically, even after the researchers accounted for factors such as gender, age, and education.[353]

## VITAMIN D

Low vitamin D levels have been associated with poor mood, impaired mental function, schizophrenia, and Alzheimer's disease.[354,355,356,357] In contrast, researchers believe that adequate levels of vitamin D influence cognitive function in a positive way by increasing a brain chemical called acetylcholine, which in turn promotes memory.[358,359,360]

Vitamin D also stimulates synthesis of nerve growth factor which is believed to be helpful in protecting against stroke damage, preventing memory loss, and minimizing other neurodegenerative diseases (such as Alzheimer's).[361,362,363,364,365]

Vitamin D has been found to reduce the incidence of seizures in epileptic mice and an analog of vitamin D has been found to cause regression of brain tumors like glioblastoma and astrocytoma in some suffering from these forms of cancers.[366,367] Early symptoms of vitamin D deficiency include profuse sweating, restlessness, and irritability.[368] Other symptoms are muscle aches, muscle weakness, and bone pain at any age.[369] More extensive coverage of vitamin D is provided in the chapter of this book covering light therapy. If you don't get regular exposure in the sun, ensure that you take 1000-4000 I.U. of vitamin D a day.[370,371]

## VITAMIN E

Vitamin E intake in food and supplements may help slow decline in mental functioning among older people, according to the results of a study led by Dr. Martha Clare Morris, professor of internal medicine at Rush-Presbyterian-St. Luke's Medical Center in Chicago, Illinois. In her study, Dr. Morris found that high amounts of vitamin E from foods appear to protect against cognitive decline.[372] Deficiencies of vitamin E have also been linked to impaired thinking. Deficits of this vitamin are rare in the developed world, occurring almost exclusively in individuals with an inherited or acquired inability for absorption.[373] A table detailing some of the highest healthy choices of vitamin E is provided in **Figure 11.17**.

## VITAMIN K

Vitamin K is closely associated with coagulation of blood in the body. The "K" itself was actually derived from a European spelling for the word coagulation (Koagulation).[374] Anticoagulant drugs (such as warfarin) are

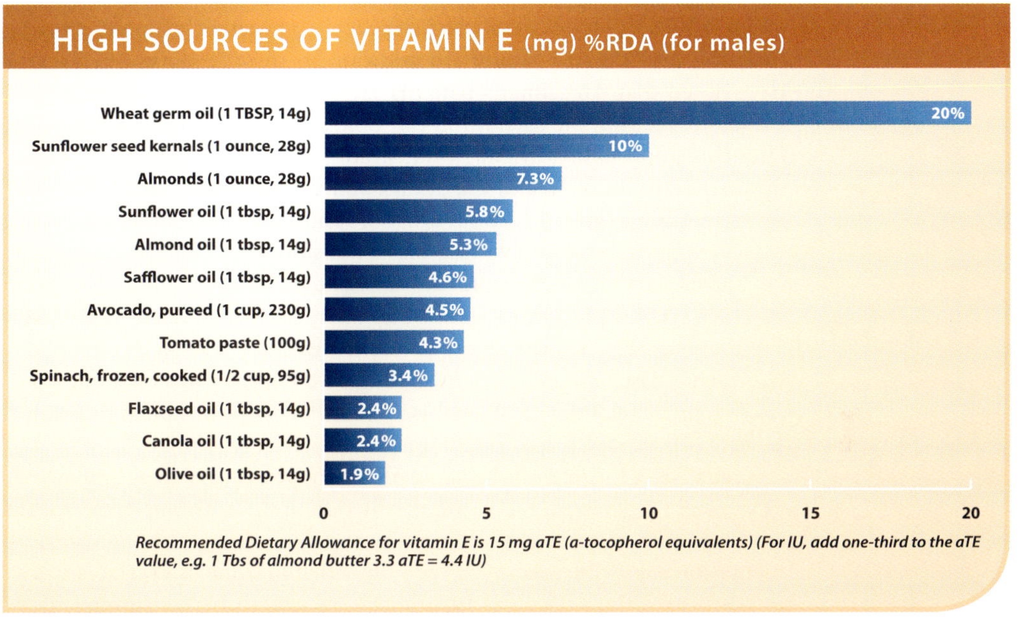


***Figure 11.17***

another reason the role of vitamin K in blood coagulation has received much attention in the medical world.[375] Such drugs work by impairing the activity of the body's natural vitamin K-dependent anticoagulant molecules. Although the emphasis on vitamin K relates to blood coagulation, an increasing body of research has highlighted additional important roles vitamin K plays in the body. By keeping calcium in the bones and out of the arteries, vitamin K appears to be particularly critical to calcium regulation.[376] This function alone gives it potential as a weapon against both heart disease and osteoporosis.

In one animal study, scientists from the Netherlands found that vitamin K significantly reduced the amount of calcium in the aortas of rats that had been fed a diet designed to harden their arteries. Damage to the heart valves of the rats was actually reduced by the intake of a vitamin K-rich diet.[377] In another study covering 10 years and involving more than 72,000 nurses, researchers concluded that the nurses with the highest vitamin K intake were a third less likely to suffer hip fractures than their colleagues with lower intake. In this study, vitamin K was found to be even more effective than synthetic estrogen in preventing fractures.[378]

Researchers have also found that vitamin K reduces the hormone Interleukin-6 (IL-6), a biochemical messenger that increases inflammation throughout the body.[379] IL-6 has been implicated in degenerative diseases such as arthritis, heart disease, diseases of the blood vessels, and Alzheimer's Disease.[380,381,382] By reducing IL-6, scientists now believe that vitamin K may play a significant role in the reduction of many diseases plaguing the Western World. In addition to these findings, researchers have noted that Alzheimer's patients are frequently low in vitamin K.[383] Besides regulating the calcium in our bones and arteries, vitamin K regulates this important nutrient in our brains, playing an important role in optimal brain function and the brain's ability to achieve peak mental performance. See **Figure 11.18** for a list of foods high in vitamin K.

Vitamin K (a fat-soluble vitamin) is not stored in the body. In the past, it was believed that most people had sufficient amounts of vitamin K in their bodies. Recent research has revealed that many people, especially the elderly, are not obtaining adequate amounts of this vitamin.[384] The RDA for vitamin K, which is based on body weight, is roughly 85 micrograms for adult males and 65 micrograms per day for adult females.[385] For optimal brain function it is likely that the body needs far more than the RDA requires.

The RDA for vitamin K can easily be met by eating an abundance of green, leafy vegetables. Kale is especially rich in this nutrient, but vitamin K can also be obtained in other fruits and vegetables. Although supplementation is possible, and even recommended in some cases, the best way to boost vitamin K levels is to support absorption by consuming foods high in vitamin K with dietary fat.

Note: Because the blood-thinning medication warfarin (coumadin) works by interfering with vitamin K, individuals taking this drug should not supplement with this nutrient.[386]

## FOODS RICH IN VITAMIN K

| Food Item | Serving | Vit K (mcg) |
|---|---|---|
| Lambsquarters, cooked | 1 cup/180g | 890 |
| Spinach, cooked | 1 cup/180g | 889 |
| Collards, cooked | 1 cup/190g | 836 |
| Kale, cooked or raw | 1 cup/67g | 574 |
| Swiss Chard, cooked | 1 cup/175g | 573 |
| Turnip greens, cooked | 1 cup/144g | 529 |
| Dandelion greens, raw or cooked | 1 cup/55g | 428 |
| Beet greens, cooked | 1 cup/140g | 419 |
| Amaranth leaves, raw | 1 cup/28g | 319 |
| Spinach, raw | 1 cup/30g | 145 |
| Brussels sprouts, cooked | 1 cup/78g | 109 |

*Figure 11.18*

## CALCIUM

In addition to its well-known role of promoting bone health, calcium facilitates better function of nerve and muscle cells. Like neurotransmitters, calcium serves as a type of messenger, sending electrical signals within the nervous system.

When chemical signals arrive at a brain cell, calcium ions carry the message from the outside to the inside of the cell by binding to certain important proteins.[387] These proteins, which are activated by the calcium, then cause changes in the cell.[388] The role of calcium in brain function is discussed more fully in the light therapy chapter.

## IRON

Adequate iron status, which is necessary for good athletic performance and optimal physical health, is also vital for the finest scholastic performance and cognitive function. Our bodies need iron to make and utilize neurotransmitters—chemicals that carry messages from one brain cell or nerve to another.[389]

Iron-dependent neurotransmitters include dopamine, serotonin, norepinephrine and GABA. It is unclear just how significantly iron deficiency impacts these systems. However, our growing understanding of brain chemistry argues that we maintain good iron levels to ensure optimal mental health.

Iron is necessary for the function of oligodendrocytes, the cells that produce an insulating coating on nerve cells. A lack of this mineral can result in defective nerve insulation and other serious repercussions, contributing to delayed childhood development and behavioral difficulties.[390,391]

The developing human brain is especially susceptible to iron deficiency.[392] Researchers in Jeddah, Saudi Arabia, found 20.5% of school students to be anemic. Those suffering from anemia did not do as well on class work and were more likely to fail exams. Of particular interest, two thirds of those affected were unaware that they were anemic.[393]

Although adequate iron intake is essential for top mental performance, too much iron is actually harmful to the body and brain. In excess, iron is a pro-oxidant, which is the opposite of an antioxidant. Pro-oxidants increase the production of free radicals, which increase the risk of heart disease, cancer, and dementia.[394]

When the body has plenty of iron stored already, the intestinal tract will decrease the absorption of plant-based non-heme iron to prevent the free radical production of too much iron. The intestinal tract is not able to decrease the absorption of heme iron, the iron present in the blood of meat. This leads to excessive iron stores, which further increases the risk of mental decline.[395] The result is yet another potential disadvantage of meat intake on mental performance, and precisely why it is better to seek out plant-based sources of iron.

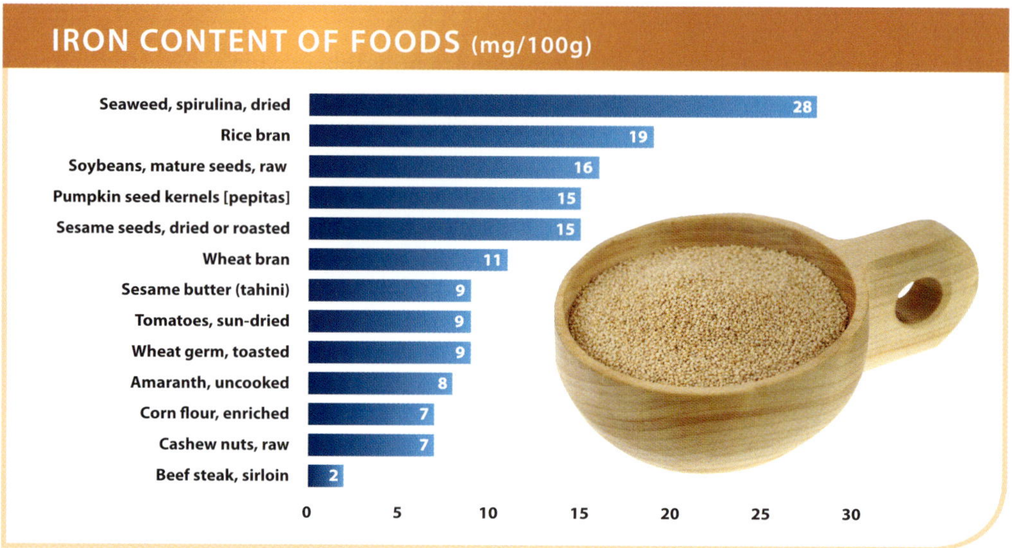


***Figure 11.19*** *recommended daily amounts of iron: 8mg adult males, women over 50; 18mg women 18-49

Soybeans are an excellent source of iron, as well as pumpkin seeds, rice bran, tahini, amaranth grain, and seaweed. A table detailing some of the highest dietary sources of iron is provided in **Figure 11.19**. Iron deficiency anemia can be caused by blood loss as well as diet, so if you're on a good diet but still deficient in iron, you may want to be evaluated for internal bleeding.

## SELENIUM

Selenium's antioxidant functions are vital to brain physiology. Selenium is a trace mineral found in whole grains, (such as wheat) grown in selenium-rich soils. Selenium helps to maintain the antioxidant capacity of glutathione, an important brain antioxidant.[396] Selenium and glutathione appear to be particularly effective in protecting a brain region (the substantia niagra), which is highly impacted by Parkinson's disease.[397] Awareness of a link between oxidative processes and neurodegenerative diseases such as Alzheimer's and Parkinson's has made antioxidant protection an even more vital issue.

A diet high in selenium (approximately 200 to 400 micrograms a day) appears to decrease the risk of a variety of cancers, including those of the lung and colon.[398,399] Lesser amounts of selenium (100 micrograms per day) alone or combined with zinc have been shown to improve immune status in older individuals.[400]

Despite the evidence of selenium's importance on a number of fronts, excessive selenium intake is toxic.[401] Surplus selenium can trigger a host of problems including hair and nail loss, bad breath, blood clotting abnormalities (prolonged prothrombin time), disruption of hormone systems (including thyroid and growth hormones), impaired white blood cells (natural killer cells), intestinal disturbances, and liver toxicity.[402,403]

Researchers from an area of China with high selenium food content—and resultant human toxicity—have concluded that the maximum safe level for selenium intake is around 400 micrograms per day.[404] Other investigators put the safe maximum level at 300 micrograms or less.[405] How can we optimize our selenium intake without getting too much? I recommend eating foods that are naturally rich in this trace mineral—and avoiding supplements. **Figure 11.20** lists some good sources of this vital mineral.

**SELENIUM SOURCES**

| Food Amount | Serving | Se (mcg) |
|---|---|---|
| Brazil nuts | 1 oz/28g | 537 |
| Wheat flour, whole grain | 1 cup/120g | 85 |
| Couscous, cooked | 1 cup/157g | 43 |
| Shiitake Mushrooms, dried | 3 oz/85g | 39 |
| Sunflower seeds, dry roasted | 1 oz/28g | 22 |
| Wheat germ | 1 oz/28g | 22 |
| Brown rice, long grain | 1 cup/195g | 19 |

*Figure 11.20*

## RESVERATROL

Flavonoids, which are beneficial phytonutrients that give the vibrant purple color to grapes, contain a second flavonoid-type compound called resveratrol.[406,407] Resveratrol, which has a protective effect on the heart, also appears to promote good brain function.[408,409] A healthy cardiovascular system generally translates into a healthy cerebrovascular system. As a result, it seems reasonable to expect that resveratrol can protect the brain against vascular dementia (the second most common type of dementia).

The connection between resveratrol and the protective effect of wine and alcohol consumption was documented in one study of 13,329 men and women in Copenhagen over 16 years. In that study, researchers found wine intake to be associated with lower risk of stroke. Flavonoid consumption (including resveratrol) and tannins were a possible explanation of those findings.[410]

Researchers have also found that resveratrol can improve blood flow in the brain by 30%. The findings, based on a study of 60 rats, found that rats subjected to an induced reduction of blood flow (ischemia) to the

## NON-WINE RESVERATROL SOURCES

| Food Item | Resveratrol (Ng/g dry sample) |
|---|---|
| Red Grapes (Merlot) | 6356 |
| Lingonberries | 5884 |
| Red Grapes (Pinot Noir) | 5746 |
| Peanuts (boiled) | 5100 |
| Blueberries | 1691 |
| Cranberries | 900 |
| Bilberries | 768 |

***Figure 11.21***

brain experienced an improved blood flow from a single dose of resveratrol.[411] This is of particular interest in relation to strokes, where blood flow to the brain is interrupted by a broken artery or blood clot.

By protecting brain cells from the ravages of free radicals, resveratrol may also provide a defense against Alzheimer's disease. A recent study examined the protective effect of black grape-skin extract, which is high in resveratrol, against toxicity caused by the protein beta-amyloid (the chief constituent of senile plaque) in human endothelial cells. Researchers found that grape-skin extract reduced free radical production associated with beta-amyloid and protected the body, helping to destroy cancerous cells and protecting against free radical-induced damage.[412]

Another study led researchers to believe that resveratrol's powerful antioxidant activity can help protect against Alzheimer's disease. Researchers in this study examined the effects of resveratrol on human neuroblastoma cells subjected to oxidative stress generated by beta-amyloid (main component of plaques found in brains of Alzheimer's patients). They found resveratrol to be effective in enhancing the levels of glutathione, an intracellular free radical scavenger that is the body's most important antioxidant. Resveratrol also helped to prevent neurotoxicity.[413]

Fortunately for those who want to avoid the many problems associated with alcohol consumption, there are a number of rich non-alcoholic sources of resveratrol. **Figure 11.21** documents some rich sources of resveratrol, which include peanuts, grapes, and a number of members of the berry family.

### BRAIN-DERIVED NEUROTROPHIC FACTOR (BDNF)

BDNF, a protein that can protect your brain from a variety of threats, has been getting more attention lately. BDNF is a neurotrophin that helps induce the survival, development, and function of brain cells, and can actually stimulate the development of new brain cells.[414] We used to think this wasn't even possible—that we each have a certain number of brain cells at birth. While it was commonly believed that the number of brain cells might expand during the first two years after birth, the number of brain cells was expected to decrease as time went on. We now know that new brain cells, or neurons, can actually be developed into new brain connections, or synapses. BDNF, which helps to develop these new synapses, appears to have a mood-elevating effect on the brain as well.

Engaging in regular exercise is one of the best natural ways to boost BDNF levels.[415] In addition, studies have shown that decreasing caloric intake by 30% may increase BDNF levels.[416]

Short periods of fasting can also increase BDNF.[417] When they had a difficult decision to make, many of the great men in history turned to a short-term fast to sharpen their thinking. In the words of Ben Franklin, "the best of all medicines are resting and fasting."

Brief, supervised fasting is an approach we have implemented with success in the 10-day residential *Nedley Depression Recovery Program.* A supervised fast for up to 72 hours is one approach we have tried for some overweight individuals with depression. At the end of the 72 hours, many patients have remarked about how much their mental outlook has improved. This is likely due to the elevation in BDNF levels. (BDNF levels begin to drop again for fasts longer than 3 days).

Other ways to increase BDNF include taking on new challenges outside of your normal comfort zone.[418] Some examples would be visiting new places, taking up a new hobby, learning a new language, mastering a musical instrument, or studying mind-expanding books (such as the Bible). Recent scientific evidence also indicates that alcohol avoidance may help optimize BDNF levels.[419]

## CHOLESTEROL: WHAT YOU SHOULD KNOW

Keeping your brain healthy through nutrition is not just about which nutrients you include in your diet, but also about the substances you avoid.

Researchers have found that patients with major depression tend to have significantly higher cholesterol as well.[420] When artery walls thicken as a result of build-up of fatty materials such as cholesterol (a condition known as atherosclerosis), this results in decreased blood flow to the frontal lobe of the brain. This syndrome can lead to decreased cognitive function and depression. Individuals with a combination of high cholesterol and atherosclerosis have a poor prognosis for depression treatment response, particularly when the treatment involves medication. If the cholesterol is brought down, however, the depression is more likely to respond to treatment.

Lowering cholesterol levels is an important step in promoting optimal brain function, and in doing so it is helpful to recognize that not all cholesterol is created equal. The fact that some forms of cholesterol are more dangerous than others was confirmed by Dr. Bruce Taylor, a New York researcher heading up some experiments involving cholesterol in rabbits and monkeys.

Dr. Taylor inadvertently left a bucket of cholesterol open. Later he found that the animals who consumed cholesterol from the open bucket suffered dramatic vascular damage within 24 hours. In contrast, animals that were fed cholesterol where the container had remained sealed experienced much less damage. The oxidized cholesterol, which had been exposed to the atmosphere for a period of time, was particularly damaging to the animals' health.

Fascinated by these findings, Dr. Taylor engaged in research designed to determine which foods were most likely to have oxidized cholesterol, and found that the most harmful foods were custards. Custards (such as ice cream), which are comprised of sugar combined with milk, eggs, or both, become heavily oxidized during the mixing process. The second most damaging product is pancake mix, which consists of powdered egg yolk that oxidizes when mixed. The third most oxidized cholesterol, parmesan cheese, is tied with lard for level of oxidation.

Though largely ignored, the dangers of such foods were pointed out more than a century ago in the classic book *Ministry of Healing*: "especially harmful are the custards and puddings in which milk, eggs, and sugar are the chief ingredients. The free use of milk and sugar together should be avoided."[421]

In searching for a low cholesterol diet, you can't go wrong with fruits, nuts, grains, and vegetables, which have no cholesterol. You don't even have to read the labels in this case. If it comes from a plant or is a plant, there's no cholesterol in it.

In contrast, most animal products, including milk, eggs, cheese, meat, butter, and fish, contain cholesterol. The only exception to this rule is egg whites. Studies have actually shown that if you add fish to the diet of a vegetarian, that individual's cholesterol will go up. **Figure 11.22** shows some of the foods with the highest levels of dietary cholesterol.

## OVEREATING AND OBESITY

Even if you are eating a nutrient-rich diet full of healthy foods, too much food is not nourishing to your body or mind. Overeating is a surefire way to reduce cognitive ability. In contrast, a reduced calorie intake contributes to better brain function. In one study, Italian researchers demonstrated that while rats on a normal diet lose mental function as they age, elderly rats that had been on a low calorie diet since birth had mental abilities as good as their younger counterparts.[422]

## CHOLESTEROL IN SELECTED FOODS

| Food Item | Serving | Chol. (mg) |
|---|---|---|
| Chicken liver, cooked | 3 oz/85g | 474 |
| Whitefish, dried | 3oz/85g | 222 |
| Egg | 1 large | 211 |
| Heavy whipping cream | 1 cup/120g | 164 |
| Egg substitute, powder | 1 oz/28g | 160 |
| Cheddar Cheese | 1 oz/28g | 139 |
| Chicken, roasted, chopped | 1 cup/140g | 119 |
| Pork, ground, cooked | 3 oz/85g | 80 |
| Salmon, smoked, canned | 3 oz/85g | 78 |
| Cod liver oil | 1 Tbs/14g | 77 |
| Turkey, roasted | 3 oz/85g | 75 |
| Fish oil (salmon) | 1 Tbs/14g | 66 |
| Beef steak, sirloin (1/8" fat) | 3 oz/85g | 64 |
| Ice Cream | 1 cup/132g | 58 |
| Cream cheese | 1 oz/28g | 31 |
| Butter | 1 Tbs/14g | 30 |
| Milk, whole | 1 cup/244g | 24 |
| Milk, 1%, low fat | 1 cup/246g | 10 |
| Mayonnaise, light | 1 Tbs/15g | 5 |
| Egg white | 1 large | 0 |
| Grains, nuts, fruits, vegetables | | 0 |

***Figure 11.22***

Obesity is also associated with low energy levels and a decline in mood. Blood sugar levels that exceed 140 one hour after a meal can cause fatigue or sluggish thinking. Researchers at Toulouse University School of Medicine in France, who published their results in the journal *Neurology*, report that obesity (as measured by Body Mass Index) does affect cognitive function.[423] After analyzing data for more than 2,000 middle-aged healthy individuals at a 5-year interval, the researchers noted that a higher BMI was associated with lower cognitive scores, even after adjustments

for other variables (such as age, sex, education, blood pressure, and diabetes) were made. Embarking on a weight control program that results in a loss of even 5 pounds can increase energy levels and improve mood right away.

For individuals interested in improving cognitive function through weight loss, I recommend a five-part program (as outlined in **Figure 11.23**)[424] to get things rolling right away. As many of my patients have proven, if you combine these four tips with daily moderate exercise, you will lose weight.

### BREAKFAST FOR YOUR BRAIN

Good breakfast habits are essential for maximum efficiency, both mentally and physically, particularly during the late morning hours. For the best brain health, each day should begin with a high-quality breakfast that includes a balanced selection of plant sources of nutrition. I prefer a

## STRATEGIES FOR WEIGHT LOSS SUCCESS

**#1: Eliminate snacks**

One out of three overweight people in our society are so not because of what they eat at mealtime, but because of what they eat in between.

**#2: Drink only water between meals**

No pop, juice, or coffee. If you eat a good diet, you won't be hungry. When hunger crops up between meals, it's a sign your diet is deficient.

**#3: Eat a good breakfast, moderate lunch, and no evening meal**

A study by Dr. Cupp in Louisiana showed that if you shift the calories you would've eaten in the evening over to the morning, you wouldn't gain nearly as much weight. It's the evening meal that tends to get stored as fat. If you do eat in the evening, choose whole fruit.

**#4: Nix foods high in sugar and fat and get plenty of fiber**

Refined sugar and free fats in the diet should be either eliminated or greatly reduced. At the same time, emphasize foods high in fiber.

**#5: Get at least 45 minutes of aggressive physical exercise daily.**

Choose a few vigorous activities that you enjoy and alternate them from day to day to avoid boredom

*Figure 11.23*

**MENTAL PERFORMANCE BENEFITS OF BREAKFAST**

- more efficient problem solving
- improved memory
- reversal of mild age-related memory problems
- more creativity
- increased verbal fluency
- improved attention span
- better attitudes
- more positive mood; less depressive symptoms
- improved handling of stress and greater calmness
- better scholastic scores
- improved spatial memory performance

***Figure 11.24***

variety of fruits and whole grains along with a few nuts. Whether you're a student, a middle-aged adult, or a senior citizen, breakfast appears to provide a mental edge. **Figure 11.24** lists the benefits of a good breakfast.[425]

Worldwide, research literature links breakfast with better cognitive (mental) performance.[426,427] Swedish studies reveal that children who were served larger breakfasts showed improved mental functioning compared to those who ate a smaller meal to start their day. Jamaican school children who ate daily breakfasts for two weeks showed an increase in "creative ideas." In Saudi Arabia, 14.9% of students reported skipping breakfast. Those who missed the morning meal tended to perform poorer in school. Research from both the United States and South America shows that undernourished children fare worse mentally when they miss breakfast.[428] Breakfast eating yields cognitive benefits even in well-nourished kids.[429]

In August of 1995, the Pediatrics Department at the University of California at Davis hosted a number of psychologists, neuroscientists, nutritionists, and physiologists who reviewed the scientific studies on breakfast. The researchers concluded that the "eating of breakfast is important to learning, memory, and physical well-being in both children and adults."[430]

For anyone in need of a memory boost, breakfast is indeed the most important meal of the day. In support of this fact, researchers had 22 men and women aged 61 to 79 perform memory tests after ingesting one of four "meals," given on separate mornings. Each morning, participants had a drink containing either pure carbohydrate, protein, fat, or a non-calorie placebo. The investigators found that, compared with the placebo drink, carbs, protein, and fat combined to boost memory performance 15 minutes after ingestion. On tests taken later, the three nutrients had differing effects, with carbohydrates tending to have greater benefits one hour after ingestion, although fat still tended to improve attention one hour out.[431,432]

Research also suggests that consistent breakfast eating may have mood elevating benefits. Allgower and colleagues from London, England, who studied over 5,000 male and female university students, documented a significant relationship between skipping breakfast and depressive symptoms.[433]

In a controlled trial involving 144 volunteers (mean age, 21) another British group found that, compared to fasting, breakfast eaters had a more positive mood, performed better on a spatial memory task, and felt calmer at the end of a testing session. Furthermore, despite conventional wisdom, morning caffeine did not improve mood or working memory.[434]

Breakfast's brain-boosting benefits are not confined to children and young adults. Early-morning consumption of glucose or breakfast cereals can enhance cognitive functions in elderly individuals. Carbohydrate-rich breakfasts appear to be particularly effective at improving one's ability to retrieve and verbally articulate memories (technically referred to as "verbal declarative memory").[435]

A carbohydrate-rich breakfast can also brighten your mood. In another study, Reid and Hammersley demonstrated that increased carbohydrate intake at breakfast promoted calmness several hours later.[436] In contrast, higher fat breakfasts suppressed both alertness and mood.[437]

## THE MEDITERRANEAN DIET

**The traditional Mediterranean diet is good for your brain.**

An increasing body of research has shown the Mediterranean diet to be one that promotes mental and physical health. Led by Nikolaos Scarmeas, researchers studied 1393 cognitively normal subjects and monitored how well they followed the Mediterranean diet and their cognitive decline as they aged.

For purposes of the study, the Mediterranean diet was defined as one characterized by a high intake of fish, vegetables, legumes, fruits, cereals, and unsaturated fatty acids (mostly in the form of olive oil) and a low intake of dairy products, meat, and saturated fatty acids.

The researchers found that individuals with a higher adherence to the Mediterranean Diet had a reduced risk of developing mild cognitive impairment. If they had the impairment, they also had a reduced risk that impairment would convert to Alzheimer's Disease.[438]

People who follow the average Mediterranean diet eat less saturated fat than those who eat the average American diet. In addition, more than half the fat calories in a Mediterranean diet come from monounsaturated fats (mainly from olive oil). Monounsaturated fat doesn't raise blood cholesterol levels the way saturated fat does. A table showing dietary sources of monounsaturated fat is provided in **Figure 11.25**.

## BEST FOODS FOR THE BRAIN

A liberal supply of fruits, vegetables, and grains provides the best nourishment for the frontal lobe. They are also proven winners in the fight to stave off dementia, with some research suggesting that these powerful plant foods may even turn back the cognitive clock. Though there's hardly a poor choice among them, here are some of the best of the plant-based bunch when it comes to feeding your brain:

**Berries** contain antioxidants that help boost cognition, coordination, and memory. Blueberries are among the best brain foods on earth as they boost the potency of neuron signals. Nicknamed the "brain berry," they are known to protect the brain from oxidative stress and may reduce the effects of age-related conditions such as Alzheimer's disease and dementia. Antioxidant-rich strawberries can prevent age-related neurological declines by improving brain cell abilities to send and receive the signaling molecules. The brain uses these signaling molecules to communicate. Blackberries are rich in nutrients called anthocyanins that help protect our brain from oxidation stress, which in turn fights degenerative brain diseases.

**Cruciferous vegetables** seem to put the brakes on age-related declines in memory and thinking, turning back the cognitive clock by as much as a year and a half. Harvard researchers have reported that women

**FOODS HIGH IN MONOUNSATURATED FAT**

| Food Item | Serving | Fat (g) |
|---|---|---|
| Macadamia nuts | 1 oz/28g | 17 |
| Hazelnuts | 1 oz/28g | 13 |
| Pecans | 1 oz/28g | 10 |
| Avocado | ½ fruit | 10 |
| Olive oil | 1 Tbs/14g | 10 |
| Almonds | 1 oz/28g | 9 |
| Cashews | 1 oz/28g | 7 |
| Sesame seeds | 1 oz/28g | 5 |
| Olives, large | 10 ea | 3 |

*Figure 11.25*

in the Nurses' Health Study who ate the most broccoli, cauliflower, and other cruciferous vegetables performed better on memory tests than women the same age who ate the least.[439]

**Garlic** is one of the most nutritious foods on the planet. Famous for reducing bad cholesterol and strengthening the cardiovascular system, it also exerts a protective antioxidant effect on the brain. Garlic may also help protect against stroke, dementia, and Alzheimer's disease.

**Green leafy vegetables** such as spinach and kale are high in iron and among the richest sources of folate.[440] Kale, for example, contains compounds that fight many forms of cancer, optimize cells' ability to detoxify, lower the risk of cataracts, promote lung health, support the immune system, and help keep an aging brain sharp.[441,442] Spinach, kale, chard, romaine, and other green leafy vegetables should be consumed on a regular basis.

**Nuts** contain generous amounts of protein, fiber, and beneficial fats. They also contain plenty of vitamin B, E, and magnesium, which are essential to cognitive function. As positive mood enhancers, nuts (in small amounts) can also help you think more clearly. Filberts, hazelnuts, cashews, and walnuts are great choices, with almonds being the king of nuts. If you are overweight, don't eat more than a handful of nuts every day.

**Olive oil** is rich in antioxidants needed for clear thinking, good memory, and a balanced mood. The extra virgin organic variety is best because the oil is produced without chemical treatment. Unprocessed organic olive oil also contains fiber and protein. In contrast, processed fats can alter the brain's communication pathways in unhelpful ways.

**Pomegranates** contain blueberry-like levels of antioxidants, offering brain and memory protection. Pomegranates are a rich source of vitamin C, A, and E, as well as fiber, iron, and potassium. In addition, the anti-inflammatory attributes of pomegranates strengthen the immune system.

**Seeds** contain a lot of protein, beneficial fat, and vitamin E, as well as stress-fighting antioxidants and important brain-boosting minerals like magnesium. Seeds such as sunflower seeds, sesame seeds, flax seeds, and chia seeds can boost both brainpower and mood.

**Tomatoes** are also brain food due to their high lycopene content. Research suggests that lycopene, a powerful antioxidant, could help protect against the kind of free radical damage to cells which occurs in the development of dementia, particularly Alzheimer's.

**Whole grains** like brown rice are essential for maintaining concentration throughout the day and improving memory, because they contain the perfect mix of carbohydrates and fiber to fuel your brain while keeping you full. The low-glycemic index complex carbohydrate present in brown rice is excellent for people sensitive to gluten who still want to maintain cardiovascular health. Whole grain breads and cereals are also rich in folate and vitamin $B_6$.

## NUTRITIONAL BRAIN DRAINS

Some foods, beverages, and habits will positively work against your efforts at clear thinking. Items to steer clear of include sugary drinks, colas, processed foods, and foods containing high-fructose corn syrup, refined white sugars, alcohol, nicotine, trans fats, and partially-hydrogenated oils. Below is a detailed overview of food categories to watch out for.

**Alcohol** interferes with dopamine production and decreases activity of the frontal lobe of the brain. Any resveratrol-related benefits obtained through alcohol can also be received by drinking grape juice. The healthiest course of action is to steer clear of alcoholic beverages.

**Corn syrup and sugar** not only lead to health problems such as diabetes and obesity: they are a drain on the brain. Sugary fruit drinks, sodas, colas, and juices are among the worst offenders. The best policy is to limit sweets to special occasions, or as an infrequent treat.

**High carbohydrate meals** loaded with refined foods, sugar, or junk food also deter mental performance.[443] The consumption of sugary food causes the blood sugar to rise and fall quickly. When refined sweets enter the digestive system, the blood sugar rises dramatically and the body reacts as if it were just exposed to a great volume of natural food. In contrast, when blood sugar falls low enough, frontal lobe function can suffer due to inadequate fuel supplies. Scientific research has shown that boys who ate a diet low in refined sugar had a higher attention span and responded more accurately to questions than a control group of boys with higher levels of sugar in their diet. The difference in scores could not be explained by IQ or the parent's social or educational status.[444]

**High-fat diets** also deter mental performance. Researchers have found that saturated fat found in margarine, butter, and cheese may increase the risk of mental decline in old age.[445] Another study concluded that those with elevated intake of harmful fats (arachidonic and palmitic) and low intakes of omega-6 fats had an decline in verbal fluency.[446]

**Nicotine** may soothe jittery nerves, but it also constricts blood flow to the brain, reducing thinking ability. Effects are cumulative.

**Meat-based diets** contain arachidonic acid, which decreases the synthesis and storage of acetylcholine. Excess arachidonic acid found in meat impairs optimal functioning of the brain center for wisdom, judgment, and foresight—the frontal lobe.[447] Meat and other animal products, which contain no phytochemicals, are also high in saturated fats and cholesterol. While the intake of animal products increases the risk of heart disease, cancer, and parasites, the excess protein in meat robs calcium from the bones. In contrast, plant-based foods are rich in phytochemicals, high in fiber, low in fat, moderate in calories and cholesterol-free. One of the best ways to cut back on meat in the diet is to begin eliminating it from your meals at least two days per week. The second step of this process is to limit meat to only one meal per day, on the days that you do eat meat.

**It typically takes 3-14 days for the results of a healthier diet to be noticeable. Improvement will continue and peak at about 3-6 months.**

After you have adjusted to this regimen, eliminate meat from your diet 4-5 days per week. The final step is to progress to a total plant-based diet.

## DIDEROT'S PROVERB

The French philosopher Denis Diderot wrote that "doctors are always working to preserve our health and cooks to destroy it, but the latter are often more successful." That doesn't have to be true if we retrain the cooks.

The Standard American Diet (SAD) leaves us vulnerable to anxiety disorders and depression. As shown in this chapter, it's not just what we are eating that hurts us; it is also what we are not eating that compounds our trouble. Fortunately, the solution to these challenges is clear: ensure that your diet contains adequate amounts of the amino acids, nutrients, and "good fats" that have been shown to promote optimal brain function, while avoiding the tainted sources of those vital nutrients and other harmful substances.

The positive effects of dietary changes do not become evident overnight, but the results are worth the effort. The outcome of such actions is sure to be clearer thinking, as good nutrition is a vital step in achieving peak mental performance. Why not take control of your life by nourishing your brain?

# References

238. Molteni R., et al. "A high-fat, refined sugar diet reduces hippocampal brain-derived neurotrophic factor, neuronal plasticity, and learning." *Neuroscience* 112 (2002): 803+.
239. Winocur G, Greenwood C. "Studies of the effects of high fat diets on cognitive function in a rat model." *Neurobiology of Aging* 26.1 (1996): 46+.
240. Blackman JD, et al. "Hypoglycemic thresholds for cognitive dysfunction in humans." *Diabetes* 39.7 (1990): 828+.
241. Parker G, Parker I, Brotchie H. "Mood state effects of chocolate." *Journal of Affective Disorders* 92.2-3 (2006): 149+.
242. Goetz CG. "Hypokinesia and Hyperkinesia." Goetz: *Textbook of Clinical Neurology*. 3rd ed. Philadelphia, PA: Saunders, 2007.
243. Goetz CG. "Mood, Emotion, and Thought." Goetz: *Textbook of Clinical Neurology*. 3rd ed. Philadelphia, PA: Saunders, 2007.
244. Cooper JR, Bloom FE, Roth RH. *The Biochemical Basis of Neuropharmacology*. 8th ed. New York, Oxford University Press, 2002. 12, 299.
245. Wurtman RJ, et al. "Effects of normal meals rich in carbohydrates or proteins on plasma tryptophan and tyrosine ratios." *American Journal of Clinical Nutrition* 77.1 (2003): 128+.
246. Banderet LE, Lieberman HR. "Treatment with tyrosine, a neurotransmitter precursor, reduces environmental stress in humans." *Brain Res Bull.* 1989 Apr;22(4):759-62.
247. Thomas JR, Lockwood PA, Singh A, Deuster PA. "Tyrosine improves working memory in a multitasking environment." *Pharmacol Biochem Behav.* 1999 Nov;64(3):495-500.
248. Shukitt-Hale B, Stillman MJ, Lieberman HR. "Tyrosine administration prevents hypoxia-induced decrements in learning and memory." *Physiol Behav.* 1996 Apr-May;59(4-5):867-71.
249. Yeghiayan SK, Luo S, Shukitt-Hale B, Lieberman HR. "Tyrosine improves behavioral and neurochemical deficits caused by cold exposure." *Physiol Behav.* 2001 Feb;72(3):311-6.
250. Wurtman RJ, et al. "Effects of normal meals rich in carbohydrates or proteins on plasma tryptophan and tyrosine ratios" *American Journal of Clinical Nutrition*, Vol. 77, No. 1, 128-132, January 2003.

251. Markus CR, Panhuysen G, Tuiten A, Koppeschaar H, Fekkes D, Peters ML. "Does carbohydrate-rich, protein-poor food prevent a deterioration of mood and cognitive performance of stress-prone subjects when subjected to a stressful task?" *Appetite*. 1998 Aug;31(1):49-65.
252. USDA National Nutrient Database for Standard Reference, http://www.nal.usda.gov/fnic/foodcomp/search/.
253. Lucca A, Lucini V, Piatti E, Ronchi E, Smeraldi E. "Plasma tryptophan levels and plasma tryptophan/neutral amino acids ratio in patients with mood disorder, patients with obsessive-compulsive disorder, and normal subjects." *Psychiatry Res*. 1992 Nov;44(2):85-91.
254. USDA National Nutrient Database for Standard Reference, http://www.nal.usda.gov/fnic/foodcomp/search/.
255. USDA National Nutrient Database for Standard Reference, http://www.nal.usda.gov/fnic/foodcomp/search/.
256. Petursdottir AL, et al. "Effect of Dietary n-3 Polyunsaturated Fatty Acids on Brain Lipid Fatty Acid Composition, Learning Ability, and Memory of Senescence-Accelerated Mouse." *The Journals of Gerontology*. Washington: Nov 2008. Vol. 63A, Iss. 11; p. 1153.
257. Jacobson JL, et al. "Beneficial Effects of a Polyunsaturated Fatty Acid on Infant Development: Evidence from the Inuit of Arctic Quebec." *Journal of Pediatrics* 152.3 (2008).
258. Fontani G, et al. "Cognitive and physiological effects of Omega-3 polyunsaturated fatty acid supplementation in healthy subjects", *European Journal of Clinical Investigation* (2005) 35, 691–699
259. Fontani G, et al. "Cognitive and physiological effects of Omega-3 polyunsaturated fatty acid supplementation in healthy subjects", *European Journal of Clinical Investigation* (2005) 35, 691–699
260. Nash K, "Salmon not the only hook to anti-aging", *Dermatology Times*; Mar 2003; 24, 3
261. Lopez PM, Ortega RM. "Omega-3 fatty acids in the prevention and control of cardiovascular disease", *European Journal of Clinical Nutrition* (2003) 57, Suppl 1, S22–S25.
262. Kemper KJ, "Complementary and Alternative Medicine Therapies to Promote Healthy Moods", *Pediatric Clinics of North America* - Volume 54, Issue 6 (December 2007).
263. Mori TA, et al., " Overweight Men Vascular Reactivity of the Forearm Microcirculation in Hyperlipidemic, Differential Effects of Eicosapentaenoic Acid and Docosahexaenoic Acid on Overweight Men Vascular Reactivity of the Forearm Microcirculation in Hyperlipidemic, Overweight Men", *Circulation* 2000;102;1264-1269.
264. Mischoulon D, "Update and critique of natural remedies as antidepressant treatments.", *Psychiatr Clin North Am* - 01-MAR-2007; 30(1): 51-68.
265. Farkas E, Luiten, PGM. "Cerebral microvascular pathology in aging and Alzheimer's disease", *Progress in Neurobiology* 64 (2001) 575–611.
266. Peet M, Horrobin DF. "A Dose-ranging Study of the Effects of Ethyl-eicosapentaenoate in Patients With Ongoing Depression Despite Apparently Adequate Treatment With Standard Drugs." *Archives of General Psychiatry* 59 (2002): 913+.
267. Dewailly E, et al., "n-3 Fatty acids and cardiovascular disease risk factors among the Inuit of Nunavik", *Am J Clin Nutr* 2001;74:464–73.
268. Puskas LG, et al. "Short-term administration of omega 3 fatty acids from fish oil results in increased transthyretin transcription in old rat hippocampus." *Proceedings of the National Academy of Sciences of the U.S.A.* 100.4 (2003).
269. Gretchen V. "Cognition, Aging, and Omega-3 Fatty Acides", *Journal of Applied Nutrition*, Volume 55, Number 1, 2005.
270. Biomed Pharmacother. 2002 Oct;56(8):365-79. *The importance of the ratio of omega-6/omega-3 fatty acids*. Simopoulos AP. The Center for Genetics, Nutrition and Health, Washington, DC, 20009, USA.
271. *Biomed Pharmacother*. 2002 Oct;56(8):365-79.,The importance of the ratio of omega-6/omega-3 essential fatty acids.,The Center for Genetics, Nutrition and Health, Washington, DC 2009, USA.
272. Leviticus 11. The Holy Bible. Authorized King James Version.
273. Walker CH. *Organic Pollutants: An Ecotoxicological Perspective, Second Edition* (November 18, 2008), P. 113.
274. Goetz CG. "Organic Mercury." *Goetz: Textbook of Clinical Neurology*. 3rd ed. Philadelphia, PA: Saunders, 2007.
275. Joyce C McCann and Bruce N Ames, "Is docosahexaenoic acid, an n3 long-chain polyunsaturated fatty acid, required for development of normal brain function? An overview of evidence from cognitive and behavioral tests in humans and animals", Am J Clin Nutr 2005;82:281–95.
276. Buettner D. *The Blue Zones: Lessons for Living Longer From the People Who've Lived the Longest.*
277. Phillips RL, Lemon FR, et al. "Coronary heart disease mortality among Seventh-day Adventists with differing dietary habits." *Am J Clin Nutr* 1978 Oct; 31 (10 Suppl): S191-S198.
278. Innis SM. "Dietary (n-3) Fatty Acids and Brain Development." *J. Nutr*. 2007 137: 855-859.

279. Report during question and answer session given by Gary Fraser, M.D. principle investigator of Adventist Health Study-2, after the lecture on DHA by A. Leaf from Harvard— 5th International Congress on Vegetarian Nutrition March 4-6, 2008 at Loma Linda University.
280. Hill, et al. "Combining Fish-oil Supplements with Regular Aerobic Exercise Improves Body Composition and Cardiovascular Disease Risk Factors." *Am J Clin Nutr.*, 85:1267-1274 (2007).
281. Fruend-Levi Y, et al. "Omega-3 Fatty Acid Treatment in 174 Patients With Mild to Moderate Alzheimer Disease: OmegAD Study," October 23, 2006, *Arch. Neurol.*, 63: 1402-1408 (2006).
282. Wozniak J, et al. "Omega-3 fatty acid monotherapy for pediatric bipolar disorder: A prospective open-label trial," February 12th, 2007, *Eur Neuropsychopharmacol.* Epub ahead of print(2007).
283. Nemets H, et al. "Omega-3 Treatment of Childhood Depression: A Controlled, Double-Blind Pilot Study," June 6th, 2006, *Am. J. Psychiatry*, 163 :1098-1100 (2006).
284. Buydens-Branchey L, Branchey M. "Long-chain n-3 polyunsaturated fatty acids decrease feelings of anger in substance abusers." *Psychiatry Research.* 157(1-3):95-104, (2008).
285. Buydens-Branchey L, Branchey M. "Long-chain n-3 polyunsaturated fatty acids decrease feelings of anger in substance abusers." *Psychiatry Research.* 157(1-3):95-104, (2008).
286. Berger GE, et al. "Ethyl-Eicosapentaenoic Acid in First-Episode Psychosis: A Randomized, Placebo-Controlled Trial." *Journal of Clinical Psychiatry.* 68(12): 1867-1875. (2007).
287. Schlanger S, et al. "Diet enriched with omega-3 fatty acids alleviates convulsion symptoms in epilepsy patients." *Epiplepsia.* 43(1): 103-104, 2002.
288. Yuen AWC, et al. "Omega-3 fatty acid supplementation in patients with chronic epilepsy: A randomized trial." *Epilepsy & Behaviour.* 7: 253-258, 2005.
289. Moralez de Silva, et al. "Depression in Parkinson's disease: a double-blind, randomized, placebo-controlled pilot study of omega-3 fatty-acid supplementation." *Journal of Affective Disorders* 111: 351-359, 2008.
290. Nordvik K, et al. "Effect of dietary advice and n-3 supplementation in newly diagnosed MS patients." *Acta Neurol Scand.* 102: 143-149, 2000.
291. Weinstock-Guttman B, et al. "Low fat dietary intervention with n-3 fatty acid supplementation in multiple sclerosis patients. Prostaglandins, Leukotrienes and Essential Fatty Acids." 73: 397-404. 2005
292. Hibbeln J, et al. "Maternal seafood consumption in pregnancy and neurodevelopmental outcomes in childhood (ALSPAC study): an observational cohort study." *Lancet*, 369: 578-585 (2007).
293. Su KP, et al. "Omega-3 Fatty Acids for Major Depressive Disorder During Pregnancy: Results from a Randomized, Double-Blind, Placebo-Controlled Trial." *J. Clin. Psychiatry.* 69:4:644-51, 2008.
294. Judge MP, et al. "Maternal Consumption of a Docosahexaenoic Acid-Containing Functional Food During Pregnancy: Benefit for Infant Performance on Problem-Solving but not on Recognition Memory Tasks at Age 9 months." *American Journal of Clinical Nutrition.* 85:1572-1577 (2007).
295. Sinn N, Bryan JJ. "Effect of Supplementation with Polyunsaturated Fatty Acids and Micronutrients on Learning and Behavior Problems Associated with Child ADHD." *Dev Behav Pediatr.* 28: 82-91 (2007).
296. Dalton, et al. "A Randomized Control Trial in Schoolchildren Showed Improvement in Cognitive Function After Consuming a Bread Spread, Containing Fish Flour From a Marine Source." *Prostagl., Leuk., and EFAs.* 80: 143-149, 2009.
297. Effect of Supplementation with Polyunsaturated Fatty Acids and Micronutrients on Learning and Behavior Problems Associated with Child ADHD. Sinn N and Bryan J. J Dev Behav Pediatr. 28: 82-91 (2007).
298. Kim JL, et al. "Fish Consumption and school Grades in Swedish Adolescents : a study of the large general population." *Acta Paediatrica*, 99: 72-77 , 2010.
299. Stamp LK, et al. "Diet and rheumatoid arthritis: A review of the literature." *Seminars in Arthritis.* 35:77-94, 2005.
300. Sundstrom B, et al. "Supplementation of omega-3 fatty acids in patients with ankylosing spondylitis." *Scand J Rheumatol.* 35:359-362 (2006).
301. Maroon JC, Bost JW. "Omega-3 Fatty acids (fish oil) as an anti-inflammatory: an alternative to nonsteroidal anti-inflammatory drugs for discogenic pain." *Surgical Neurology*, 65 : 326-311 (2006).
302. Kelley DS, et al. "DHA Supplementation Decreases Serum C-Reactive Protein and Other Markers of Inflammation in Hypertriglyceridemic Men." *J. Nutr.* 139 :495-501, 2009.
303. Chua B, et al. "Dietary Fatty Acids and the 5-Year Incidence of Age-Related Maculopathy." *Arch Ophthalmol.* 124:981-986 (2006).

304. Chang, ET, et al. "Nutrient Intake and Risk of Non-Hodgkin's Lymphoma." *Am J Epidemiol.* 164:1222-1232 (2006).
305. Kuriki K, et al. "Risk of Colorectal Cancer Is Linked to Erythrocyte Compositions of Fatty Acids as Biomarkers for Dietary Intakes of Fish, Fat, and Fatty Acids." *Cancer Epidemiol Biomarkers Prev.* 15(10):1791-1798 (2006).
306. Geelen, et al. "Fish Consumption, n-3 Fatty Acids, and Colorectal Cancer: A Meta-Analysis of Prospective Cohort Studies." *American Journal of Epidemiology.* 166(10):1116-1125 (2007).
307. Black HS, Rhodes LE. "The potential of omega-3 fatty acids in the prevention of non-melanoma skin cancer." *Cancer Detection and Prevention.* 30: 224-232, 2006.
308. Hakim, et al. "Fat intake and risk of squamous cell carcinoma of the skin." *Nutr. Cancer.* 36: 155-162, 2000.
309. Lee JH, et al. "Omega-3 Fatty Acids for Cardioprotection." *Mayo Clin Proc.* 83:324-332, (2008).
310. Wang S, et al. "Fish Oil Supplementation Improves Large Arterial Elasticity in Overweight Hypertensive Patients." *European Journal of Clinical Nutrition.* Ahead of Publication (2007).
311. Balk EM, et al. "Effects of omega-3 fatty acids on serum markers of cardiovascular disease risk: A systematic review." *Atherosclerosis.* 2006.
312. Bhalodkar NC, et al. "Accuracy of the ratio of triglycerides to high-density lipoprotein cholesterol for predicting low-density lipoprotein cholesterol particle size, phenotype B, and particle concentrations among Asian Indians." *Am. J. Cardiol.* 97:1007-9, 2006.
313. Cullen P. "Evidence the triglycerides are an independent coronary heart disease risk factor." *Am. J. Cardiol.* 86:943-949, 2000.
314. *Omega-3 Learnings for Health & Medicine.* Medical Findings. http://www.omega3learning.purdue.edu/medical-findings/
315. Benton D, Donohoe RT. "The effects of nutrients on mood." *Public Health Nutr.* 1999 Sep;2(3A):403-9.
316. Beers MH. "Nutritional disorders - Thiamin". *The Merck Manual of Diagnosis and Therapy, Eighteenth Edition.*
317. Calingasan NY, Gibson GE. "Vascular endothelium is a site of free radical production and inflammation in areas of neuronal loss in thiamine-deficient brain." *Ann N Y Acad Sci.* 2000 Apr;903:353-6.
318. Calingasan NY et al., "Disturbances of the Blood-Brain Barrier without Expression of Amyloid Precursor Protein-Containing Neuritic Clusters or Neuronal Loss during Late Stages of Thiamine Deficiency in Guinea Pigs." *Dev Neurosci* 1998;20:454-461.
319. Rodriguez-Martin JL, Qizilbash N, Lopez-Arrieta JM. "Thiamine for Alzheimer's disease." *Cochrane Database Syst Rev.* 2001;(2):CD001498.
320. McCully KS, "Homocysteine, vitamins, and vascular disease prevention." *Am J Clin Nutr.* 2007 Nov;86(5):1563S-8S.
321. Chiaki I. "Increase of total homocysteine concentration in cerebrospinal fluid in patients with Alzheimer's disease and Parkinson's disease". *Life Sciences Volume 77*, Issue 15, 26 August 2005, Pages 1836-1843.
322. Goetz. *Textbook of clinical neurology.* "Vitamin deficiencies", 3rd edition.
323. Goetz. *Textbook of clinical neurology.* "Vitamin deficiencies", 3rd edition.
324. Gibson GE, Blass JP. "Nutrition and Brain Function" *Basic Neurochemistry: Molecular, Cellular and Medical Aspects, Sixth Edition.* Philadelphia, PA: Lippincott Raven Publishers. 1999. 697.
325. Munro HN. *Human Vitamin B6 Requirements.* National Academy Press. June 1978. 283.
326. Marcus R, Coulston AM. Water-soluble vitamins. *Goodman and Gilman's The Pharmacologic Basis of Therapeutics—7th edition.* New York, NY: MacMIllan Publishing Company, 1985. 1559-1562.
327. Reynolds EH. "Folic acid, ageing, depression, and dementia". BMJ 2002;324;1512-1515.
328. Coppen A. "Enhancement of the antidepressant action of fluoxetine by folic acid: a randomised, placebo controlled trial." *Journal of Affective Disorders*, Volume 60 , Issue 2 , Pages 121 - 130.
329. Durga J. "Folic Acid Supplementation Improved Cognitive Function in Older Adults". *J Clin Outcomes Manage* 2007 Mar;14(3):134-135.
330. Su LJ, Arab L. "Salad and Raw Vegetable Consumption and Nutritional Status in the Adult US Population: Results from the Third National Health and Nutrition Examination Survey."*Journal of the American Dietetic Association.* Volume 106, Issue 9 (September 2006).
331. Lawson W. "Brain food". *Psychology Today.* May/Jun 2003; 36, 3.
332. Goetz. *Textbook of clinical neurology. 3rd edition.* "Cobalamin (Vitamin B12)".

333. Lerner V, Kanevsky M. "Acute Dementia with Delirium Due to Vitamin B-12 Deficiency: A Case Report." *International Journal of Psychiatry in Medicine.* Amityville: 2002/2003. Vol. 32, Iss. 2; p. 215.
334. Jones KM. "Prevalent Vitamin B-12 Deficiency in Twelve-Month-Old Guatemalan Infants Is Predicted by Maternal B-12 Deficiency and Infant Diet". *J. Nutr.* 137: 1307–1313, 2007.
335. Mozafar A. "Enrichment of some B-vitamins in plants with application of organic fertilizers". *Plant and Soil* 167:305-311, 1994.
336. Watanabe F. "Vitamin B12 Sources and Bioavailability". *Exp Biol Med* 232:1266–1274, 2007.
337. Mischoulon, Fava. *American Journal of Clinical Nutrition* 2002 Nov;76(5):1158S-61S.
338. Gibson GE, Blass JP. "Nutrition and Brain Function" *Basic Neurochemistry: Molecular, Cellular and Medical Aspects, Sixth Edition*. Philadelphia, PA: Lippincott Raven Publishers. 1999. Chapter 33.
339. Craciunescu CN, Albright CD, Mar MH, Song J, Zeisel SH. "Choline availability during embryonic development alters progenitor cell mitosis in developing mouse hippocampus." *J Nutr.* 2003 Nov;133(11):3614-8.
340. McKeon-O'Malley C, Siwek D, Lamoureux JA, Williams CL, Kowall NW. "Prenatal choline deficiency decreases the cross-sectional area of cholinergic neurons in the medial septal nucleus." *Brain Res.* 2003 Jul 11;977(2):278-83.
341. Zeisel SH. "Nutritional Importance of Choline for Brain Development". *Journal of the American College of Nutrition*, Vol. 23, No. 6, 621S–626S (2004).
342. Guo-Ross SX, Jones KH, Shetty AK, Wilson WA, Swartzwelder HS. "Prenatal dietary choline availability alters postnatal neurotoxic vulnerability in the adult rat." *Neurosci Lett.* 2003 May 1;341(2):161-3.
343. Blount PJ, et al. "Clinical use of cholinomimetic agents: A review". *The Journal of Head Trauma Rehabilitation*; Aug 2002; 17, 4
344. Alvarez XA, Laredo M, Corzo D, Fernandez-Novoa L, Mouzo R, Perea JE, Daniele D, Cacabelos R. "Citicoline improves memory performance in elderly subjects." *Methods Find Exp Clin Pharmacol.* 1997 Apr;19(3):201-10.
345. Spiers PA, Myers D, Hochanadel GS, Lieberman HR, Wurtman RJ. "Citicoline improves verbal memory in aging." *Arch Neurol.* 1996 May;53(5):441-8.
346. Adibhatla RM, Hatcher JF, Dempsey RJ. "Cytidine-5'-diphosphocholine affects CTP-phosphocholine cytidylyltransferase and lyso-phosphatidylcholine after transient brain ischemia." *J Neurosci Res.* 2004 May 1;76(3):390-6.
347. Davalos A, et al. "Oral citicoline in acute ischemic stroke: an individual patient data pooling analysis of clinical trials." *Stroke.* 2002 Dec;33(12):2850-7.
348. Davalos A, et al. "Oral citicoline in acute ischemic stroke: an individual patient data pooling analysis of clinical trials." *Stroke.* 2002 Dec;33(12):2850-7.
349. Zeisel SH, Mar MH, Howe JC, Holden JM. "Concentrations of choline-containing compounds and betaine in common foods." *J Nutr.* 2003 May;133(5):1302-7.
350. Buchman AL, et al. JPEN *J Parenter Enteral Nutr.* 2001 Sep-Oct;25(5):260-8.
351. Zeisel SH, Mar MH, Howe JC, Holden JM. "Concentrations of choline-containing compounds and betaine in common foods." *J Nutr.* 2003 May;133(5):1302-7.
352. Zeisel SH, Mar MH, Howe JC, Holden JM. "Concentrations of choline-containing compounds and betaine in common foods." *J Nutr.* 2003 May;133(5):1302-7.
353. Perrig WJ, et al. "The Relation Between Antioxidants and Memory Performance in the Old and Very Old", *J Am Geriatr Soc* 1997 (Jun); 45 (6): 718–24.
354. Wilkins CH, et al. "Vitamin D deficiency is associated with low mood and worse cognitive performance in older adults." *Am J Geriatr Psychiatry* 2006; 14:1032-1040.
355. Jorde R. "Neuropsychological function in relation to serum parathyroid hormone and serum 25-hydroxyvitamin D levels". *J Neurol* (2006) 253 : 464–470.
356. McGrath J. "Vitamin D supplementation during the first year of life and risk of schizophrenia: a Finnish birth cohort study." *Schizophrenia Research*, Volume 67 , Issue 3. 237-245.
357. Evatt ML. "Prevalence of Vitamin D Insufficiency in Patients With Parkinson Disease and Alzheimer Disease." *Arch Neurol*. 2008;65(10):1348-1352.
358. Garcion E, et al. "New clues about vitamin D functions in the nervous system". *TRENDS in Endocrinology & Metabolism* Vol.13 No.3 April 2002.
359. Levitan IB, et al. "The Neuron: Cell and Molecular Biology". 2002. 226.

360. Institute of Medicine (U.S.). Committee on Optimization of Nutrient Composition of Military Rations for Short-Term, High-Stress Situations, "Nutrient Composition of Rations for Short-term, High-intensity Combat Operations". 2006. 77.
361. Apel C. "The neuroprotective effect of dental pulp cells in models of Alzheimer's and Parkinson's disease". *J Neural Transm* (2009) 116:71–78.
362. Heese K. "Nerve Growth Factor, Neural Stem Cells and Alzheimer's Disease". *Neurosignals* 2006–07;15:1–12.
363. Brown J. "1,25-Dihydroxyvitamin D3 induces nerve growth factor, promotes neurite outgrowth and inhibits mitosis in embryonic rat hippocampal neurons." *Neuroscience Letters* 343 (2003) 139–143.
364. Koji A. "Therapeutic Potential of Neurotrophic Factors and Neural Stem Cells Against Ischemic Brain Injury". *Journal of Cerebral Blood Flow and Metabolism* 20:1393–1408.
365. De Rosa R. "Intranasal administration of nerve growth factor (NGF) rescues recognition memory deficits in AD11 anti-NGF transgenic mice". *PNAS*, March 8, 2005, vol. 102, no. 10, 3811–3816.
366. Kalueff AV. "Anticonvulsant effects of 1,25-dihydroxyvitamin D in chemically induced seizures in mice." *Brain Res Bull.* 2005 Sep 30;67(1-2):156-60.
367. Trouillas P. "Redifferentiation therapy in brain tumors: Long-lasting complete regression of glioblastomas and an anaplastic astrocytoma under long term 1-alpha-hydroxycholecalciferol". *Journal of Neuro - Oncology.* Dordrecht: Jan 2001. Vol. 51, Iss. 1; 57.
368. Springhouse. "Professional Guide to Diseases". Lippincott Williams & Wilkins; Ninth Edition edition (February 1, 2008). 553.
369. Beers MH. "Nutritional disorders - Vitamin D", *The Merck Manual of Diagnosis and Therapy, Eighteenth Edition.*
370. *UC Berkely Wellness Letter*, October 2005, 2.
371. Canadian Cancer Society, press release 8 June 2007. Access from: http://www.cancer.ca/Canada-wide/About%20us/Media%20centre/CW-Media%20releases/CW-2007/Canadian%20Cancer%20Society%20Announces%20Vitamin%20D%20Recommendation.aspx?sc_lang=en — Accessed Jan-9-2009.
372. Morris MC, et al. "Vitamin E and Cognitive Decline in Older Persons". *Arch Neurol.* 2002;59:1125-1132.
373. Beers MH. "Nutritional disorders - Vitamin E". *The Merck Manual of Diagnosis and Therapy, Eighteenth Edition.*
374. Dam, H. "The Antihaemorrhagic Vitamin Of The Chick", *Biochemical Journal* XXIX (82): 1273–1285.
375. Harvey RA, et al. "Lippincott's Illustrated Reviews: Pharmacology", 4th Edition. 240.
376. Van Winckel M, et al. "Vitamin K, an update for the paediatrician", Feb 2009. Vol. 168, Iss. 2; pg. 127, 8 pg.
377. Schurgers LJ, et al. "Regression of warfarin-induced medial elastocalcinosis by high intake of vitamin K in rats", *Blood.* 2007; 109:2823-2831.
378. Feskanich D, et al. "Vitamin K intake and hip fractures in women: a prospective study", *Am J Clin Nutr* 1999;69:74–9.
379. Cees V, et al. "Beyond Deficiency: Potential benefits of increased intakes of vitamin K for bone and vascular health", *Eur J Nutr* (2004) 43 : 325–335.
380. Anonymous. "Arthritis; Research findings from Vanderbilt University update understanding of arthritis", *Heart Disease Weekly.* Atlanta: Nov 2, 2008. 81.
381. Rauscher FM, et al. "Aging, Progenitor Cell Exhaustion, and Atherosclerosis", *Circulation.* 2003;108:457-463.
382. Zuliani G, et al. "High interleukin-6 plasma levels are associated with functional impairment in older patients with Vascular dementia", *Int J Geriatr Psychiatry* 2007; 22: 305–311.
383. Presse N, et al. "Low Vitamin K Intakes in Community-Dwelling Elders at an Early Stage of Alzheimer's Disease", American Dietetic Association. *Journal of the American Dietetic Association.* Chicago: Dec 2008. Vol. 108, Iss. 12; 2095.
384. Anonymous. "Vitamin K Deficiency In the Elderly", *Nutrition Health Review.* Haverford: 2007. 16.
385. World Health Organization. "Vitamin and Mineral Requirements in Human Nutrition", World Health Organization, Food and Agriculture Organization of the United Nations - Medical - 2004, 121.
386. Aschenbrenner DS, Venable SJ. "Drug Therapy in Nursing", Lippincott Williams & Wilkins; Third Edition edition (February 1, 2008), 608.
387. Alberts B. "Voltage-gated Ca2++ Channels convert electrical signals into chemical signals at nerve terminals". *Essential Cell Biology: An Introduction to the Molecular Biology of the Cell.* 2004. 417.
388. Rhoades, RA. "Electromechanical and pharmacomechanical coupling triggers contractions in gastrointestinal muscles". *Medical Physiology: Principles for Clinical Medicine.* 2008. 465.

389. Agarwal KN. "Iron and the brain: neurotransmitter receptors and magnetic resonance spectroscopy", British Journal of Nutrition (2001), 85, Suppl. 2, S147–S150.
390. Morath DJ, et al, "Iron Deficiency during Embryogenesis and Consequences for Oligodendrocyte Generation in vivo", *Developmental Neuroscience*. Basel: Mar-Jun 2002. Vol. 24, Iss. 2-3; 197.
391. Lozoff B, et al. "Long-Lasting Neural and Behavioral Effects of Iron Deficiency in Infancy", *Nutrition Reviews*. Washington: May 2006. Vol. 64, Iss. 5; p. S34.
392. Lozoff B, et al., "Long-Lasting Neural and Behavioral Effects of Iron Deficiency in Infancy", *Nutrition Reviews*. Washington: May 2006. Vol. 64, Iss. 5; S34.
393. Abalkhail B, Shawky S. "Prevalence of daily breakfast intake, iron deficiency anaemia and awareness of being anaemic among Saudi school students." *Int J Food Sci Nutr*. 2002 Nov;53(6):519-28.
394. *Blood*. 2002 Aug 1;100(3):879-87.
395. Jeney V, et al. "Pro-oxidant and cytotoxic effects of circulating heme.", *Clinics in Geriatric Medicine*, Volume 18, Number 3, August 2002.
396. Mandell, Bennett, & Dolin: *Principles and Practice of Infectious Diseases*, 6th ed.; Chapter 10 - Nutrition, Immunity, and Infection.
397. Harris RS, Mattes RD. "Appetite and Food Intake: Behavioral and Physiological Considerations", *CRC*; 1 edition (February 21, 2008), P. 327,238.
398. Gray J, et al. "Lung Cancer Chemoprevention ACCP Evidence-Based Clinical Practice Guidelines (2nd Edition)", *Chest* - Volume 132, Issue 3 (September 2007).
399. Reid ME, et al. "Selenium supplementation and colorectal adenomas: an analysis of the nutritional prevention of cancer trial", *Int J Cancer* - 1-APR-2006; 118(7): 1777-81.
400. Wardwell L, et al. "Nutrient Intake and Immune Function of Elderly Subjects", *J Am Diet Assoc*. 2008;108:2005-2012.
401. Feldman. *Sleisenger & Fordtran's Gastrointestinal and Liver Disease*, 8th ed. CHAPTER 15 - Nutritional Assessment and Management of the Malnourished Patient.
402. Vinceti M, Wei ET, Malagoli C, Bergomi M, Vivoli G. "Adverse health effects of selenium in humans." *Rev Environ Health*. 2001 Jul-Sep;16(4):233-51.
403. Yang G, Yin S, Zhou R, Gu L, Yan B, Liu Y, Liu Y. Studies of safe maximal daily dietary Se-intake in a seleniferous area in China. Part II: Relation between Se-intake and the manifestation of clinical signs and certain biochemical alterations in blood and urine. J Trace Elem Electrolytes Health Dis. 1989 Sep;3(3):123-30.
404. Yang G, Zhou R. Further observations on the human maximum safe dietary selenium intake in a seleniferous area of China. J Trace Elem Electrolytes Health Dis. 1994 Dec;8(3-4):159-65.
405. Vinceti M, Wei ET, Malagoli C, Bergomi M, Vivoli G. Adverse health effects of selenium in humans. Rev Environ Health. 2001 Jul-Sep;16(4):233-51.
406. Vine RP, et al. "Winemaking: From Grape Growing to Marketplace", Springer; 2nd edition (October 2002), 113.
407. Barnes S. "Nutritional Genomics, Polyphenols, Diets, and Their Impact on Dietetics", *J Am Diet Assoc*. 2008;108:1888-1895.
408. Najm W, Lie D. "Dietary Supplements Commonly Used for Prevention", *Prim Care Clin Office Pract* 35 (2008) 749–767.
409. Han Y, al. "Neuroprotective effects of resveratrol against beta-amyloid-induced neurotoxicity in rat hippocampal neurons: involvement of protein kinase C", *Br J Pharmacol*. 2004 March; 141(6): 997–1005.
410. Truelsen T, et al. "Intake of Beer, Wine, and Spirits and Risk of Stroke The Copenhagen City Heart Study", *Stroke*. 1998;29:2467-2472.
411. Tsai SK, et al. "Resveratrol neuroprotective effects during focal cerebral ischemia injury via nitric oxide mechanism in rats", *Journal of Vascular Surgery* Volume 46, Issue 2, August 2007, 346-353.
412. Jang JH, Surh YJ. "Protective effect of resveratrol on Beta-amyloid-induced oxidative PC12 cell death", *Free Radical Biology and Medicine* Volume 34, Issue 8, 15 April 2003, Pages 1100-1110.
413. Savaskan E, et al. "Red wine ingredient resveratrol protects from beta-amyloid neurotoxicity", *Gerontology*. 2003 Nov;49(6):380-3.
414. Pencea V, et al. "Infusion of Brain-Derived Neurotrophic Factor into the Lateral Ventricle of the Adult Rat Leads to New Neurons in the Parenchyma of the Striatum, Septum, Thalamus, and Hypothalamus", *The Journal of Neuroscience*, September 1, 2001, 21(17):6706-6717.

415. Araya AV, et al. "Effect of Exercise on Circulating Brain Derived Neurotrophic Factor (BDNF) in Overweight and Obese Subjects", Poster presented at the Endocrine Society;s 90th Meeting. June 15-18 (2008). San Francisco, CA.
416. Duan, Wenzhen, et al. "Reversal of Behavioral and Metabolic Abnormalities, an Insulin Resistance Syndrome, by Dietary Restriction in Mice Deficient in Brain-Derived Neurotrophic Factor", *Endocrinology* 144(6):2446–2453.
417. Duan, Wenzhen, et al. "Dietary restriction normalizes glucose metabolism and BDNF levels, slows disease progression, and increases survival in huntingtin mutant mice", PNAS March 4, 2003 vol. 100 no. 5 2911-2916.
418. Tsai SJ et al., "Association study of brain-derived neurotrophic factor and apolipoprotein E polymorphisms and cognitive function in aged males without dementia", Neurosci Lett - 12-MAR-2008; 433(2): 158-62.
419. Terao T, Pesaresi L. "Mood Stabilizers for Alcoholism: BDNF Hypothesis", *Psychiatry* 2008; 11: 16-20.
420. Antti Tanskanen et al., "Fish Consumption and Depressive Symptoms in the General Population in Finland", *Psychiatr Serv* 52:529-531, April 2001.
421. White, Ellen G. *Ministry of Healing*. p. 301.
422. Algeri S. et al. "Age-related ability of rats kept on a life-long hypocaloric diet in a spatial memory test. Longitudinal observations", *Neurobiol Aging*. 1991 Jul-Aug;12(4):277-82.
423. Cournot M. "Relation between body mass index and cognitive function in healthy middle-aged men and women", *Neurology* 2006;67:1208-1214.
424. Carter JP, Brown J. "Dr. Cupp's Simple Approach to Weight Loss." Journal of the Louisiana State Medical Society 1985;137 (6):35-38
425. Mathews R. "Importance of breakfast to cognitive performance and health." *Perspectives in Applied Nutrition* 1996;3(3):204-212.
426. Fernald L, Ani CC, Grantham-mcgregor S. "Does school breakfast benefit children's educational performance?" *Afr Health*. 1997 Sep;19(6):19-20.
427. Abalkhail B, Shawky S. "Prevalence of daily breakfast intake, iron deficiency anaemia and awareness of being anaemic among Saudi school students." *Int J Food Sci Nutr*. 2002 Nov;53(6):519-28.
428. Cueto S. "Breakfast and performance." *Public Health Nutr*. 2001 Dec;4(6A):1429-31.
429. Marquez Acosta M, Sutil de Naranjo R, Rivas de Yepez CE, Rincon Silva M, Torres M, Yepez RD, Portillo Z. "Influence of breakfast on cognitive functions of children from an urban area in Valencia, Venezuela". Article in Spanish. *Arch Latinoam* Nutr. 2001 Mar;51(1):57-63.
430. Mathews R. "Importance of breakfast to cognitive performance and health." *Perspectives in Applied Nutrition* 1996;3(3):210.
431. Morley JE. "Food for thought", *Am J Clin Nutr* 2001;74:567–8.
432. Kaplan RJ. "Dietary protein, carbohydrate, and fat enhance memory performance in the halthy elderly", Am J Clin Nutr 2001;74:687–93.
433. Allgower A, Wardle J, Steptoe A. "Depressive symptoms, social support, and personal health behaviors in young men and women." *Health Psychol*. 2001 May;20(3):223-7.
434. Smith AP, Clark R, Gallagher J. "Breakfast cereal and caffeinated coffee: effects on working memory, attention, mood, and cardiovascular function." *Physiol Behav*. 1999 Aug 1;67(1):9-17.
435. Korol DL. "Enhancing cognitive function across the life span." *Ann N Y Acad Sci*. 2002 Apr;959:167-79.
436. Reid M, Hammersley R. "The effects of sucrose and maize oil on subsequent food intake and mood." *Br J Nutr*. 1999 Dec;82(6):447-55.
437. Wells AS, Read NW. "Influences of fat, energy, and time of day on mood and performance." *Physiol Behav*. 1996 Jun;59(6):1069-76.
438. Scarmeas N, et al. "Mediterranean Diet and Mild Cognitive Impairment", *Arch Neurol*. 2009;66(2):216-225.
439. Kang J. "Fruit and vegetable consumption and cognitive decline in women." Presented at: 9th International Conference on Alzheimer's Disease and Related Disorders; July 18, 2004; Philadelphia, Pa.
440. USDA National Nutrient Database for Standard Reference, http://www.nal.usda.gov/fnic/foodcomp/search/.
441. Talalay P, Fahey JW. "Phytochemicals from Cruciferous Plants Protect against Cancer by Modulating Carcinogen Metabolism." *J. Nutr*. 2001 131: 3027S-3033.
442. Beliveau R, Gingras D. "Role of nutrition in preventing cancer." *Can Fam Physician* 2007 53: 1905-1911.
443. Bellisle F. "Effects of diet on behaviour and cognition in children." British Journal of Nutrition (2004), 92: S227-S232 Cambridge University Press.

444. Prinz RJ, Riddle DB. "Associations Between Nutrition and Behavior in 5-year-old Children." *Nutr Rev* 1986 May;44 Suppl:151-158.

445. Morris MC, et al., "Dietary Copper and High Saturated and trans Fat Intakes Associated With Cognitive Decline", *Arch Neurol*, Aug 2006; 63: 1085 - 1088.

446. Beydoun MA, et al., "Plasma n–3 fatty acids and the risk of cognitive decline in older adults: the Atherosclerosis Risk in Communities Study", *American Journal of Clinical Nutrition*, Vol. 85, No. 4, 1103-1111, April 2007.

447. Moriyama T, Uezu K, et al. "Effects of dietary phosphatidylcholine on memory in memory deficient mice with low brain acetylcholine concentration." *Life Sci* 1996:58(6):PL111-118.

Chapter 12

TOXINS ARE NOT ONLY FOUND IN OBVIOUS PLACES MARKED BY A "HAZARDOUS MATERIALS" SIGN.

# Protect Against Toxins

## *Exposure to environmental toxins compromises your mental performance.*

Local Ohio doctors initially thought 15-year old Richard Johnson's problems were "all in his head." After all, he didn't appear acutely ill, and his complaints—aches, irritability, and inability to think clearly— sounded like mere excuses for his declining school performance. However, upon further evaluation, Richard's physicians made a chilling realization: his symptoms were due to elemental mercury poisoning. In fact, Richard's urine mercury measurement was more than 40 times higher than acceptable levels.

When checked a couple of weeks later, his 11-year-old sister, Susie, had urine mercury levels nearly double that of her brother! In addition to neuropsychiatric impairment, Susie's mercury poisoning caused severe arm and leg weakness. Although prompt treatment was instituted once the diagnosis was made, it took nearly three months before Susie could walk even short distances on her own.[448]

Surely every parent would be motivated to ensure his or her children are never exposed to toxic levels of mercury. What mistake did Richard and Susie's parents make?

Case investigation by the Columbus, Ohio Health Department revealed a problem no parent could have reasonably suspected. The tenant who had lived in the apartment prior to the Johnsons had spilled a large jar of "quicksilver" (elemental mercury) on the premises. Once that history was obtained, a series of air mercury measurements confirmed a "worst case" scenario: throughout the apartment mercury levels registered 100 to nearly 1,000 times over acceptable limits.

Although the Johnson's exposure was from inhaled mercury, far more cases are attributed to ingested mercurial compounds. This environmental catastrophe was recognized in the 1950s and 60s when literally hundreds of residents of Minamata City in Southwestern Japan were stricken with a neurologic illness. Ultimately the problem was traced to consumption of mercury-laden local seafood. The mercury source? A manufacturing waste product the Chisso chemical company had been dumping into nearby Minamata Bay for years.[449] In 2001, the Japanese government certified that 2,265 persons had been stricken by the poisoning.

Mercury is just one of many toxins that can impair brain health. And like the case of the Johnsons or the residents around Minamata Bay, those affected by such poisons often don't realize their danger until their situation is far advanced.

In this chapter, we'll discuss some of the most dangerous mental health-robbing environmental toxins. You'll gain insights into how to decrease your risk of exposure, as well as some practical insights as to what to do if you're already encountering problems. First, let's take a look at sources of toxin exposure where we work, live, and play.

## HAZARDS IN THE WORKPLACE

Industry has brought tremendous advantages to society, while at the same time adding greatly to our global toxic burden. It is beyond the scope of this chapter to give an exhaustive list of toxins found in industrial settings. However, regardless of your line of employment, it behooves you to become familiar with every chemical being used in your workplace. Your employer is required to have MSDS (material safety data sheets) available, which give detailed information about all potential on-the-job exposures. I recommend you invest the time to be cognizant of the risks and safety precautions related to compounds to which you may become exposed.

City life exposes residents to a host of pollutants in the air.

## URBAN LIVING AND LEAD EXPOSURE

Lead paint, especially on older structures, continues to be a problem, even in America. Many exposures are a result of soil contamination—and ensuing toxin laden dust. Consequently, more densely populated urban housing environments increase the risk that you and your family will be exposed to lead from another person's home—even if yours is lead free.

Another factor linked with higher blood lead levels is living in congested urban areas, especially where leaded gasoline is currently used (or has been used to a significant extent in the past).[450] Further increasing the risk of lead exposure in urban areas is the close proximity to factories and other industries. A recent study carefully analyzed soil samples for heavy metals and found the closer one got to industrial facilities, the greater the soil contamination with lead and other potentially toxic metals like arsenic, barium, chromium, manganese and nickel.[451]

Lead is a toxin widely recognized for its harmful effects on children. The negative consequences are greater than could be feasibly described in detail here. However, because few are aware of lead's dangers during and before pregnancy, several comments are warranted. First of all, lead exposure can prevent a couple from ever conceiving a child as it has been linked to male infertility.[452,453]

Secondly, lead has adverse fetal effects (summarized in **Figure 12.1**). In general, the more lead in a mother's bones, the lower her child's birth weight. By measuring bone lead levels, researchers at Mexico's National Institute for Public Health were able to estimate mothers' total exposure to this heavy metal. When women were divided into four groups based on bone lead levels, babies born to women in the highest exposure category weighed 156 grams (5.5 ounces) less, on average, than offspring of the women with the lowest bone lead levels.[454]

Birth length and head circumference (a predictor of later intelligence) also decreased as bone lead levels increased.[455] In addition, children of heavily lead-exposed mothers grow slower in their first month of life.[456] Exclusively breastfed infants fare best in the weight gain department, yet those benefits are partially offset by increased maternal lead stores. During lactation, lead is apparently mobilized from the bone into the bloodstream and then into breast milk.

Other researchers have documented additional fetal problems stemming from *in utero* lead exposure. These include fetal death (stillbirth), growth restriction, seizures, brain impairment (including developmental problems affecting speech and language), lower I.Q., and attention deficit problems.[457]

### ADVERSE FETAL EFFECTS FROM MATERNAL LEAD EXPOSURE

- growth restriction
- seizures
- fetal death or stillbirth
- low birth weight
- lower I.Q.
- brain impairment
- attention deficit problems
- developmental issues

***Figure 12.1***

Women need to be cognizant of lead exposure long before they contemplate pregnancy. This is because lead remains in human bones for many years. Thus, distant exposure can affect the fetus as lead is mobilized from the bone and enters the maternal and then fetal circulation.[458] Therefore, every female of present or future reproductive capacity should be familiar with potential sources of lead exposure.

Before leaving the subject of lead's effects on brain health, let me emphasize that anyone, regardless of area of residence, can face lead exposure problems. For example, heavy use of canned foods has been linked to increased lead exposure. Similarly, plumbing fixtures may be sources of this toxic metal. The use of lead-glazed pottery, especially when employed for cooking food, is another major source of exposure in many parts of the world. On the other hand, calcium intake has been associated with lower lead levels (unless a person is using a calcium supplement that is contaminated with lead).

Even exposures of other family members from outside the home at a distant work place can present problems for a pregnant woman. Consider the situation with auto radiator repair workers. Dust lead levels in the homes of such workers are nearly 40 times higher than in homes where no one works in a lead-related trade.[459] This leads to a greater concern: blood lead measurements in those households. Perhaps this can be seen best by looking at exposures in the most vulnerable group—children—as illustrated in **Figure 12.2**.

Because of a variety of habits (playing on the floor, putting their hands in their mouths, etc.), children tend to receive greater exposure from a given amount of lead dust in the home. However, the spouses of radiator repair workers, or others who are exposed to a high lead working environment, also tend to have higher blood lead levels as a result of increased dust lead concentrations.[460] Of course, if a woman herself works

**CHILDHOOD LEAD EXPOSURE BASED ON PATERNAL OCCUPATION**

| Father's Occupational Setting | Average Childhood Blood Lead Level |
|---|---|
| Fathers working in home-based workshops repairing radiators | 22.4 micrograms/dl |
| Fathers working in an external radiator repair workshop | 14.2 micrograms/dl |
| Fathers with no lead exposure | 5.6 micrograms/dl |

***Figure 12.2***

in such a high exposure occupation, we would expect her blood levels to be strikingly elevated.

## UNSUSPECTED LEAD EXPOSURE

A number of recent scientific reports have raised concerns about an often-unanticipated source of lead exposure: candles.[461,462,463,464,465] While we've made progress by eliminating lead from most U.S. gasoline sources, still some 900,000 American children less than 6 years of age have elevated lead levels.[466] With sales in the range of $2 billion yearly, candles may be a significant source of lead exposure.[467]

In 2002, Environmental Protection Agency (EPA) researchers published results on their analysis of 100 different types of candles—all of which had wicks that either appeared to contain a metal core or were covered by a metallic pigment.[468] (Metallic wicks are popular because the wick stays vertical, rendering it easier to light; candles with these wicks also burn slower, an attractive quality in the scented candle market.)

In the EPA study, among metal-wicked candles, 1 in 12 had wicks that were partially or largely composed of lead (lead composition ranged between 39 and 74 percent). Burning the lead-wicked candles in an enclosed research environment liberated sufficient amounts of lead to have adverse human health consequences.

Other research demonstrated that 20 percent of the lead contained in such wicks is volatilized, releasing microscopic, highly respirable particles into the air.[469] This lead is either inhaled or deposited on home surfaces (where small children are at high risk of ingesting it).

Based on such information, Australian lead poisoning expert Michael van Alphen concluded: "Child blood lead levels could readily exceed levels of 10 micrograms/dl, largely due to exposure to emissions from burning Pb [lead] wick core candles for several hours once per week."[470] (Blood lead levels of 10 micrograms/dl can lower intelligence and adversely affect other aspects of behavior and childhood development.)[471,472] Van Alphen went on to state, "The regular burning of multiple candles in small, poorly ventilated spaces could readily be associated with clinical Pb [lead] poisonings and death."

These dangers are not overblown. San Antonio, Texas-based physician, Claudia Miller, MD, MS, described how in her work in the Lower Rio Grande Valley, she frequently encounters many religious candles, some with lead wicks, in the very homes of children with respiratory problems like asthma. She wonders whether parents with sick children are more likely to pray and, ironically, burn religious candles because of their child's illness, oblivious to the fact that this very practice may be contributing to their child's poor health.[473]

Are candles safe if you avoid those with leaded wicks? Probably relatively so.[474] German researchers Lau and colleagues looked at organic pollutants given off by burning candles. Although candles emit a variety of toxic compounds including dioxins, dibenzofurans, polycyclic aromatic hydrocarbons (PAH), and some volatile organic compounds (VOC), all of these emissions are at extremely low concentrations. If you want to keep such exposures to an absolute minimum, you'll no doubt want to avoid even safe-wicked candles. However, I personally see no great danger in using candles periodically for special occasions.

## COUNTRY LIVING, WELL WATER, AND BRAIN HEALTH

**Well water isn't always free of toxins.**

A growing list of "sick-building" horror stories is enough to convince some to leave high-rise urban dwellings and businesses in favor of rural America. However, moving to the country does not guarantee freedom from environmental toxins. Consider a recent study from America's Great Lakes region.

In 2006 Wisconsin Department of Health researchers studied private drinking-water wells from 19 rural townships in their state. When their analysis of 2,233 household wells was completed they discovered 20% of the wells exceeded the federal drinking-water standard of 10 micrograms of arsenic per liter (mcg/L), with 11% showing levels greater than double that standard. One well topped the charts at a stunning 3,100 mcg/L.[475]

Although municipal water also may be drawn from arsenic-tainted waters, wells for public water supplies are constructed differently than home wells. Theses differences tend to decrease arsenic in "city water" as compared to private rural wells. As expressed by Dr. Melinda Erickson in her 2005 dissertation: "Public water system well construction practices such as seeking a thick, coarse aquifer and installing a long well screen, yield good water quantity. These well construction practices also, coincidentally, often yield low arsenic."[476]

Other researchers have probed the connection between arsenic, along with other metallic toxins, and brain health. 2010 saw the publication of an alarming hypothesis for all those taking comfort in rural residence as a haven for optimal mental health. After summarizing data connecting arsenic exposure to reduced memory and intellectual abilities in children and adolescents, researchers with the Department of Neurology at Texas Tech University Health Sciences Center dropped the latest bombshell: arsenic exposure may be a significant risk factor for Alzheimer's disease.[477]

If you live in a rural area and use water from a private well, it would be wise to have the source tested for arsenic levels.

## FARM CHEMICALS AND BRAIN THREATS

Agricultural chemicals pose yet another brain health threat to rural citizens. In a medical review examining potential causes of another neurodegenerative (brain-wasting) condition, Parkinson's disease, researchers at the U.S. National Institutes of Health, Environmental Health Sciences

**NEUROTOXIC PESTICIDES THAT MAY LEAD TO PARKINSON'S DISEASE**

- Pyridinium (paraquat)
- Dithiocarbamate (maneb)
- Complex inhibitor (rotenone)
- Organochlorine (dieldrin)

***Figure 12.3***

Division, looked at the agrochemical connection. These investigators found strong evidence suggesting a connection between Parkinson's and pesticide exposure.[478] Specifically, four different classes of common agricultural chemicals were linked to Parkinson's in the human observational studies and animal models they reviewed. These chemicals, which are neurotoxic to the dopamine-sensitive brain regions involved in Parkinson's Disease, appear in **Figure12.3**.

Although rural wells and agrochemicals can present mental health risks, this is no reason to eschew country living. Evidence suggests urban dwellers often face more dangerous and prevalent neurotoxins. I find environmental health topics often fuel the debate of whether rural or urban living is better for decreasing toxic exposures. So, let me make this clear: although both rural and urban living have risks and benefits from a toxic exposures perspective, you are much better off living in the country if you want the most favorable venue for brain health for you and your loved ones. I have at least two reasons for saying this. First, many of the toxin exposures in urban settings you have limited opportunity to mitigate, whereas in the country environment, you often have more control over key exposures. Second, country living provides unique opportunities for "environmental enrichment," a key component in protecting us from the consequences of toxic onslaughts that we'll explore later in this chapter.

## RETURN TO NATURE?

The Luddites among us may feel the urban-rural debate on such data is misdirected. Some might posit humankind's tampering with the environment is the source of all neurotoxic insults. Such a conclusion might lead one to relocate to a remote location and live off the things of nature: hunting, fishing, growing your own food, and collecting rain water.

However, there are two major flaws with such thinking. First, no matter where you live, it's impossible to escape the toll humanity has exacted on the environment. Second, nature itself can expose man to neurotoxins that are sometimes more devastating than many man-made threats.

As an illustration of the first, later in this chapter we'll consider the case of fish caught in "pristine" waters. The broad range of waters many fish traverse, combined with their tendency to concentrate toxins (as we learned in the previous chapter), render many fish toxin-laden.

With respect to natural neurotoxic threats, consider the example of a human illness designated as "possible estuarine-associated syndrome" (PEAS) by the U.S. Centers for Disease Control and Prevention (CDC). In a series of well-documented cases, Ritchie Shoemaker and Kenneth Hudnell (of the U.S. Environmental Protection Agency) illustrate how natural toxins can cause serious brain health threats.[479]

A 32-year-old fisherman exposed to fish infected with a germ called Pfiesteria piscicida, developed memory impairment, headache, hypersensitivity to bright light, weakness, fatigue, loss of appetite, and an extremely low level of higher mental ("executive") functioning. A 41-year-old soil scientist with similar exposure to estuarine-associated neurotoxins developed memory impairment, mild confusion, a severe throbbing headache, as well as other systemic symptoms. The authors documented three other cases in recreational fisherman and crab hunters ranging in age from 28 to 75. Symptoms included memory impairment, confusion, headache, hypersensitivity to bright light, and fatigue.

Although PEAS may sound like a very esoteric condition (indeed, it is unfamiliar to even many physicians), it underscores an extremely important point. Nature is replete with toxic and other environmental threats to our mental health—apart from any human involvement.

Clearly, there is no place we can move to avoid all environmental threats. Rather than further magnifying potential risks wherever we live (and provide additional material that might only fuel depressive thoughts), my goal is to make this chapter extremely practical and encouraging. Throughout this chapter, I'll provide information and counsel aimed at achieving three goals (summarized in **Figure 12.4**).

The first goal is to help you identify, or assess the significance of, neurotoxic threats in your environment. The second is to show you how to mitigate or avoid neurotoxic threats that may be present. The last aim is to

STEPS TO PROTECT AGAINST TOXINS

**1.** Identify threats in your environment.

**2.** Avoid or mitigate toxic exposure.

**3.** Overcome past exposure and unavoidable present exposures.

***Figure 12.4***

provide you with strategies to decrease your risk of brain-health problems in view of past toxic exposures (or ongoing unavoidable exposures).

Make it a priority to eliminate toxic habits. Your body, and brain, will thank you.

## THE MOST DANGEROUS ENVIRONMENTAL EXPOSURES

Ironically, for many of us, the greatest environmental risks we face are not those related to workplace toxins, chemicals discharged by nearby plants, or contaminated wells. Instead, some of the most brain-toxic environmental exposures are things we choose ourselves. Many people are concerned about exposure to the toxins in their environment that they can't control, while they continue to engage in activities that subject them to common toxins that they have complete control over. For example, alcohol, caffeine, tobacco, and certain elective medications all take a toll on mental performance.

In our increasingly medicated society, a host of popular drugs can seriously compromise brain health. If you think about it, this entire book has been about changing your environment. I've recommended you change your mental environment (how you think), your kitchen environment (the foods you keep in your home), and your environment as it relates to physical activity. Optimal brain health calls for changes in the pharmaceutical agents that we bring into our environment—into intimate contact with our bodies.

## AVOIDING SELF-INFLICTED NUTRITIONAL "TOXINS"

Typically, when I talk to audiences about the health benefits of nutrition, some are not content with my message of eating more fruits, whole grains, and vegetables. They want something more—and, perhaps, something less.

Think about it. Maintaining a healthy diet requires effort, planning, and resolve, especially if you aim to dramatically increase your consumption of plant foods. Many feel taking supplements is an easier way to reap nutritional benefits. They attempt to improve their diet, not by eating substantially better, but by adding vitamin and mineral supplements to their same cherished eating patterns. Unfortunately, tanking up on vitamins may not only fail to help—it can actually cause harm. And some of that harm comes in the form of impairing the brain. Some supplements of concern, listed in **Figure 12.5**, are discussed on the following pages.

No class of vitamins can be removed from scrutiny categorically. For example, B vitamins are water-soluble and thus easily eliminated. Consequently, those lacking a thorough biochemistry background might erroneously think these vitamins are nontoxic. Such is not the case. High doses of niacin (vitamin $B_3$) can result in delirium. Vitamin $B_6$ (pyridoxine) in large amounts can damage sensory nerves, cause coordination problems, and interfere with L-dopa, a medication used to treat Parkinson's disease.[480,481,482]

| TOO MUCH OF A GOOD THING: DIETARY SUPPLEMENTS OF CONCERN |
|---|
| • B Vitamins |
| • Folic Acid |
| • Fat Soluble Vitamins (A, D, E, K) |

***Figure 12.5***

Folic acid, although generally considered to be relatively non-toxic, can present problems in special situations. Doses of more than 400 μg per day can worsen seizure tendencies in individuals with epilepsy.[483] Similar dosages can partially correct the anemia caused by $B_{12}$ insufficiency—thus increasing the likelihood that $B_{12}$ deficiency (which often leads to brain and nervous system-damaging consequences) will not be detected.

Fat-soluble vitamins like vitamins A, D, E, and K are more difficult for the body to eliminate. As a result, relatively minor excesses on a daily basis can lead to major problems over the long haul. For example, many individuals have become ill as a result of taking modest amounts of additional vitamin A from supplements. A dose of 25,000 IU (7500 μg) of vitamin A per day (about eight times the recommended intake for an adult male) can cause a wide range of problems including neurological problems like headaches, fatigue, and coordination problems.[484,485,486,487]

Furthermore, loading up on vitamin A has been linked to dangerous rises in brain pressure (called "increased intracranial pressure" or "pseudotumor cerebri"). Such elevated pressures, if persistent, can cause vision loss.[488]

As we get up in years, the potential for vitamin A toxicity progressively increases.[489] Older individuals do not remove vitamin A from their bloodstreams efficiently. Therefore, potentially toxic vitamin A compounds called "retinyl esters" can persist in their circulation for about a week (as opposed to several hours in younger individuals).[490] For this reason, the older we are, the more careful we should be not to exceed vitamin A intake recommendations (900 μg or 3,000 IU for men; 700 μg or about 2300 IU for women).

Although I often emphasize our need for vitamin D because many fail to secure optimal amounts of this important vitamin/hormone, excessive vitamin D intake can cause severe problems. Among the mental health effects are headache, loss of appetite, confusion, weakness, dementia, and coma.[491,492,493,494] These varied manifestations result because excessive amounts of vitamin D lead to dangerous elevations in calcium and phosphorus blood levels. Toxicity is extremely unlikely if taking less than 2,000 IU daily. However, the most reliable way to ensure vitamin D adequacy—and guard against excess—is by periodically having your 25-OH vitamin D level measured.

Vitamin E also may be toxic in high amounts (above 1,200 IU or 800 mg daily), causing neuropsychiatric problems such as weakness, fatigue, headache, blurred vision, and sexual dysfunction.[495,496] Many Americans seem to think vitamin E will help them prevent heart disease and other circulatory disorders. However, a 2004 Archives of Internal Medicine paper put the vitamin E-circulatory connection in perspective.[497] After analyzing 14 years' worth of international scientific research, the authors identified seven high quality studies (representing, collectively, over 106,000 subjects) that examined whether vitamin E actually had heart preventive benefits. Careful statistical analysis of these studies revealed a stunning conclusion: vitamin E provided no heart benefits and even showed a trend toward increasing the risk of bleeding strokes—a serious threat to brain health.

What implications does this information have on taking a simple multiple vitamin pill or eating a bowl of Product 19 or Total cereal? Unlike many high potency supplements, most standard once-a-day vitamins or fortified foods don't provide excessive amounts of nutrients. It is, therefore, unlikely that serious repercussions will arise from using such products. Furthermore, multi-vitamin and mineral supplements are generally unnecessary for healthy individuals following sound eating practices.

Large doses of vitamins can sometimes benefit certain disease states. However, before using nutrients to treat disease, find a health professional who will work with you—preferably one who is well aware of the risks and benefits of such approaches. As we have seen in this section, indiscriminate use of vitamin supplements may well increase health problems rather than decreasing them.

**In the case of some supplemental nutrition, it is possible to get too much of a good thing.**

If you are concerned about getting sufficient nutrients for optimal health, simply prioritize plant foods like fruits and vegetables.[498,499] Such benefits simply have not been demonstrated with the use of vitamin pills.

Nutrient researcher Gilbert Omenn, MD, PhD, of the University of Michigan, recently summarized the world literature relating to nutrients and disease prevention: "Persons who eat a relatively large quantity of vegetables, fruits, and grains have a profoundly lower risk of death, particularly from cardiovascular disease and cancer."[500]

Interestingly, in his commentary, Omenn quoted a lay source of wisdom: *Forbes* magazine. "Take any new reports of disease-preventing vitamins with a grain of salt. When this is all sorted out, it could turn out that we will all have to take 50 or 60 different nutrients to get real benefit. 'That's a possibility,' says [Dr. Gary] Goodman, of the Hutchinson Cancer Research Center. 'It's called broccoli.'"[501]

## WARNING SIGNS & SYMPTOMS OF ADHD

- "always on the go"
- aggression; anger outbursts
- impatience
- taking dangerous risks
- restlessness
- procrastination
- poor relationships: at school/ work, with friends, in the home
- resistance to authority figures
- forgetfulness
- poorly organized work
- carelessness
- disorganization
- frequently late
- poor self esteem
- distractibility, failure to stick with and complete tasks

**Note: these characteristics can vary in their manifestations at different ages*

***Figure 12.6***

Dr. Omenn's emphasis is shared by many experts. Simply put, medical research indicates that taking supplements in no way comes close to offering the benefits of a plant food-rich diet. Rather than rushing to the nearest health food store or pharmacy to stock up on supplements, avail yourself of the true key to better health by eating more plant foods.

### EVALUATION FOR TOXIC EXPOSURES

There are a number of settings in which a person might suspect he or she has been exposed to a significant toxin load. These include direct testing of your water supply, physical signs and symptoms of possible toxin-related illness, public media reports about a toxic release, or a workplace announcement about an event that put employees at risk. Regardless of what your concern may be, how does one go about being evaluated for this possibility?

There is no substitute for working with a knowledgeable health professional. Individuals with special training in this area include toxicologists, industrial hygienists, occupational medicine specialists, and a variety of public health professionals. One good place to start is with a call to your state or local health department. Of course you can always work with your primary care provider, but not all such physicians are equally experienced in dealing with environmental health issues. Working with someone of experience is vital to ensure you have a proper, timely evaluation, and that costly, unnecessary tests are not ordered.

The area of toxic diagnosis is complex as different toxins are best evaluated with different testing strategies. **Appendix I** provides an example of some of the different tests used to evaluate for toxic exposures. Unless otherwise noted, all of this information is drawn from the federal Agency for Toxic Substances and Disease Registry (ATSDR), a division of the U.S. Centers for Disease Control (CDC), a worthwhile place to get toxin-related answers (www.atsdr.cdc.gov).

## ARE TOXINS INVOLVED IN THE DEVELOPMENT OF ADHD?

Attention-deficit/hyperactivity disorder (ADHD) is one of the Western world's major blights. With as many as 6% of children affected, few in the United States have not been impacted by this malady.[502,503]

However, familiarity with this condition has led to misconceptions regarding its nature. Although many lay people feel competent to judge someone as "hyperactive," hyperactivity is often, surprisingly, not present in ADHD. Instead, the diagnosis rests on two specific criteria: (1) persistent inattention or easy distractibility, and (2) behavioral and emotional impulsivity. Fewer than half of those affected manifest the classic hyperactivity or severe restlessness.[504] **Figure 12.6** provides an overview of some of the diverse signs and symptoms associated with ADHD.[505]

**Dangerous levels of toxins and allergic reactions have been linked to the development of ADHD in children.**

Even a quick glance at the list reveals ADHD is much more than an inconsequential "nuisance" problem. The disorder typically interferes with every aspect of a child's life: at home, at school, and with friends. Furthermore, ADHD has deleterious long-term effects on scholastic performance, career success, and both social and emotional development.[506] For example, fully one quarter of children with ADHD must repeat at least one school grade even though their academic abilities are otherwise adequate.[507] Affected adults also can experience far-ranging consequences. Therefore, it behooves every family, community, and nation to do what it can to prevent ADHD. Prompt diagnosis and treatment are also vital.

## FOODS AND ADDITIVES THAT PROVOKE ADHD SYMPTOMS

The classic approach to identifying food allergies and sensitivities is through something called an "elimination diet." An elimination diet begins by drastically limiting food choices. Which foods are excluded depends on the philosophy of the practitioner recommending the diet. Common foods eliminated on ADHD regimens include those with artificial colorings, flavorings, and preservatives as well as dairy, corn, citrus, chocolate, and wheat.[508,509] (Note: these agents should be completely excluded. Anything with these ingredients—even items like medications and toothpaste—should not be used.)[510] Many of the food categories I've listed were excluded in Feingold's famous protocol, published in 1973.

If the patient shows signs of improvement while following such a limited diet, then excluded foods are gradually re-introduced (one at a time) after a period of three weeks. If adding a certain food worsens symptoms, that food is labeled a potential contributor to ADHD symptoms and is again excluded. After several months of avoidance, even some of these foods may be used infrequently without provoking symptoms.[511]

Over a decade ago, British researchers Carter and colleagues used such an approach with 78 hyperactive children.[512] Fifty-nine of them improved with an elimination diet. In 19 of these dietary responders, the researchers were able to identify offending foods or additives that would reproduce behavioral problems even when concealed in other dishes.

More recently, another U.K. group found that certain compounds should be removed from the diet and not reintroduced. In a study of over 1,800 three-year-olds, Bateman and colleagues discovered that artificial colorings as well as the preservative, sodium benzoate, caused deterioration in behavior—whether or not the child had ADHD.[513]

The data is convincing enough that I believe all parents should consider an elimination diet for their children with ADHD. Although theoretically an educated parent could do so without medical supervision, the prudent course is to identify a doctor who can assist the family in implementing such a regimen. And by all means, don't leave off any medications (due to ingredient concerns or other reasons) without first consulting with the prescribing practitioner.

## TESTING THE WATERS: ASSURE A PURE SOURCE

Rather than waiting to develop symptoms or running expensive blood or hair analyses, I recommend you be proactive. Check the things you can in your environment and take steps to address any toxic issues before problems arise. One of the most prudent and cost-effective places to start is with water analysis.

Water analysis is important not only for sodium content but also to check for other water-borne impurities. The more we learn about biochemistry, metabolism, and the influence of toxins, the more we get

### ELIMINATION DIET FOR ADHD SYMPTOMS

1. Eliminate ALL consumption of possible sources of symptom inducement (such as artificial colorings, dairy, corn, citrus, chocolate, or wheat.)
2. After three weeks, slowly introduce the avoided foods one at a time to determine the problem substances.

*Figure 12.7*

concerned about current levels of water pollutants. It comes as no surprise that tainted water can negate many of the benefits of this vital fluid.

Microbiologically contaminated water is to be absolutely avoided, if at all possible, because it can cause both short- and long-term problems. Water-borne germs can cause troublesome and sometimes even fatal diseases. As a result, Western municipalities carefully monitor water for microbiological purity. However, chemically contaminated waters typically inflict their damage over the long haul. These insidious threats are often of greater concern in developed nations.

**Municipal water supplies may be considered safe, but toxin levels that are deemed insignificant in the short term can build up over time.**

For example, consider the widespread pollution of U.S. water supplies with nitrates. Although your water may come from a lake, stream, or other source of "surface water," over half of all Americans get their water supplies from "ground water." Ground water is the subterranean supply that is tapped by wells or emerges in the form of springs and is especially susceptible to nitrate contamination. These chemicals are derived from nitrogen-containing sources such as commercial fertilizers, animal manure, nitrogenous industrial wastes, septic systems, and even automobiles.[514] Because of the pervasive use of nitrogen in agriculture, water-soluble nitrates have passed through the soil and into ground water sources. These compounds persist for decades, so very high amounts can easily accumulate.

In the past, nitrate-tainted water primarily interested those focused on infant health. Newborns who ingest high levels of nitrates compromise their bloods' oxygen-transporting abilities, resulting in the potentially brain-damaging or fatal "blue baby" disorder. However, recent studies have raised concerns for linkages between nitrates and adult health problems such as cancer.[515]

Although discussing all potential water contaminants is beyond the scope of this chapter, several generalizations are warranted. If your "tap" water is obtained from a municipal source, it is likely to be relatively pure microbiologically (i.e., free of infectious agents). In this case, I recommend a reverse osmosis system to help eliminate other toxins from your water.

However, if you are drinking water from a private well, distillation combined with charcoal filtration may be a better option. Compared to municipal sources, well water is more often contaminated with germs; distillation's boiling phase provides thorough disinfection. Remember to use a system that combines a charcoal filter with the distiller. Otherwise you risk failing to extract certain organic toxins from your drinking water. They too evaporate during the boiling process.

Not convinced about whether or not your tap water requires additional treatment? That's OK. It's not difficult to get some hard facts about your water quality. **Appendix II** provides some sources of water quality information as well as options for addressing water contamination.

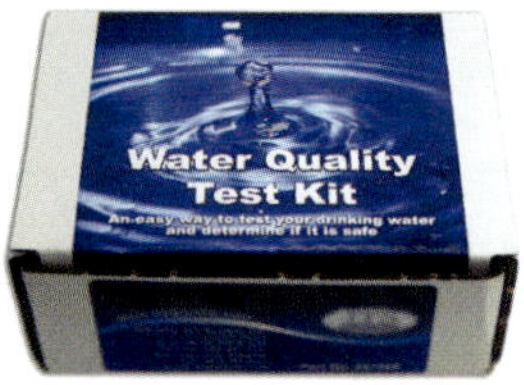


Have the quality of your tap water tested to determine if it is safe to drink unfiltered.

A final concern with water quality is worth mentioning. Factors which impact the purity of drinking water vary with time. Therefore, keep periodic tabs on your water's quality. As far as chemical contaminants, referring to an annual consumer confidence report should be adequate. If you use a private well or other non-regulated source, periodically have your water assessed. I recommend at least once every other year.

The situation with biological agents in the water is different. Breaks in disinfection processes can render your water microbiologically unsafe, even when it was safe the day before. How can you guard against this possibility?

First, if there have been any recent major environmental changes, listen to the news for any warnings about water safety or call your local water provider. Heavy rains, flooding, fires, tornadoes, power outages, and earthquakes are some examples of environmental situations that can disrupt the quality of your water supply.[516]

A second safeguard requires no more than looking at your tap water. Simply fill a clear glass from the tap. Let the water sit for a short while until all the air bubbles clear. Then look at the water. If it is at all cloudy, you are looking at an indication of excess particles. Those particles can be innocuous things like silt or clay residues, but they may also be related to germ contamination. Recent studies from Philadelphia suggest that water cloudiness (technically called "turbidity") is a risk factor for infectious illness especially in the most susceptible populations.[517,518]

What should you do if your water looks cloudy? Don't drink from the tap that day, or simply boil it prior to use. The Centers for Disease Control and Prevention state that, at sea-level, one minute at a rolling boil is sufficient to kill all water-borne germs of concern. If you live at an elevation above 6562 feet (2 kilometers), increase the boiling time to three minutes (the higher the altitude, the lower the boiling temperature of water).[519]

## PUTTING WATER FEARS IN PERSPECTIVE

If discussing sources of water contamination leaves you feeling inclined to bypass the water cooler, reconsider the pros and cons of hydrating your body versus the possible toxin exposure. In the short term, most domestic water is safe, and you can gain an extra measure of protection by applying the common sense strategies mentioned here.

There's no need to lay awake at night worrying about the implications of water pollution; you can rest easy in the knowledge that what's in your drinking water is not likely to inspire nightmares. On the other hand, recognizing water pollution's biggest danger may leave you tossing and turning in bed—especially if you frequently eat fish. That's right; when it comes to the toll of water pollution you are much more likely to have ill health effects from eating fish than from anything you drink.

The reason for this is that these water-dwelling creatures tend to concentrate toxins in their tissues. The larger the fish, the longer it lives, and the more carnivorous its diet, the greater the likelihood that it will be laced with significant amounts of toxins.

A classic example of this was given in chapter 11 of this book, recording a study of a lake in California. The carnivorous creatures at the top of the food chain had a concentration of DDD that was a whopping 125,000 times the amount in the water itself. This is not an unusual scenario. The EPA has gone on record saying, "Aquatic organisms may bioaccumulate environmental contaminants to more than 1,000,000 times the concentrations detected in the water..."[520]

This accumulation of DDT and its metabolites is a worldwide phenomenon because DDT and related organochlorine compounds (like TCCD of "Agent Orange" infamy) remain in the environment for decades and accumulate in human fatty tissues. Although many countries banned or significantly restricted the majority of these compounds in the 1970s, experts believe the most dangerous agents are still being used in many international jurisdictions.[521] Combined with the volatility of the compounds (which allows them to travel for literally thousands of miles in air currents before settling on land or in water sources), their widespread ongoing use provides a recipe for persistent worldwide contamination. A list of some of these persistent, ubiquitous compounds is found in **Figure 12.8**.[522]

Historically—and presently—these agents have been employed for many purposes besides pest control and military operations. Organochlorines have found their way into transformer coolants, paints, lubricants, hydraulic fluids, flame retardants, and other products.

## EXAMPLES OF ORGANOCHLORINE CHEMICALS

- Polychlorinated biphenyls (PCBs)
- Polychlorinated naphthalenes (PCNs)
- Dioxins
  - TCDD ("Agent Orange" 2,3,7,8-tetrachloro-p-dioxin)
- Pesticides
  - DDT
  - Dieldrin
  - Heptachlor
  - Others

***Figure 12.8***

**"To date, no environmental contaminant... has been found to cause more harm to infants than does lack of breastfeeding. I have seen no data that would argue against breast-feeding, even in the presence of today's levels of environmental toxicants."**
*—Physician–epidemiologist Miriam Labbok, Director of the Carolina Breast-feeding Institute*

## BREASTFEEDING AND MILK QUALITY ISSUES

The impact of these persistent organic compounds has been illustrated in many studies. For example, a classic 1983 Scandinavian study revealed how persistent organic toxins (including DDT, DDE, and PCBs) were tainting the breast milk of nursing mothers. Levels were correlated with maternal dietary habits.[523] The mothers were divided into three groups based on their typical dietary practices. Those following a lacto-vegetarian diet had the lowest levels of these toxins in their breast milk. In contrast, the highest levels were found among women consuming a mixed diet with regular intake of fatty fish from the Baltic Sea. Intermediate toxin levels were found in the breast milk of those eating a mixed diet devoid of habitual Baltic fatty fish intake.

It is important to note that this Scandinavian study did not report on vegans (those who consume no animal products whatsoever). This is a significant limitation, as U.S. data suggests vegetarians who avoid dairy may further decrease their exposure to these persistent contaminants. Although the toxin load of American dairy products appears to be improving, significant levels of some contaminants are regularly detected such as PCBs, cadmium, and lead.[524] This is a further indication of the superiority of a total vegetarian (vegan) diet, as it has been identified as the best way to avoid dioxin-PCB family contaminants in the U.S. food supply.[525]

## TOXINS, MENARCHE, AND MENTAL HEALTH

Such persistent organic compounds also have brain-impairing effects later in life. Earlier menarche (the age at which a girl begins to menstruate) has been linked to higher levels of DDT, its breakdown products, and estrogenic PCBs.[526,527] These relationships have significant mental health implications since girls who develop reproductive capacity earlier in life appear to have greater risks of depression, alcohol and other substance abuse, early sexual initiation, and other mental health problems.[528,529,530,531]

Although contested by a representative of an industrial plastics group, data from Puerto Rico raised concerns that another environmental group of toxins known as phthalates may contribute to early menarche and premature female sexual development.[532,533] Phthalates are compounds used to make plastics more flexible. These chemicals are not part of the structural molecules of the plastic and can therefore easily migrate into food or beverages stored in phthalate-containing packaging or containers.[534,535] Dr. A. Michael Warhurst, an environmental chemist with the World Wildlife Federation, observes that phthalates are fat-soluble and therefore tend to concentrate in products such as butter, margarine, and cheese.[536]

These issues have implications far beyond a child's diet: pregnant women who eat liberally of pesticide-contaminated foods can increase the likelihood of earlier menarche in their daughters years later.[537] Emerging data also links PCB exposure to Parkinson's Disease.[538]

It is one thing for such toxic, pervasive compounds to get into the environment. It's another matter for those toxins to find access to human beings. Simply put, organochlorines primarily enter people through contaminated foods and beverages. And because living creatures concentrate these toxins, animal products (fish, red meat, and dairy products) tend to be the major culprits worldwide.[539,540,541,542,543,544,545]

When dealing with animal products, safety from such contaminants is difficult to ensure. For example, those who once thought farmed fish offered a safer alternative to those caught in open waters recently received a rude awakening. Researchers from Indiana University reported in the prestigious journal, *Science*, that salmon raised on farms in Northern Europe, North America, and South America generally had markedly higher levels of organochlorine contaminants than wild salmon.[546] The authors concluded: "consumption of farmed Atlantic salmon may pose health risks that detract from the beneficial effects of fish consumption."

Although some of the data is new, the overall conclusions are not. For years, authorities have advocated vegetarian or near-vegetarian diets to decrease our exposure to these compounds.[547] Further safeguards include choosing organic fruits and vegetables. Such dietary practices are ones I heartily recommend to expectant mothers, women anticipating pregnancy, and anyone else desiring to decrease their toxic exposures.

A tiny fetus is especially susceptible to toxin exposure.

## MERCURY EXPOSURE AND THE FETUS

Sorensen and colleagues from Denmark's Faroe Islands further illustrated the mental health impact of fish consumption using another bioaccumulating toxin, mercury. These researchers followed 1,000 children born in their region for seven years.[548] They found that low-level prenatal exposure to organic mercury (methylmercury), assessed by umbilical cord blood samples, was correlated with neuropsychological dysfunctions when the children were assessed as seven-year-olds.[549] The most profound deficits were in the areas of language, attention, and memory, with lesser impairments in vision-related capacities and motor functions.

The researchers concluded that, "the effects on brain function associated with prenatal methylmercury exposure therefore appear widespread, and early dysfunction is detectable at exposure levels currently considered safe."[550] The apparent source of the mercury exposure was seafood consumption; pilot whale meat was a particularly significant dietary item in this Faroe Islands population.

In view of data linking cardiovascular risks and mental health concerns to mercury exposure, I advocate that all pregnant women keep their mercury exposure as low as possible. This includes identifying any hobby- or occupationally-related mercury exposures (see **Figure 12.9**) and discontinuing as many as possible.[551] Furthermore, I strongly recommend that pregnant women avoid eating fish. Because of the positive health

### ACTIVITIES THAT MAY RESULT IN MERCURY EXPOSURE

- alcohol distillation (brewing)
- dentistry
- etching
- hat making
- leather-tannery
- painting and lithography
- taxidermy
- use of:
  - disinfectants
  - dyes
- manufacturing of other items:
  - artificial flowers
  - cosmetics
  - paints
  - paper
  - pharmaceuticals
  - pottery/ceramics
  - storage batteries

***Figure 12.9***

benefits associated with omega-3 fats, I recommend obtaining these "good fats" from plant sources like flaxseeds, walnuts, or sea plants.

Clearly, with growing links to cancer, neurodegenerative diseases, and other chronic diseases, non-biodegradable toxins are among our greatest environmental concerns.[552,553,554,555] If you want to translate this information into practice, you may be better off decreasing your fish consumption rather than restricting your water intake.

## ADDRESSING TOXIN EXPOSURES

My focus in this chapter has been to help you decrease your toxic exposure as much as possible. However, if at some point testing reveals a seriously high burden of one or more toxins, the diagnosing physician or public agency will generally make recommendations for your treatment. The particular approach will vary with the toxin. A common strategy for heavy metals, however, employs chelation therapy. Chelation involves special "binding agents" that combine with the toxic compounds and help eliminate them from your bodies. However, beware of many alternative practitioners who prescribe chelation treatments for conditions other than heavy metal poisoning. I recommend you not consent to such therapy unless you are assured that you truly have the suspected toxic condition and that the practitioner is really an expert in providing such treatment. If there is any question, obtaining a second opinion is always wise.

Even if you do not have a large enough burden of toxins to warrant aggressive treatment, there are a number of strategies that appear to offer promise for decreasing your toxic load or minimizing the damage those compounds might cause.

## PROPER NUTRITION MAY HELP COMBAT TOXIC EXPOSURES

Poor childhood nutrition is itself a risk factor for poor mental development. However, animal models suggest undernourished children may be at higher risk of toxicity from common pollutants.[556] Conversely, children with high antioxidant vitamin intake may fare better if exposed to toxic levels of lead than their less well-nourished peers.[557] Data like this is not an excuse to be complacent regarding toxic exposures. Nonetheless, it underscores the benefits of early childhood nutrition.

Children are not the only ones who can benefit from optimal nutrition with respect to combating toxic insults. For example, Dutch researchers at Wageningen Agricultural University have studied the effect of antioxidant supplements on athletes exposed to ozone. Ozone has known performance-impairing effects. However, these European investigators found that three months of once-a-day supplementation with 15 mg beta-carotene, 75 mg vitamin E, and 650 mg vitamin C protects cyclists' lungs from ozone-induced lung function compromises.[558]

Other studies suggest fruits and vegetables may actually be better at protecting long-term lung function than any mix of specific antioxidants.[559] In other data, fruits emerged as the most powerful agents in preventing Chronic Obstructive Pulmonary Disease (COPD) mortality.[560] Whole grains also appeared to have COPD preventive effects.[561] Some believe protective compounds in fruits and whole grains, including a variety of antioxidants, may confer protection by preventing some of the long-term consequences of ambient air pollution.

Furthermore, researchers are uncovering a growing list of phytochemicals (compounds found exclusively in plants) that might help individuals at any age deal with a host of environmental toxins. To help you better appreciate the diversity and health-giving potential of these plant constituents, on the following pages **Figure 12.10** presents a sampling of this ever-expanding list of phytochemicals and their benefits (as suggested by epidemiology and formal experiments).[562,563,564,565,566,567,568,569,570,571,572,573,574,575,576,577,578,579,580,581.582,583,584,585,586,587,588,589,590,591,592,593,594,595]

## PHYTOCHEMICALS THAT MAY HELP COMBAT TOXIC EXPOSURES OR MITIGATE OTHER BRAIN-HEALTH THREATS

| Phytochemical | Good Dietary Sources |
|---|---|
| Caffeic Acid *(a phenolic acid)* | Citrus fruits, olive oil, oats, coffee, artichokes[596] |
| Catechins *(a class of flavonoids)* | Grapes, apples, cocoa, green tea |
| Chlorogenic Acid *(a phenolic acid)* | Apples, cocoa |
| Chlorophyll and Chlorophyllin[600] | Green leafy vegetables |
| Curcumin *(a diketone)* | Turmeric (an herb that gives the yellow color to curry) |
| Phytic Acid *(also called "inositol hexaphosphate")* | Legumes†, whole grains (including wild rice), sesame seeds |
| Quercetin and Rutin *(flavonoids)* | Apples, berries, grapes, onions, tomatoes, potatoes, broccoli, onions, tea |

*† legumes include all members of the bean family such as black-eyed peas, lentils, garbanzo beans, pinto beans, soy beans, etc.*

**Figure 12.10**

**Suggested Roles**

May protect against the toxicity from certain chemotherapy agents (e.g., heart toxicity from doxorubicin)[597]

Antioxidant, possible resistance to brain damage following stroke[598]

Antioxidant, may protect against the toxicity from certain chemotherapy agents (e.g., heart toxicity from doxorubicin)[599]

Cancer preventive (including colon), antioxidant, decreases absorption of toxins (including aflatoxin $B_1$)[601, 602]

Cancer preventive (including colon), anti-inflammatory,[603] cataract prevention, possible protection for neurodegenerative diseases like Alzheimer's,[604] decreases platelet stickiness[605]

Potent agent for cancer prevention (including colon, breast, blood, prostate, liver, and breast),[606,607] antioxidant, enhances immune (natural killer cell) activity, possible neurotransmitter[608]

May help prevent toxin-induced Alzheimer's development.[609,610] Cancer preventive/anti-cancer (including lung, colon, melanoma, blood—leukemia), antioxidant, lowers LDL levels,[611] helps prevent LDL oxidation, osteoporosis prevention[612,613]

## EMPLOYING ENVIRONMENTAL ENRICHMENT

Our bodies make a host of brain- and nerve-health inducing compounds called neurotrophins. Research reveals that these compounds can help decrease our risk of a host of conditions that are sometimes associated with toxic exposures. These conditions are as diverse as Parkinson's Disease, Alzheimer's, ischemic stroke (stroke caused by blocked arteries as opposed to burst blood vessels), and depression. For example, a 2003 study suggested that decreased activity of brain-derived neurotrophic factor (BDNF) may explain some cases of manic-depressive illness.[614] Lower levels of BDNF have also been implicated in other models of depression.[615,616]

A variety of strategies exist to either boost neurotrophin levels or enhance their effectiveness. Since overeating tends to decrease levels of these important brain-enhancing compounds, you can boost neurotrophin levels by either reducing your caloric intake or by fasting intermittently.[617] In addition to boosting BDNF, fasting increases ketones in the blood, which in turn elevates glutathione, a natural compound with antioxidant activities. In one recent study, ketone-related rises in glutathione helped prevent against neurotoxin-induced damage.[618] Physical exercise also can help bolster supplies of neurotrophins like BDNF.[619]

Neurobiologist Dr. Lawrence Katz and colleagues at Duke University Medical Center have provided research insights that allow us to get more mileage from our neurotrophins. These scientists learned that neurons (brain cells) must be active for neurotrophins to function optimally.[620] As a result, Katz and others advocate employing as many nerve cells as possible each day. One way of doing this is by incorporating more novel behaviors into our generally stereotyped lifestyles. In his book *Keep Your Brain Alive*, Dr. Katz and coauthor Manning Rubin advocate a variety of ways to introduce such novelty into your life.[621] These activities can be as simple as putting yourself in social situations where you have to interact with strangers, taking up a new hobby, or choosing to take a vacation at a place you've never visited before. There are more contrived ways of giving your brain additional novelty: you can take a different route home from work, shop at a farmer's market instead of a grocery store, eat with your nondominant hand, or try to identify objects in your purse by feel rather than sight. Katz calls such mentally stimulating activities "neurobics," and the more senses you involve in the activity, the better.

Compared to engaging in physical exercise, mentally challenging activities like Katz's neurobics do appear to have the upper hand when it comes to maintaining cognitive function. Consider recent research from New York City's Albert Einstein College of Medicine. Researchers there found activities that constantly challenged the brain (like reading or playing a musical instrument) were superior to physical exercise in decreasing the risk of dementia.[622] However, other New York City investigators had previously identified walking as well as socializing with friends as decreasing Alzheimer's risk.[623] In working with elderly dementia patients, Belgian researchers provided evidence that exercising with music may be particularly efficacious in improving mental capacities.[624] Similar cognitive benefits from combining exercise and music were demonstrated among heart disease patients in the United States.[625]

### FINDING BALANCE

The information on toxic exposure can be overwhelming and threatens to cause excessive worry or paranoia for those who become too focused on eliminating toxins from their environment. It is helpful to recognize that you will never be able to completely avoid all contact with toxins, but you are armed with the knowledge to keep you and your family healthy. By taking steps to minimize your exposure to toxins and boosting your natural defenses through a healthy diet and lifestyle, you can attain optimal mental performance despite the occasional presence of toxins around you. Put the proactive suggestions in this chapter into practice, observe the areas of caution, and relax in the knowledge that you are doing your best to help enhance the health of your brain.

## References

448. Centers for Disease Control (CDC). Elemental mercury poisoning in a household--Ohio, 1989. *Morbidity and Mortality Weekly Report (MMWR).* 1990 Jun 29;39(25):424-5. [Note: pseudonyms were supplied for patients, as they were reported anonymously in the CDC report.]

449. Ministry of the Environment Government of Japan. "Outbreak of Minamata Disease" (Chapter 2). *Minamata Disease: The History and Measures*). Accessed 26 September 2010 at http://www.env.go.jp/en/chemi/hs/minamata2002/ch2.html

450. Brown MJ, Hu H, Gonzales-Cossio T, Peterson KE, Sanin LH, de Luz Kageyama M, Palazuelos E, Aro A, Schnaas L, Hernandez-Avila M. Determinants of bone and blood lead concentrations in the early postpartum period. *Occupational and Environmental Medicine.* 2000 Aug; 57(8):535-41.

451. Aelion CM, Davis HT, McDermott S, Lawson AB. Soil metal concentrations and toxicity: associations with distances to industrial facilities and implications for human health. *Science of the Total Environment.* 2009 Mar 15;407(7):2216-23.

452. Sheiner EK, Sheiner E, Hammel RD, Potashnik G, Carel R. Effect of occupational exposures on male fertility: literature review. *Industrial Health.* 2003 Apr;41(2):55-62.

453. For another reference connecting lead exposure to male infertility see: Sallmen M, Lindbohm ML, Anttila A, Taskinen H, Hemminki K. Time to pregnancy among the wives of men occupationally exposed to lead. *Epidemiology.* 2000 Mar; 11(2):141-7.

454. Gonzalez-Cossio T, Peterson KE, Sanin LH, Fishbein E, Palazuelos E, Aro A, Hernandez-Avila M, Hu H. Decrease in birth weight in relation to maternal bone-lead burden. *Pediatrics.* 1997 Nov; 100(5):856-62.

455. Hernandez-Avila M, Peterson KE, Gonzalez-Cossio T, Sanin LH, Aro A, Schnaas L, Hu H. Effect of maternal bone lead on length and head circumference of newborns and 1-month-old infants. *Archives of Environmental Health.* 2002 Sep-Oct; 57(5):482-8.

456. Sanin LH, Gonzalez-Cossio T, Romieu I, Peterson KE, Ruiz S, Palazuelos E, Hernandez-Avila M, Hu H. Effect of maternal lead burden on infant weight and weight gain at one month of age among breastfed infants. *Pediatrics*. 2001 May; 107(5):1016-23.
457. Simpson JL, Niebyl JR. "Occupational and Environmental Perspectives of Birth Defects" (Chapter 7) in *Obstetrics: Normal and Problem Pregnancies*, 4th ed. (Gabbe SG, Niebyl JR, Simpson JL, editors). New York: Churchill Livingstone, Inc. 2002; p. 161-169.
458. Gonzalez-Cossio T, Peterson KE, Sanin LH, Fishbein E, Palazuelos E, Aro A, Hernandez-Avila M, Hu H. Decrease in birth weight in relation to maternal bone-lead burden. *Pediatrics*. 1997 Nov; 100(5):856-62.
459. Aguilar-Garduno C, Lacasana M, Tellez-Rojo MM, Aguilar-Madrid G, Sanin-Aguirre LH, Romieu I, Hernandez-Avila M. Indirect lead exposure among children of radiator repair workers. *American Journal Industrial Medicine*. 2003 Jun; 43(6):662-7.
460. Roy A, Georgopoulos PG, Ouyang M, Freeman N, Lioy PJ. Environmental, dietary, demographic, and activity variables associated with biomarkers of exposure for benzene and lead. *Journal of Exposure Analysis and Environmental Epidemiology*. 2003 Nov; 13(6):417-26.
461. Nriagu JO, Kim MJ. Emissions of lead and zinc from candles with metal-core wicks. *Science of the Total Environment*. 2000 Apr 24;250(1-3):37-41.
462. Wasson SJ, Guo Z, McBrian JA, Beach LO. Lead in candle emissions. *Science of the Total Environment*. 2002 Sep 16;296(1-3):159-74.
463. van Alphen M. Emission testing and inhalational exposure-based risk assessment for candles having Pb metal wick cores. *Science of the Total Environment*. 1999 Dec 15;243-244:53-65.
464. Miller C. Heavy Metals: Mercury, Lead and Arsenic. Presented at The Biennial Scientific Symposium on Children's Health as Impacted by Environmental Contaminants. 2002. Accessed October 1, 2004 at www.cehi.org/PDFs/151_155_heavymetals.pdf.
465. Sobel HL, Lurie P, Wolfe SM. Lead exposure from candles. *Journal of the American Medical Association (JAMA)*. 2000 Jul 12;284(2):180.
466. Agency for Toxic Substances and Disease Registry. Toxicological profile for lead. Atlanta, Georgia: US Department of Health and Human Services, Agency for Toxic Substances and Disease Registry, 1999. Accessed October 6, 2004 at http://www.atsdr.cdc.gov/toxprofiles/tp13.html.
467. National Candle Association. Candle Industry Facts. Accessed October 6, 2004 at http://www.candles.org/CandleIndustry/index.htm.
468. Wasson SJ, Guo Z, McBrian JA, Beach LO. Lead in candle emissions. *Science of the Total Environment*. 2002 Sep 16;296(1-3):159-74.
469. van Alphen M. Emission testing and inhalational exposure-based risk assessment for candles having Pb metal wick cores. *Science of the Total Environment*. 1999 Dec 15;243-244:53-65.
470. van Alphen M. Emission testing and inhalational exposure-based risk assessment for candles having Pb metal wick cores. *Science of the Total Environment*. 1999 Dec 15;243-244:53-65.
471. U.S. Centers for Disease Control and Prevention. Update: blood lead levels--United States, 1991-1994. *Morbidity and Mortality Weekly Report (MMWR)*. 1997 Feb 21;46(7):141-6.
472. Agency for Toxic Substances and Disease Registry. Toxicological profile for lead. Atlanta, Georgia: US Department of Health and Human Services, Agency for Toxic Substances and Disease Registry, 1999. Accessed October 6, 2004 at http://www.atsdr.cdc.gov/toxprofiles/tp13.html.
473. Miller C. Heavy Metals: Mercury, Lead and Arsenic. Presented at The Biennial Scientific Symposium on Children's Health as Impacted by Environmental Contaminants. 2002. Accessed on line October 1, 2004 at www.cehi.org/PDFs/151_155_heavymetals.pdf.
474. Lau C, Fiedler H, Hutzinger O, Schwind KH, Hosseinpour J. Levels of selected organic compounds in materials for candle production and human exposure to candle emissions. *Chemosphere*. 1997 Mar-Apr;34(5-7):1623-30.
475. Knobeloch LM, Zierold KM, Anderson HA. Association of arsenic-contaminated drinking-water with prevalence of skin cancer in Wisconsin's Fox River Valley. *Journal of Health, Population and Nutrition*. 2006 Jun;24(2):206-13.
476. Erickson ML. Arsenic in upper Midwest ground water: occurrence and geochemical mobilization mechanisms (University of Minnesota Doctoral Dissertation). 2005. Accessed 12 September 2010 at wrs.umn.edu/prod/groups/cfans/@pub/@cfans/.../cfans_asset_186401.pdf.
477. Gong G, O Bryant SE. The Arsenic Exposure Hypothesis for Alzheimer Disease. *Alzheimer Disease and Associated Disorders*. 2010 May 13.

478. Liu B, Gao HM, Hong JS. Parkinson's disease and exposure to infectious agents and pesticides and the occurrence of brain injuries: role of neuroinflammation. *Environmental Health Perspectives.* 2003 Jun;111(8):1065-73.
479. Shoemaker RC, Hudnell HK. Possible estuary-associated syndrome: symptoms, vision, and treatment. *Environmental Health Perspectives.* 2001 May;109(5):539-45.
480. Cetaruk EW. Vitamins (Chapter 34) in *Clinical Toxicology*, 1st Ed. (editors: Ford MD, Delaney KA, LJ Ling, Erickson T). Philadelphia: W.B. Saunders Company. 2001; pages 296-304.
481. Schaumburg H, Kaplan J, Windebank A, Vick N, Rasmus S, Pleasure D, Brown MJ. Sensory neuropathy from pyridoxine abuse. A new megavitamin syndrome. *The New England Journal of Medicine.* 1983 Aug 25;309(8):445-8.
482. Ritchie CS, McClave SA. Part II. Common nutritional issues in older adults. Dis Mon. 2002 Nov;48(11):713-24.
483. Mason JB. Consequences of Altered Micronutrient Status (Chapter 231) in *Cecil Textbook of Medicine*, 21st ed. (Editors: Goldman L, Bennett JC). Philadelphia: W.B. Saunders Company. 2000. pages -1170-1178.
484. Cetaruk EW. Vitamins (Chapter 34) in *Clinical Toxicology*, 1st Ed. (editors: Ford MD, Delaney KA, LJ Ling, Erickson T). Philadelphia: W.B. Saunders Company. 2001; pages 296-304.
485. Mason JB. Consequences of Altered Micronutrient Status (Chapter 231) in *Cecil Textbook of Medicine*, 21st ed. (Editors: Goldman L, Bennett JC). Philadelphia: W.B. Saunders Company. 2000. pages -1170-1178.
486. Michaelsson K, Lithell H, Vessby B, Melhus H. Serum retinol levels and the risk of fracture. *The New England Journal of Medicine.* 2003 Jan 23;348(4):287-94.
487. Feskanich D, Singh V, Willett WC, Colditz GA. Vitamin A intake and hip fractures among postmenopausal women. *Journal of the American Medical Association (JAMA).* 2002 Jan 2;287(1):47-54.
488. Brust JCM. Nutritional Disorders of the Nervous System (Chapter 489) in *Cecil Textbook of Medicine*, 21st ed. (Editors: Goldman L, Bennett JC). Philadelphia: W.B. Saunders Company. 2000. pages 2175-2178.
489. Russell RM. The vitamin A spectrum: from deficiency to toxicity. *The American Journal Clinical Nutrition.* 2000 Apr;71(4):878-84.
490. Russell RM. The vitamin A spectrum: from deficiency to toxicity. *The American Journal Clinical Nutrition.* 2000 Apr;71(4):878-84.
491. Cetaruk EW. Vitamins (Chapter 34) in *Clinical Toxicology*, 1st ed. (editors: Ford MD, Delaney KA, LJ Ling, Erickson T). Philadelphia: W.B. Saunders Company. 2001; pages 296-304.
492. Brust JCM. Nutritional Disorders of the Nervous System (Chapter 489) in *Cecil Textbook of Medicine*, 21st ed. (editors: Goldman L, Bennett JC). Philadelphia: W.B. Saunders Company. 2000. pages 2175-2178.
493. Fairfield KM, Fletcher RH. Vitamins for chronic disease prevention in adults: scientific review. *Journal of the American Medical Association (JAMA).* 2002 Jun 19;287(23):3116-26.
494. Carlton S, Clopton D, Cappuzzo KA. Vitamin D deficiency: appropriate replenishment therapies and the effects of vitamin D toxicity. *Consultant Pharmacist.* 2010 Mar;25(3):171-7.
495. Fairfield KM, Fletcher RH. Vitamins for chronic disease prevention in adults: scientific review. *Journal of the American Medical Association (JAMA).* 2002 Jun 19;287(23):3116-26.
496. Napier K. Too Many Vitamins? *Harvard Health Letter* 1996 Jan 21(3):1-3.
497. Eidelman RS, Hollar D, Hebert PR, Lamas GA, Hennekens CH. Randomized trials of vitamin E in the treatment and prevention of cardiovascular disease. *Archives of Internal Medicine.* 2004 Jul 26;164(14):1552-6.
498. Bazzano LA, Serdula MK, Liu S. Dietary intake of fruits and vegetables and risk of cardiovascular disease. *Current Atherosclerosis Reports.* 2003 Nov;5(6):492-9.
499. Joshipura KJ, Ascherio A, Manson JE, Stampfer MJ, Rimm EB, Speizer FE, Hennekens CH, Spiegelman D, Willett WC. Fruit and vegetable intake in relation to risk of ischemic stroke. *Journal of the American Medical Association (JAMA).* 1999 Oct 6;282(13):1233-9.
500. Omenn GS. Human lung cancer chemoprevention strategies: Parker B. Francis lecture. *Chest.* 2004 May;125(5 Suppl):123S-7S.
501. Ross PE. Spinach in a pill. *Forbes.* 1996; 4:354–355
502. Dey AN, Bloom B. Summary health statistics for U.S. children: National Health Interview Survey, 2003. *Vital and Health Statistics, Series 10.* 2005 Mar;(223):1-78.
503. National Institutes of Health. Diagnosis and treatment of attention deficit hyperactivity disorder (ADHD). *NIH Consensus Statement.* 1998 Nov 16-18;16(2):1-37.
504. Dodson WW. Attention Deficit-Hyperactivity Disorder (Chapter 56) in *Psychiatric Secrets*, 2nd ed. (editors: Jacobson JL, Jacobson AM) Philadelphia: Hanley and Belfus, Inc. 2001. Page 302-4.

505. Adapted from: Dodson WW. Attention Deficit-Hyperactivity Disorder (Chapter 56) in *Psychiatric Secrets*, 2nd ed. (editors: Jacobson JL, Jacobson AM) Philadelphia: Hanley and Belfus, Inc. 2001. Page 303.
506. National Institutes of Health. Diagnosis and treatment of attention deficit hyperactivity disorder (ADHD). *NIH Consensus Statement*. 1998 Nov 16-18;16(2):1-37.
507. Dodson WW. Attention Deficit-Hyperactivity Disorder (Chapter 56) in *Psychiatric Secrets*, 2nd ed. (editors: Jacobson JL, Jacobson AM) Philadelphia: Hanley and Belfus, Inc. 2001. Page 306.
508. Anthony HM, Maberly DJ, Birtwistle S. Attention deficit hyperactivity disorder. *Archives of Disease in Childhood*. 1999 Aug;81(2):189.
509. Beseler L. Effects on Behavior and Cognition: Diet and Artificial Colors, Flavors, and Preservatives. *International Pediatrics*. 1999;14(1):41-43.
510. Anthony HM, Maberly DJ, Birtwistle S. Attention deficit hyperactivity disorder. *Archives of Disease in Childhood*. 1999 Aug;81(2):189.
511. Anthony HM, Maberly DJ, Birtwistle S. Attention deficit hyperactivity disorder. *Archives of Disease in Childhood*. 1999 Aug;81(2):189.
512. Carter CM, Urbanowicz M, Hemsley R, Mantilla L, Strobel S, Graham PJ, Taylor E. Effects of a few food diet in attention deficit disorder. *Archives of Disease in Childhood*. 1993 Nov;69(5):564-8.
513. Bateman B, Warner JO, Hutchinson E, Dean T, Rowlandson P, Gant C, Grundy J, Fitzgerald C, Stevenson J. The effects of a double blind, placebo controlled, artificial food colourings and benzoate preservative challenge on hyperactivity in a general population sample of preschool children. *Archives of Disease in Childhood*. 2004 Jun;89(6):506-11.
514. Nolan BT, Ruddy BC, Hitt KJ, Helsel DR. A national look at nitrate contamination of ground water. *Water Conditioning and Purification* 1998 Jan;39(12):76-79.
515. De Roos AJ, Ward MH, Lynch CF, Cantor KP. Nitrate in public water supplies and the risk of colon and rectum cancers. *Epidemiology*. 2003 Nov; 14(6): 640-9.
516. For example: Gaffield SJ, Goo RL, Richards LA, Jackson RJ. Public health effects of inadequately managed stormwater runoff. *American Journal of Public Health*. 2003 Sep;93(9):1527-33.
517. Schwartz J, Levin R, Goldstein R. Drinking water turbidity and gastrointestinal illness in the elderly of Philadelphia. *Journal of Epidemiology and Community Health*. 2000 Jan;54(1):45-51.
518. Schwartz J, Levin R, Hodge K. Drinking water turbidity and pediatric hospital use for gastrointestinal illness in Philadelphia. *Epidemiology*. 1997 Nov;8(6):615-20.
519. CDC. Assessment of Inadequately Filtered Public Drinking Water - Washington, D.C., December 1993. *Morbidity and Mortality Weekly Report (MMWR)*; September 16, 1994 Vol. 43 No. 36. Pp. 661-669.
520. U.S. EPA. Office of Science and Technology. Office of Water. Guidance for assessing chemical contaminant data for use in fish advisories. *Volume 1: Fish Sampling and Analysis*. 2nd ed. September 1995. EPA 823-R-95-007; p. 1-1.
521. Abelsohn A, Gibson BL, Sanborn MD, Weir E. Identifying and managing adverse environmental health effects: 5. Persistent organic pollutants. *Canadian Medical Association Journal (CMAJ)*. 2002 Jun 11;166(12):1549-54.
522. Phuong NT, Hung BS, Schecter A, Vu DQ. Dioxin levels in adipose tissues of hospitalized women living in the south of Vietnam in 1984-89 with a brief review of their clinical histories. *Journal of Women's Health*. 1990;16(1):79-93.
523. Noren K. Levels of organochlorine contaminants in human milk in relation to the dietary habits of the mothers. *Acta Paediatrica Scandinavica*. 1983 Nov;72(6):811-6.
524. Schaum J, Schuda L, Wu C, Sears R, Ferrario J, Andrews K. A national survey of persistent, bioaccumulative, and toxic (PBT) pollutants in the United States milk supply. *Journal of Exposure Analysis and Environmental Epidemiology*. 2003 May;13(3):177-86.
525. Schecter A, Cramer P, Boggess K, Stanley J, Papke O, Olson J, Silver A, Schmitz M. Intake of dioxins and related compounds from food in the U.S. population. *Journal of Toxicology and Environmental Health, Part A*. 2001 May 11;63(1):1-18.
526. Denham M, Schell LM, Deane G, Gallo MV, Ravenscroft J, DeCaprio AP; Akwesasne Task Force on the Environment. Relationship of lead, mercury, mirex, dichlorodiphenyldichloroethylene, hexachlorobenzene, and polychlorinated biphenyls to timing of menarche among Akwesasne Mohawk girls. *Pediatrics*. 2005 Feb;115(2):e127-34.
527. Krstevska-Konstantinova M, Charlier C, Craen M, Du Caju M, Heinrichs C, de Beaufort C, Plomteux G, Bourguignon JP. Sexual precocity after immigration from developing countries to Belgium: evidence of previous exposure to organochlorine pesticides. *Human Reproduction*. 2001 May;16(5):1020-6.
528. Gaudineau A, Ehlinger V, Vayssiere C, Jouret B, Arnaud C, Godeau E. Factors associated with early menarche: results from the French Health Behaviour in School-aged Children (HBSC) study. *BMC Public Health*. 2010 Mar

30;10:175.

529. Downing J, Bellis MA. Early pubertal onset and its relationship with sexual risk taking, substance use and anti-social behaviour: a preliminary cross-sectional study. *BMC Public Health*. 2009;9:446.

530. Joinson C, Heron J, Araya R, Lewis G. Early menarche is associated with an increased risk for depressive symptoms in adolescent girls in a UK cohort. *Journal of Epidemiology and Community Health* 2009;63:17.

531. Stice E, Presnell K, Bearman SK. Relation of early menarche to depression, eating disorders, substance abuse, and comorbid psychopathology among adolescent girls. *Developmental Psychology*. 2001 Sep;37(5):608-19.

532. McKee RH; Toxicology Research Task Group, Phthalate Esters Panel American Chemistry Council. Phthalate exposure and early thelarche. *Environmental Health Perspectives*. 2004 Jul;112(10):A541-3.

533. Colon I, Caro D, Bourdony CJ, Rosario O. Identification of phthalate esters in the serum of young Puerto Rican girls with premature breast development. *Environmental Health Perspectives*. 2000 Sep;108(9):895-900.

534. Agency for Toxic Substances and Diesease Registry. ToxFAQs™ for Diethyl Phthalate. September 1996. Accessed 18 October 2005 at http://www.atsdr.cdc.gov/tfacts73.html.

535. Agency for Toxic Substances and Diesease Registry. ToxFAQs™ for Di(2-ethylhexyl)phthalate (DEHP). September 2002. Accessed 18 October 2005 at http://www.atsdr.cdc.gov/tfacts9.html.

536. Warhurst AM. Introduction to Hormone Disrupting Chemicals: Phthalates. Accessed 20 October 2005 at http://website.lineone.net/~mwarhurst/phthalates.html.

537. Vasiliu O, Muttineni J, Karmaus W. In utero exposure to organochlorines and age at menarche. *Human Reproduction*. 2004 Jul;19(7):1506-12. Epub 2004 May 6.

538. Liu B, Gao HM, Hong JS. "Parkinson's Disease and Exposure to Infectious Agents and Pesticides and the Occurrence of Brain Injuries: Role of Neuroinflammation." Neuropharmacology Section, Laboratory of Pharmacology. *Environmental Health Perspectives.* 111:1065–1073 (2003).

539. Abelsohn A, Gibson BL, Sanborn MD, Weir E. Identifying and managing adverse environmental health effects: 5. Persistent organic pollutants. *Canadian Medical Association Journal (CMAJ)*. 2002 Jun 11;166(12):1549-54.

540. Hall RH. A new threat to public health: organochlorines and food. *Nutrition and Health*. 1992;8(1):33-43.

541. Kannan K, Tanabe S, Williams RJ, Tatsukawa R. Persistent organochlorine residues in foodstuffs from Australia, Papua New Guinea and the Solomon Islands: contamination levels and human dietary exposure. *Science of the Total Environment*. 1994 Aug 15;153(1-2):29-49.

542. Martinez MP, Angulo R, Pozo R, Jodral M. Organochlorine pesticides in pasteurized milk and associated health risks. *Food and Chemical Toxicology*. 1997 Jun;35(6):621-4.

543. Domingo JL. Polychlorinated naphthalenes in animal aquatic species and human exposure through the diet: a review. *Journal of Chromatography A*. 2004 Oct 29;1054(1-2):327-34.

544. Kannan K, Corsolini S, Imagawa T, Focardi S, Giesy JP. Polychlorinated-naphthalenes, -biphenyls, -dibenzo-p-dioxins, -dibenzofurans and p,p'-DDE in bluefin tuna, swordfish, cormorants and barn swallows from Italy. *Ambio*. 2002 May;31(3):207-11.

545. Gerstenberger SL, Dellinger JA. PCBs, mercury, and organochlorine concentrations in lake trout, walleye, and whitefish from selected tribal fisheries in the Upper Great Lakes region. *Environmental Toxicology*. 2002 Dec;17(6):513-9.

546. Hites RA, Foran JA, Carpenter DO, Hamilton MC, Knuth BA, Schwager SJ. Global assessment of organic contaminants in farmed salmon. *Science*. 2004 Jan 9;303(5655):226-9.

547. Hall RH. A new threat to public health: organochlorines and food. *Nutrition and Health*. 1992;8(1):33-43.

548. Sorensen N, Murata K, Budtz-Jorgensen E, Weihe P, Grandjean P. Prenatal methylmercury exposure as a cardiovascular risk factor at seven years of age. *Epidemiology*. 1999 Jul;10(4):370-5.

549. Grandjean P, Weihe P, White RF, Debes F, Araki S, Yokoyama K, Murata K, Sorensen N, Dahl R, Jorgensen PJ. Cognitive deficit in 7-year-old children with prenatal exposure to methylmercury. *Neurotoxicology and Teratology*. 1997 Nov-Dec;19(6):417-28.

550. Grandjean P, Weihe P, White RF, Debes F, Araki S, Yokoyama K, Murata K, Sorensen N, Dahl R, Jorgensen PJ. Cognitive deficit in 7-year-old children with prenatal exposure to methylmercury. *Neurotoxicology and Teratology*. 1997 Nov-Dec;19(6):417-28.

551. Bolla KI, Cadet JL. Exogenous Acquired Metabolic Disorders of the Nervous System: Toxins and Illicit Drugs (Chapter 39). *Textbook of Clinical Neurology*, 2nd ed. (Goetz CG, ed.). Philadelphia: Saunders/Elsevier Science. 2003; p. 841-843.

552. Falck F Jr, Ricci A Jr, et al. Pesticides and polychlorinated biphenyl residues in human breast lipids and their relation to breast cancer. *Archives of Environmental Health*. 1992 Mar-Apr;47(2):143-146.

553. Igbedioh SO. Effects of agricultural pesticides on humans, animals and higher plants in developing countries. *Archives of Environmental Health.* 1991 Jul-Aug;46(4):218-224.
554. Rosenman KD. Dioxin, polychlorinated biphenyls, and dibenzofurans. *Environmental and Occupational Medicine.* 2nd ed. (editor: WN Rom). Boston MA: Little Brown and Co., 1992. p. 927-933.
555. Colborn T. Animal/Health Connection. In: Proceedings of the US Environmental Protection Agency's National Technical Workshop "PCBs in Fish Tissue." September 1993. EPA/823-R-93-003; p. 2-27 to 2-30.
556. Ferri A, Duffard R, Sturtz N, Evangelista de Duffard AM. Iron, zinc and copper levels in brain, serum and liver of neonates exposed to 2,4-dichlorophenoxyacetic acid. *Neurotoxicology and Teratology.* 2003 Sep-Oct;25(5):607-13.
557. Hsu PC, Guo YL. Antioxidant nutrients and lead toxicity. *Toxicology.* 2002 Oct 30;180(1):33-44.
558. Grievink L, Jansen SM, van't Veer P, Brunekreef B. Acute effects of ozone on pulmonary function of cyclists receiving antioxidant supplements. *Journal of Occupational and Environmental Medicine.* 1998 Jan;55(1):13-7.
559. Tabak C, Smit HA, Rasanen L, Fidanza F, Menotti A, Nissinen A, Feskens EJ, Heederik D, Kromhout D. Dietary factors and pulmonary function: a cross sectional study in middle aged men from three European countries. *Thorax.* 1999 Nov;54(11):1021-6.
560. Walda IC, Tabak C, Smit HA, Rasanen L, Fidanza F, Menotti A, Nissinen A, Feskens EJ, Kromhout D. Diet and 20-year chronic obstructive pulmonary disease mortality in middle-aged men from three European countries. *European Journal of Clinical Nutrition.* 2002 Jul;56(7):638-43.
561. Tabak C, Smit HA, Heederik D, Ocke MC, Kromhout D. Diet and chronic obstructive pulmonary disease: independent beneficial effects of fruits, whole grains, and alcohol (the MORGEN study). *Clinical and Experimental Allergy.* 2001 May;31(5):747-55.
562. Adlercreutz H. Phyto-oestrogens and cancer. *The Lancet Oncology.* 2002 Jun;3(6):364-73.
563. World Cancer Research Fund and American Institute for Cancer Research. Other Bioactive Compounds (Chapter 5.8). *Food, Nutrition and the Prevention of Cancer: a Global Perspective.* Washington, D.C: The American Institute for Cancer Research.1997, pages 421-427.
564. Hecht SS. Chemoprevention of lung cancer by isothiocyanates. *Advances in Experimental Medicine and Biology* 1996;401():1-11.
565. Kris-Etherton PM, Hecker KD, Bonanome A, Coval SM, Binkoski AE, Hilpert KF, Griel AE, Etherton TD. Bioactive compounds in foods: their role in the prevention of cardiovascular disease and cancer. *American Journal of Medicine.* 2002 Dec 30;113 Suppl 9B:71S-88S.
566. Jang M, Cai L, Udeani GO, et al. Cancer chemopreventive activity of resveratrol, a natural product derived from grapes. *Science.* 1997 Jan 10;275(5297):218-220.
567. Murray MT, Pizzorno JE Jr. Role of dietary fiber in health and disease (Chapter 57) in *Textbook of Natural Medicine*, 2nd ed. (Pizzorno JE Jr, Murray MT, editors). New York: Churchill Livingstone, Inc.1999, pages 507-516.
568. Bloedon LT, Szapary PO. Flaxseed and cardiovascular risk. *Nutr Rev.* 2004 Jan;62(1):18-27.
569. Hudson EA, Dinh PA, Kokubun T, Simmonds MS, Gescher A. Characterization of potentially chemopreventive phenols in extracts of brown rice that inhibit the growth of human breast and colon cancer cells. *Cancer Epidemiol Biomarkers Prev.* 2000 Nov;9(11):1163-70.
570. Walaszek Z, Hanausek M, Slaga TJ. Mechanisms of chemoprevention. *Chest.* 2004 May;125(5 Suppl):128S-33S.
571. Viner JL, Umar A, Hawk ET. Chemoprevention of colorectal cancer: problems, progress, and prospects. *Gastroenterology Clinics of North America. 2002 Dec;31(4):971-99.*
*572. Wagner KH, Elmadfa I. B*iological relevance of terpenoids. Overview focusing on mono-, di- and tetraterpenes. *Annals of Nutrition and Metabolism.* 2003;47(3-4):95-106.
573. Dragsted LO, Strube M, Larsen JC. Cancer-protective factors in fruits and vegetables: biochemical and biological background. *Pharmacololy and Toxicology.* 1993;72 Suppl 1:116-35.
574. Ross ZM, O'Gara EA, Hill DJ, Sleightholme HV, Maslin DJ. Antimicrobial properties of garlic oil against human enteric bacteria: evaluation of methodologies and comparisons with garlic oil sulfides and garlic powder. *Applied and Environmental Microbiology.* 2001 Jan;67(1):475-80.
575. Baublis AJ, Lu C, Clydesdale FM, Decker EA. Potential of wheat-based breakfast cereals as a source of dietary antioxidants. *Journal of the American College of Nutrition.* 2000 Jun;19(3 Suppl):308S-311S.
576. Yuan JM, Gago-Dominguez M, Castelao JE, Hankin JH, Ross RK, Yu MC. Cruciferous vegetables in relation to renal cell carcinoma. *Internatinal Journal of Cancer.* 1998 Jul 17;77(2):211-6.
577. Muti P, Awad AB, Schunemann H, Fink CS, Hovey K, Freudenheim JL, Wu YW, Bellati C, Pala V, Berrino F. A plant food-based diet modifies the serum beta-sitosterol concentration in hyperandrogenic postmenopausal women.

*Journal of Nutrition*. 2003 Dec;133(12):4252-5.

578. Garcia-Closas R, Berenguer A, Jose Tormo M, Jose Sanchez M, Quiros JR, Navarro C, Arnaud R, Dorronsoro M, Dolores Chirlaque M, Barricarte A, Ardanaz E, Amiano P, Martinez C, Agudo A, Gonzalez CA. Dietary sources of vitamin C, vitamin E and specific carotenoids in Spain. *British Journal of Nutrition*. 2004 Jun;91(6):1005-11.
579. Millen AE, Tucker MA, Hartge P, Halpern A, Elder DE, Guerry D 4th, Holly EA, Sagebiel RW, Potischman N. Diet and melanoma in a case-control study. *Cancer Epidemiology, Biomarkers and Prevention*. 2004 Jun;13(6):1042-51.
580. [No authors listed]. Calcium-D-glucarate. *Alternative Medicine Review*. 2002 Aug;7(4):336-9.
581. Steinmetz KA, Potter JD. Vegetables, fruit, and cancer prevention: a review. *Journal of the American Dietetic Association*. 1996 Oct;96(10):1027-39. Murray MT, Pizzorno JE Jr. Beta-carotene and other carotenoids (Chapter 67). *Textbook of Natural Medicine*, 2nd ed.
582. (Pizzorno JE Jr, Murray MT, editors). New York: Churchill Livingstone, Inc.1999, pages 603-610.
583. Ronzio RA. Naturally occurring antioxidants (Chapter 99). *Textbook of Natural Medicine*, 2nd ed. (Pizzorno JE Jr, Murray MT, editors). New York: Churchill Livingstone, Inc.1999, pages 831-846.
584. Lee KW, Kim YJ, Kim DO, Lee HJ, Lee CY. Major phenolics in apple and their contribution to the total antioxidant capacity. *Journal of Agricultural and Food Chemistry*. 2003 Oct 22;51(22):6516-20.
585. Dashwood RH. Early detection and prevention of colorectal cancer (review). *Oncol Rep*. 1999 Mar-Apr;6(2):277-81.
586. Heber D, Bowerman S. Applying science to changing dietary patterns. *Journal of Nutrition*. 2001 Nov;131(11 Suppl):3078S-81S.
587. Ferguson LR, Philpott M, Karunasinghe N. Dietary cancer and prevention using antimutagens. *Toxicology*. 2004 May 20;198(1-3):147-59.
588. Yilmaz Y, Toledo RT. Major flavonoids in grape seeds and skins: antioxidant capacity of catechin, epicatechin, and gallic acid. *Journal of Agricultural and Food Chemistry*. 2004 Jan 28;52(2):255-60.
589. Zheng Q, Hirose Y, Yoshimi N, Murakami A, Koshimizu K, Ohigashi H, Sakata K, Matsumoto Y, Sayama Y, Mori H. Further investigation of the modifying effect of various chemopreventive agents on apoptosis and cell proliferation in human colon cancer cells. *Journal of Cancer Research and Clinical Oncology*. 2002 Oct;128(10):539-46.
590. Sies H, Stahl W. Non-nutritive bioactive constituents of plants: lycopene, lutein and zeaxanthin. *International Journal of Vitamin and Nutrition Research*. 2003 Mar;73(2):95-100.
591. Boyer J, Liu RH. Apple phytochemicals and their health benefits. *Nutrition Journal*. 2004 May 12;3(1):5.
592. Radtke J, Linseisen J, Wolfram G [Phenolic acid intake of adults in a Bavarian subgroup of the national food consumption survey]. Z Ernahrungswiss1998; 37(2):190-7.
593. Grey CE, Adlercreutz P. Ability of antioxidants to prevent oxidative mutations in Salmonella typhimurium TA102. *Mutation Research*. 2003 Jun 19;527(1-2):27-36.
594. Nishikawa A, Furukawa F, Lee IS, Tanaka T, Hirose M. Potent chemopreventive agents against pancreatic cancer. *Current Cancer Drug Targets*. 2004 Jun;4(4):373-84.
595. Murkies AL, Wilcox G, Davis SR. Clinical review 92: Phytoestrogens. *Journal of Clinical Endocrinology and Metabolism*. 1998 Feb;83(2):297-303.
596. Rechner AR; Pannala AS; Rice-Evans CA. Caffeic acid derivatives in artichoke extract are metabolised to phenolic acids in vivo. *Free Radical Research*. 2001 Aug; 35(2): 195-202.
597. Chlopcikova S, Psotova J, Miketova P, Sousek J, Lichnovsky V V, Simanek V. Chemoprotective effect of plant phenolics against anthracycline-induced toxicity on rat cardiomyocytes Part II. caffeic, chlorogenic and rosmarinic acids. *Phytotherapy Researcg*. 2004 May;18(5):408-413.
598. Suzuki M, Tabuchi M, Ikeda M, Umegaki K, Tomita T. Protective effects of green tea catechins on cerebral ischemic damage. *Medical Science Monitor*. 2004 Jun 1;10(6):BR166-BR174.
599. Chlopcikova S, Psotova J, Miketova P, Sousek J, Lichnovsky V V, Simanek V. Chemoprotective effect of plant phenolics against anthracycline-induced toxicity on rat cardiomyocytes Part II. caffeic, chlorogenic and rosmarinic acids. *Phytother Res*. 2004 May;18(5):408-413.
600. Harttig U, Bailey GS. Chemoprotection by natural chlorophylls in vivo: inhibition of dibenzo[a,l]pyrene-DNA adducts in rainbow trout liver. *Carcinogenesis*. 1998 Jul;19(7):1323-6.
601. Sudakin DL. Dietary aflatoxin exposure and chemoprevention of cancer: a clinical review. *Journal of Toxicology - Clinical Toxicology*. 2003;41(2):195-204.
602. Egner PA, Wang JB, Zhu YR, Zhang BC, Wu Y, Zhang QN, Qian GS, Kuang SY, Gange SJ, Jacobson LP, Helzlsouer KJ, Bailey GS, Groopman JD, Kensler TW. Chlorophyllin intervention reduces aflatoxin-DNA adducts in individuals at high risk for liver cancer. *Proceedings of the National Academy of Sciences USA*. 2001 Dec 4;98(25):14601-6.

603. Baek OS, Kang OH, Choi YA, Choi SC, Kim TH, Nah YH, Kwon DY, Kim YK, Kim YH, Bae KH, Lim JP, Lee YM. Curcumin inhibits protease-activated receptor-2 and -4-mediated mast cell activation. *Clinica Chimica Acta.* 2003 Dec;338(1-2):135-41.
604. Kang G, Kong PJ, Yuh YJ, Lim SY, Yim SV, Chun W, Kim SS. Curcumin suppresses lipopolysaccharide-induced cyclooxygenase-2 expression by inhibiting activator protein 1 and nuclear factor kappab bindings in BV2 microglial cells. *Journal of Pharmacological Sciences.* 2004 Mar;94(3):325-8.
605. Shah BH, Nawaz Z, Pertani SA, Roomi A, Mahmood H, Saeed SA, Gilani AH. Inhibitory effect of curcumin, a food spice from turmeric, on platelet-activating factor- and arachidonic acid-mediated platelet aggregation through inhibition of thromboxane formation and Ca2+ signaling. *Biochem Pharmacol.* 1999 Oct 1;58(7):1167-72.
606. Tantivejkul K, Vucenik I, Shamsuddin AM. Inositol hexaphosphate (IP6) inhibits key events of cancer metastasis: II. Effects on integrins and focal adhesions. *Anticancer Research.* 2003 Sep-Oct;23(5A):3681-9.
607. Tantivejkul K, Vucenik I, Shamsuddin AM. Inositol hexaphosphate (IP6) inhibits key events of cancer metastasis: I. In vitro studies of adhesion, migration and invasion of MDA-MB 231 human breast cancer cells. *Anticancer Research.* 2003 Sep-Oct;23(5A):3671-9.
608. Vucenik I, Shamsuddin AM. Cancer inhibition by inositol hexaphosphate (IP6) and inositol: from laboratory to clinic. *Journal of Nutrition.* 2003 Nov;133(11 Suppl 1):3778S-3784S.
609. Kim H, Park B, Lee K, Choi C, Jang SS, Kim YH, Lee SE. Effects of naturally occurring compounds on fibril formation and oxidative stress of beta-amyloid. *Journal of Agricultural and Food Chemistry.* 2005 Nov 2;53(22):8537-41.
610. Heo HJ, Lee CY. Protective effects of quercetin and vitamin C against oxidative stress-induced neurodegeneration. *Journal of Agricultural and Food Chemistry.* 2004 Dec 15;52(25):7514-7
611. Arai Y, Watanabe S, Kimira M, Shimoi K, Mochizuki R, Kinae N. Dietary intakes of flavonols, flavones and isoflavones by Japanese women and the inverse correlation between quercetin intake and plasma LDL cholesterol concentration. *Journal of Nutrition.* 2000 Sep;130(9):2243-50.
612. Horcajada-Molteni MN, Crespy V, Coxam V, Davicco MJ, Remesy C, Barlet JP. Rutin inhibits ovariectomy-induced osteopenia in rats. *Journal of Bone Mineral Research.* 2000 Nov;15(11):2251-8.
613. Wattel A, Kamel S, Prouillet C, Petit JP, Lorget F, Offord E, Brazier M. Flavonoid quercetin decreases osteoclastic differentiation induced by RANKL via a mechanism involving NF kappa B and AP-1. *Journal of Cellular Biochemistry.* 2004 May 15;92(2):285-95.
614. Green E, Craddock N. Brain-derived Neurotrophic Factor As a Potential Risk Locus for Bipolar Disorder: Evidence, Limitations, and Implications. *Current Psychiatry Reports.* 2003 Dec;5(6):469-76.
615. Altar CA, Whitehead RE, Chen R, Wortwein G, Madsen TM. Effects of electroconvulsive seizures and antidepressant drugs on brain-derived neurotrophic factor protein in rat brain. *Biological Psychiatry.* 2003 Oct 1;54(7):703-9.
616. Altar CA. Neurotrophins and depression. *Trends in Pharmacological Sciences.* 1999 Feb;20(2):59-61.
617. Mattson MP. Gene-diet interactions in brain aging and neurodegenerative disorders. *Annals of Internal Medicine.* 2003 Sep 2;139(5 Pt 2):441-4.
618. Cheng B, Yang X, An L, Gao B, Liu X, Liu S. Ketogenic diet protects dopaminergic neurons against 6-OHDA neurotoxicity via up-regulating glutathione in a rat model of Parkinson's disease. *Brain Research.* 2009 Aug 25;1286:25-31.
619. Brené S, Werme M, Widenfalk J, Thorén P, Olson L. Mechanisms of Gene Induction After Chronic Cocaine and Voluntary Running: A Role for Neuropeptides and Trophic Factors. Neurotrophins Meeting Summary Abstracts. National Institute on Drug Abuse 2001. Accessed 10 November 2003 at http://www.drugabuse.gov/MeetSum/ameetsum.html.
620. McAllister AK, Katz LC, Lo DC. Neurotrophin regulation of cortical dendritic growth requires activity. *Neuron.* 1996 Dec;17(6):1057-64.
621. Katz LC, Rubin M. *Keep Your Brain Alive.* New York: Workman Publishing Co. 1999.
622. Verghese J, Lipton RB, Katz MJ, Hall CB, Derby CA, Kuslansky G, Ambrose AF, Sliwinski M, Buschke H. Leisure activities and the risk of dementia in the elderly. *New England Journal of Medicine.* 2003 Jun 19;348(25):2508-16.
623. Scarmeas N, Levy G, Tang MX, Manly J, Stern Y. Influence of leisure activity on the incidence of Alzheimer's disease. *Neurology.* 2001 Dec 26;57(12):2236-42.
624. Van de Winckel A, Feys H, De Weerdt W, Dom R. Cognitive and behavioural effects of music-based exercises in patients with dementia. *Clinical Rehabilitation.* 2004 May;18(3):253-60.
625. Emery CF, Hsiao ET, Hill SM, Frid DJ. Short-term effects of exercise and music on cognitive performance among participants in a cardiac rehabilitation program. *Heart and Lung.* 2003 Nov-Dec;32(6):368-73.

Chapter 13

PHYSICAL EXERCISE HAS BEEN SHOWN TO HAVE A POSITIVE IMPACT ON COGNITIVE ABILITY, AND EVEN TO HELP PREVENT SENILITY.

# Tune-up Your Body

***Optimal physical health is an important precursor to achieving peak mental performance.***

Ralph had been retired for decades, yet at the age of 95, showed no intention of slowing down or letting up for that matter. An active member of the men's tennis club in his Florida retirement community, Ralph took pleasure in not only playing a good game of tennis, but winning his share of games against the "young" 75-year-olds in the group.

"I'd invite you to my birthday party next year," Ralph often teased the 'young bucks' as he called them, "but I don't know if you'll be around." Apparently no one had told Ralph that he really was "too old" to play tennis. If someone had tried, it's likely he wouldn't have listened anyway.

"I can hardly wait until I retire," John gazed dreamily out the window behind his office cubicle.

"What will you do then?" John's buddy Ed wanted to know.

"Nothing at all—won't that be grand?" After the hectic life he had lived in the corporate world, John envisioned long days basking on a sunny beach.

"I like to be busy myself," Ed replied. "Sure, I'd love to spend some time on the beach. But I've got trips to take, grandkids to play with, and the homeless shelter downtown where I like to volunteer. Retirement will be a nice change of pace, to be sure, but I have no plans to slow down."

After a life of working hard to try and make ends meet, people often dream of the day they can kick back and slow down—and who can blame them? Truth be told, however, an extra-leisurely lifestyle doesn't bode well for achieving peak mental performance.

Research suggests there may be a connection between retirement and mortality in apparently healthy people. The findings surfaced in a study of nearly 17,000 adults. Researchers found that those who were retired upon enrollment in the study were 51% more likely to die during the study period than their same age counterparts who were still working. This trend was observed across all age groups. For example, among men who were younger than 55 at the study entry, 9% of retirees died versus just over 1% of those who were still working. The difference narrowed but was still evident in the older men. The research team found that for every 5-year increase at the age of retirement, there was a 10% decrease in mortality risk. Even when researchers accounted for other factors (such as age, education, smoking habits, and weight), there was still a correlation between retirement status and the odds of dying during the study.

People looking forward to an early retirement may want to rethink those plans. If they are going to retire from their usual jobs, they may want to be involved in productive work on a regular basis after retirement.

## A WORKOUT FOR THE BRAIN

Exercise is extremely beneficial to the body and mind of young, old, healthy, and ailing people. The physical results of consistent exercise translate into significant mental advantages as well. It is especially critical for individuals at risk for cognitive impairment (such as senior citizens). Even relatively short exercise interventions can restore some of the losses in brain volume associated with aging. One study of 1,020 senior housing residents, all of whom were free of dementia, found that the risk of becoming disabled fell 7% for every additional hour spent each week being physically active. In addition, the risk of dying over the next several years fell by 11% for each hour of added weekly activity.[626] Some of the cognition-related benefits of regular aerobic exercise are listed in **Figure 13.1**. An added benefit is weight loss, which can also result in improved cognition.

## ACTIVITY IMPROVES FOCUS

Active octogenarians appear to be more focused and less easily distracted than their less active peers, according to research involving 106 seniors whose average age was 80.[627] In this study, participants completed a survey detailing how much time they spent each week participating in five physical activities—vigorous exercise, leisure walking, moving, standing, and sitting. Afterwards, the seniors were tested on ability to focus mentally.

Physically active seniors were better able to focus on a task at hand, even when distractions were present, than their less active peers. Weight training or an all-out fitness regimen was not a prerequisite to benefit, as researchers noted that a moderate level of physical activity appeared to lead to an improvement in cognitive ability. A study by the National Academy of Sciences found that people who were in better shape had much more activity in attention-related parts of the brain.[628] In the study, 41 people who had no signs of dementia underwent an exercise test to evaluate physical fitness. Researchers also measured the brain activity of the participants while they were performing a task requiring them to pay close attention.

Older adults who had a high level of physical fitness performed better on the activity. In addition, participants who were in better shape demonstrated much more activity in parts of the brain which are believed to be involved in attention. In a second related study, participants were randomly assigned to one of two exercise groups.[629] One group engaged in stretching and toning activities several days a week, while the other group focused on aerobic activity such as walking. At the end of the 6-month program, older adults in the aerobic group experienced a significant improvement in cardiovascular health, attention activity, and increase in brain activity in areas related to attention. In contrast, there were no significant changes in people in the stretching and toning group.

## FITNESS PRESERVES COGNITION

Another study involving 460 seniors from the United Kingdom found that seniors who performed well on a series of fitness tests also tended to score higher on tests of cognitive abilities such as verbal skills, proficiency with numbers, and spatial organization.[630] Each of the 79-year-olds in the study had taken a test in 1932 that measured their I.Q. at age 11.

### BENEFITS OF AEROBIC EXERCISE

- increases serotonin, norepinephrine, and dopamine levels in the brain
- a natural remedy for preventing, reducing, or treating depression, which is just as effective as medication and more effective than traditional counseling
- alleviates anxiety, substance abuse disorders, and ADHD

***Figure 13.1***

In 2000, the participants took the same cognitive tests they had taken 68 years before, as well as fitness tests. Their physical fitness was measured in three ways: a walking test, a test of handgrip strength, and a test of lung function. The participant's childhood I.Q. was considered to be an important factor because, in addition to affecting adulthood cognitive ability, it could affect an individual's odds of staying fit into old age. Researchers did find that higher childhood I.Q. was related to better lung function at age 79. However, no relationship was found between childhood I.Q. and handgrip strength or performance on the walking test.

Of special interest was the fact that physical fitness seemed to preserve mental acuity regardless of childhood I.Q. The individuals who scored highest on the I.Q. test at age 79 were not necessarily those who scored highly at age 11. Rather, the seniors with the highest level of cognitive function were those who scored highest on the walking test, test of handgrip strength, and test of lung function. In other words, a direct relationship was found between physical health at age 79 and cognitive function for the participants involved. A review of published studies on the subject supports the conclusion that exercise keeps not only the body, but also the mind, in tip-top shape.

## AEROBICS ENHANCES MEMORY

Middle-aged individuals—and even those up into their 80s who do not suffer from Alzheimer's disease—have shown a measurable improvement in memory following aerobic exercise programs of nine or ten weeks in duration.[631] In fact, older Americans have a progressive improvement in mental function as they increase their amount of exercise. As one research article put it: "There was a clear linear relationship between the level of activity and the level of cognitive [mental] ability."[632]

Vascular dementia, which ranks second only to Alzheimer's as the most common form of dementia, is caused by an impaired blood flow to the brain. Individuals with diseases that damage blood vessels throughout the body (such as high blood pressure or diabetes) are at increased risk for vascular dementia.

Taking regular walks can help older adults lower their risk of vascular dementia, according to a study recently published by Italian researchers.[633] The study, which included 749 adults who were 65 years of age or older, showed that adults who walked or got other forms of moderate exercise had about ¼ the risk of developing vascular dementia over the next four years as their more sedentary counterparts.

In another study, researchers found that individuals who participated twice weekly in leisure time physical activity had a reduced risk of dementia later in life. Pooled data from 18 intervention studies support the positive influence of fitness training, particularly on "executive" functions such as planning, scheduling, working memory, and multi-tasking. Under more sedentary conditions, many of these processes often show substantial decline with age. While moderate physical activity can certainly result in improved mental processing, fitness training may help even more.

## PLAY DEVELOPS BRAINS

Children are just as much at risk of suffering from a sedentary lifestyle as their age-endowed counterparts. A study reported in the *Archives of Pediatric & Adolescent Medicine* demonstrates this, with researchers concluding that "kids need outside playtime" and that "unstructured playtime, which seems to be steadily disappearing, needs to be restored to children's lives."[634]

Play is essential to development because it contributes to the cognitive, physical, social, and emotional well-being of children. Play allows children to be creative while developing imagination and dexterity. Undirected play allows children to learn how to work in groups, share, negotiate, resolve conflicts and learn self-advocacy skills. Play also offers an excellent opportunity for children to conquer their fears while practicing adult roles and, in the end, improving their emotional intelligence.[635]

Recreation is most beneficial for children's mental growth in a 3D environment (as opposed to computers and television). Hands-on learning allows young people to explore how the world works in a practical way, gain an understanding of materials and processes, and make informed judgments about abstract concepts. Research has shown that increasing time spent on the virtual world of computers is displacing hands-on play. Brain development of children from the Western world is being threatened by their failure to work with their hands in school and at home. Certain classes in school are becoming much less popular, and many schools do not even offer classes in areas that involve working with the hands due to lack of interest. These classes include woodworking, metal work, crafts, agriculture, music, home economics, and auto mechanics.

Apparently, children would rather play computer games and take computer classes than work with their hands. Despite this trend, a recent report confirmed that working with one's hands in a real-world 3D environment is imperative for the full cognitive and intellectual development of young people. The report was released by Dr. Aric Sigman, who was commissioned by the Ruskin Mill Educational Trust. According to Sigman, the Western world is fast becoming "a software instead of a screwdriver society." Many people in our culture today consider working with one's hands to be for the lower class.

Dr. Sigman's report pointed out that many 11-year olds have deficits in certain areas of their cognitive development that were not present in children of the same age a generation or two ago. There has also been a decline in the ability of young engineers and apprentices to conceptualize straightforward mechanical problems. The findings of Dr. Sigman's report clearly emphasize the need for strengthening the role of 3D learning and crafts in education today. It also underscores the need for parents to take the responsibility to ensure that their children get more physical play.

## EXERCISE REDUCES ANXIETY

Highly stressed students who engaged in less exercise reported 21 percent more anxiety than students who exercised more frequently. Exercise helped them get their mind away from their stressors, providing a time-out period.[636] The physical movement also triggers the release of chemicals in the brain that promote a more balanced, relaxed mood. This is supported by the findings listed in **Figure 13.2** by researchers who have found exercise to be beneficial in reducing stress in laboratory rats.[637]

People who physically exercise on a regular basis experience less depression and anxiety.[638] People who are already depressed or anxious will improve with regular physical exercise; the improvement is similar to the improvement experienced with medications but without the side effects.[639]

As I pointed out in the book *Depression: the Way Out*, physical exercise is vital to induce and maintain healthy emotional balance.[640] Exercise has value when it comes to quelling anxious thoughts.

## MOVEMENT MANAGES DEPRESSION

It should not be surprising that exercise can help to fend off depression. Physical activity boosts the brain's natural antidepressants. Researchers who gave mice a week's worth of workouts on a running wheel found that activity in a total of 33 genes had been altered by the exercise. [641] Most notably, exercise enhanced activity in the gene for a nerve growth factor known as VGF. (Nerve growth factors are small proteins important in the development and maintenance of nerve cells.) In their efforts to measure the effects of VGF on the mice, the researchers infused a synthetic version of VGF into the brains of the mice. The result was a "robust antidepressant effect" in standardized tests of animals placed in stressful situations.

Another study, involving humans with Major Depressive Disorder (MDD) in a 16-week treatment program, found that exercise was just as effective in reducing depression as antidepressants.[642] Although the antidepressants facilitated a more rapid initial response in some cases, the results were virtually the same over time. This led researchers to conclude that an exercise training program may be an alternative to antidepressants for treatment of depression in older persons. The findings in this study would certainly be supported by my experience in the *Nedley Depression Recovery Program*, where exercise is an important tool in the arsenal used against this disease. In my experience, it takes at least a week of daily exercise before depressive symptoms begin to improve in most individuals.

Even if you're not depressed, exercise is good for the mind. A study by the National Institutes of Health observed 1,900 healthy subjects. It showed that women who exercise only occasionally or not at all have twice the risk of developing major depression within eight years compared with those that exercised moderately at least several times a week.[643]

Physical exercise brings about better results than most counseling approaches and is certainly much more cost effective.[644] Another study showed that as little as eight minutes of daily vigorous exercise on an inclined treadmill to the point of exhaustion reduced symptoms of depression as well as tension, anger, and fatigue.[645] In another study, memory and other mental abilities were improved after four months of regular aerobic exercise.[646]

## GARDENING SUPPORTS INTELLIGENCE

Researchers at Kansas State University, who had found previously that gardening results in improvements in mental health and depression, now report that gardening can fulfill the daily recommendation for exercise prescribed by the Centers for Disease Control (CDC) and Prevention and the American College of Sports Medicine (ACSM). Results of this study were published in the doctoral dissertation of Sin-Ae Park (entitled "Gardening as a physical activity for health in older adults").

The researchers, who studied 14 gardeners aged 63-86 years, took measurements of the gardener's heart rates, oxygen intake, and energy expenditure. Participants in the study also kept weekly logs of their gardening activity. The researchers also found that senior gardeners had better hand coordination and other physical functions than non-gardeners. Furthermore, gardening was found to be a predictor for leading a physically active lifestyle and high life satisfaction in older adults.

### EXERCISE HELPS WITH THE "RAT RACE"

Exercise has even been shown to reduce the stress of laboratory rats. Rats that exercised regularly:

- had lower levels of damaging protein in stress-related parts of their brains
- released less adrenal norepinephrine, a stress hormone
- appeared to recover more quickly from infections

*Figure 13.2*

**RESULTS OF REGULAR EXERCISE**

- benefit to mental health and well-being
- short-term reductions in stress such as anxiety and tension
- long-term reductions in anxiety
- long-term reductions in depression in moderately-depressed individuals
- reduction in muscle tension, heart rate, and stress hormone levels

*Figure 13.3*

Tending a garden is an enjoyable and productive way to encourage physical activity for young and old alike. Garden-based nutrition-education programs for youth are gaining popularity in some sections of the U.S., and for good reason. A review of eleven scientific studies published between 1990 and 2007 found that garden-based nutrition intervention programs may have the potential to promote increased fruit and vegetable intake among youth and increased willingness to taste fruits and vegetables among younger children.

Getting youngsters to eat what they grow is only one of the benefits attributed to the gardening programs springing up around the country. Leaders of programs such as the "Edible Schoolyard" in California and "National Farm-to-School Program" report positive benefits in a wide range of characteristics among youth, including improved environmental attitudes, community spirit, social skills, self-confidence, leadership skills, volunteerism, motor skills, scholastic achievement, and open attitudes toward good nutrition.

The usefulness of gardening to promote health and intellect, as well as being a good teaching tool, was promoted in the 1800's by well-known author Ellen White, who wrote that "as a rule, the exercise most beneficial to the youth will be found in useful employment. The little child finds both diversion and development in play; and his sports should be such as to promote not only physical, but mental and spiritual growth. As he gains strength and intelligence, the best recreation will be found in some line of effort that is useful. That which trains the hand to helpfulness, and teaches the young to bear their share of life's burdens, is most effective in promoting the growth of mind and character."[647]

## JOGGING MAKES YOU SMARTER

Another study found that individuals consistently scored higher on intellectual tests after embarking on a 3-month running program.[648] The study involved seven healthy young people, who each ran for 30 minutes, 2-3 times per week for at least 12 weeks. Each of the runners also took a series of complex computer-based tests, to compare memory skills before and after the 3-month jogging program.

After 12 weeks of jogging, scores on all of the tests "significantly increased" in the runners, as did their reaction times in completing the tests. The researchers, who pointed out that the runners had no time to practice the tests between evaluations, concluded that the joggers had a clear improvement in prefrontal lobe function. Interestingly enough, the scores began to fall when participants stopped their running routine.

Several animal studies also support the idea that aerobic training (such as jogging) has a positive effect on the brain.[649,650] Exercise that gets your heart pumping improves blood flow in the brain, encourages the formation of new neurons, and increases the number of connections called synapses that form between neurons. All in all, regular exercise can improve your quality of life, as detailed in **Figure 13.3**.

## BEAGLE BRAINS BENEFIT TOO

Even our canine friends need exercise and a proper diet to keep them healthy and spry, according to a study reported in the journal Neurobiology of Aging.[651] In a two-year experiment that scientists said "could teach humans a thing or two," researchers found that exercise and a diet fortified with vitamins, fruits, and vegetables helped older dogs learn new tricks. The study divided thirty beagles into three groups. One set of dogs received a diet supplemented with tomatoes, carrot granules, citrus pulp, spinach flakes, and other nutrients, as well as a play and exercise routine. A second group received only the supplemented diet without the exercise. The third set of dogs received a standard diet and no special exercise.

**When they exercised and ate right, senior beagles were much more efficient at finding treats.**

The researchers tested the intelligence of the beagles by having them find a hidden treat. All of the dogs that got the supplemented diet and exercise could solve a difficult problem. In contrast, 80% of the dogs that got the enriched diet alone could find the treat and only 25% of the dogs that got no special treatment could solve the problem. Researchers concluded that the combination of an antioxidant diet and exercise significantly improved the brain function of the senior beagles in in the study.

## RAPID RESULTS

The good news is that a four-component lifestyle program can improve memory and brain efficiency in as little as two weeks.[652] This was shown in a 14-day study of 34 adults with normal memory. The participants were randomly assigned to two groups. One group engaged in a memory improvement plan with a diet rich in omega-3 fats, olive oil, healthy whole grain carbohydrates, and antioxidants. They also engaged in cardiovascular exercise. In contrast, the second group made no behavior modifications.

At the conclusion of the 14-day study, PET scans were taken of the participant's brains. Researchers noted that adults who followed the memory improvement plan experienced a marked decrease in brain metabolism in an area of the brain linked to working memory and other cognitive functions, suggesting that they were using their brains more efficiently.

In other words, people with better memories actually used up less brain power. This would be similar to the effect of a weight-lifting routine on the body. After a few weeks of training, you can lift more weights—while actually using less energy to do it. So, as your brainpower increases, you can actually achieve better cognitive function with less effort.

The results of this study, which included participants ranging from 35 to 70 years of age, were basically the same for all age categories, leading researchers to conclude that it's never too late or too early to get started on a healthy lifestyle in order to improve brain health.

## TIPS FOR EXERCISE SUCCESS

As with any lifestyle change, you may not notice any significant benefits or improvement in your first week of exercise. Stay with your positive new exercise routine consistently, however, and improvement will come. Introduce a new sport or exercise into your routine or listen to classical music as you exercise. Changing it up, if you are able, will keep freshness and excitement in your life. If you live in a climate that makes it difficult

### CHECK WITH YOUR DOCTOR

The risks of physical activity are very low compared to the benefits, so most adults don't need a medical evaluation before beginning a moderate intensity exercise program. However, the following individuals should see a doctor before starting a vigorous program:

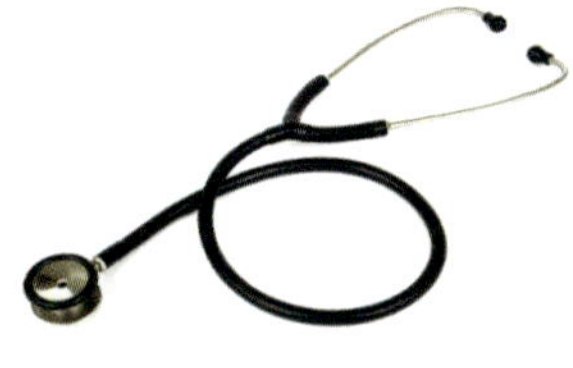

- people with known cardiovascular disease
- men over 40 with multiple cardiovascular risk factors
- women over 50 with multiple cardiovascular risk factors

**Figure 13.4**

## WALKING WITH A PEDOMETER SPURS WEIGHT LOSS

Researchers have found that simply strapping on a pedometer and trying to walk more steps per day is enough to help most people lose a modest amount of weight. Pedometers are small devices usually worn at the waist that count the number of steps a person takes. While some people use pedometers during long walks, the most effective strategy is to wear one all day and see how many steps you can accumulate. 10,000 steps is widely recommended as a goal to strive for daily.

***Figure 13.5***

to exercise outdoors part of the year, many indoor shopping malls encourage walkers. Another option is an aerobic exercise video. Is disability threatening to keep you from exercising? Remember, exercise is a vital key to your wellness, so talk to someone familiar with exercise (for example: a trainer at a gym, YMCA, or community center) who can suggest a routine which works with your limitations. If you suffer from any of the conditions listed in **Figure 13.4**, check with a doctor before getting started.

If you're not up to jogging, don't worry. Walking, which is one of the easiest and most effective exercises, can also benefit cognition. One of the best ways to get started on a walking program is to strap on a pedometer, as documented in **Figure 13.5**.[653] To prevent strain, warm up your muscles by doing ankle circles or leg swings, or start out walking slowly for three to five minutes before safely picking up your pace. Remember to stretch again after you finish walking.

Many people think they get more out of their exercise if they push themselves harder and longer until they are completely exhausted. But scientific research shows that by adding a short portion of rest into every minute of our exercise, we more efficiently build up our muscles and cardiovascular fitness. It's how our muscles and bodies were designed to perform best so we get more for less! Interval Training (I.T.) is a way to exercise that helps incorporate rest as a natural part of activity. I.T. teaches that rest makes the work more effective, and is an excellent choice for those who are unfit or who desire to maximize their exercise minutes without muscle soreness.

With a proper understanding of Interval Training, you can realize that the old saying, "no pain, no gain," is not completely true. You'll be much more inclined to exercise on subsequent days if you don't hurt yourself on the previous day's program, which is what makes I.T. such an excellent idea. Newcomers are often hesitant to exercise because they dread muscle soreness. In those who are unfit, frequent 30-second periods of rest will prevent this from happening. You can do almost any physical activity in the style of I.T. – simply choose your favorite exercise and follow the guidelines in **Figure 13.6**.

The fact is, when done right, exercise can be an enjoyable way to increase our quality of life and mood. There are so many different things that qualify as exercise that you can easily incorporate energy and excitement into getting started. Pick a fitness program that works well with your schedule, ability, and physical aptitude.

## GAIN WITHOUT PAIN—GETTING STARTED WITH I.T.

Entire books have been written on this subject, but these are the basics.

- Begin with 5 to 10 minutes of gentle stretching.
- Next, warm up your circulatory system with 5 minutes of slow, comfortable walking at a continuous pace.
- Start your chosen exercise at a vigorous pace; continue for 60 seconds.
- "Rest" for 30 seconds by easing off to a gentler pace until your heart rate slows slightly. (Don't stop completely!)
- Begin your vigorous pace again for the next interval of 60 seconds.
- Slow your pace again for 30 seconds. (Continue to perform your exercise less vigorously.)

- Continue alternating between very active then milder exercise intervals until your total time is achieved.
- To finish, do some gentle stretching and slow, comfortable walking for 5-10 minutes to cool down.

You will eventually be able to extend the length of your exercise intervals to several minutes as your physical fitness improves.

*Figure 13.6*

| EXPEND 150 CALORIES* WITH MODERATE EXERCISE | |
|---|---|
| Volleyball | 45 minutes |
| Brisk walking | 30 minutes |
| Raking leaves or active gardening | 30 minutes |
| Swimming laps | 20 minutes |
| Playing basketball | 15-20 minutes |
| Running (1.5 miles) | 15 minutes |

*time/calorie calculations based on a 150 lb/68.2 kg person.

***Figure 13.7***

**Activity in the fresh morning air, such as a brisk walk or tending a garden, is one of the best ways to get your blood circulating freely.**

## WHAT ARE YOU WAITING FOR?

It is never too late to begin an exercise program. The benefits of exercise extend far beyond cognitive function. Exercise and a healthy immune system go hand-in-hand. Research has shown that regardless of how out of shape a person is, the risk of death from all causes could be reduced by merely becoming fit through a regular exercise program.[654] Studies have shown that an increase in physical activity that burns as few as 500 calories decreases mortality risk. Although the greatest benefit will be experienced by those who expend at least 3500 calories per week in physical exercise, significant benefit can be derived with a program that burns 750 calories per week.[655] **Figure 13.7** provides a list of calorie-burning activities.

Medical research continues to uncover more and more science showing the positive benefits of exercise on quality of life. Without a doubt, exercise is an important part of a healthy lifestyle. The benefits of regular physical activity are enormous, while the risks are few. So what are you waiting for? Ramp up your body—and mind—today!

## References

626. Boyle PA, et al. "Physical activity is associated with incident disability in community-based older persons." *Journal of the American Geriatrics Society* 55.2 (2007): 195+.

627. Bixby W. North American Society for Psychology of Sport and Physical Activity Conference in Hunt Valley, Maryland.

628. Colcombe SJ, et al. "Cardiovascular fitness, cortical plasticity, and aging." *Proceedings of the National Academy of Sciences* 101.9 (2004): 3316+.

629. Colcombe SJ, et al. "Cardiovascular fitness, cortical plasticity, and aging." *Proceedings of the National Academy of Sciences* 101.9 (2004): 3316+.
630. Deary IJ, et al. "Physical fitness and lifetime cognitive change." *Neurology* 67.7 (2006).
631. Bowers RW, et al. "Memory Dependent Reaction Time and Improved Cardiovascular Fitness in Middle-aged Adults." *Medicine and Science in Sports and Exercise* 15 (1983).
632. Clarkson-Smith L, Hartley AA. "Relationships between physical exercise and cognitive abilities in older adults." *Psychology and Aging* 4.2 (1989): 183+.
633. Ravaglia G. "Physical activity and dementia risk in the elderly. Findings from a prospective Italian study." *Neurology Online* (2007).
634. Burdette, HL and RC Whitaker. "Resurrecting free play in young children: Looking beyond fitness and fatness to attention, affiliation, and affect." Archives of Pediatrics and Adolescent Medicine 159.1 (2005): 46+.
635. Ginsburg K. "The Importance of Play in Promoting Healthy Child Development and Maintaining Strong Parent-child Bonds." *Pediatrics* 119.1 (2007): 182+.
636. Carmack CL. "Aerobic fitness and leisure physical activity as moderators of the stress-illness relation." *Annals of Behavioral Medicine* 21.3 (1999): 251+.
637. ScienceDaily. "CU Studies Suggest Exercise Protects Body Against Negative Effects of Stress From Brain to Cell." 27 October 1999. 21 April 2008 <http://www.sciencedaily.com/releases/1999/10/991027072350.htm>.
638. Martinsen EW. "Physical fitness, anxiety, and depression." *British Journal of Hospital Medicine* 43.3 (1990): 194, 196+.
639. Hales RE, Stolt J. "Exercise as a treatment option for anxiety and depressive disorders." *Military Medicine* 152.6 (1987): 299+.
640. Byrne A, Byrne DG. "The effect of exercise on depression, anxiety and other mood states: A review." *Journal of Psychosomatic Research* 37.6 (1993): 565+.
641. Hunsberger J, et al. "Antidepressant actions of the exercise-regulated gene VGF." *Nature Medicine* 13.12 (2007): 1476+.
642. Blumenthal JA, et al. "Effects of exercise on older patients with major depression." *Archives of Internal Medicine* 159.19 (1999): 2349+.
643. Farmer ME, et al. "Physical Activity and Depressive Symptoms: The NHANES I Epidemiological Follow-up Study." *American Journal of Epidemiology* 128.6 (1988): 1340+.
644. Tkachuk GA, Martin GL. "Exercise Therapy for Patients With Psychiatric Disorders: Research and Clinical Implications." *Professional Psychology: Research and Practice* 30.3 (1999): 275+.
645. Moore KA. Study presented by Duke University at the Society of Behavioral Medicine, San Francisco, California, April 17, 1997.
646. Babyak M, et al. "Exercise Treatment for Major Depression: Maintenance of Therapeutic Benefit at 10 Months." *Psychosomatic Medicine* 62 (2000): 633+.
647. White EG *Education* (1903) Manual Training Chapter 24 p. 215.
648. Richardson CR, et al. "A Meta-analysis of Pedometer-based Walking Interventions and Weight Loss." *Annals of Family Medicine* 6.1 (2008).
649. Taeko H, Okagawa S, Kubota K. "Jogging improved performance of a behavioral branching task: Implications for prefrontal activation." *Neuroscience Research* 49.3 (2004): 325+.
650. O'Callaghan RM, Ohle R, Kelly AM. "The effects of forced exercise on hippocampal plasticity in the rat: A comparison of LTP, spatial and non-spatial learning." *Behavioural Brain Research* 176.2 (2007): 362+.
651. Milgram NW, et al. "Learning ability in aged beagle dogs is preserved by behavioral enrichment and dietary fortification: A two-year longitudinal study." *Neurobiology of Aging* 26.1 (2005): 77+.
652. Small GW, et al. "Effects of a 14-Day Healthy Longevity Lifestyle Program on Cognition and Brain Function." *American Journal of Geriatric Psychiatry* 14 (2006): 538+.
653. Van der Broght K, et al. "Exercise improves memory acquisition and retrieval in the Y-maze task: Relationship with hippocampal neurogenesis." *Behavioural Neuroscience* 121.2 (2007): 324+.
654. Blair, SN, et al. "Physical Fitness and All-Cause Mortality: A Prospective Study of Healthy Men and Women." *JAMA*. 1989;262(17):2395-2401.
655. Paffenbarger RS Jr, Hyde RT, et al. "The association of changes in physical activity level and other lifestyle characteristics with mortality among men." *N Engl J Med* 1993 Feb 25;328(8):538-545.

Chapter 14

SUNSHINE IS A VITAL INGREDIENT IN OPTIMAL OVERALL HEALTH. IT IS ALSO CRITICAL FOR PEAK MENTAL PERFORMANCE.

# Turn On the Bright Lights

***Bright light therapy plays an important role in brain function, from alleviating symptoms of depression to balancing circadian rhythms.***

Tracy stood hesitantly in her front hall for a few moments before tentatively opening the front door of her home. It was the first spring-like day after a lengthy Michigan winter. The snow had melted and the trees were starting to bud.

Tracy squinted a bit as she stepped out into the bright morning sunshine, happy to confirm that her toes were not freezing inside her slippers. The birds trilled happy little songs, the sun beamed down on the sidewalk, and the promise of spring permeated the fresh morning air. Tracy stood on her porch basking in the warmth and light, feeling her skin tingle under the sun's rays.

Then something incredible happened, or it least it seemed so to Tracy. She hadn't thought she had been depressed, yet suddenly everything seemed so much better.

"It literally felt like a ton of bricks was lifted from off my shoulders," Tracy later said to a friend, "a ton of bricks I hadn't realized was there."

Unwittingly, and like so many others who have shared her plight, Tracy's mood had been affected by Seasonal Affective Disorder (SAD), a form of depression triggered by lack of sunshine.

## MODERN DAY SUNSHINE DISRUPTIONS

The importance of sunlight to health and well-being has been recognized since ancient times. Songs, poems, stories, and folklore all support the association between sunshine and happiness. John Denver's song "Sunshine on my Shoulders" and the hymn "There is Sunshine in My Soul Today" are both examples of this. In contrast, a lack of sunshine is frequently associated with sadness or "the blues."

*"When my heart is heavy, the sun helps make it light."*
—Astrid Alauda

Technology has allowed us to miss out on much-needed sunshine by providing us with an environment in which we can live and function indoors at any hour of the day or night. Regardless of its usefulness, such unnatural lighting is often discordant with natural body rhythms. In addition, most artificial (incandescent and standard fluorescent) lighting lacks the intensity of natural sunlight, as well as the complete balanced spectrum of light which the sun so ably provides.

Windows, windshields, eyeglasses, smog, and suntan lotions all contribute to this "mal-illumination" by filtering out segments of the light spectrum. Compounding the problem is the fact that as the days become shorter in the fall, many people do not get enough light to end the body's internal night. As a result, bodies fail to shut off production of melatonin when morning comes. The effects of this failure set off a cascade of responses, resulting in the Seasonal Affective Disorder (SAD) as experienced by Tracy in the previous story. The condition, which has the identical symptoms to depression, resolves when the individual is exposed to bright light.

## BENEFITS OF BRIGHT LIGHT

As light enters the eyes, photoreceptors convert it into nerve impulses that travel along the optic nerve to the brain. These impulses trigger the hypothalamus gland, which in turn sends neurotransmitters to regulate the automatic functions of the body (such as blood pressure, body temperature, respiration, digestion, pulse, moods, immune and hormonal modulation, and circadian rhythm).[656,657]

SAD is a common condition in the Northern Latitudes like the Scandinavian countries and Alaska. People from the Arctic Circle in Norway understand the value of sunlight: in the winter virtually all of them suffer from SAD.[658] They address the problem by placing light stations on many street corners (just as we have gas stations on many street corners here).

Moderate amounts of sunshine may also be beneficial in cancer prevention. Researchers at the University of Washington found that men from the Northern states (who might naturally be exposed to less sunshine) had colon cancer rates 50 to 80 percent higher than men from the Southern states. The effect also seemed to hold true for women, although it was not as profound.[659] The effectiveness of bright light therapy is something that makers of Viagra®, Cialis®, and Levitra® would just as soon you didn't know. Though these drugs are sold very commonly in America, they wouldn't be nearly as common if the men taking them made some light-related lifestyle changes.

Researchers have found that men who are exposed to an hour of bright light first thing in the morning experience an increase in luteinizing hormone. Luteinizing hormone, which is produced by the pituitary gland, helps regulate reproductive processes in males and females. In men, this hormone stimulates the production of testosterone. Determining the amount of luteinizing hormone present is a common step in investigating infertility in both sexes.[660] Bright light also contributes to hormonal regulation in women. In one study, researchers found that bright light helped regulate the monthly cycles of women who had long and irregular menstrual periods.[661]

In the more agricultural societies of the past, farmers and their wives were outside getting their bright light each morning as they did chores. This could explain why erectile dysfunction and irregular menstrual cycles were much less common in those days. Our male ancestors had healthy sexual function into their 60s, 70s, and even 80s. In many cases, this would be due to the positive effects of bright light through the eyes.

*"I do know that sunshine activates our happiness glands."*

—Jessi Lane Adams

## LIGHT UP YOUR MENTAL PERFORMANCE

Sunlight has beneficial effects on the mood in general and the frontal lobe in particular. Among other things, sunshine is capable of increasing serotonin production in the daytime. This, in turn, helps prevent depression and fatigue.[662] Animal research indicates that exposure to natural daylight also results in significantly higher evening melatonin levels than an equal amount of exposure to artificial light.[663] The role of melatonin, in turn, promotes sound sleep and may help to boost frontal lobe function the following day.

Research has shown that serotonin and melatonin regulation play a role in mental performance, and that the body's regulation of these compounds is influenced by light.[664] Scientists from the University of Alabama recently studied 16,800 participants in the "stroke belt" (a high-stroke mortality region consisting of the 8 southeastern states) to determine if sunlight exposure was related to cognitive impairment. In individuals with a history of depression, the researchers found that low levels of sunlight exposure were associated with a more than 2.5 times increase in risk of impaired cognitive function. Even after allowing for seasonal differences, the researchers found a significant correlation between cognitive impairment and a lack of sunlight exposure.[665]

Bright light therapy is also an effective remedy for partum and postpartum depression. This condition is caused by a reduction in hormones related to the fact that the placenta is no longer present. Missed sleep and other lifestyle changes also contribute to the stress faced by new mothers.

As a result, two thirds of women suffer from "the blues" within two weeks of delivery and up to 15% end up with major depression after giving birth, a condition which could be alleviated to some degree by additional morning sunlight.[666]

Even filtered sunlight, streaming through an office window, appears to promote better brain function. Researchers who evaluated various work factors (such as privacy, an office with a "view," and sunlight) found access to sunlight in the office to be one of several factors that improved both mood and mental performance.[667]

## OUTDOOR LIGHT: WHAT YOU NEED TO KNOW

The light produced by the sun is incredibly more intense than the artificial variety. Outdoor light can reach 80,000 lux on a bright sunny day.[475] A bright indoor environment may provide only 400 lux, less than 1% of daylight brightness.[476]

If you are in a geographic area where the sun doesn't shine as long or strong as other areas, consider investing in a medical grade blue light (470 nn wavelength) that simulates the blue sky. Some of the blue-light generators are even available with an alarm clock built-in, so the light comes on at the time you need to get up. This will assist you in obtaining your bright light first thing in the morning. You will only need 15-20 minutes of exposure with this light.

Blue light is actually more effective than other light in halting the body's production of melatonin, and thus is a specific treatment for SAD. However, if you cannot obtain a medical grade blue light, another option is using a 10,000 lux white light for 30 minutes.

## SETTING YOUR BODY CLOCK

**$R_x$ for a balanced daily rhythm:**

**30 minutes of sunshine or bright light therapy within 10 minutes of waking.**

You've probably heard of something called "circadian rhythm." The word circadian comes from two Latin words: circa, meaning "around," and dian, which means "day." What this phrase is referring to is our daily rhythms.[668] Balancing your daily rhythms is vital to emotional and mental wellness. Waking up with the sun each morning and taking in the natural light is an easy way to find this balance. If the sun rises later than you do, purchase a therapeutic bright light box and alarm clock to set your circadian rhythm. It will be a valuable investment in your health.

Bright light in the morning sets your body clock and is absolutely critical for people who are fatigued, have disordered sleep, or depression or SAD. Maintaining a regular sleep schedule (as discussed in chapter 16) is the other component in the equation. Because light is one factor that suppresses melatonin production in humans, it is also important to avoid bright light exposure in the evening before going to bed.[669] When light is necessary during the night (e.g., waking up to use the bathroom), use a dim light if possible.

## VITAMIN D: THE SUNSHINE VITAMIN

Because the skin makes it from ultraviolet rays, vitamin D is nicknamed the "sunshine vitamin." Vitamin D is a fat-soluble vitamin that is necessary to regulate many body systems such as the immune system, the thyroid gland, and the circulatory system. Vitamin D also regulates absorption and the blood level of various minerals, particularly calcium.[670]

Though once relegated to the field of bone health, vitamin D has emerged as a powerful, wide-ranging, health-enhancer. Recent reviews by international vitamin D authority Dr. Michael Holick report an amazing list of benefits linked to this nutrient which are documented in **Figure 14.1**.[671] Medical research suggests that maintaining optimal vitamin D status can help preserve mental function and stave off neurodegenerative disorders throughout the lifespan. Evidence from animal studies also suggests that vitamin D has a protective effect on neurons and may regulate the production of certain neurotransmitters.[672]

Although there are some dietary sources of vitamin D, sunlight is the best way to obtain this valuable nutrient. It's not easy to obtain enough of this essential vitamin through food alone. For example, a person would have to drink 10 large glasses of vitamin D fortified milk each day just to reach a minimal daily level. Individuals with limited sun exposure, especially those with darker skin, should consider vitamin D supplementation. (1-4,000 IU per day is considered a safe level). The best "supplementation," however, remains a good sunbath.

### HEALTH BENEFITS OF VITAMIN D

- enhanced calcium absorption and bone health
- increased muscle function (speed, strength, and fall prevention)
- reduced risk of cancer and certain lymphomas
- improved cardiovascular health (helps lower high blood pressure and treat congestive heart failure)
- superior immune system function and decreased risk of rheumatoid arthritis and type 1 diabetes, as well as certain infectious illnesses such as tuberculosis
- prevention of pregnancy complications
- better mental function and lower risk of conditions such as multiple sclerosis, depression, schizophrenia, insomnia, and fatigue

*Figure 14.1*

## D-EFICIENCY DANGERS

One study reported that when all risk factors are considered, having a low level of vitamin D increases the risk of heart attack just as much as high blood pressure or smoking.[673] Another study, which included 22 clinical investigations of patients with pain, found that those with chronic back pain almost always had inadequate levels of vitamin D.[674] Deficiency can also precipitate or exacerbate osteopenia and osteoporosis.[675]

In a large-scale study of senior citizens, researchers from the Peninsula Medical School, the University of Cambridge and the University of Michigan recently identified a relationship between vitamin D and cognitive impairment. The study, which involved 1766 adults aged 65 and over, demonstrated that levels of cognitive impairment increased as levels of vitamin D decreased. Seniors with the lowest levels of vitamin D were more than twice as likely to be cognitively impaired as those with optimum levels.[676]

**An Irish Blessing**

**May flowers always line your path and sunshine light your day.**

**May songbirds serenade you every step along the way.**

**May a rainbow run beside you in a sky that's always blue.**

**And may happiness fill your heart each day your whole life through.**

New research involving 3,133 European men suggests that vitamin D may also boost cognitive function in middle-aged and older brains. Scientists in the study, which was published in the *Journal of Neurology, Neurosurgery, and Psychiatry*, found that men (ages 40-70) with higher levels of vitamin D performed consistently better on a test that measured attention and how fast the brain processes information. Though the researchers didn't see an association between vitamin D and memory, they did see a link between lower blood levels of vitamin D and reduced performance on a test that assessed the processing speed of the brain. (The association between vitamin D and processing speed was strongest in men aged 60 and older).[677]

The connection between vitamin D and mood disorders has also been scientifically established. A study at the University of Newcastle in Australia tested the effects of supplemental vitamin D intake versus a placebo in a group of healthy subjects in late winter. The subjects receiving vitamin D had a dramatic improvement in mood scores versus the placebo group.[678] Researchers in the Netherlands, who studied more than 1000 individuals who were over 65 years of age, found a connection between depression and lower vitamin D levels.[679]

Another recent study tested the effects of vitamin D supplementation on subjects suffering from Seasonal Affective Disorder (SAD) for a one-month period. Again, the subjects receiving vitamin D had a measurable improvement when evaluated using depression scale tests versus subjects not receiving supplementation.[680]

Maternal deficiencies of this vitamin are now generating greater concern for a variety of reasons. One of them is emerging research suggesting an important role for vitamin D in mammalian brain development. A number of animal models show mothers deficient in this "sunshine vitamin" give birth to offspring with neurodevelopmental abnormalities.[681,682]

One current controversy in the human research literature is whether or not prenatal vitamin D deficiency predisposes the fetus to psychiatric disorders.[683,684,685,686] Although there is no conclusive answer yet, the discussion underscores the growing concerns with vitamin D's importance in brain development.

Scientists are also finding links between low vitamin D levels and other mental disorders. Marian Evatt, MD and her colleagues at Emory University in Atlanta recently reported a striking association between low vitamin D levels and Parkinson's disease.[687] It is too soon to say whether vitamin D deficiency is a cause or a result of the condition (for example, Parkinson's patients may be less likely to get outside in the sunshine). However, other evidence suggests a causal relationship.

The *subtantia nigra*, the brain region hardest hit by Parkinson's disease, has an abundance of vitamin D receptors, suggesting this vitamin-hormone is especially needed in this important center of movement coordination.[688] A recent report in the *Journal of Alzheimer's Disease* suggests a broader connection between low vitamin D levels and neurodegenerative disorders—including Alzheimer's.[689]

*"I think you might dispense with half your doctors if you would only consult Dr. Sun more."*

—Henry Ward Beecher

## THE CALCIUM CONNECTION

No discussion of bright light therapy or vitamin D would be complete without addressing the role this essential nutrient plays in optimal calcium absorption. Research suggests that part of vitamin D's brain benefits may be related to its favorable effects on calcium status.[690] The far-ranging benefit of calcium on all aspects of nervous system function is supported by numerous studies.

Some of the emerging areas of calcium's role in brain and nerve function involve how calcium may have important signaling roles even on the outside of nerve cells.[691] In this context, calcium deficiency can depress transmission of certain nerve impulses. An impressive body of evidence has also linked dietary calcium to prevention of known risk factors for depression and other conditions that impair brain health. That list includes high blood pressure, stroke prevention, and blood fat abnormalities.[692,693,694]

Susan Thys-Jacobs, an endocrinologist at St. Luke-Roosevelt Hospital, found that calcium supplementation can relieve the physical and emotional toll of PMS by almost 50%. At least half of the 497 women she studied who took calcium supplementation (1,200 mg. daily) experienced fewer mood swings and feelings of depression, sadness, anxiety, nervousness, or other PMS-related symptoms.[695] Clearly, the achievement of optimal mental and physical health is directly related to sufficient calcium in the diet—which can only be properly absorbed in the presence of adequate vitamin D.

Soy beans and greens are a good natural source of calcium. Some green leafy vegetables—like collards and lambsquarters—have even more calcium per serving than soybeans. Furthermore, these foods are lower in protein and therefore should not extract calcium from our bones. A helpful list of food calcium sources is provided in **Figure 14.2**.[696]

## BAD PRESS FOR THE SUN

Despite the value of sunlight as the best method of procuring vitamin D for the body, it is possible to get "too much of a good thing." Sunburn, the result of overexposure to the ultraviolet rays of the sun, causes both immediate and long-term damage to both surface skin and the supporting tissue below the skin. Visual evidence may take years to develop, but once it has happened, it is irreversible. Marked wrinkling, a leathery thickening of the skin, patchy increases in pigmentation, or wart-like lumps (called

**CALCIUM IN COMMON FOODS** *RDA is 1000mg adults

| Food Item | Serving | Ca (mg) |
|---|---|---|
| Lambsquarters | 1cup | 464 |
| Carob flour | 1cup | 358 |
| Collard greens | 1cup | 357 |
| Nonfat skim milk | 1cup | 301 |
| Amaranth grain | 1cup | 298 |
| Whole milk | 1cup | 290 |
| Figs (dried) | 10 ea | 269 |
| Green soybeans | 1cup | 261 |
| Filberts/Hazelnuts (dried) | 1cup | 254 |
| Turnip greens | 1cup | 249 |
| Kale | 1cup | 179 |
| Blackstrap cane molasses | 1 Tbs | 176 |
| Sesame seeds (dried) | 2 Tbs | 176 |
| Baked beans | 1cup | 154 |
| Mustard greens | 1cup | 152 |
| Dandelion greens | 1cup | 147 |
| Rutabagas | 1cup | 115 |
| Quinoa grain | 1cup | 102 |
| Lentils | 1cup | 38 |
| Oatmeal | 1cup | 19 |

*Figure 14.2*

solar keratoses) are all common in middle-aged or elderly individuals who have spent much of their lives outdoors exposed to the weather and the sun. Individuals who have had several episodes of sunburn are more likely to develop skin cancer. People with long-term sun exposure who have never been sunburned are also at risk, however. Skin cancer is the most serious risk of repeated overexposure to the sun. About 95 percent of skin cancers are of two types: squamous cell and basal cell.[697] Both types of cancer are increased by substantial cumulative lifetime exposure to the sun. The good news is that squamous cell and basal cell skin cancer are slow growing and usually remain confined to the skin.

*"The light is pleasant, and it is good for the eyes to see the sun."*

—Ecclesiastes 11:7 NASV

A third type of skin cancer, melanoma, is much more deadly. While melanoma accounts for about three percent of skin cancer cases, it's responsible for more than 75 percent of skin cancer deaths.[698] Despite medicine's success in fighting some of the other more common cancers, the rate of melanoma diagnoses continues to rise. Approximately 68,720 melanomas were diagnosed in 2009, with nearly 8,650 resulting in death.[699,700]

Despite these concerns, the number of skin cancer fatalities (from all types) each year is less than one percent of new diagnoses for the disease. Furthermore, such fatalities occur mostly in those who fail to get prompt and complete removal of the cancer. While overexposure to sunlight and sunburn in particular should be avoided, warnings to "stay out of the sun" can be overblown. Some researchers believe that the health benefits of exposure to sunlight outweigh the risk of skin cancer.

Dr. Edward Giovannucci, a Harvard University professor of medicine and nutrition, contends that the number of annual cancer deaths prevented by sunlight exposure far exceeded the number of deaths from skin cancer. Dr. Giovannucci laid out his case in a keynote lecture at a recent American Association for Cancer Research meeting, stating that vitamin D from sun exposure might help prevent 30 deaths for each one caused by skin cancer.

"I would challenge anyone to find an area or nutrient or any factor that has such consistent anti-cancer benefits as vitamin D," Giovannucci told the cancer scientists. "The data is really quite remarkable."[701] Given the significant benefits to be derived from obtaining adequate sunlight, I recommend that (where possible) exposure to judicious amounts of sunshine be part of the daily routine.

## DAILY DOSES OF SUNSHINE

In order to achieve peak mental performance, we really need to be exposed to daylight for at least thirty minutes a day.[702] Our brains can't make enough serotonin without bright light, and we need that light through the eyes as well as on our skin. The further from the equator, the longer exposure to the sun is needed in order to generate adequate vitamin D. People with dark skin pigmentation may need 20-30 times as much exposure to sunlight as fair-skinned people to generate the same amount of vitamin D.[703] Fair-skinned individuals may receive enough UVB to produce about 10,000 international units of vitamin D simply by going outside for 10 minutes each midday in shorts and a tank top with no sun screen.

The amount of exposure needed also depends on the time of the year, location, amount of cloud cover, and pollution. In the northern hemisphere, the UVB is more intense during the summer months and less intense during the winter months. People living north of 42-degrees latitude (which corresponds to a line on the map drawn from Boston, Massachusetts, west to Chicago, and on to the northern border of California), won't be able to get enough vitamin D from sunlight from November through February, so supplementation or blue light therapy may be necessary.

Since vitamin D is stored in the body's fatty cells, outdoor workers employed in the summer sun may not need to supplement with vitamin D during the winter months. While sunlight exposure will never result in an overdose of vitamin D, it is possible to overdose with dietary vitamin D supplementation. Individuals who are orally taking more than 4,000 units of vitamin D daily may wish to check blood vitamin D levels to ensure that their bodies aren't becoming toxic through consumption of excess vitamin D.

### BASK IN THE GLOW OF LIGHT THERAPY

Unfortunately, people who live where sunshine is much more prevalent tend to take it for granted and stay indoors much of the time. The resultant lack of sunlight takes a toll on the brain and is one of the controllable lifestyle factors that can impede mental performance or even trigger depression. It is not coincidental that people who spend time outside in the sun appear healthy and satisfied. Use the sun judiciously and your serotonin levels will be brought up, mood will improve, vitamin D levels will rise, calcium will be more adequately absorbed, and your probability of achieving peak mental performance will be greatly enhanced.[704]

## References

656. Rostand SG. "Ultraviolet Light May Contribute to Geographic and Racial Blood Pressure Differences." *Hypertension* 30: 150-156.
657. Surtman RJ. "The Effect of Light on the Human Body." *Scientific American*. 1975.
658. Haggag A, Eklund B, LInaker O, Götestam, KG. "Seasonal mood variation: an epidemiological study in northern Norway." Acta Psychiatrica Scandinavica VL 81 IS 2 1990.
659. Emerson JC, Weiss NS. "Colorectal cancer and solar radiation." *Cancer Causes and Control.* Volume 3, Number 1. January, 1992.
660. *Neuroscience Letters* 2003;341:25-28.
661. Dewan EM, Menkin MF, Rock J. "Effect of Photic Stimulation on the Human Menstrual Cycle." *Photochemistry and Photobiology*. Volume 27 Issue 5, Pages 581 - 585.
662. Muller-Oerlinghausen RMB, et al. "The influence of phototherapy on serotonin and melatonin in non-seasonal depression." *Pharmacopsychiatry* 1990 May;23(3):155-158.
663. Laakso M, Porkka-Heiskanen T, et al. "Twenty-four-hour patterns of pineal melatonin and pituitary and plasma prolactin in male rats under 'natural' and artificial lighting conditions." *Neuroendocrinology* 1988 Sep;48(3):308-313.
664. Srinivasan V, et al. "Melatonin in mood disorders." *World J Biol Psychiatry* 2006, 7:138-151.
665. Kent ST, et al. "Effect of sunlight exposure on cognitive function among depressed and non-depressed participants: a REGARDS cross-sectional study." *Environmental Health* 2009.
666. O'hara MW, Swain AM. "Rates and risk of postpartum depression—a meta-analysis." *International Review of Psychiatry*, 1996, 8(1), 37-54.
667. Wang, N. "In broad daylight: An investigation of the multiple environmental factors influencing mood, preference, and performance in a sunlit workplace." *DAI-A* 70/06, Dec 2009.
668. *Illustrated Stedman's Medical Dictionary* 24th Edition, 282.
669. Sack RL, et al. "Morning vs Evening Light Treatment for Winter Depression: Evidence That the Therapeutic Effects of Light Are Mediated by Circadian Phase Shifts." *Arch Gen Psychiatry*. 1990;47(4):343-351.
670. Ooms ME, et. al. "Vitamin D status and sex hormone binding globulin: Determinants of bone turnover and bone mineral density in elderly women." *Journal of Bone and Mineral Research*. VL: 10 NO: 8 PG: 1177-1184. 1995.
671. Holick MF. "High Prevalence of Vitamin D Inadequacy and Implications for Health." *Mayo Clinic Proceedings*. March 2006 vol. 81 no. 3 353-373.
672. Garciona E, et. al. "New clues about vitamin D functions in the nervous system." *Trends in Endocrinology and Metabolism*. Volume 13, Issue 3, 1 April 2002, Pages 100-105.
673. Zitterman A, Schleithoff SS, Koerfer R. "Putting cardiovascular disease and vitamin D insufficiency into perspective." *British Journal of Nutrition*, (2005) 94 , pp 483-492.
674. Leavitt SB. "Vitamin D–A Neglected 'Analgesic' for Chronic Musculoskeletal Pain." *Pain Treatment Topics.*
675. Holick MF. "Vitamin D Deficiency." *New England Journal of Medicine.* Volume 357:266-281. July 19, 2007.
676. Llewellyn DJ, Langa KM, Lang IA. "Serum 25-Hydroxyvitamin D Concentration and Cognitive Impairment." *J Geriatr Psychiatry Neurol* 2009 22: 188-195.
677. Lee DM. "Association between 25-hydroxyvitamin D levels and cognitive performance in middle-aged and older European men." *J Neurol Neurosurg Psychiatry*. December 2009.
678. Lansdowne AT, Provost SC, "Vitamin D3 enhances mood in healthy subjects during winter." *Psychopharmacology* (Berl). 1998 Feb;135(4):319-23.
679. Witte JG, et al. "Depression Is Associated With Decreased 25-Hydroxyvitamin D and Increased Parathyroid Hormone Levels in Older Adults." *Arch Gen Psychiatry*. 2008;65(5):508-512.
680. Gloth FM 3rd, Alam W, Hollis B. "Vitamin D vs broad spectrum phototherapy in the treatment of seasonal affective disorder." *J Nutr Health Aging*. 1999;3(1):5-7.
681. Burne TH, Feron F, Brown J, Eyles DW, McGrath JJ, Mackay-Sim A. Combined prenatal and chronic postnatal vitamin D deficiency in rats impairs prepulse inhibition of acoustic startle. *Physiol Behav*. 2004 Jun;81(4):651-5.
682. Burne TH, Becker A, Brown J, Eyles DW, Mackay-Sim A, McGrath JJ. Transient prenatal Vitamin D deficiency is associated with hyperlocomotion in adult rats. *Behav Brain Res*. 2004 Oct 5;154(2):549-55.
683. McGrath J. Hypothesis: is low prenatal vitamin D a risk-modifying factor for schizophrenia? *Schizophr Res*. 1999 Dec 21;40(3):173-7.

684. McGrath J, Eyles D, Mowry B, Yolken R, Buka S. Low maternal vitamin D as a risk factor for schizophrenia: a pilot study using banked sera. *Schizophr Res.* 2003 Sep 1;63(1-2):73-8.
685. Ozer S, Ulusahin A, Ulusoy S, Okur H, Coskun T, Tuncali T, Gogus A, Akarsu AN. Is vitamin D hypothesis for schizophrenia valid? Independent segregation of psychosis in a family with vitamin-D-dependent rickets type IIA. *Prog Neuropsychopharmacol Biol Psychiatry.* 2004 Mar;28(2):255-66.
686. Kendell RE, Adams W. Exposure to sunlight, vitamin D and schizophrenia. *Schizophr Res.* 2002 Apr 1;54(3):193-8.
687. Evatt ML, et al. "Prevalence of Vitamin D Insufficiency in Patients With Parkinson Disease and Alzheimer Disease." *Arch Neurol.* 2008;65(10):1348-1352.
688. Eylesa DW, et al. "Distribution of the Vitamin D receptor and 1α-hydroxylase in human brain." *Journal of Chemical Neuroanatomy.* Volume 29, Issue 1, January 2005, Pages 21-30.
689. Grant, WB. "Does Vitamin D Reduce the Risk of Dementia?" *Journal of Alzheimer's Disease* 17:1 (May 2009).
690. Dawson-Hughes B, et al. "Effect of Calcium and Vitamin D Supplementation on Bone Density in Men and Women 65 Years of Age or Older." *N Engl J Med* 1997 337: 670-676.
691. Ghosh A, Greenberg ME. "Calcium signaling in neurons: molecular mechanisms and cellular consequences." *Science.* 1995 Apr 14;268(5208):239-47.
692. Frizel D, et al. "Plasma magnesium and calcium in depression." *Br J Psychiatry* 1969;115:1375-7.
693. Mu JJ, Liu ZQ, Liu WM, et. al. "Reduction of blood pressure with calcium and potassium supplementation in children with salt sensitivity: a 2-year double-blinded placebo-controlled trial." *J-Hum-Hypertens.* 2005 Jun; 19(6): 479-83.
694. Hiroyasu I, Meir J, et al. "Prospective Study of Calcium, Potassium, and Magnesium Intake and Risk of Stroke in Women." *Stroke* 30: 1772-1779.
695. Thys-Jacobs S, et al. "Calcium carbonate and the premenstrual syndrome: Effects on premenstrual and menstrual symptoms." *American Journal of Obstetrics and Gynecology.* 1 August 1998 (volume 179 issue 2 Pages 444-452).
696. USDA National Nutrient Database for Standard Reference, http://www.nal.usda.gov/fnic/foodcomp/search/.
697. US Preventive Services Task Force. "Screening for skin cancer—including counseling to prevent skin cancer." *Guide to Clinical Preventive Services—2nd edition.* 1996 p. 141-152.
698. American Cancer Society. "2009 Cancer Facts and Figures." www.cancer.org/downloads/STT/500809web.pdf.
699. World Health Organization. "Solar ultraviolet radiation: Global burden of disease from solar ultraviolet radiation." *Environmental Burden of Disease Series,* N.13. 2006.
700. American Cancer Society. "2009 Cancer Facts and Figures." www.cancer.org/downloads/STT/500809web.pdf.
701. Marchione M. "Research On Vitamin D Makes Doctors Consider Prescribing Sunshine." *Associated Press.* 2005.
702. Byrne B. "Seasonal Affective Disorder and Light Therapy." *Sleep Medicine Clin* June 2008; 3(2); 307-315.
703. Clemens TL, Adams JS, Henderson SL, Holick MF. "Increased skin pigment reduces the capacity of skin to synthesize vitamin D3." *Lancet* 1982;1:74–6.
704. Corral M. "Morning light therapy for postpartum depression."*Arch Womens Ment Health* 01-JAN-2007; 10(5): 221-4.

Chapter 15

WE CAN LIVE WEEKS WITHOUT FOOD, DAYS WITHOUT WATER, BUT ONLY MINUTES WITHOUT AIR.

# Take a Deep Breath

## *Deep breathing is a good habit with many positive side benefits, including improved cognition.*

A perplexing "murder mystery" was playing out in major cities across the country. Literally thousands of people were dying from strokes and heart attacks, and at first, scientists were at a loss for a "weapon." They were able to connect the rise in death rates, however, with a spike in the tiny particles that spew from the exhaust of diesel trucks, buses, and coal-burning factories, known as microscopic pollution.

Researchers at Northwestern University's Feinberg School of Medicine finally solved a key piece of the mystery with a study that identified how tiny pieces of soot kill people at risk for strokes and heart attacks. Inflammation in the lungs caused by these tiny air pollutants was leading to death from cardiovascular disease. People with previous blockages in the coronary or carotid arteries are at the highest risk.

The risk of dying from a heart attack or ischemic stroke jumps an eye-opening 30 percent for each 10 micrograms of pollution in the air (there is no "safe" level for these pollutants). Particulate matter pollution is highest near expressways or truck routes, so it's hard for commuters to escape exposure.[705]

Exercise during "soot spikes" increases the risk of trouble by flooding the lungs with more polluted air. For example, runners may take in five times more polluted air than someone sitting on a park bench.

The air cycle is a wonderful sequence of giving and receiving. Plants take in carbon dioxide from the air and release oxygen, which provides fresh air for us to breathe. Our cells use the oxygen to give energy to the body, producing carbon dioxide, which is released through our lungs into the air.

Running near an expressway can be particularly detrimental, especially for an individual already at risk for a heart attack or stroke. The mysterious "assassin" in these cases was pollution...and it is still at large.

## WHAT MAKES FRESH AIR FRESH?

Wherever water interfaces with the earth's atmosphere, fresh air is found. The ocean surf, evergreen trees, and waterfalls are all great sources of fresh air. The air after a rain storm, and particularly a thunderstorm, is very beneficial. Being exposed to areas such as this will definitely provide a boost to mental health.[706] Ocean air from the mid-Pacific contains about 15,000 particles (e.g. pollutants) per cubic inch. In contrast, air from big cities contains about 5,000,000 particles per cubic inch.[707]

While oxygen and the absence of pollutants certainly help to make fresh air "fresh," ionization is another important factor in the equation. Ions are tiny, electrified particles of matter. Fresh air may contain as many as 5-10 times more negative ions than stale air.

Numerous studies have associated negative ions with health benefits, as listed in **Figure 15.1.**[708,709,710,711,712,713,714] Negatively charged "fresh" air has also been shown to kill germs, vitalize the blood, slow tumor growth, and decrease the survival of airborne bacteria and viruses. In contrast, positively charged air has been shown to result in headaches, dizziness, nausea, and fatigue.[715]

## COMBATING POLLUTION

While no one would argue against the importance of fresh air, the best strategies for combating air pollution, both indoors and out, are not always clear-cut.

### BENEFITS OF FRESH AIR

- improved sense of well-being
- decreased anxiety and relaxed mind
- better concentration and improved learning
- improvement in hay fever and asthma symptoms
- decreased severity of stomach ulcers
- enhanced immune system
- cleaner lungs and open air passageways
- lower body temperature and resting heart rate
- increased rate and quality of growth in plants

*Figure 15.1*

## WAYS TO IMPROVE INDOOR AIR QUALITY

- Avoid unnecessary pollutants such as cigarette and cigar smoke, pet dander, or chemicals from "air-freshening" devices.
- Make sure your home and workplace are well-ventilated.
- Open windows and air out your home or office whenever appropriate.
- Direct ventilation from range hoods and bathroom exhaust fans to the outside, rather than into an attic.
- Minimize heat and humidity to decrease off-gassing of formaldehyde and other volatile compounds from common household items.
- Change air conditioning filters at least monthly.
- Add potted plants to your home or office environment.
- Use low emission (low fume) paints, varnishes, and carpets.
- Securely seal all containers with volatile contents (such as paints, paint strippers, and pesticides).
- Regularly service appliances that use fuels such as gas, wood, or kerosene.

***Figure 15.2***

Indoor air is two to five times more polluted than the air outside. Furniture, carpets, drapes, paint, cleaning substances, personal care products, and other household items give off toxic gases.[716] These volatile compounds are linked to asthma, kidney, central nerve damage, and sometimes cancer. In the case of indoor air pollution, the best action is to remove the problem at its source. If the source of pollution can't be removed, attempt to improve ventilation and bring in as much fresh air as possible. You can also offset the pollutants in your home or office by utilizing an air cleaning machine or air-purifying house plants.[717] A single live plant can eliminate 90% of the toxic chemicals in the air in an average room. Place a palms or ferns (which are highly purifying) around the home to revive both the air you breathe and your decor. More tips to improve the quality of indoor air are found in **Figure 15.2**.

Outdoor air pollution is more difficult to combat. If you live in a city blanketed by smog, always remain indoors during smog alerts. The air in large cities is typically cleaner in the morning, so schedule your outdoor activities for that time. Living in a large city with the heightened exhaust and factory fumes will never offer the healthiest respiration. This is why, if at all possible, you should consider relocating to a more rural area.[718]

| FRESH AIR | CITY SMOG |
|---|---|
| • vitalizes the blood | • causes coughing |
| • relaxes the mind | • leads to bronchitis |
| • kills germs | • promotes sinusitis |
| • helps clean the lungs | • contributes to emphysema |
| • boosts the immune system | • increases cancer risk |

***Figure 15.3***

Fresh air is actually food for your lungs. However, when the "food" you bring in is contaminated, great harm can result. We are actually more dependent on the air we breathe than we are on the food we eat. Breathing deeply of pure, fresh air helps to vitalize the blood. Good circulation is important to overall health, and anyone interested in a long and active life should do what they can to improve their circulation by breathing deeply and often of pure, invigorating fresh air. The benefits of fresh air are contrasted with the dangers of inhaling smog in **Figure 15.3**.

## LUNG CAPACITY

The inside of your lungs actually resembles a sponge filled with about 300 million tiny pockets called alveoli.[719] All together, these tiny pockets provide over 70 square yards of surface area for the exchange of gases in and out of the blood stream.[720] The average adult breathes in about 16 times per minute, taking in about one pint of air per breath. This intake adds up to about 2,000 gallons of air per day.

The maximum amount of air a person can expel from the lungs after first filling them and then exhaling to the maximum extent (about 4,600 milliliters) is called vital capacity or forced vital capacity.[721] Your lung capacity is influenced by a number of factors, including smoking, air pollution, posture, exercise, weight, and how deeply you breathe.[542,543,544,545,546]

If your lung capacity seems somewhat limited, not to worry. Improving vital capacity is possible by engaging in deep breathing exercises on a regular basis. Doing so will extend longevity and boost cognition.[722,723]

## "AIR-OBICS" FOR THE LUNGS

Deep breathing exercises should be learned to make the best use of time in fresh air. These exercises, often associated with Eastern meditational styles, can be practiced for stress relief without the use of meditation. One study showed that slow deep breathing contributes to increased oxygen consumption, decreased heart rate, decreased blood pressure, increased parasympathetic activity, and the experience of alertness and reinvigoration.[724] Breathing exercises have also been found to improve the symptoms of asthma and reduce the need for some asthma medications.[725]Low blood oxygen levels cause the problems listed in **Figure 15.4**.[726]

After eight weeks of using a breathing muscle trainer, participants in another study had enhanced breathing muscle strength and better performance on treadmill tests.[727]

Deep breathing aids digestion by massaging the abdominal organs. Blood is assisted in its return to the chest by the negative pressure that is developed with each deep breath. This pressure helps to reduce the chances of congestion headaches, the pooling of blood in the legs, and aids in the digestive process.[728] Deep breathing gets more oxygen into the blood with each breath, allowing the heart to slow down a little.[729]

A good habit is to go outside in the fresh air and take 10-20 slow, deep, abdominal breaths after each meal and just before retiring for the night. Another good exercise is to breathe deeply once every 10 seconds while timing yourself with a stopwatch. The only way to breathe six times a minute and not get short of breath is by taking deep breaths. Studies show that this breathing exercise will improve your oxygen saturation throughout the entire day.

### HOW TO BREATHE PROPERLY

Proper breathing is important for optimal performance. Unfortunately many adults are getting into the habit of shallow breathing without the proper use of the abdomen. Inadequate breathing then leads to fatigue, exhaustion, anemia, and depression.[730] Shallow breathing habits deny our bodies the optimal levels of oxygen needed for better health.[731]

**LOW OXYGEN LEVELS YIELD POOR RESULTS**

Studies show that failing to breathe deeply results in low blood-oxygen.

Shallow breathing leads to:

- exercise intolerance
- impaired muscle performance
- reduced metabolic function
- muscle atrophy
- restricted brain efficiency
- fatigue & lethargy

***Figure 15.4***

## BENEFITS OF DEEP BREATHING

- relaxes the body
- oxygenates the brain for clear thinking
- helps prevent respiratory infections
- induces sound sleep
- improves mood

*Figure 15.5*

Early signs of insufficient oxygen are impaired judgment and memory, dulling of intellect, and a tendency to impatience and irritability.[732]

Slow, deep abdominal breathing is the correct way to breathe. Some major health benefits of deep breathing are listed on **Figure 15.5**. Use the diaphragm to "suck" air into the lower portion of the lungs and the abdominal muscles to "push" it out. One way to check yourself is to lie down with a book on your stomach. Now breathe in such a way as to make the book go up and down each time you breathe in and out.[733]

Tight clothing around the chest or abdomen makes proper breathing difficult, as does restrictive clothing that does not allow the free movement of the arms above the head.[734] Wear clothes that fit loosely and do not constrict your diaphragm.

Good posture while sitting and standing is necessary for proper breathing. Many people stoop or sit slumped over for much of the day. Poor posture is actually a depression-related impediment to mental performance.

## HOW TO GET FRESH AIR

- Breathe in deeply through your nose.
- Wear loose-fitting clothing.
- Combat air pollution.
- Avoid smoking and secondhand smoke.
- Exercise in fresh air.
- Keep bedroom windows open when possible.

*Figure 15.6*

It's simply impossible to breathe as deeply as you should when you slump in your chair. Maintaining good posture, taking stretch breaks often, and getting exercise whenever you can, will serve as an aid to proper breathing and maintaining a strong set of lungs. Sound advice on how to get fresh air is summarized in **Figures 15.6**.

**Fresh air is one of the best natural remedies.**

## A BREATH OF FRESH AIR

As you seek to breathe more deeply, never forget to watch the quality of the air you are breathing.

Try to spend as much time as possible outdoors in rural locations such as large parks, near the ocean, or other natural settings.

Practice slow deep breathing for optimal oxygen intake and improved alertness, and exercise in the early morning in the great, fresh out-of-doors whenever possible. The result—clearer thinking and a longer, healthier life—will no doubt be well worth the effort.

## References

705. Mutlu GM. *J Clin Invest* - 01-OCT-2007; 117(10): 2952-61.
706. Baldwin BE. "Why is fresh air fresh?" *The Journal of Health and Healing* 11(4):26-27.
707. Tillotson D. *Patterns for preservation: a conservation text.* Great Northern Pub. Corp. 519.
708. Baldwin BE. "Why is fresh air fresh?" *The Journal of Health and Healing* 11(4):26-27.
709. Duffee RA, Koontz RH. "Behavioral effets of ionized air on rats." *Psychophysiology* 1965 Apr;1(4):347-359.
710. Jordan J, Sokoloff B. "Air ionization, age and maze learning of rats." *J. Gerentol* 1959;14:344-348.
711. Reilly T, Stevenson IC. "An investigation of the effects of negative air ions on responses to submaximal exercise at different times of day." *J Hum Ergol* (Tokyo) 1993 Jun; 22(1):1-9.
712. Mitchell BW, King DJ. "Effect of negative air ionization on airborne transmission of Newcastle disease virus." *Avian Dis* 1994 Oct-Dec;38(4):725-732.
713. Giannini AJ, Jones BT, Loiselle RH. "Reversibility of serotonin irritation syndrome with atmospheric anions." *J Clin Psychiatry* 1986 Mar;47(3):141-143.
714. Gabbay J, Bergerson O, et al. "Effect of ionization on microbial air pollution in the dental clinic." *Environ Res* 1990 Jun;52(1);99-106.
715. Verrillo EF, Gellman LM. "Chronic Fatigue Syndrome: A Treatment Guide" Macmillan 1998. 143.
716. CNN's investigative special report with Dr. Sanjay Gupta "Toxic America."
717. Anderson ME."Enviroments, indoor air quality, and children." *Pediatr Clin North Am* - 01-APR-2007; 54(2): 295-307, viii.
718. Abelsohn A. "Identifying and managing adverse environmental health effects: Outdoor air pollution." *CMAJ* - 30-APR-2002; 166(9): 1161-7.
719. Guyton AC, Hall JE. *Textbook of medical physiology 11th ed.* Elsevier Inc. 2006. 496.
720. Guyton AC, Hall JE. *Textbook of medical physiology 11th ed.* Elsevier Inc. 2006. 497.
721. Guyton AC, Hall JE. *Textbook of medical physiology 11th ed.* Elsevier Inc. 2006. 496.
722. Broczek KM. "Anthropometric chest structure of Polish centenarians." *J Physiol Pharmacol.* 01-SEP-2005; 56 Suppl 4: 9-13.
723. Carpenito-Moyet LJ. *Nursing Care Plans and Documentation: Nursing Diagnoses And Colloborative.* Lippincott Williams & Wilkins, 2005, 169.

724. Jerath R. "Physiology of long pranayamic breathing: neural respiratory elements may provide a mechanism that explains how slow deep breathing shifts the autonomic nervous system." *Med Hypotheses* - 01-JAN-2006; 67(3): 566-71.
725. Holloway EA. "Integrated breathing and relaxation training (the Papworth method) for adults with asthma in primary care: a randomised controlled trial." *Thorax* - 01-DEC-2007; 62(12): 1039-42.
726. Bernardi L, Spadacini G, Bellwon J, et al. "Influence of breathing frequency and pattern on oxygen saturation and exercise performance." *Lancet.* 1998;351:1308–1311.
727. Downey AE. "Effects of inspiratory muscle training on exercise responses in normoxia and hypoxia." *Respir Physiol Neurobiol* - 14-MAY-2007; 156(2): 137-46.
728. Morse D. *Surviving Stress: Simple, Safe, Strategic Solutions.* Virtualbookworm Publishing. 109.
729. Bernardi L, Wdowczyk-Szulc J, Valenti C, et al. "Effects of controlled breathing, mental activity and mental stress with or without verbalization on heart rate variability." *J Am Coll Cardiol* 2000;35:1462–9.
730. "Obstructive Sleep Apnea in Older Adults." *Clinics in Geriatric Medicine* - Volume 24, Issue 1 (February 2008).
731. Bernardi L, et al. "Effect of breathing rate on oxygen saturation and exercise performance in chronic heart failure." *Lancet,* 1998.
732. Wilkinson IB, Rajagopalan SR. *Oxford Handbook of Clinical Medicine.* Oxford University Press. 2004. 192.
733. Hough A. *Physiotherapy in Respiratory Care: An Evidence-Based Approach to Respiratory.* Nelson Thomas. 154.
734. Gabriel S. *Breathe for Life: How to Reduce Stress & Enhance Your Fitness.* Hardie Grant Books. 2000. 2.

Chapter 16

ADEQUATE SLEEP IS THE FOUNDATION FOR PEAK MENTAL PERFORMANCE. MISSING OUT ON SLEEP LEADS TO COMPROMISED BRAIN FUNCTION.

# Rewind in Your Sleep

***Sleep deprivation is a major factor in poor decision making and decreased mood.***

"Only two more hours of driving," Trevor climbed into the front seat of the trusty sedan next to his best friend, Tyler. It had been a great weekend filled with friends and Florida fun, but now it was time to get back to school. Having stayed up into the early morning hours, Trevor was starting to feel a bit tired. He figured he could make it through, however, by cranking up the radio and downing a double espresso for a jolt of caffeine.

Trevor didn't see the dump truck barreling down the highway before he pulled out. He never knew what hit him, either, until 30 days later when he emerged from a coma—permanently disabled and fortunate to be alive. That's when Trevor learned of an even more horrible result of the crash: Tyler had not survived.

According to the National Sleep Foundation, Trevor was involved in one of more than 100,000 accidents each year caused by drowsiness behind the wheel.[735] Many people who pride themselves on not driving under the influence don't realize that fatigue-related driving impairment is just as lethal as driving drunk.[736] Slow reaction times resulting from exhaustion increase the risk of both fatal and nonfatal accidents, which are among the top five causes of death in the Western world.[737]

Micro-sleeps, which are mini 1-2 second open-eye sleep sessions that are likely to happen during states of exhaustion, often occur in people who are fatigued behind the wheel. During a micro-sleep, attention lapses and the individual does not realize what is happening and is "frozen," even though the eyes are wide open.[738]

Slower reflexes, impaired decision-making ability, and decreased mental performance are the unfortunate, and all too frequent, results of chronic sleep deprivation.[739] Accidents on the job also occur more commonly when workers are short on sleep, working unusual hours, or otherwise fatigued.[740]

Large-scale disasters like the Chernobyl fiasco, the Exxon Valdez crash, and the Three Mile Island incident all took place in early pre-dawn hours when vigilance was at a low point.[741] Most of the "friendly fire" problems in the Persian Gulf War were also due to fatigue.[742]

## VISIBLY AFFECTED BEHAVIOR

After extended periods of wakefulness or reduced sleep, the brain's neurons begin to malfunction, visibly affecting behavior. While some muscles are able to regenerate when we simply rest or recline, the brain, especially the cerebral cortex, remains in a state of "quiet readiness" when the body is awake. In order for the brain to receive true rest and rejuvenation, it must cycle through the various stages of sleep.[743] Some of these stages assist the brain in forming new memories or generating new synaptic connections, while others help to replenish neurons within the cerebral cortex.[744]

Researchers have found the cerebral cortex, which is associated with the processing of language, to be very active in well-rested individuals who participate in learning-related tests. In contrast, sleep-deprived subjects showed no activity in the cerebral cortex during testing.[745] The effects of this inactivity are particularly prominent in individuals who have gone for prolonged periods without sleep.

The bodies of sleep-deprived individuals compensate for the loss of frontal lobe function with activity in the parietal lobe. However, well-rested research subjects who were using their frontal lobes did not require this compensatory parietal lobe activity in order to function. Despite the extra effort from other areas of the brain, the sleep-deprived subjects did not perform as well as fully rested subjects. For example, they completed math problems with less speed and accuracy than their more well-rested counterparts.[746]

Some of the most fascinating research involving sleep deprivation and mental performance involves the area of the brain associated with creative speech, moral decisions, and analytical thinking—the frontal lobe. Sleep-deprived persons have trouble thinking of imaginative words or ideas, choosing more repetitious words or phrases instead.[747] They are also less able to communicate in clear sentences, and may stutter, speak in a monotone voice, exhibit slurred speech, or talk very slowly.[748]

As a result, sleep-deprived people lack the speed or creative ability to make or implement quick and logical decisions. Researchers have also found that a dearth of sleep impairs one's ability to simultaneously focus on several different tasks, reducing both the speed and efficiency of action.[749] In other research, scientists have found that people who are learning new skills don't improve their performance in the new skill set until they complete a full eight-hour sleep cycle, including period of REM (Rapid Eye Movement).[750]

## IRREVERSIBLE DAMAGE?

In addition to reduced thinking ability and impaired reaction times, sleep deprivation may have long-term detrimental effects on the brain. Researchers have documented that brain damage occurs in sleep deprived animals, and some research suggests that damage to be irreversible.[751]

*"That we are not much sicker and madder than we are is due exclusively to that most blessed and blessing of all natural graces, sleep."*

—Aldous Huxley

PET scans confirm the reduced blood flow to the frontal lobe of the brain in chronically sleep-deprived individuals, while other areas of the brain also show a reduction in blood flow as well.[752] Irritability, belligerence, and reduced attention spans are the inevitable results of this chronic sleep shortage.[753] Other unpleasant results include rapid mood changes, diminished stress management ability, social withdrawal, and even depression.[754] I have found that most individuals must have at least four causative factors before they sink into major depression. Insomnia, however, is one of the few factors that can single-handedly trigger major depression.[755] In other words, if you are doing everything right healthwise, with the exception of getting enough sleep, you may become depressed from that factor alone.

According to a study conducted by the National Institute of Mental Health, sleepless nights and feelings of despair are closely linked. The Institute, which compared various sleep complaints and symptoms of depression in about 8,000 subjects, found that insomnia was reported by about 10% of the study participants. About 40% of those with insomnia developed a mental disorder, and the risk of major depression among insomniacs was 40 times higher than for those without insomnia. Those experiencing temporary sleeplessness had a 60% greater likelihood that they would fall prey to depression. An even greater percent of those with hypersomnia (excessive sleep) developed a mental disorder compared with the 16 percent of those with normal sleep habits.[756] Researchers have also reported that women are about 30% more likely to be insomniacs than men, and the prevalence of problems with sleep increases as people age. In older adults, insomnia not only contributes to depression, but also to memory impairment.

Other mental issues suffered by extreme non-sleepers are delusions and hallucinations.[757] In addition, some individuals who were diagnosed to be schizophrenic were later found to be simply deprived of sleep.[758]

Losing even three hours of sleep on any given night can cut the effectiveness of your immune system in half, resulting in greater susceptibility to colds, diarrhea, gastroenteritis, and other infections.[759] A number of immune alterations occur with sleep deprivation: antibody levels are decreased while interleukins-1 and -2 fail to experience the rise that occurs with deeper stages of sleep. Growth hormone (GH) requires sleep for optimal release. Absence of GH further impairs immunity as important immune defenders, the cytotoxic T cells (a type of white blood cell), are dependent on this hormone.[760] Chronic fatigue also increases the risk of problems that may not be so obvious: heart disease, heart related deaths, and stomach and intestinal problems.[761]

In the United States, fatigue is one of the 10 most common reasons for visiting a physician. 3.3 million Americans visit their doctors each year for insomnia alone.[762] Sixty percent of Americans are troubled by sleep-related problems such as insomnia, daytime fatigue, waking up too early, or falling asleep frequently in the middle of the day.[763]

A common cause of inadequate sleep is stress. Experiencing stress can interfere with sleep, and without sufficient sleep a person is less capable to cope with stress. As illustrated in **Figure 16.1**, the combination of stress and sleep deprivation can easily snowball into a vicious cycle.

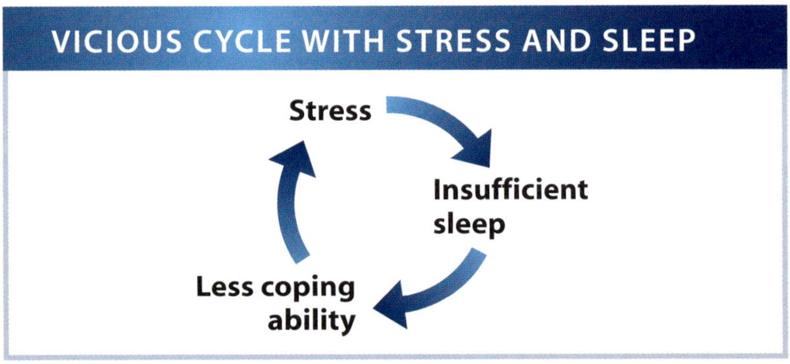


*Figure 16.1*

## SLEEP FACILITATES LEARNING

Sleep facilitates learning by increasing the production of proteins, which are used to replenish neurons in the brain, while reducing the rate at which they are broken down. Without the regenerated neurons, the synapses may not be formed, thus limiting the amount of information a sleep-deprived individual can process.[764]

One of the most serious negative effects of sleep deprivation is the inability of an exhausted individual to realize just how tired they really are.[765] According to research performed by Dr. Hans P.A. Van Dongen, assistant professor of sleep and chronobiology at the University of

Pennsylvania School of Medicine, people who experience chronic sleep deprivation convince themselves that sleep debt is actually normal. They also frequently believe that, while things are not optimal, they will manage "somehow."[766] No doubt this explains why so many people who cause sleep-related car crashes don't perceive they are sleepy just before the crash.

In a study similar to Van Dongen's, Israeli scientists reported that children who slept just one hour less per night than their peers scored significantly worse on various memory and attention tests. In both of the aforementioned studies, researchers concluded that missing just one hour or two of sleep on a regular basis can have devastating results on mental performance.[767]

Researchers have found that students with lower grade point averages (GPAs) were more likely to have restless/aching legs when trying to fall asleep, snoring at night, difficulty waking in the morning, and difficulty concentrating and staying awake during the day. Evidence indicates that sleep disturbances occur at high frequencies in adolescents and significantly affect daytime performance as measured by GPA. Even after statistically controlling for other variables such as age and household income, sleep disturbances (or lack of sleep) were shown to have a significant and detrimental effect on school performance.[768] A 9 o'clock bedtime allows for the highest production of melatonin, and post-midnight bedtimes have been shown to significantly reduce melatonin levels.

In another study, researchers found that people who burn the candle on both ends nightly for two weeks can accumulate a sleep debt equal to a total of two full nights of sleep deprivation.[769] Sleep four hours or less per night over a period of two weeks, and your brain reacts as though you have not slept at all for three consecutive nights!

## NAPPING AND MENTAL PERFORMANCE

Researchers led by Matthew Turner, of the City University of New York, have shown that even taking a nap with no REM sleep can improve mental performance. In Tucker's study, volunteers were instructed to memorize pairs of words (a test of factual learning). They also practiced tracing images in a mirror (a test of action learning). The volunteers were tested immediately and then again 6 hours later. Test subjects who were allowed a nap of up to 1 hour before the second test scored 15% higher on the factual test than the non-nappers (there was no significant difference in the action test scores).[770]

## THE MELATONIN CONNECTION

Melatonin, the "fix and rejuvenate" night-time hormone, is extremely important to restful, refreshing sleep.[771] Produced in the pineal gland of the brain, melatonin helps regulate the body's sleep and wake cycles

## HEALTH IMPACT OF MELATONIN

- increases the ability to experience pleasure
- lowers cholesterol, blood pressure, and risk of heart rhythm problems
- protects against free radical damage
- prevents or fights tumors
- delays some effects of aging
- assists in coping with stress
- lowers risk of osteoporosis
- enhances immune system

***Figure 16.2***

(also known as the "internal clock" or circadian rhythm). In addition to sleep-related functions, melatonin impacts the body in a number of positive, health-promoting ways (see **Figure 16.2** for a summary).[772] Our lifestyle choices can affect the body's ability to produce optimal levels of melatonin.

The human body begins the process of making melatonin when the pineal gland draws tryptophan, an amino acid, from the blood. The pineal gland then converts the tryptophan to serotonin (a light-dependent reaction). As a final step, the serotonin is converted to melatonin (a process which requires darkness, sufficient calcium, sufficient vitamin D, and vitamin B-6).[773] You must provide your body with these nutrients to start the process.

As illustrated in **Figure 16.3**, under normal conditions melatonin levels rise in the mid-to late evening, remain high for most of the night, and then decline in the early morning hours.[774] When you don't sleep during these hours, your melatonin levels are thrown off. Natural melatonin production is also partly affected by light. (For a more complete discussion of this, see chapter 14). During the shorter days of the winter months, melatonin production may start earlier or, more often, later. Using light and dark to stimulate and slow down melatonin production at the appropriate times is very effective in supporting healthy sleep cycles.

Natural melatonin levels decline gradually with age, with some older adults producing very small amounts of melatonin or none at all.[775] The decline begins before age 10 and continues through age 70, at which time it is reduced to only about two percent of the amount produced by a young child. This decline is partly due to lifestyle practices that interfere with the production of this important sleep aid, such as insufficient nutrients, staying up too late, and not getting enough bright light during the day.

In addition to doing what you can to promote healthy melatonin production, it is important to obtain sufficient amounts of "vitamin R" – Rest.

## VITAMIN $R_1$ (NIGHTLY REST)

If rest could be sold as a pill, it would be one of the hottest selling supplements on the market today. Vitamin $R_1$, as I like to call it, is available in four forms today. Nightly rest, which we have discussed thus far in the chapter, is what I call vitamin $R_1$. Although sleep is what people generally think of when we talk about rest, it is only one of four facets of rest.

## VITAMIN $R_2$ (WEEKLY REST)

A second vital component of rest is found in vitamin $R_2$, or weekly rest. Most people understand that the body has a 24-hour cycle which is actually set by sunlight. Our hormones, heart rate, blood pressure, and many other physical factors are regulated around this 24-hour cycle.[776] However, many are not aware that our bodies also have a seven-day rhythm. Medical research has demonstrated the connection between

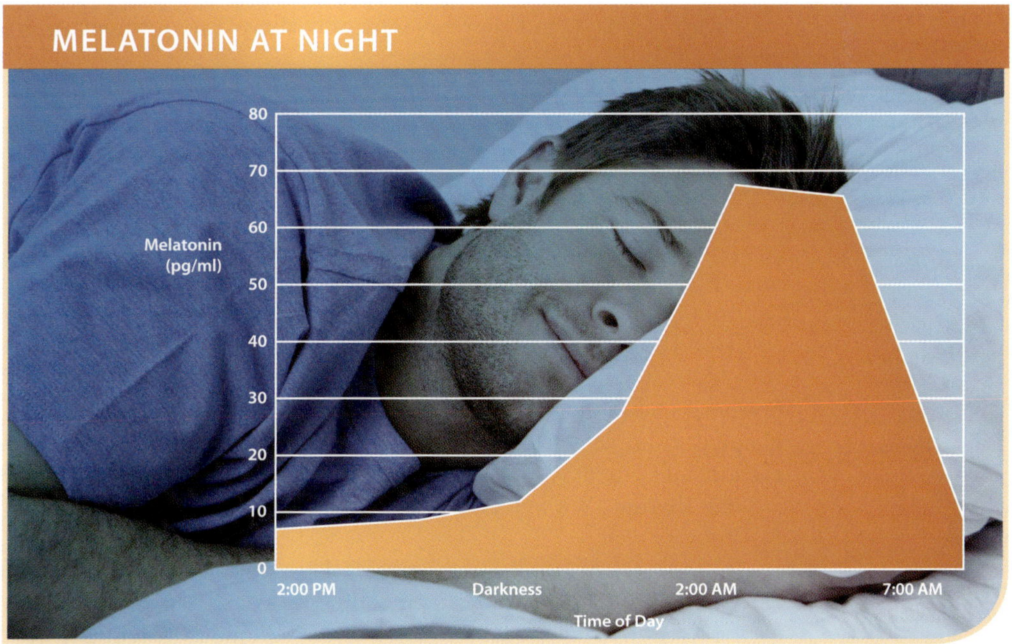


*Figure 16.3*

weekly rhythms and a variety of physiological functions. Some that have been identified include heart rate, natural hormones in human breast milk, swelling after surgery, and rejection of transplanted organs.[777,778,779,780,781,782,783,784,785]

To understand the significance of these rhythms, consider the latter two items in the list. A person will tend to have an increase in swelling on the seventh and then the fourteenth day after surgery. Similarly, a person with a kidney transplant is more likely to reject the organ seven days and then fourteen days after the surgery.[786] An increasing number of scientists now believe that the 7-day rhythm is a normal built-in feature of our physiology. The importance of the 7-day rhythms should not be underestimated; they are a part of who we are; not just a function of the fact that we happen to keep a 7-day week in our culture. It has been demonstrated that this 7-day rhythm does not depend on the external week cycle.

**A regular weekly day of rest is as important as a daily time of rest. Not only does it help physically, but it can also strengthen family relationships.**

From a historical perspective the weekly cycle is of great interest. We keep a 24-hour day based on the earth revolving on its axis. We keep a monthly cycle based on the periodicity of the moon. The year is based on the earth's circling the sun. But what is the week based on? For many years, it was thought that the 7-day week was simply a part of religious culture or tradition. During the French Revolution, anti-religious sentiment led the French to experiment with the metric or 10-day week. Under the French system, each day was divided into ten hours, and each hour was divided into one hundred minutes. The weekend only occurred once every ten days, and churches were only allowed to open once every ten days.[787]

Benefits expected by the French from this 10-day week included increased productivity and a more scientific, enhanced society. Instead, mental institutions were filled to capacity. An alarming array of physical problems also came to the surface. Soon there weren't enough hospital beds for those who were sick, especially with mental illness. During this crisis, the French mathematician Laplace advised the new French government to return to the 7-day week because so many problems were resulting from implementation of the more "scientific" metric week.[788]

Unfortunately, not everyone learned from the experience of France with regard to the 7-day week. Under the leadership of Josef Stalin, the Bolsheviks attempted a 5-day week.[789] The tribes of the Congo also attempted to implement 4-day, 5-day, and 8-day weeks.[790] None of these experiments lasted very long, because our body cycles revolve around a 7-day rhythm. We humans simply do not adapt to any other weekly rhythm very well.

In the book of Exodus, the 7-day weekly cycle is described as part of God's design in creation. That cycle is described as consisting of six days of work followed by a Sabbath day of rest.[791] Some thinkers have seen significance in the Sabbath concept in relation to circaseptan rhythms, recognizing it as a "zeitgeber" ("time-giver" in German). Zeitgebers keep our weekly rhythms synchronized by pausing one day in seven for a time of rest.[792] In order for these time-givers to work, they must come at the same time each week. It is not sufficient to get one day in seven off; it is optimal to get a specific day in seven off on a regular basis.

My own experience agrees with this body of medical research. I personally need one day in seven where I set things aside and experience a true rest. That does not mean I sleep the whole day. Instead, I use it as a day for recreation, reflection, meditation, and focusing on spiritual values. Whether you keep the seventh day of the week as I do or a different 24-hour period, there is a benefit to observing one specific day in seven as a day of rest. Many have learned by experience that in order for the daily rest of sleep to happen, it must be treated as a priority. Even if your work is not completed, it is best to go to bed on time. The same principle holds true for the weekly rest. Even if your work is not done, it is best to take time for the weekly rest.

Jesus said that the seventh day, which is known as the Sabbath, was made for man.[793] The ancient Ten Commandments, which were etched in stone by the finger of God, admonish us to remember the weekly rest of the Sabbath.[794] The word used in the commandments is to "remember." Apparently God knew that a lot of people would forget to take rest, which has been a challenge not only in America, but in the rest of the world as well. Jesus, who needed to achieve peak mental performance to endure the ordeal of the cross, kept the weekly rest of the Sabbath. Those who wish to achieve optimal mental, physical, and spiritual health can learn by His example.[795]

## VITAMIN $R_3$ (RECREATION)

Another component of healing rest is recreation—a word that is best understood by dividing it into two parts: re and creation. True recreation rejuvenates, replenishes, and restores. Unfortunately, the number one and two forms of recreation today (TV and the Internet) provide little if any rest or rejuvenation. Healthy doses of vitamin $R_3$ come not through entertainment, but through being out in nature, drinking in fresh air and sunlight.

The major difference between recreation and entertainment (which can sometimes be called "wreck creation") is made clear when you consider the official definitions of the words. The Merriam-Webster dictionary defines recreation as "refreshment of strength and spirits after work." In contrast, entertainment is defined as "amusement or diversion provided especially by performers." Both activities are diversionary; engaging in either serves to take our minds off of work and other obligations or concerns. But while recreation is the purposeful attempt to restore or refresh creative energy, too much entertainment has a mind numbing effect—failing to rekindle mental energy.[796]

Hiking by lakes, streams, or the ocean surf is a great way to receive life-enhancing negative ions, rejuvenating heart and mind while building muscle as well. Those pursuing optimal mental health will avoid so-called "recreation" that exhausts, rather than refreshes, the brain.

### VITAMIN $R_4$ (REFLECTION)

The fourth form of vitamin R is that of meditation, which simply means reflection. One of the best forms of meditation (with benefits that have been scientifically demonstrated) is prayer. The relaxation found in prayer to God actually results in improved frontal lobe function. This is in contrast to the "feel good" meditation practiced by many Eastern religions, where the frontal lobe is actually suppressed through self-hypnotic techniques.[797] Another form of meditation that increases frontal lobe function is Bible study combined with reflection.

**Babies need considerably more sleep than adults, but many adults don't realize they need more sleep than they think.**

### HOW MUCH SLEEP DO YOU NEED?

While the average individual needs 7 or 8 hours of sleep per night, some need as many as 9 hours of sleep.[798] A third of adults—or more—are missing out on this "recommended daily allowance."[799] How do you know if you're sleep deprived? If you have to use an alarm clock to wake up, you suffer from sleep deprivation. People who have accumulated the amount of rest they need wake up spontaneously. In addition, if you do not feel wide awake and energetic throughout your waking hours, you could be sleeping too little. Fatigue or a profound lack of energy are other signs that a reorganization of your schedule to accommodate more sleep may be in order.

### HOW TO IMPROVE YOUR SLEEP

There are number of steps we can take to enhance melatonin production, and with it, the soundness and quality of our sleep.

#### Step #1: Watch where you sleep.

For an improvement in sleep quality, sleep in a cool, dark, quiet, tidy, room. A comfortable bed is obviously very important to restful sleep, but studies have actually shown that people sleep better when the room is neat and clean.[625] Sleeping in complete darkness is best for melatonin production.[800] Consider using a fan or, if possible, opening a screened window in cooler months to keep fresh air circulating.

#### Step #2: Set your body's "light" clock.

You'll also want to increase exposure to natural light during non-sleep time while minimizing artificial light exposure.[801] Some people make the mistake of staying up late with the idea that, by making themselves tired, they will fall asleep more easily. Exposure to artificial light while staying up late interferes with melatonin production, however, ultimately robbing the night owl of much-needed rest.

### Step #3: Avoid the "sleep robbers."

Drugs that interfere with melatonin production should be avoided, as well as activities that deter restful sleep. A number of prescription drugs, such as those listed in **Figure 16.4**, inhibit the body's production of that important hormone.[802,803]

Alcohol and caffeine consumption also interferes with sound sleep. The consumption of caffeine cuts melatonin production in half for 6 hours, and significantly worsens sleep quality by decreasing the deepest, most restorative stages of sleep.[804] Alcohol results in a 41% reduction deep sleep cycles.[805,806] Scientists at the University of Wisconsin in Madison found that the more alcoholic drinks that men have at any time of day, the greater the risk of breathing problems during sleep.[807] After the researchers accounted for the effects of body size, smoking, and medications that can trigger breathing problems, they found that for every additional drink a man took per day, his risk of sleep apnea increased by twenty-five percent. (Sleep apnea occurs when your oxygen level drops during sleep, and breathing temporarily stops. Alcohol consumption, along with obesity, is one of the major causes of sleep apnea.)

Other sleep robbers include TV and the Internet. The more time you spend in these activities, the less you will have for sleep. If you are tempted to stay up and watch just one more show or visit just one more website, ask yourself if it's worth feeling wiped out the next day. Earlier bedtimes are also beneficial to quality of sleep, since the earlier you turn in, the more melatonin your body will make.

**DRUGS THAT MAY IMPEDE SLEEP**

- non-steroidal anti-inflammatory drugs
- beta and calcium channel blockers
- anti-anxiety drugs and sleep aids
- vitamin $B_{12}$ (>3 mg a day)
- anti-depressants
- breathing medications
- certain antibiotics
- anti-seizure drugs
- steroids

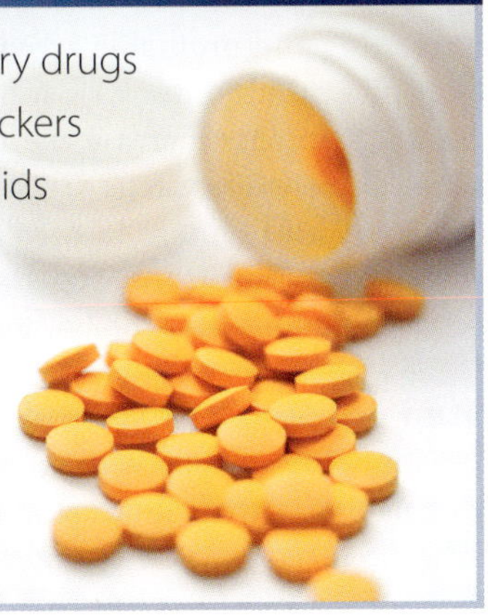

*Figure 16.4*

### Step #4: Make healthy dietary lifestyle choices

As discussed in chapter 11, adequate vitamin D and calcium is also critical to melatonin production and peaceful, restorative sleep. Many people who don't consume enough calcium-rich foods should consider a calcium supplement, which can promote quality rest with an adequate melatonin peak at night. In addition to obtaining plenty of calcium in the diet, consume foods rich in melatonin, tryptophan, and vitamin $B_6$.[808,809810,810809,811] Rich plant-based sources of melatonin would include oats, corn, rice, ginger, tomatoes, bananas, and barley.[812,813] The timing of the last meal before bed is also important. Eating just before retiring or eating a heavy meal in the evening often contributes to heartburn or acid reflux, and insomnia can result. When the evening meal is eaten three to four hours before retiring, digestion will usually be completed, and superior, more efficient rest will be experienced. Insomnia will also improve when the order of meals is reversed, shifting the bulk of the day's calories to the breakfast and lunch meals, and choosing light and easily digested foods for the evening meal.

A simple fruit meal is an excellent choice for the third meal. For some individuals, cutting out the evening meal altogether may prove to be a very helpful sleep aid. If there is a feeling of hunger, try drinking 8 to 12 ounces of cool water. With the stomach resting through the night, both mind and body will be more rested in the morning.

Restricting food intake increases melatonin production.[813] Fasting, especially in the evening hours, is one of the best ways to accomplish this. Even a daytime fast produces as much melatonin as people normally get at night, since the entero-chromafin cells in the gut produce melatonin during periods of fasting.[814]

### Step #5: Keep yourself busy, and remember to exercise

Inactivity can also contribute to sleepless nights. Filling the day with interesting and profitable activities that keep you active will prepare your body and mind to rest well at night. Because of its stress-reducing effects, exercise can also increase the energy obtained from a given amount of sleep. Those who exercise vigorously, regularly, and aerobically sleep more efficiently and require less sleep than their less active peers.[815] They also wake less frequently during the night. However, just before bedtime is best avoided because the body needs time to transition to a restful state.

### Step #6: Set your worries aside

Inability to cope with stress contributes to fitful sleep.[816]When individuals reprioritize duties and develop a healthier perspective, it becomes easier to relax, experience inner peace, fall asleep at night, and stay asleep. Attempt to quickly curb the cycle of stress and insomnia before it becomes out of control.

When you get into bed, it is important to set your anxieties and worries aside. Having a clear conscience helps, since guilt can cause insomnia or even major depression. Another means of inducing sleep is to engage in a calming activity such as reading spiritual material or listening to soothing music for 15 to 30 minutes before retiring. A season of prayer, though certainly not recommended solely for the purpose of inducing sleep, may also have a calming effect. A summarized list of best practices for sleep improvement is provided in **Figure 16.5**.

## MAKE THE RIGHT CHOICES

Sleep patterns can definitely either deter or enhance mental performance. Lifestyle changes that may ensure a good night's rest frequently offer other health benefits as well, including weight loss and increased energy levels. Improved sleep habits in combination with other lifestyle changes can be a powerful aid in achieving peak mental performance.

### TO IMPROVE SLEEP QUALITY

- Exercise daily.
- Ensure a good supply of fresh air.
- Avoid daytime boredom.
- Manage stress effectively.
- Avoid caffeine, alcohol, and nicotine.
- Eliminate drugs that interfere with sleep.
- Avoid eating for at least 3 hours before bed.
- Eliminate the bedroom clock.
- Establish a regular sleeping/waking schedule.
- Sleep in a cool, dark, comfortable, and tidy room.
- Keep the room completely quiet (or use white noise).
- Lie still shortly after going to bed to calm your mind and body.
- Set anxieties, worries, and anger aside before going to bed.
- If needed, listen to soothing music, read spiritual material, or pray.

***Figure 16.5***

## References

735. National Sleep Foundation, "Teens and Sleep." http://www.sleepfoundation.org/article/sleep-topics/teens-and-sleep.
736. Pizza F, et al. "Sleep quality and motor vehicle crashes in adolescents." *J Clin Sleep Med* 2010; 6(1):41-45.
737. Centers for Disease Control and Prevention, http://www.cdc.gov/nchs/fastats/lcod.htm.
738. Chokroverty S. *Sleep Disorders Medicine: Basic Science, Technical Considerations, and Clinical Aspects. Saunders.* 2009. 19-20. 23.
739. Williamsona AM, Feyerb A. "Moderate sleep deprivation produces impairments in cognitive and motor performance equivalent to legally prescribed levels of alcohol intoxication." *Occup Environ Med* 2000;57:649-655.
740. National Commission on Sleep Disorders Research, R*eport of the National Commission on Sleep Disorders Research*, submitted to the United States Congress and to the secretary of the U.S. Department of Health and Human Services, January 1993.
741. Maas JB. *Power Sleep*. Quill. 2001. 11, 57.
742. Kushida C A. *Sleep Deprivation: Clinical Issues, Pharmacology, and Sleep Loss Effects.* Informa Healthcare. 2004. 291.
743. Bentley E. *Awareness: biorhythms, sleep, and dreaming.* Routledge. 1999.
744. Chokroverty S. *Sleep Disorders Medicine: Basic Science, Technical Considerations, and Clinical Aspects. Saunders.* 2009. 19-20.
745. Drummond SPA, et al. "Sleep deprivation-induced reduction in cortical functional response to serial subtraction." *NeuroReport*, 1999. 10 (18), 3745-3748.
746. Chee, MW, Chuah L, Venkatraman V, Chan W, Dinges PP. "Functional imaging of working memory following normal sleep and after 24 and 35 h of sleep deprivation: Correlations of fronto-parietal activation with performance." *Neuroimage* 2006 Jan 18.
747. Nelson CS, et al. "Residents' performance before and after night call as evaluated by an indicator of creative thought." *J Am Osteopath Assoc* 1995;95(10):600-3.
748. Boyce S, Macauslan J, Bradlow A, Smiljanic R. "Landmark-based analysis of sleep-deprived speech." *J Acoust Soc Am* 2008;123(5):3887.
749. Haavisto M, et al. "Sleep restriction for the duration of a work week impairs multitasking performance." *Journal of Sleep Research*. April 9, 2010 (online).
750. Scharff R. "Effects of sleep deprivation on auditory and visual memory tasks." *Percept Mot Skills* 2005;101(2):451-67.
751. Gopalakrishnan A, Cirelli C. "Sleep Deprivation and Cellular Responses to Oxidative Stress." *Sleep* 2004;27(1):27-35.
752. Chokroverty S. *Sleep Disorders Medicine: Basic Science, Technical Considerations, and Clinical Aspects. Saunders.* 2009. 19-20. 127.
753. Friedman RC, Kornfeld DS, Bigger TJ. "Psychological problems associated with sleep deprivation in interns." PMID: 4699420.
754. Lopez MC. "Non-REM sleep instability in patients with major depressive disorder: subjective improvement and improvement of non-REM sleep instability with treatment (Agomelatine)." *Sleep Med* - 01-DEC-2007; 9(1): 33-41.
755. Holsboer-Trachsler E, Seifritz E, "Sleep in depression and sleep deprivation: a brief conceptual review." *World J Biol Psychiatry* 2000 Oct;1(4):180-6.
756. Kushida CA. *Sleep Deprivation: Clinical Issues, Pharmacology, and Sleep Loss Effects.* Informa Healthcare. 2004. 21-22.
757. Lee-Chiong T. *Sleep Medicine: Essentials and Review.* Oxford University Press. 2008. 289.
758. Reite M, Weissberg MP, Ruddy J. *Clinical Manual for Evaluation and Treatment of Sleep Disorders.* American Psychiatric Publishing, Inc. 2008. 124.
759. Spiegel K, Leproult R, Van Cauter E. "Impact of sleep debt on physiological rhythms." *Rev Neurol* ( Paris ). 2003 Nov;159(11 Suppl):6S11-20.
760. Irwin M, et al. *Journal of the Federation of American Societies for Experimental Biology.* 10 (1996): 643-653.
761. Moore-Ede M. *The Twenty-Four-Hour Society* (New York: Addison Wesley, 1993).
762. Radecki SE, Brunton SA. "Management of Insomnia in Office-Based Practice National Prevalence and Therapeutic Patterns." *Archives of Family Medicine*, Volume II, November 1993.
763. National Center on Sleep Disorders Research, http://www.nhlbi.nih.gov/health/prof/sleep/sleep.txt.
764. Chokroverty S. *Sleep Disorders Medicine: Basic Science, Technical Considerations, and Clinical Aspects. Saunders.* 2009. 19-20. 112.
765. Maas JB. *Power Sleep*. Quill. 2001. 61-62.
766. Maas JB. *Power Sleep*. Quill. 2001. 61-62.

767. Sadeh A, Gruber R, Raviv A. "The Effects of Sleep Restriction and Extension on School-Age Children: What a Difference an Hour Makes." *Child Development*:74:2:444-455. 2003.
768. Pagel JF. "Adolescent sleep disturbance and school performance: the confounding variable of socioeconomics." *J Clin Sleep Med* - 15-FEB-2007; 3(1): 19-23.
769. Dinges DF, et al. "Cumulative sleepiness, mood disturbance, and psychomotor vigilance performance decrements during a week of sleep restricted to 4-5 hours per night." *Sleep*. 1997 Apr;20(4):267-7.
770. *Neurobiology of Learning and Memory*, vol 86, p 241.
771. Rao ML, et al. "Selective slow-wave sleep deprivation influences blood serotonin profiles and serum melatonin concentrations in healthy subjects." *Biological Psychiatry* 1996;40(7):664-7.
772. Paerpoli W. *The Melatonin Miracle*. Pocket. 1996. 4, 14-15, 24, 85, 88, 185, 202.
773. Yu H, Reiter RJ. *Melatonin: biosynthesis, physiological effects, and clinical applications.* CRC Press. 1992. 3.
774. Cajochen C, Kräuchi K, Wirz-Justice A. "Role of melatonin in the Regulation of Human Circadian Rhythms and Sleep." *Journal of Neuroendocrinology*, Volume 15, Number 4, April 2003 , pp. 432-437(6).
775. Bassil N. "Endocrine aspects of healthy brain aging." *Clin Geriatr Med* - 01-FEB-2010; 26(1): 57-74.
776. Singh R. "Circadian heart rate and blood pressure variability considered for research and patient care ." *International Journal of Cardiology*, Volume 87 , Issue 1 , Page 9.
777. "Individual differences in entrainment of mood to the weekly calendar." *Journal of personality and Social Psychology* 1990, Vol. 58, No. 1, 164-171.
778. Campbell J. *Winston Churchill's afternoon nap: a wide-awake inquiry into the human nature of time.* Simon and Schuster. 1986.
779. "Antioxidants and Cardiovascular Disease." *Alpha Science Int'l Ltd.* 260.
780. Siegelová J. "Circaseptan rhytmm in blood pressure and heart rate in newborns." *Scripta medica*, (CZE). ISSN 1211-3395. Volume 69, number Suppl. 2, pp. 63-70.
781. Rawson MJ, Cornelissen G. "Circadian and Circaseptan Components of Blood Pressure and Heart Rate During Depression." *Scriptamedica* (BRNO). 73 (2): 117–124, April 2000.
782. "Individual differences in entrainment of mood to the weekly calendar." *Journal of personality and Social Psychology* 1990, Vol. 58, No. 1, 164-171.
783. Zerubavel E. *The Seven Day Circle.* Chicago: Univ. of Chicago Press. 1985. 43.
784. Nicolau G, Haus E, Popescu M. "Orcadian, Weekly, and Seasonal Variations in Cardiac Mortality, Blood Pressure, and Catecholamine Excretion." *Chronobiology International*, Volume 8, Issue 2 1991. 149-159.
785. de la Pena S, et al. "Circadian and circaseptan (about-7-day) free-running physiologic rhythms of a woman in social isolation." Proc. 2nd Ann. IEEE Symp. on Computer-Based Medical Systems, Minneapolis, June 26–27 1989 Washington DC: Computer Society Press 1989, 273-278. OpenURL
786. DeVecchi A, et al. "Circaseptan rhythmic aspectsof rejection in treated patients with kidney transplant." *Chronopharmacology and Chronotherapeutics*, Florida A & M University Foundation, Tallahassee, Florida, 1981, 339-353.
787. Palmer RR. *The World of The French Revolution*. Harper & Row. New York. 1971. 120.
788. Gillespie CC, et al. *Pierre-Simon Laplace, 1749-1827: A Life in Exact Science.* Princeton University Press. 2000. 154.
789. Freeze GL. *Russia: a history*. Oxford University Press. 2002. 376.
790. Article "Week." *Encyclopedia Britannica, Eleventh Edition*, 1910.
791. Philippians 2:3. *The Holy Bible.* Authorized King James Version.
792. Merriam Webster Dictionary online. http://www.merriam-webster.com/dictionary/zeitgeber
793. Mark 2:27. *The Holy Bible.* Authorized King James Version.
794. Exodus 20:11. *The Holy Bible.* Authorized King James Version.
795. Luke 4:16. *The Holy Bible.* Authorized King James Version.
796. Merriam Webster Dictionary online. http://www.merriam-webster.com/netdict/recreation
797. Cohen DL. "Cerebral blood flow effects of yoga training: preliminary evaluation of 4 cases." *J Altern Complement Med* - 01-JAN-2009; 15(1): 9-14.
798. Wingard DL. "Berkman LF. Mortality risk associated with sleeping patterns among adults." *Sleep* 1983;6(2);102-107.

799. "Perceived Insufficient Rest or Sleep — Four States, 2006." Centers for Disease Control and Prevention. http://www.cdc.gov/mmwr/preview/mmwrhtml/mm5708a2.htm.
800. Levy AJ, Wehr TA, et al. "Light suppresses melatonin secretion in humans." *Science* 1980 Dec 12;210(4475):1267-1269.
801. Laakso ML, Porkka-Heiskanen T, et al. "Twenty-four hour patterns of pineal melatonin and pituitary and plasma prolactin in male rats under 'natural' and artificial lighting conditions. *Neuroendocrinology* 1988 Sep;48(3):308-313.
802. Reiter, RJ, Robinson, Jo. *Melatonin*. Bantam. 1996. 238, 244, 246.
803. "Plasma melatonin levels in depressed patients before and after treatment with antidepressant medication." *Biological Psychiatry*, Volume 25, Issue 1, Pages 33-38.
804. Reiter RJ, Robinson J. "Drugs That Deplete Melatonin." *Melatonin: You Body's Natural Wonder Drug*. New York, NY: Bantam Books, 1995. 188.
805. Gates J. "Getting Melatonin Naturally." *Nutrition Advocate,* Vol. 3, No. 9 - September 2005.
806. Ekman AC, Leppaluoto J, et al. "Ethanol inhibits melatonin secretion in healthy volunteers in a dose-dependent randomized double blind cross-over study." *J Clin Endocrinaol Metab* 1993 Sep:77(3):780-783.
807. Aldrich MS. Neurobiology of sleep." *Sleep Medicine*. New York: Oxford, 1999. 27-38.
808. Morton DJ, Reiter RJ. "Involvement of calcium in pineal gland function." *Prog. Exp. Biol. Med.* 197 (1991), pp. 378–383.
809. Hattori A, Migitaka H, et al. "Identification of melatonin in plants and its effects on plasma melatonin levels and binding to melatonin receptors in vertebrates." *Biochem Mol Biol Int* 1995 Mar;35(3):627-634.
810. Yaga K, Reiter RJ, Richardson BA. "Tryptophan loading increases daytime serum melatonin levels in intact and pinealectomized rats." *Life Sci* 1993;52(14):1231-1238.
811. Dakshinamurti K, Paulose CS, et al. "Neurobiology of pyridoxine." *Ann N Y Acad Sci* 1990;5850:128-44.
812. Dubbels R, Reiter RJ, et al. "Melatonin in edible plants identified by radioimmunoassay and by high performance liquid chromatography-mass spectrometry." *J Pineal Res* 1995 Jan;18(1):28-31.
813. Reiter RJ, Robinson J. "Drugs That Deplete Melatonin." *Melatonin: You Body's Natural Wonder Drug*. New York, NY: Bantam Books, 1995. 188.
814. Reiter RJ. "The Ageing pineal gland and its physiological consequences." *Bioessays* 1992 Mar;14(3):169-175.
815. Ramakrishnan K. "Treatment options for insomnia." *Am Fam Physician.* 15-AUG-2007; 76(4): 517-26
816. Basta M. "Chronic Insomnia and the Stress System." *Sleep Medicine Clin* - June 2007; 2(2); 279-291.

Chapter 17

WATER IS FOR MORE THAN DRINKING - IT CAN TRANSFORM YOUR HEALTH INSIDE AND OUT.

# Hydrate Yourself

***The therapeutic use of water, internally and externally, is an effective way to improve cognition.***

Jill is a courtroom reporter in the state of Oklahoma, and also one of my patients. Having a number of years of experience, she took great pride in her ability to accurately record virtually everything said in a courtroom.

Things were going well for Jill in her job, until one embarrassing day when, right in the midst of a heated courtroom discussion, she began to feel faint. Before she could say a word or even realize what was happening, Jill passed out—right on the courtroom floor. As might be imagined, proceedings in the courtroom came to a rather abrupt halt. The judge and other onlookers were naturally concerned for Jill, and wanted to make sure she was fine. In addition, there was no way court could proceed without the services of a court reporter. Unfortunately for Jill and her employer, her fainting in the courtroom began to happen with an unnerving degree of regularity.

"I think I have hypoglycemia," Jill said when she came to my office, anxious to get to the root of the problem. She certainly had manifested some of the symptoms of hypoglycemia during her fainting spells, which led her to this self-diagnosis.

She had tried every diet she could find on the internet for hypoglycemia, but to no avail. In addition to a diet high in complex carbohydrates and fiber, I decided to try an additional approach.

"How much water are you drinking each day?" I asked Jill. I then instructed her to drink 12 glasses per day from then on. This created a different sort of dilemma for Jill in the courtroom, as she now felt the need for regular restroom breaks. But after the increase in water intake, Jill never passed out in the courtroom again.

## WATER'S IMPORTANCE

It goes without saying that water is a very important ingredient, utilized by virtually every area of our bodies. Water makes up 83% of your blood, 75% of your lean muscle tissue, 74% of your brain, and 22% of even your bones.[817] All in all, about 60% of your body weight is really comprised of water.[818]

Adequate water intake is vital to every function of your body, including your brain.

Many people who feel sluggish late in the day think they are just running out of energy. More often than not, however, their sluggishness is due to dehydration.[819] Water improves energy, increasing both mental and physical performance.[820,821,822,823] Marathon runners know they need water to keep their energy and endurance up. That's why they drink it throughout the race.

Fiber is great, but when a person is dehydrated, constipation and abdominal discomfort are often the result. Dehydration is actually one of the most common causes of constipation.[824]

Water helps detoxify the liver and kidneys. Without adequate $H_2O$, these critical organs have a much more difficult job ridding themselves of toxins and waste.[825] And of course, waste build-up in the body is not good: it can cause nausea and sluggishness, among other symptoms.

Because water removes toxins and waste products from the body, it can actually keep the skin healthier.[826] When the body is properly hydrated, the skin has more of a beautiful, glowing color. Hydration can also be helpful in the battle against obesity.[827] Often when people feel they are hungry, that hunger is actually a sign of needing more water.[828] If you are overweight and feel hungry, I suggest you drink more water instead. This strategy will help reduce your hunger pains and assist in weight loss.

Water is also vital to your body's ability to digest and absorb water-soluble vitamins and minerals. Any nutrient that is water-soluble actually requires water to get through the digestive system. A partial list of water-soluble vitamins and minerals is provided in **Figure 17.1**.

Good hydration is important for the development of strong muscles, and also for the health of the brain.[829,830] The work of your brain really occurs in the synapses, when one neuron communicates with another. This is where brain chemistry really happens, and the target of every pharmaceutical company trying to manipulate mental processes and mood. There is a liquid between these synapsis which helps them to work, and that liquid is not soda pop, coffee, milk, or juice. It's good old-fashioned water.[831]

## WATER SOLUBLE VITAMINS

| Vitamin | Actions | Vegetarian sources |
|---|---|---|
| **$B_1$** (thiamin) | Helps your body use carbohydrates for energy; good for your nervous system | Legumes, nuts, enriched whole-grain products |
| **$B_2$** (riboflavin) | Helps your body process protein, carbohydrates and fats; helps maintain healthy skin | Legumes, nuts, enriched whole-grain products |
| **$B_3$** (niacin) | Helps your body process protein and fats; helps maintain a healthy nervous system, skin, and digestion | Peanuts, beans, yeast, enriched whole-grain breads and cereals |
| **$B_5$** (pantothenic acid) | Helps your body process nutrients; helps your body make red blood cells | Peanuts, peas, beans, lentils, broccoli, yeast, cereals, whole grains |
| **$B_6$** (pyridoxine) | Helps the body use protein & fat; supports nervous & immune systems; helps blood carry oxygen to the body's tissues; breaks down copper & iron; prevents anemia; helps maintain normal blood sugar levels | Peanuts, bananas, carrots, yeast, fortified cereals |
| **$B_{12}$** (cobalamin) | Maintains healthy nerve cells & red blood cells; needed to make genetic material in cells; prevents one type of anemia | Fortified cereals, Red Star Nutritional Yeast |
| **C** (ascorbic acid) | Helps form connective tissues, such as cartilage and tendons; acts as an antioxident and protects your body's cells from damage from free radicals; good for your immune system | Broccoli, green peppers, spinach, brussels sprouts, citrus fruits, tomatoes, potatoes, strawberries, cabbage |
| **H** (biotin) | Helps the body use nutrients; good for nervous system; forms red blood cells | Peas, beans, nuts, tomatoes, yeast |
| **Folic Acid** (folate) | Helps your body make and sustain new cells; prevents one type of anemia; prevents neural tube birth defects | Dark leafy vegetables, dry beans and peas, oranges, fortified cereals, and grain products |

*Figure 17.1*

When we have enough water in the system, the brain communicates with itself much more effectively.[832] We have fewer headaches, better neuronal function, better concentration, and better endurance overall.[833,834,835,836]

The importance of water consumption to overall health cannot be emphasized enough. Proper hydration is the foundation that supports every other healthy lifestyle habit.

## BLOOD LIKE MOLASSES

**Good hydration is a natural blood-thinner beneficial for those with diabetes, risk of stroke, and high blood pressure.**

Good circulation is vital, because this is how the blood delivers nutrients to the body. If the body is dehydrated, the blood becomes thick with a consistency like molasses.[837] When the viscosity of blood increases, the heart must pump harder to send it through the system. Blood pressure rises, and the adverse effect is felt through the entire body, including the brain.[838] The more water you drink, the more freely your blood can flow.

The thinning of the blood which results from adequate hydration can be particularly helpful to diabetics. Diabetic complications worsen when the blood is thick, but the reverse is true when the blood flows more freely.[839] Strokes, which are tragic because a part of the brain actually dies, are much more likely when the blood is thick.[840] The effect of a large stroke can be pretty dramatic, affecting memory, the ability to reason, the vision, and even the ability to move one side of the body. To think that the risk of stroke could be reduced by simply drinking more $H_2O$ should make each of us reach for some water.

Drinking eight cups of water per day can also help lower high blood pressure for people who are chronically dehydrated.[841] It's fairly common knowledge that thickness in the blood is associated with heart disease, and a lot of people think the best way to thin the blood is to take an aspirin. Aspirin is pretty inexpensive, and it is true that aspirin thins the blood. In some patients with heart disease, we might recommend both aspirin and water: aspirin to reduce the platelets from clotting, and water to thin the blood. But aspirin does not decrease blood viscosity, and of the two remedies, water is the more effective blood thinner.

## INCREASE WATER INTAKE AND DECREASE RISK

One study, which considered more than 20,000 individuals over the course of many years, found that those who drank less than two glasses of water per day had a much higher risk of heart disease than those who drank five or more cups of water per day. As illustrated in **Figure 17.2**, researchers in this study found that women who drank five or more cups of water daily had a 40% reduction in heart disease. The improvement was even greater for men—who experienced an impressive 60% reduction in heart disease when they drank five or more cups of water.

This study was not just about fluids, it was about water. A lot of people think if they drink enough fruit juice, milk, coffee, or pop, they'll be fine. Women in the study who drank other fluids besides water actually had a much higher risk of heart disease mortality than their water-drinking, non-water-drinking, and non-fluid-drinking counterparts.[842] There is no substitute for water! These findings are both important and dramatic. You can reduce your risk of premature death, plus improve your quality of life, simply by drinking adequate water.

Water is also an important ally in the work of the gall bladder. Three different studies have shown that water intake decreases the risk of gallstone formation.[843] Gall bladder removal is one of the most common surgeries in the western world.[844] There are two main reasons why gallstones develop: cholesterol and dehydration. By cutting your cholesterol consumption and increasing your water intake, you can prevent developing gallstones or related complications such as pancreatitis.

Drinking more water also decreases the chances of kidney stones by diluting the mineral content in the urinary system.[845] Kidney stones are quite a painful problem. Many of my female patients who bore children through natural childbirth tell me that kidney stone passage is actually worse than labor and delivery. On the male side of the equation, many of my patients have told me that passing a kidney stone was the most painful experience they ever had in their lives.

Drinking more water may also decrease the risk of urinary tract infections.[846] Take to heart the expression "an ounce of prevention is worth a pound of cure," and consider that drinking more water can be the simple step in reducing your risk of major health issues.

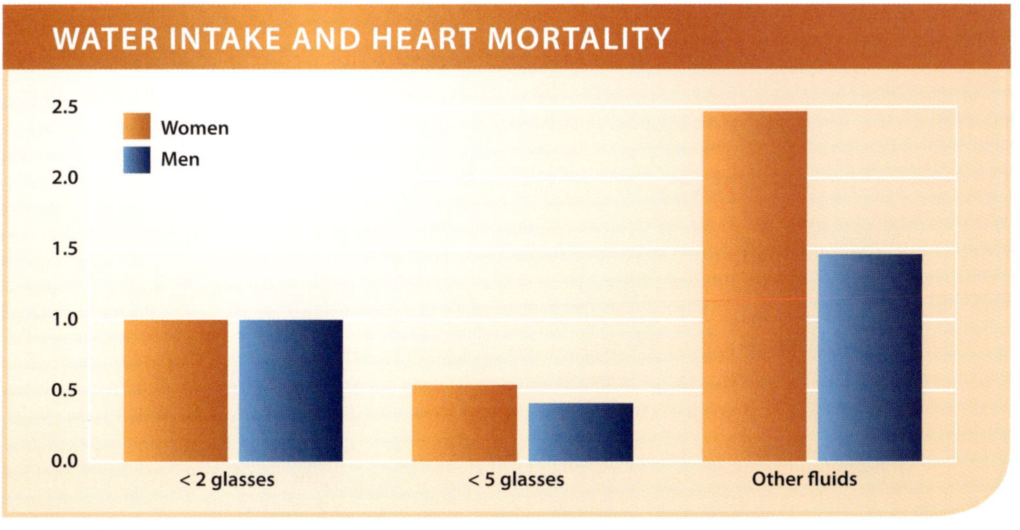


*Figure 17.2*

## TOO MUCH OF A GOOD THING?

Of course, it is possible to get too much of a good thing, even water. One Boston marathon runner was so convinced of the value of water that she drank huge amounts of it throughout the marathon. Towards the end of the race she collapsed and died, a victim of an electrolyte imbalance due to too much water.[847]

If you aren't exercising, yet you regularly drink more than a gallon of water per day, you are probably drinking too much water. However, if you're outside and really sweating it out, you may need to drink that much or more.

When the body is properly hydrated, the urine should have a slight yellow tinge. If it's yellow or perfectly clear, you are most likely erring on one or the other ends of the spectrum.

## WATER FOR CLEANLINESS

Often illness is actually due to a lack of not only water consumption, but cleanliness and a failure to use clean water. Many ailments, such as diarrhea and pneumonia, can be prevented by washing the hands thoroughly with soap and water. Pneumonia is one of the leading causes of death worldwide, and many cases of pneumonia are due to not washing the hands.[848,849]

Hands should be washed whenever there is contact with body secretions. Proper hand washing with soap before meals and after using the toilet can reduce the number of cases of diarrhea by 47% and acute respiratory illness by 30%.[850]

Not having access to a clean water source is a grave concern for millions of people worldwide, leading to the spread of many diseases. In 2006, the World Health Organization called infectious disease due to the lack of clean water an "impending global crisis." **Figure 17.3** provides some alarming statistics with regard to this trend.[851]

Clean water on the outside plays as vital a role in disease prevention and reducing health risks as consuming adequate clean water inside.

## WATER ON THE OUTSIDE (HYDROTHERAPY)

Hydrotherapy, the therapeutic use of water, has been used successfully for centuries to treat a variety of physical and mental ailments. In the *Nedley Depression Recovery Program*, we introduce the participants to a type of hydrotherapy that involves a rotating treatment of hot and cold water. This "contrast bath" stimulates the body's circulatory and nervous systems by achieving a push-and-pull effect, which results in dramatic improvements in both energy and brain chemistry. The treatment actually has a positive effect similar to electric shock therapy, without the harsh jolt of electricity. Hydrotherapy has the advantage of utilizing the body's natural responses and avoiding the negative side effects of electric therapies.

## STARTLING STATS ABOUT CLEANLINESS AND MORBIDITY

- 1.8 million people die every year from diarrheal diseases (including cholera); 90% are children under 5, mostly in developing countries. 88% of diarrheal disease is attributed to an unsafe water supply, inadequate sanitation, and poor hygiene.
- An estimated 160 million people are infected with schistosomiasis, a disease that causes tens of thousands of deaths every year, mainly in sub-Saharan Africa. It is strongly related to unsanitary excreta disposal and absence of nearby sources of safe water. Basic sanitation reduces the disease by up to 77%.
- 500 million people are at risk from trachoma, which impairs vision or results in blindness in many. The disease is strongly related to lack of face washing, often due to absence of nearby sources of safe water.

***Figure 17.3***

Contrast baths take advantage of water's unique ability to store and transmit both cold and heat. The cold water has a depressant effect on the body's functions, decreasing activity and constricting blood vessels by numbing nerves, which pushes lymph fluids away from the treated area. The body's response to the hot water, on the other hand, is dilation of blood vessels as the body attempts to throw off the excess heat and keep body temperature from rising. This results in increased circulation to the area being treated, thus bringing blood nutrients and oxygen to nourish the body.[852,853,854] This is why hydrotherapy is so effective in increase circulation and boosting the immune system.

One of the best treatments for migraine headaches is a hot foot bath - immersing both feet in hot water and placing a cold cloth on the forehead. This alleviates migraine congestion in the brain by drawing the blood toward the feet and away from the head, relieving the headache.

There are many forms of hydrotherapy. The effect of the contrast bath can easily be achieved at home as well. Contrast showers offer a variation of the same treatment for individuals without access to tubs. As with any new physical program, some precautions should be observed. Those with heart disease, blood pressure problems, or other serious health

## CONTRAST SHOWERS

1. Warm water for 3-5 minutes
   (as warm as you can tolerate, but no hotter than 104°F/40°C)
2. Cool water for 1 minute
   (as cool as you can stand, but no colder than 55°F/13°C)

Repeat the cycle 3 times, ending with cold water.

*Figure 17.4*

conditions should not use contrast showers. You will also need to take care not to scald your skin (you can set your water heater to control the maximum temperature.)

The therapy can be completed in less than twenty minutes and repeated every time you shower if desired. Simply alternate the temperature of the water flow as explained in **Figure 17.4**. When you have completed your therapy, always rest in bed for at least thirty minutes, keeping warm and comfortable. This is a very important step because your body needs to rest to properly benefit from the treatment. You will find the treatment breathtaking—but also truly invigorating and refreshing.

### DRINK YOUR WATER

As simple as it may sound, the correct and adequate use of water really is key to achieving peak mental performance. Some best practices for water consumption are provided below.

- Start drinking water as soon as you get out of bed. If you are cold in the morning, drink warm water instead of dehydrating coffee and tea, which can actually cause more dehydration.

- Set an alarm time to remind you to drink water and keep a bottle of water with you whenever possible. If you work at home, you can set 8 or 10 glasses up on the counter to remind yourself that you need to drink them during the day.

- Don't wait until you are thirsty to drink water. By the time your body alerts you to thirst, you are already dehydrated.

- Compensate for the "thieving" diuretics that steal water from your body. If you drink coffee, tea, or sodas with caffeine, drink a few extra glasses of water to make up for the water these beverages leach from your system.

- If you live in an area of high altitude or work outside in the heat each day, your body will require more water to remain hydrated.

By using plenty of water inside and out, you will improve your endurance, energy, and ability to think with clarity and precision.

## References

817. U. S. Department of the Interior. "The Water in You." http://ga.water.usgs.gov/edu/propertyyou.html.
818. Maughan RJ. "Impact of mild dehydration on wellness and on exercise performance." *European Journal of Clinical Nutrition* (2003) 57, Suppl 2, S19–S23.
819. Maughan RJ. "Impact of mild dehydration on wellness and on exercise performance." *European Journal of Clinical Nutrition* (2003) 57, Suppl 2, S19–S23.
820. Schols JMGA, et al. "Preventing and Treating Dehydration in the Elderly During Periods of Illness and Warm Weather." *Journal of Nutrition*. February, 2009.
821. Lieberman,HR. "Hydration and cognition: a critical review and recommendations for future research." *Journal of the American College of Nutrition*, (2007). 26(5 Suppl), 555S-561S.
822. Lieberman,HR. "Hydration and cognition: a critical review and recommendations for future research." *Journal of the American College of Nutrition*, (2007). 26(5 Suppl), 555S-561S.
823. Maughan RJ. "Impact of mild dehydration on wellness and on exercise performance." *European Journal of Clinical Nutrition* (2003) 57, Suppl 2, S19–S23.
824. Batmanghelidj F. *Water: For Health, for Healing, for Life: You're Not Sick, You're Thirsty!* Grand Central Publishing. 2003. 118.
825. Colbert D. *Toxic Relief.* Siloam. 2003. 57,118.
826. Batmanghelidj F. *Water: For Health, for Healing, for Life: You're Not Sick, You're Thirsty!* Grand Central Publishing. 2003. 34.
827. Kleiner SM. "Water: an essential but overlooked nutrient." *J Am Diet Assoc.* 1999 Feb;99(2):200-6.
828. Batmanghelidj F. *Your Body's Many Cries for Water*. Global Health Solutions, Inc. 2008. 100.
829. Greiwe JS, et al. "Effects of dehydration on isometric muscular strength and endurance." *Medicine & Science in Sports & Exercise:* February 1998 - Volume 30 - Issue 2 - pp 284-288.
830. Lieberman HR. "Hydration and cognition: a critical review and recommendations for future research." *Journal of the American College of Nutrition*, 26(5 Suppl), 555S-561S. (2007).
831. Remal RA. *Water*. Urotext. 2009. 314.
832. Maughan RJ. "Impact of mild dehydration on wellness and on exercise performance." *European Journal of Clinical Nutrition* (2003) 57, Suppl 2, S19–S23.
833. Warren JL, Bacon WE, Harris T, McBean AM, Foley DJ & Phillips C (1994): "The burden and outcomes associated with dehydration among US elderly." *Am. J. Pub. Health* 84, 1265–1269.
834. Batmanghelidj F. *Your Body's Many Cries for Water*. Global Health Solutions, Inc. 2008. 51.
835. D' Anci KE, Constant F, Rosenberg IH. "Hydration and Cognitive Function in Children. *Nutrition Reviews* VL 674, IS 10. Blackwell Publishing LTD. 1753-4887.
836. von Duvillard SP, Braun WA, Markofski M, Beneke R, Leithäuser R. "Fluids and hydration in prolonged endurance performance." *Nutrition* - July 2004 (Vol. 20, Issue 7, Pages 651-656).

837. Froom P. "Blood Viscosity and the Risk of Death from Coronary Heart Disease." *European Heart Journal* (2000) 21, 513–514.
838. Batmanghelidj F. *Water: For Health, for Healing, for Life: You're Not Sick, You're Thirsty!* Grand Central Publishing. 2003. 93-95.
839. Hill MA, Court JM, Mitchell GM. "Blood rheology and microalbuminuria in type I diabetes mellitus." *Lancet* 1982 Oct 30;2(8305):985.
840. Isselbacher JJ, Braunwald E, et al. "Atherosclerosis and Other Forms of Ateriosclerosis." *Harrison's Principles of Internal Medicine—13th edition* (CD-ROM). New York, NY: McGraw-Hill, Inc. Health Professions Division, 1994. 1113-1119.
841. Batmanghelidj F. *Water: For Health, for Healing, for Life: You're Not Sick, You're Thirsty!* Grand Central Publishing. 2003. 304.
842. *American Journal of Epidemiology* Vol. 155, No. 9 : 827-833
843. Kleiner SM. "Water: an essential but overlooked nutrient." *J Am Diet Assoc.* 1999 Feb;99(2):200-6.
844. U. S. Department of Health and Human Services, Agency for Healthcare Research and Quality. "Top Ten All-listed Procedures." http://www.ahrq.gov/data/hcup/factbk9/factbk9b.htm.
845. Schols JMGA, et al. "Preventing and Treating Dehydration in the Elderly During Periods of Illness and Warm Weather." *Journal of Nutrition.* February, 2009.
846. Schols JMGA, et al. "Preventing and Treating Dehydration in the Elderly During Periods of Illness and Warm Weather." *Journal of Nutrition.* February, 2009.
847. "Doctors: Marathoner Died From Too Much Water—Hyponatremia A Danger In Long-Distance Sports." http://www.thebostonchannel.com/newscenter5/1610699/detail.html.
848. Department of Health and Human Services. Center for Disease Control and Prevention. http://webapp.cdc.gov/sasweb/ncipc/leadcaus10.html.
849. Luby SP, et al. "Effect of handwashing on child health: a randomised controlled trial." *Lancet.* 2005 Jul 16-22;366(9481):225-33.
850. Kmietowicz Z. "Cricket legend Tendulkar tells Indian children to wash their hands." *British Medical Journal* 2008;337:a2011.
851. http://www.who.int/water_sanitation_health/publications/facts2004/en/index.html
852. Higgins, TR, Heazlewood, IT, and Climstein, M. A random control trial of contrast baths and ice baths for recovery during competition in U/20 rugby union. J Strength Cond Res 24(x): 000-000, 2010.
853. Petrofsky J, et al. The Effects of Aging on the Skin Blood Response to Warm, Cold, and Contrast Warm and Cold Baths. Physical & Occupational Therapy in Geriatrics 2007 25:3, 19-33
854. Burke DT. Effects of Hydrotherapy on Pressure Ulcer Healing. American Journal of Physical Medicine & Rehabilitation: September/October 1998 - Volume 77 - Issue 5 - pp 394-398.

Chapter 18

FAMILY RELATIONSHIPS PLAY AN IMPORTANT ROLE IN COGNITIVE HEALTH AND DEVELOPMENT.

# Nurture Your Network

## *Research indicates that positive family and social networks are vital to optimal brain function. How strong are your ties?*

Eighteen-month-old Mimi stared blankly across the room in her orphanage. One of thousands of infants in Romanian orphanages, Mimi seemed to lack the sparkle that would have brought her extra attention. Listless and joyless, she was easily ignored by overworked caregivers cooing over more responsive babies.

Mimi did have a blanket. She was kept clean, her diapers were changed, and the people in the orphanage really did care. There was just so little time, and so many babies to love. Mimi's life changed dramatically in 2001, when she became one of the "lucky ones." Chosen as part of a study to show the effects of a family atmosphere on previously institutionalized children, Mimi was placed in a loving foster home. When Mimi arrived, she was chronically ill and undersized to the point of being pathetic. Unable to feed herself, she could neither totter nor talk.

Nearly five years later, researchers found that Mimi's I.Q. had risen into near normal range. Her size and weight are slightly below average, but she's grown faster than the orphans in the institutionalized control group.[855] While still a somber child, she has a very winning smile. Mimi's experience resulted from the unfortunate social experiment led by the late Romanian dictator, Nicolae Ceauşescu, who championed population growth as a political goal of the Romanian government. One of the sad results of these errant political policies was a huge increase in the number of orphaned children. These touch-deprived children, who received little intimacy early in life, tended to develop a greater susceptibility to stressful events. They also were found to have higher cortisol levels.[856]

Research has shown that individuals who are constantly under stress develop elevated cortisol levels, which are detrimental to health over time.[857] A partial list of detrimental effects associated with elevated cortisol levels is provided in **Figure 18.1**.[858,859,860,861,862,863] One of the best ways to handle stress better and thereby improve mental performance is to improve social health. By social health, I mean the quality of our social relationships with our parents, siblings, other family members, and friends. A list of social factors that may impair mental performance is provided in **Figure 18.2**.[864,865,866,867,868]

These findings concur with results of a study released by the journal *Science* which found that toddlers placed in foster families developed significantly higher I.Q.s by age 4, on average, than children who spent those years in an orphanage. The I.Q. difference in this study was significant—a full 8 points. The sooner in life the child was placed in a traditional family setting, the higher the boost in I.Q.. The I.Q. tests, which were taken when the children were 4.5 years old, found the institutionalized children in the study to have an average I.Q. of 73. In contrast, children placed in foster care had an average I.Q. of 81 at that age, while children living with their biological families had an average I.Q. of 109.

## ELEVATED CORTISOL IMPEDES BRAIN FUNCTION

Elevated cortisol levels have been shown to have a negative impact on brain function, by contributing to:

- depression
- panic
- anxiety
- impaired memory
- dementia
- shrinkage of the brain
- anorexia (aversion to food)
- obsessive-compulsive disorder

***Figure 18.1***

## SOCIAL FACTORS THAT MAY IMPAIR MENTAL PERFORMANCE

- negative, stressful events
- the absence of social support
- low social class
- codependency
- sexual abuse
- parental separation
- unexpected guardianship of children

***Figure 18.2***

One of the major factors cited by researchers as affecting the intellectual development of these children was their limited access to caregivers, who in some instances were responsible for more than 20 children at a time.[869]

## A GOOD SOCIAL START

Research has shown that human relationships early in life affect how we handle stress as adults. This is true even in the animal world. Scientists removed baby rats from their mothers for a short time early in life. Months later, those baby rats were shown to be more susceptible to stress than rats who had not been removed from their mothers.[870] In an unrelated study, another set of researchers found that rats who got more attention early in life (such as maternal licking and grooming) tend to be more resilient in the face of stress.[871]

In other research, baby monkeys that were separated from their mothers demonstrated overt symptoms of despair.[872] The same type of results have been demonstrated in the human race.

Even in less-than-optimal child-rearing environments, effective parenting or caregiving is a major predictive factor in how well a child will handle stress later in life. One study, which examined low-income families from a high-stress, inner-city environment, found that the major factor predicting how well children reared in this environment would handle stress was the parenting skills of their caregivers.[873]

Even in an atmosphere which often included neighborhood violence, family turmoil, and family separation, nurturing parents with good mental health were able to project more positive expectations into their children's future. Interestingly enough, this same study found that the most nurturing parents were not necessarily reared in a positive way themselves. The encouraging news is that individuals who experience abuse or neglect in their childhood can overcome that background and become better parents.

Children are not the only ones who receive benefit from touch and intimacy. Researchers have found that parents may receive benefit as well. For example, one study found that breast-feeding provides a protective health benefit for mothers as well as their infants.[874]

## THE VALUE OF FAMILY CONNECTIONS

According to the Harvard Mastery of Stress Study, close family connections do more than foster emotional well-being. They are also a very potent form of preventative medicine. This landmark study demonstrated a significant connection between close parent/child relationships and health for the offspring well into adulthood.

In the early 1950's, 126 men were randomly chosen and questioned about their relationship with their parents. Study participants were asked to rank their relationship to each of their parents as either "very close," "warm and friendly," "tolerant," "strained," or "cold." A follow-up to the study, which took place 35 years later and was published in 1997, showed that 87% of the participants who rated their parents as uncaring had contracted a major medical illness by the time they reached their mid-50s. In contrast, only 25% of the men who rated their parents as loving and caring had had a major illness.

Men who did not have a perceived warm relationship with their mothers were especially at risk. By mid-life, 91% of those men had been diagnosed with serious illnesses such as coronary artery disease, high blood pressure, duodenal ulcers, and alcoholism. In contrast, only 45% of the men who had perceived themselves to have warm relationships with their mothers had developed a serious illness.

A disconnection between the men and their fathers was also extremely damaging. 82% of participants who had low warmth and closeness with their fathers had diagnosed diseases in midlife, compared with only 50% of those who felt close to their fathers.

Most damaging of all was a disconnect between the offspring and both parents. Every single one of the study participants (that's 100%) who ranked their mothers and fathers low in warmth and closeness in the 1950s had been diagnosed with a serious illness within the 35 years following the start of the study.

Researchers in the Harvard Mastery of Stress Study also delved into the negative and positive nature of answers provided during the 1950's. They accomplished this simply by counting the number of positive words the study participants had used when describing each parent. At the 35-year follow-up, researchers found that an alarming 95% of subjects who rated their parents low in parental caring and had few positive words had been diagnosed with diseases in midlife. In contrast, only 29% of study participants who rated their parents highly in the 1950's had been diagnosed with a major medical illness in midlife.[875]

As this study so powerfully illustrates, the parent/child relationship is a significant factor in the future health of the offspring, even into adulthood. In addition, the importance of maintaining positive parent/child relationships is abundantly clear. Some of the benefits of strong social support are listed in **Figure 18.3**.[876,877]

## CLOSE RELATIONSHIPS KEEP YOUR MIND SHARP

Good support from family and friends is not only vital to infant health and strongly influential in adulthood; it can also can also protect the health of an aging brain. Research conducted by the Rush University Medical Center in Chicago found that many elderly people had the tangles and plaques in the brain associated with Alzheimer's disease, yet had never shown signs of cognitive impairment or dementia. The scientists, who examined the brains of 89 deceased elderly individuals, believed that the social network surrounding many of the seniors offered somewhat of a "protective reserve," which inhibited the clinical manifestations of Alzheimer's disease.

Participants in the study underwent clinical evaluations and 21 cognitive performance tests each year. To determine the size and impact of the social network, participants were asked numerous questions about their relationships with their children, spouses, or other family members.

Researchers noted how many of these individuals the seniors saw at least monthly and whether the participants felt at ease in the relationships (e.g. could share private matters or ask for help if needed). Researchers found that the larger the social network, the greater the protective-reserve capacity that seemed to help deter Alzheimer's disease. As a result of this study, they concluded that healthy and frequent interactions with friends and family have important implications for the prevention of disease, as well as a positive impact on cognition.[878]

### SOCIAL SUPPORT IS VITAL

- A sense of belonging improves mood and mental health.
- Social support reduces risk of death following a heart attack.
- A busy social life does not guarantee a sense of belonging.
- Close family members and/or friends provide a basic need.

*Figure 18.3*

*"Friendship isn't a big thing - it's a million little things."*
—Unknown

## SOCIAL SUPPORT: GOOD FOR YOUR HEART

In a study of patients who had recently undergone heart surgery, the higher levels of social participation were associated with better health six months after surgery.[879] Researchers who followed 887 heart attack patients in the year after the attack found that about a third of the patients became mildly or moderately depressed early in the recovery process. Patients who were depressed were more than three times as likely to die during the year after having the heart attack. However, the effect of depression on survival depended on the perceived social support of the patient. The risk of dying were highest in depressed people who felt they didn't get enough support from family and friends. In contrast, the depressed patients who felt the strongest support from friends and family were not any more likely to die than the non-depressed patients. In addition, symptoms of depression were more likely to improve in depressed patients who felt well supported.[880]

## BENEFITS OF GETTING INVOLVED

There is a segment of the population in today's self-centered society that doesn't understand the concept of value in "getting involved." To such people, the idea of volunteerism seems foreign. Researchers have found, however, that participating in the lives of others on a social basis can have significant physiological benefits to the giver.[881]

While there is a certain joy received in the act of giving, the benefits to the giver go beyond joy. Helping others provides a sense of meaning and purpose in life that is critical in dealing with certain stressors. Committing to an honorable cause that helps others is an excellent way to fight stress, and in turn improve mental performance. Those who go through life fulfilling their own personal desires, without thought of the needs of others, actually deprive themselves of the health-giving benefits of altruism and loving-kindness. (The health benefits of altruism are discussed in chapter 23, "Love to Live.") Also, once you find a cause that helps others, you are much more likely to find close friends with similar goals.

In another study, researchers found that there is something even more important than social support. This study, which was conducted in Michigan, found that from all social factors considered, a sense of belonging is the best predictor of what an individual might experience in terms of protecting the person from depressive symptoms.[882]

## THE STORY OF LINDA

One patient who came to me for the treatment of depression (which is a form of impaired frontal lobe or brain function which impedes mental performance) actually had quite a lot going for her. Linda had truly impressive knowledge about wellness and health. Her hobbies included cultivating a magnificent flower garden. She also had developed her own fitness routine to manage her diet, exercise, and need for rest.

In spite of all these positive things, however, Linda had been unable to manage the mood swings that left her feeling unmotivated and dull. Sometimes, she felt terribly despondent. In studying the possible causes of Linda's symptoms, we realized that loneliness might be one of the roots of her depression. Linda had recently left her job for a new one. While this could be a good thing, Linda's social network (and support) had been unsettled. The stress from this lack of social support was disturbing her mental health. She needed to make new connections. While loneliness or situational depression (caused by recent temporary circumstances can deter peak mental performance, the impact of such factors is most often controllable. Although adverse social factors may very well contribute to less-than-optimal thinking patterns, they never happen in a vacuum. People who become clinically depressed after the break-up of a relationship, for example, generally have other factors contributing to the depression.

## NEEDED: SOCIAL RELATIONSHIPS

People who prefer to deal with problems by themselves, rather than reaching out to others for comfort, may face higher stress levels and increased health risks. As members of the human race, each of us needs real support from other people. Individuals who develop a "hermit-type" attitude, keeping to themselves and refusing to acknowledge their relationship needs, are more likely to feel overwhelmed and besieged by life.

*"A friend is someone who comes in when the whole world has gone out."*
—Grace Pulpit

A primary factor which leads some people to withdraw from developing relationships is a simple distrust of others. They have been hurt in the past, and don't want to be hurt again. By developing habits of isolation, they hope to avoid, or at least minimize, the pain. Unfortunately, isolation is not the only negative effect of distrust. The level of overall health and longevity you reach will ultimately be impacted by whether you see the people in your life as benevolent and kind-hearted, or malicious and frustrating.

A personal policy of isolation is quickly followed by loneliness, which in turn leads to increased stress, a weakened immune system, and ultimately an increased risk of disease. Isolation leads to depression and withdrawal in both animals and humans.[883] In contrast, social support and a sense of belonging leads to improved mood and optimal mental and physical health.[884] One of the things that makes certain addictions (such as excessive internet usage or video gaming) so dangerous is the tendency of such patterns to lead to isolation.

In a 1998 study reported in American Psychologist, researchers provided Internet access to 169 people who had not previously been able to log on from home. The researchers found that the more time these people spent online, the less time they spent with their families, the smaller their social circles became, and the more depressed and lonely they felt. More information on the dangers of excessive internet usage is provided in **Figure 18.4** on the following page.[885,886,887,888,889]

## INTERNET ADDICTION?

How long have you been sitting there, staring at that screen? Are you spending more and more of your time clicking and typing, typing and clicking? Is there nothing else you'd rather do? The answers to these questions may say a lot about your mental health.

A growing body of research suggests that excessive Internet use can lead to:

- social isolation
- depression
- failure at work or school
- struggling marriages
- ruined careers

Internet addicts experience the same feelings as those "hooked" on other habits: a building of tension before using, a rush of relief afterwards, distortions of mood, and binging. For many, the Internet is an escape from the cares and perplexities of life.

In a venue where information is limitless, even innocent inquiries can become an obsession when each informative site is linked to more interesting information. Hours slip by easily...time that could have been spent building marriages, nurturing children, or even fixing the car. The internet is a great educational tool, but is not without hazard. Use the internet wisely - once you find the information you need, log off. Don't forget there's a real life waiting for you just beyond the screen.

*Figure 18.4*

Although some people have forged healthy friendships by meeting online, many others are hurting face-to-face relationships through excessive internet use and other addictions that promote isolation. (For more information on addictions and mental performance, see chapter 21, "Make Smarter Choices.") While the importance of strong social support has been emphasized in addiction recovery programs, it should not be underestimated for any individual.

In short, the quality of your physical as well as mental health will be significantly impacted by whether you have nourishing—and flourishing—social relationships.

## FIVE TIPS FOR RELATIONSHIP-BUILDING

The ability to enter into warm personal relationships is one of the most enjoyable aspects of living. Despite the value of healthy relationships, many people have difficulty cultivating and maintaining long-term friendships. Lack of peak mental performance can be the reason for loss of close friends.

If you have few or no close friends, your mental performance could be improved by following the principles in this book. Then, as mental performance improves, the development of close friends will become much more likely. Following are five tips that should help you as you strive to keep things in balance while strengthening family and friendship ties:

*"A man that hath friends must shew himself friendly."*
—Proverbs 18:24

### Tip #1: Get involved!

If you do not have a sense of belonging or have no close family or friends, consider involving yourself in certain community or church projects that are consistent with your personal goals. It is likely you will form close relationships in the process, and with a sense of common purpose, soon feel like you "belong." This in turn will help to reduce your stress level and assist you in the goal of reaching improved brain function and optimal mental health.

### Tip #2: Be the type of friend you want.

If you have given much thought to choosing your friends, you probably realize that you would prefer mentally healthy friends. Instead of dragging you down, stable friends can actually lift you up. You can increase your circle of friends by being the type of person other people would like to be around. While we all have our moments of self-searching and doubt, people don't like to be around a "downer" all the time. Cultivate a great attitude and cheerful disposition, and others will enjoy being wherever you are.

Mentally healthy people actually prefer friends who are stronger and more independent. Friends who spend all their time filling the inappropriate demands of needy friends will get tired. People who require constant

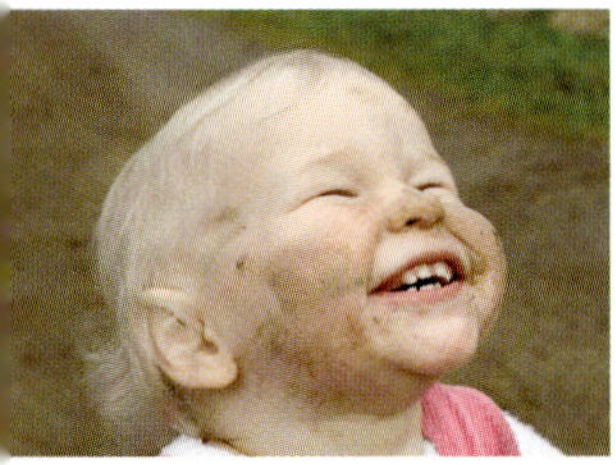

*"Only your real friends will tell you when your face is dirty."*
—Sicilian Proverb

attention, are obsessed with themselves, or spend an inordinate amount of time trying to get their own needs met make poor friends. They are too busy focusing on themselves to reach out to anyone else.

This does not mean we must cut such people off. They may very well need your friendship, as well as a helping hand. To be balanced, it may not be best to include such people in your inner circle of close friends, or you may be dragged down. The most enjoyable relationships we can have are close friendships. By investing in your "friendship accounts," you can build relationships that truly will last a lifetime.

### Tip #3: Never "own" anybody.

Some people, whether married or simply close friends, get the idea that they "own" each other. This is especially true in relationships where one of the parties feels unfulfilled. People who are not getting what they want out of a relationship often try to manipulate a partner by claiming some level of ownership. This tactic rarely works for long. People don't like to be owned. In addition, making demands doesn't exactly endear us to others. Good relationships are a voluntary thing. If someone does not willingly give his or her heart to another person, then all the threats in the world will not make a relationship work. Determine what is really causing the strain in the relationship and address the problem directly before you are tempted to feel jealousy or ownership. True friends or lovers do not have to be possessive.

### Tip #4: Adhere to the truth

Most people would agree: honesty and integrity are pivotal to solid relationships. Nothing unbalances a relationship more quickly than dishonesty and lies. If you want to build a friendship, keep your word.

### Tip #5: Improve Your Mental Performance

More often than not, peak mental performance programs improve relationships. Many of my patients that came to me for depression have marital problems, and after they begin the path to peak mental performance, their marriage suddenly improves.

## RELATIONSHIPS ARE VITAL TO HEALTH

Cultivating strong and healthy relationships is certainly an important step toward improved physical and mental health. Take care not to overrate the value of social connections, however. Building relationships is an important part of a balanced and healthy life, but some individuals mistakenly believe their personal level of success, happiness, and peace is totally dependent on their current social relationships. Social support has a great impact, but it is only one piece of the pie.

It is also important to make wise choices in friends, marriage partners, and business partners. Selecting associates who have similar values and purposes and are mentally healthy will benefit your health. In contrast, if your beloved or associate is difficult to be around or a bad influence, your ability to think clearly will likely be affected again and again for years to come.

Some timeless thoughts on the value of positive friendships are provided in **Figure 18.5**. If you have become too busy, distracted, or stressed to cultivate personal relationships, why not make nurturing those "ties that bind" an important priority in your life, starting today? The end result should be well worth the effort: improved physical and mental performance for both yourself and the people you care for.

## THOUGHTS ON FRIENDSHIP

"A friend accepts us as we are yet helps us to be what we should." —*Unknown*

"You can always tell a real friend: when you've made a fool of yourself he doesn't feel you've done a permanent job." —*Laurence J. Peter*

"A friend is one of the nicest things you can have, and one of the best things you can be." —*Douglas Pagels*

"It takes a long time to grow an old friend." —*John Leonard*

"No road is long with good company." —*Turkish Proverb*

"A true friend is one who thinks you are a good egg even if you are half-cracked." —*Unknown*

"The friend who holds your hand and says the wrong thing is made of dearer stuff than the one who stays away." —*Barbara Kingsolver*

"Faithful are the words of a friend, but the kisses of an enemy are lavish and deceitful." —*Proverbs 27:6, Amplified Bible*

"Never correct a conceited man, he will hate you for it. But if you correct a wise man, he will respect and love you for it." —*Proverbs 9:8, TEV*

***Figure 18.5***

## References


855. Nickerson C. "Study on Orphans Sees Benefit in Family Care." *Boston Globe*. November 11, 2006.
856. Gunnar MR, Morison SJ, Chisholm K, Schuder M. "Salivary cortisol levels in children adopted from Romanian orphanages." *Development and Psychopathology* 13 (2001). 611-628.
857. Kuningas M, et al. "Mental Performance in Old Age Dependent on Cortisol and Genetic Variance in the Mineralocorticoid and Glucocorticoid Receptors." *Neuropsychopharmacology* (2007) 32, 1295–1301.
858. Vreeburg SA, et al. "Salivary Cortisol Levels in Persons With and Without Different Anxiety Disorders." *Psychosom Med* 2010 72: 340-347.
859. Kirschbaum C, et al. "Stress and treatment-induced elevations of cortisol levels associated with impaired declarative memory in healthy adults." *Life Sciences*, Volume 58, Issue 17, 22 March 1996, Pages 1475-1483.
860. Lupien SJ, et al. "Increased cortisol levels and impaired cognition in human aging: implication for depression and dementia in later life." *Rev Neurosci.* 1999;10(2):117-39.
861. O'Brien JT, et al. "A Longitudinal Study of Hippocampal Volume, Cortisol Levels, and Cognition in Older Depressed Subjects." *Am J Psychiatry* 2004 161: 2081-2090.
862. Walsh BT, et al. "The Production Rate of Cortisol Declines during Recovery from Anorexia Nervosa." *J. Clin. Endocrinol. Metab.* 53: 203-205.
863. Catapanoa F, et al. "Melatonin and cortisol secretion in patients with primary obsessive-compulsive disorder." Volume 44, Issue 3, December 1992, Pages 217-225.
864. Evans GW, Schamberg MA. "Childhood poverty, chronic stress, and adult working memory." *Proc Natl Acad Sci* U S A. 2009 April 21; 106(16): 6545–6549.
865. Baumeister RF, Twenge JM, Nuss C. "Effects of social exclusion on cognitive processes: Anticipated aloneness reduces intelligent thought." *Journal of Personality and Social Psychology*, 83, 817-827.
866. Stein ZA, Susser M. "Measured intelligence in childhood, social class and adult outcomes across Poland's sociopolitical transitions, 1945–1995." *International Journal of Epidemiology*, Volume 33, Number 1, pp. 227-230.
867. McGowan PO, et al. "Epigenetic regulation of the glucocorticoid receptor in human brain associates with childhood abuse." *Nature Neuroscience*. 2009.
868. Fearon P, et al. "The Significance of Insecure Attachment and Disorganization in the Development of Children's Externalizing Behavior: A Meta-Analytic Study." *Child Development*, Vol 81, Issue 2.
869. Carroll M. "Orphanages and Fostering in Romania." *Science* 21 December 2007 318: 1829.
870. Stanton ME, Wallstrom J, Levine S. "Maternal contact inhibits pituitary-adrenal stress responses in preweanling rats." *Developmental Psychobiology*. Vol. 20 Issue 2, 131-145.
871. Caldji C, Tannenbaum B, Sharma S, Francis D, Plotsky PM, Meaney MJ. "Maternal care during infancy regulates the development of neural systems mediating the expression of fearfulness in the rat." *Proc Natl Acad Sci U S A.* 1998 Apr 28;95(9):5335-40.
872. Seay B, Harlow HF. "Maternal Separation in the Rhesus Monkey." *The Journal of Nervous and Mental Disease:* June 1965. Volume 140, Issue 6. 434-441.
873. Elder Jr GH, Eccles JS, Ardelt M, Lord S. 1995. "Inner-city Parents under Economic Pressure: Perspectives on the Strategies of Parenting." *Journal of Marriage and the Family* 57(August): 771-784.
874. Heinrichs M, Neumann I, Ehlert U. "Lactation and stress: protective effects of breast-feeding in humans." *Stress.* 2002 Sep;5(3):195-203.
875. Funkenstein D, King S, Drolette M. "Mastery of Stress." Cambridge, MA: Harvard University Press, 1957; Russek LG, Schwarts GE. "Narrative descriptions of parental love and caring predict health status in midlife; a 35-year follow-up of the Harvard Mastery of Stress study." *Alternative Therapies in Health and Medicine,* 1996, 2;55-62.
876. Hagerty, Bonnie M. Williams, Reg A. Coyne, James C. Early, Margaret R. "Sense of belonging and indicators of social and psychological functioning." *Archives of Psychiatric Nursing.* Volume 10, Issue 4, August 1996, Pages 235-244
877. Czajkowski SM. "Effects of Treating Depression and Low Perceived Social Support on Clinical Events After Myocardial Infarction—The Enhancing Recovery in Coronary Heart Disease Patients (ENRICHD) Randomized Trial." *JAMA.* 2003;289:3106-3116.
878. Bennett DA, et al. "The effect of social networks on the relation between Alzheimer's disease pathology and level of cognitive function in old people: a longitudinal cohort study." *The Lancet Neurology*, Volume 5, Issue 5, Pages 406 - 412, May 2006.

879. Leifheit-Limson EC, et. al. "The Role of Social Support in Health Status and Depressive Symptoms After Acute Myocardial Infarction: Evidence for a Stronger Relationship Among Women." *Circ Cardiovasc Qual Outcomes* 2010;3:143-150.

880. Frasure-Smith N, Lespérance F, Gravel G, Masson A, Juneau M, Talajic M, Bourassa MG. "Social support, depression, and mortality during the first year after myocardial infarction." Presented in part at the *American Psychosomatic Society* Meeting, Vancouver, Canada, March 1999.

881. Schwartz CE, Sendor MS. "Helping others helps oneself: response shift effects in peer support." *Social Science & Medicine*, Volume 48, Issue 11, June 1999, Pages 1563-1575.

882. University Of Michigan (1999, August 11). "Low Sense Of Belonging Is A Predictor Of Depression." *ScienceDaily*.

883. Karelina K, et al. "Social isolation alters neuroinflammatory response to stroke. Proceedings of the National Academy of Sciences." 2009.

884. Leifheit-Limson EC, et al. "The Role of Social Support in Health Status and Depressive Symptoms After Acute Myocardial Infarction: Evidence for a Stronger Relationship Among Women." *Circ Cardiovasc Qual Outcomes* 2010;3:143-150.

885. Shapira NA, Goldsmith TD, Keck PE, Khosla UM, McElroy SL. "Psychiatric features of individuals with problematic internet use." (2000) *J Affect Disord*, 57(1-3):267-272.

886. Young KS. "Internet addiction: A new clinical phenomenon and its consequences" (2004) *American Behavioral Scientist*, 48(4):402-415.

887. Christakis DA, Moreno MA. "Trapped in the net: Will internet addiction become a 21st-century epidemic?" (2009) *Arch Pediatr Adolesc Med*, 163(10):959-960.

888. Kaltiala-Heino R, Lintonen T, Rimpelä A. "Internet addiction? potentially problematic use of the internet in a population of 12–18 year-old adolescents." (2004) *Addiction Research & Theory*, 12(1):89-96.

889. LaRose R, Eastin MS, Gregg J. "Reformulating the Internet paradox: Social cognitive explanations of Internet use and depression." (2001) *Journal of Online Behavior*.

Chapter 19

"MUSIC IS THE ART OF THINKING WITH SOUNDS." —*JULES COMBARIEU*

# Choose Brain-boosting Music

## *How balanced, melodious music can improve thinking ability and mood.*

Those who are familiar with ancient history may have heard the story of Israel's first monarch, King Saul. Being a very good-looking, tall, and impressive man, King Saul had a rather fine start in life. Things began to turn sour for him, however, sometime during his reign. The Bible records that Saul became moody and emotionally troubled. He developed the rather bad habit, when entrenched in one of his anger episodes, of hurling javelins at people he was jealous of.[890]

The monarch's moods were of great concern to Saul's hired help, who were developing anxiety disorders of their own as a result of their master's unpredictable mental state. No doubt this explains why Saul's staff suggested that he find an expert musician to play soothing songs.[891]

Fortunately for all involved, King Saul's helpers found their man. And so a fresh-faced shepherd lad, gifted with nerves of steel, exceptional musical talent, and javelin-dodging speed, became the first musical therapist on record. The Bible says David took a harp and played with his hand: so Saul was refreshed, and the evil spirit departed from him.[892]

Saul's advisors were not alone in their steadfast belief in the power of music. The ancient Greeks regarded music as an important part of their lives, regulating it as a function of the state for the ethical and moral growth of the citizen. The Greeks claimed that music softened the manners, promoted civilization, expressed the passions, inspired brutality, guarded chastity, calmed riotous crowds, stirred military valor, prevented murder, and cooled a fever.[893]

The Greek poet Homer recommended music to avoid negative passions such as anger, sorrow, worry, fear, fatigue—and also to promote healthful recreation for the elevation of body and soul.[894] Pythagorus is said to have cured mental illnesses through the use of specially prepared musical compositions—specific melodies for cases of despondency, anger, or "desires."[895]

"Music is a moral law," wrote Plato. "It gives a soul to the universe, wings to the mind, flight to the imagination, a charm to sadness, gaiety and life to everything. It is the essence of order, and leads to all that is good, just, and beautiful, of which it is the invisible, but nevertheless dazzling, passionate, and eternal form."[896]

Aristotle, the famous Greek philosopher, recognized the impact music plays in shaping the character (and therefore the frontal lobe) centuries ago, writing that "… when one listens to music that imitates a certain passion he becomes imbued with the same passion. If over a long time he habitually listens to the kind of music that rouses ignoble [degraded or vulgar] passions, his whole character will be shaped to an ignoble form. In short, if one listens to the wrong kind of music he will become the wrong kind of person; conversely, if he listens to the right kind of music he will tend to become the right kind of person."[897]

## MUSIC TASTES IMPACT YOUR LIFE

Certain classes of music have historically aroused a specific set of emotions. For example, what would it be like to listen to marches such as "Stars and Stripes Forever" at bedtime, funeral dirges at weddings, lullabies at parades and Gregorian chants while shopping?

### BENEFITS OF SEDATIVE MUSIC

- reduced anxiety
- optimized brain rhythm and function
- increased relaxation
- reduced need for pain relievers during cancer treatment and childbirth
- increased socialization
- decreased symptoms in "disturbed and inaccessible" psychiatric patients

**Figure 19.1**

## MUSIC THERAPY FACTS

- The mental health benefits of music have been well-proven.
- Not all kinds of music are beneficial.
- Melodic classical music has been found to be most effective, even among those who do not know it or even prefer it.

***Figure 19.2***

The fact is, the nonverbal portion of music moves through the brain's auditory cortex, arriving directly at the center of the limbic system. This system governs emotional experiences and basic metabolic responses such as body temperature, blood pressure, and heart rate. It has the power to create new neuropathways in the brain, activate the flow of stored memory and imagined material across the corpus collosum (bridge between left and right hemispheres of the brain), and stimulates the immune system.[898]

Music can also excite peptides in the brain and stimulate the production of endorphins, which are natural opiates secreted by the hypothalamus, which produces a feeling of natural euphoria, positively shifting mood and emotion.[899]

### RESEARCH CHIMES IN

Many of the claims of the ancients have now been substantiated by scientific research. One study reported in *The Journal of the National Cancer Institute*, for example, revealed that sedating classical music has many benefits, as shown in **Figure 19.1**.[900] Some other important discoveries regarding music therapy are provided in **Figure 19.2**.[901,902,903,904]

Another study involving music psychotherapy showed that certain music can improve mood and reduce stress. Even "normal," healthy adults showed improved scores on tests of overall mood. After six sessions of music therapy held over a 12-week period, the volunteers, ages 23-45, also reported feeling less fatigue and depression. The improvement was more than just subjective. The patients blood levels of the steroid hormone cortisol, which elevates with stress, also fell significantly.

In the music therapy sessions, volunteers listened to specific, selected sequences of classical music in sessions of approximately 45 minutes every two weeks. Selections included portions from the music of Respighi, Ravel, Bach, and Brahms. To encourage introspection while listening, participants were asked to identify one to three areas of concern in their lives.

Later they shared and discussed the spontaneous images that came to mind while listening to the music selections. Thirteen weeks into the study, test scores revealed that mood disturbance, fatigue, and depression were significantly decreased. The changes persisted at a follow-up six weeks later. However, no significant changes in test scores or cortisol levels were found among the control subjects who did not undergo classical music therapy.[905]

These positive effects of music therapy were enhanced by engaging the frontal lobe through visualization. If you would like to try the exercise mentioned above, I recommend Handel's Concerto Grossos and some of the music of Mantovani. The orchestral hymn arrangements of Mantovani, with their cascading style, can set the mood for reflective thought. This music is not just for people struggling with depression or mental disorders. It will benefit anyone interested in achieving peak mental performance. **Appendix III** lists the songs from two popular albums, with examples of reflective visualization, as an example. I have selected some classics which, based on the scientific literature, help promote brain function. They are organized into two collections, and these brain-boosting CDs are available on my website, drnedley.com.

*"Music speaks what cannot be expressed, soothes the mind and gives it rest, heals the heart and makes it whole, flows from heaven to the soul."*

—Unknown

Researchers reported in the *Journal of Psychosomatic Medicine* that elderly patients who listened to music during eye surgery had significantly lower blood pressure and feelings of stress. The patients chose from a selection of tapes including classical guitar, folk music, and music from the 1940s and 1950s. Researchers measured each patient's blood pressure a week before surgery, the morning of surgery, and continuously during the surgery. Half of the 40 patients involved in the study listened to music during the procedure, while half did not. All patients experienced significant spikes in blood pressure on the morning of the surgery, indicating a high degree of anxiety in anticipation of the procedure. The blood pressure of the patients who listened to music returned to normal within 5 minutes of hearing the music. In contrast, patients in the "no music" group continued to experience high blood pressure throughout the surgery.[906]

The famed brain surgeon, Dr. Ben Carson, believed classical music to be so important that he hand-selected the music to be played during this "impossible" but successful operation where he separated two Siamese twins who were joined at the head.[907]

"Without music, life would be a mistake," Nietzsche wrote in 1889. An article in the *Journal of the American Medical Association* put a new twist on Nietzsche's statement: "Our data prompts us to ponder if, without music, surgery would be a mistake."[908]

## THE FRONTAL LOBE CONNECTION

Few people understand the powerful influence of music upon the frontal lobe. While all music enters the brain through its emotional regions, some music also stimulates responses in the frontal lobe. Thus, depending on the type of music, and whether it predominantly stimulates the frontal lobe or lower emotional centers, the net influence can be either beneficial or detrimental to mental performance.[909] An overview of the interaction between music and the frontal lobe is provided in **Figure 19.3**.[910]

Some years ago, researchers Schreckenberg and Bird (a neurobiologist and a physicist) teamed up to test the impact of listening to rock music on thinking ability. They designed an eight-week study to evaluate neurological reactions in mice to different musical rhythms. At the beginning of the study, all the mice went through a standard maze test (searching for food at the end of a maze). All three groups performed equally well, groping about the maze until they located the food. During the next eight weeks, the investigators kept the mice divided into three groups. One group constantly heard rock-like disharmonic drum beats softly playing, a second group heard only classical music, while the third group heard no music at all.

By the end of eight weeks the second and third groups had learned the direct path to the food. The "rock group," however, was still groping about, taking much longer to find the food than the other two groups. The researchers then allowed a three-week break in maze training where no music was played. At the end of the break, the mice were re-tested. Again the rock group performed poorly and continued to have difficulty remembering where to get to their food. They seemed to have an irreversible learning handicap, appearing to start from scratch each time as they groped disorientedly about the maze. In contrast, both the control group and the classical group retained what they learned from earlier sessions. As a result they found their food quickly and could run the maze considerably faster than their rock music counterparts.

*"I regard music therapy as a tool of great power... because of its unique capacity to organize or reorganize cerebral function..."*
—Oliver Sacks, M.D.

## MUSIC AND THE FRONTAL LOBE

- Music enters the brain through its emotional regions, which include the temporal lobe and the limbic system.
- From there, some kinds of music tend to produce a positive frontal lobe response that influences the will, moral values, and reasoning power.

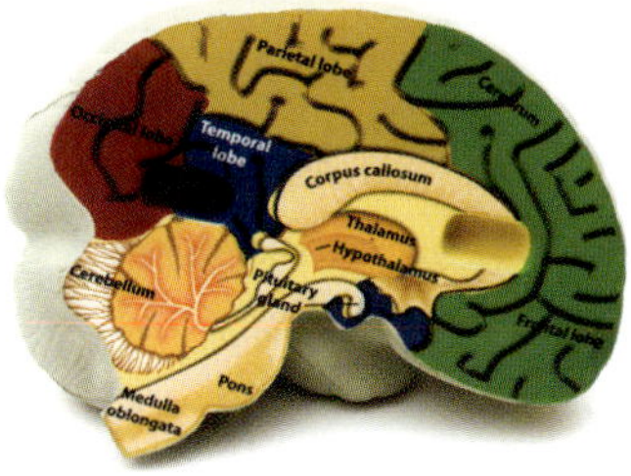


- Other kinds of music will evoke very little frontal lobe response, while producing a large emotional response with very little logical or moral interpretation.

***Figure 19.3***

At the end of the study, the researchers examined the brains of the mice. They were looking specifically for changes in the hippocampus, a region of the brain that lies deep in the temporal lobe and affects emotions, memory, and learning. In the "rock music mice," Schreckenberg and Bird found visible evidence of abnormal branching and sprouting of the nerve cells, as well as disruptions in the messenger RNA, a chemical crucial to memory storage. A summary of their findings is provided in **Figure 19.4**. The researchers concluded that music rhythms—not harmonic or melodic structure—caused the memory and learning problems. They theorized that certain musical rhythms help synchronize natural biological rhythms and enhance body functions, while other rhythms tend to clash with or disrupt internal rhythms. When natural rhythms are disrupted, detrimental effects result, including permanent learning difficulties. In addition to hippocampus damage, Schreckenberg and Bird's research linked rock-like music to frontal lobe shrinkage.[911]

If such results were carried over to humans, we would expect deleterious effects on moral values, learning, and reasoning power from music driven by a heavy beat. Furthermore, because there is a link between frontal lobe impairment and depression, we might also anticipate a link between rock music and depression.

Research involving 121 Midwest high school students appeared to confirm this link, In the study, researchers found that 75% of the girls who preferred heavy metal music had considered suicide, in comparison to 35% of the girls who preferred other types of music. The results for boys were similarly conclusive: nearly 50% of the boys who preferred heavy metal had considered suicide, compared with 15% of the boys who listened to "nonmetal" music.[912]

## EFFECTS OF MUSIC ON LABORATORY MICE

- Eight weeks of a soft-rock beat led to impaired memory.
- Three weeks after the music stopped, memory had not come back.
- Permanent brain damage could be seen.
- Eight weeks of classical music had no detrimental effect.

***Figure 19.4***

## GOOD MUSIC IMPROVES MENTAL PERFORMANCE

Research also suggests a strong link between intelligence and musical ability. The College Entrance Examination Board has reported that students taking courses in music performance and music appreciation scored higher on the SAT test than students with no arts participation. Music performance students scored 53 points higher on the verbal and 39 points higher on the math. Music appreciation students scored 61 points higher on the verbal and 42 points higher on the math.[913]

When the University of Montreal researched brain imaging techniques to study brain activity during musical tasks, researchers concluded that the tasks of sight-reading musical scores and playing music "activate regions in all four of the cortex's lobes" and "parts of the cerebellum are also activated during those tasks."[914]

Through the use of brain scans, researchers in Leipzig discovered that musicians had a larger planum temporale, the region of the brain associated with reading skills. Also, musicians had a thicker corpus callosum, the nerve fibers that connect the two halves of the brain.[915]

A statewide survey of schools in Texas revealed that students involved in extracurricular or cocurricular activities were less likely to engage in substance abuse than their peers. Secondary students who participated in band, orchestra, or choir reported the lowest lifetime use of all substances.[916]

In Rhode Island, other research indicated that sequential, skill-building instruction in art and music integrated with the rest of the curriculum greatly improves the reading and writing performance of the children.[917]

Researchers at the University of Toronto found that, over a year's time span, children who took music lessons experienced greater gains in I.Q. (7 points over the course of the year) than those who did not (a gain of 3 points in one year). These advances in I.Q. seemed unrelated to the musical giftedness of the children. It was their involvement in music, not level of talent, that mattered.[918]

*"Where words fail, music speaks."*

—Hans Christian Anderson

In another study, volunteers who listened to Vivaldi's "Four Seasons" while exercising on a treadmill did much better on a test of verbal ability than when they exercised without music. Researchers involved in the study believed that listening to music during exercise increased cognitive arousal, while helping to organize cognitive input.[919]

Some people wonder if the stress-relieving benefits of music truly result from the music itself, or simply result from cultural "cues" to relax. At least one answer to this question can be found by considering the effect of music on newborn babies. Though fetuses are certainly exposed to sounds in the womb, they have not learned relaxation techniques in connection with their exposure to music. As featured in **Figure 19.5** on the following page, a Florida study found that music did have a profound impact on children who were too young to have their musical tastes significantly influenced by their upbringing or friends.[920]

## AN ACTUAL OR "CULTURAL" IMPACT?

Case Study: 52 low birth weight babies in stable condition, restricted to hospital incubators in the hospital.

Variable: Half were exposed to lullabies and children's music three times a day (no rock). The other half had no music.

Observed: weight, caloric intake, length of hospital stay, and stress behaviors.

Findings: The babies exposed to music had greater weight gain, increased appetite, a reduced length of hospital stay, and fewer stress behaviors.

*Figure 19.5*

### PRINCIPLES FOR CHOOSING GOOD MUSIC

As evidenced by the studies previously mentioned, the type of music listened to matters as much as the presence of music. Fortunately, there are a number of time-honored principles that can, if applied, help you make choices in music that will optimize your thinking ability. The remainder of this chapter will be focused on those principles, together with some musical recommendations to get you started and a checklist that can help you evaluate musical options.

If you were raised listening to a detrimental type of music and think you would have trouble learning to appreciate anything else, don't be discouraged. A taste for good music can be developed over time. In addition, your mind will still benefit from good music, even if you do not care for it at first. Broadening your horizons through exposure to uplifting music is one of the best ways to strengthen the mind. As you work in that direction, perhaps the primary question should be not so much "do I really like this music?" as "is this the best music to promote health for my body and mind?"

### BEWARE OF SWEEPING ASSUMPTIONS

Some people prefer to simplify the question of "what is good music?" by classifying all religious music or classical music as the best. It is not safe to make sweeping assumptions, however. There are many uplifting religious praise songs, but much of the music under the "religious" label is filled with hypnotic, frontal-lobe suppressive, repetitive rhythms. The fact that a song purports to be religious does not automatically mean that it will be good music for your brain.

Sweeping assumptions are also unsafe in the realm of classical music. History records that some classical music composers suffered from depression or mental instability. Music is an expression of emotion, which is why dark mental states can be so clearly portrayed in the discordant, jerky, clashing, excessively minor, or even alarming compositions of disturbed musicians, such as the music of Prokofiev.

The best music for promoting peak mental performance follows a set of mathematical rules—rules which cause the mind to feel comforted, encouraged, and safe. Baroque classical music, which is organized and melodic, is one genre which follows this set of rules. There is something "brain improving," soothing, metered, and organized about Pachelbel's Canon that brings a sense of calm and relaxation to those who listen. In contrast, music that goes against the rules can result in a nervous state of tension, frontal lobe suppression, sexual stimulation, or an addictive high.

*"The aim and final end of all music should be none other than the glory of God and the refreshment of the soul."*

—Johann Sebastian Bach

This may be one of the reasons why, when the Bible refers to harps, they are so frequently mentioned in conjunction with heavenly music. Harps, which are melodic and reflective, can't shock the senses with overwhelming volume or rhythm. One of my favorite authors wrote about what the music of heaven may be like. She described simple songs of praise sung in a natural tone (as opposed to long, drawn out notes and operatic singing), and also spoke of words uttered clearly, in a musical tone, sung from the heart with spirit, understanding, and devotion. "The keynote of the song of heaven is thanksgiving," she wrote, and the themes of the songs are love, praise, adoration to God and thanks for the wonderful beauties of creation. Songs of praise are a living connection with God, an effective tool to help resist evil, and a valuable way to impress spiritual truth upon the heart. Although I am sure there will be some grand and triumphal music in heaven, the characteristics listed in **Figure 19.6** on the following page are helpful when deciding what music to listen to and contemplate.[921]

## BALANCE IS KEY

Good music strikes an integrated balance between the major elements of melody, harmony, and rhythm, which are emphasized in that order.[922] There must also be a synergy between the types of chords used. An over-emphasis on augmented or diminished chords can lead to mental tension and lack of clarity, a fact that jazz musicians understand well and implement with effect.

In addition, the timing and tempo utilized in the rhythm, as well as the elements of volume and pitch, affect the emotional impact of music. Though beautiful orchestral music may deviate from the natural balance of music at times in order to showcase the talents of the composer or the dexterity of the performers, it should always return to balance.

## CHARACTERISTICS OF HEAVENLY MUSIC

Based on scripture, the music of heaven has been described in this way:

- mellow-toned
- harmonious
- happy
- joyful
- rich
- melodious
- perfect
- subdued
- the sweetest music
- like the singing of the birds

***Figure 19.6***

A mismatch between music and words can result in confusion. Despite the importance of words, the music itself is still the primary vehicle of expression. Putting religious words to nightclub music does not significantly change the end result. The message primarily conveyed is that of the music, not of the words. This is one area where country music—with its doleful emphasis on alcoholism and marital infidelity—has it right. The sorrowful music often matches the hard-luck words.

### UNDERSTANDING THE MUSICAL ELEMENTS

The melody is the "story line" or most prominent part of the music. A good melody rises and falls. If the melody is static or stays on one note, there can be a hypnotic effect. Like a good story, an excellent melody has satisfying proportions between the beginning, middle, and ending. The melody should reach a climax or resolution at some point, providing a sense of completion when the piece is complete. The harmony in a piece, which is produced by the chord structure involved, should blend and support the melody, adding beauty and personality to the composition.

While the major chords or intervals generally express pleasure or joy, the minors frequently convey deep thought, but may also convey depression, pain, or anguish. For example, the major third expresses happiness or pleasure, while a falling minor third (which is one of the operative notes in the mournful blues style), conveys depression. The sharp fourth, an unresolved chord, is actually known as the "diabolus" in music. This is the chord that Saint-Saens used in the *Danse Macabre* to represent the character of death tuning its fiddle.[923]

During the 19th century, or "Romantic Period" of classical music, much more emphasis was placed on emotion and freedom of form. Dissonant chords which had not been used so much previously, and which create disturbance and tension, became much more common.[924] Such dissonant or discordant music is not beneficial for those trying to soothe troubled minds or promote harmonious mental function.

## THE IMPORTANCE OF RHYTHM

The musical components of melody and harmony must unfold together, and it is rhythm—the beat of the music—which makes this simultaneous unfolding both interesting and possible. Rhythm provides the essential energy and heartbeat of music. It is what makes music move. Without it, music is often boring, or worse yet, dead.

> ***"Music creates order out of chaos; rhythm imposes unanimity upon the divergent, melody imposes continuity upon the disjointed, and harmony imposes compatibility upon the incongruous."***
> —Yehudi Menuhin

Despite the importance of rhythm, in brain-enhancing music it should be more like an undergirding or foundation than a driving force. One of the most important aspects of musical rhythm, known as timing, plays an important role in developing the emotional impact of a piece. Music in double-time tends to be more controlled, while triple-time rhythms can be more relaxed and abandoned. Irregular timing, such as is common in much of pop music today, produces a high state of nervous tension.

Tempo, or the pace of the music, can also stimulate heightened or depressed emotions. A fast or allegro tempo often accompanies music that is tumultuous or joyful, although too much presto (very fast) can be used to create a sense of hysteria. In contrast, music performed at a moderate tempo creates a more easy-going mood. Adagio (or slow) reflects serenity, while lento (extremely slow) could convey feelings of resignation or grief (Chopin's Funeral March is a good example of this).[925]

Using dotted notes, which increases the duration of certain notes, is one way that composers play with the standard tempo of a piece. Dotted rhythms can create strong tension and energy when played at a fast tempo, or a weary dragging feeling when played in "adagio."

In brain-enhancing music, rhythm is usually organized into regular recurring beats which are known as the "meter" or "metrical pattern" of the music. The beats come in patterns of two, three, or four, which are divided by measures. The strongest beat in the pattern (measure) is the downbeat (the first beat in the pattern). If the pattern has four beats, the strongest beat will be the first, and the next second strongest beat will be the third.

## SYNCOPATION: A COMPOSING TOOL

Composers utilize syncopation, or a shift in the emphasized notes, to disrupt the regular flow of the rhythm. Syncopation places the rhythmic stresses or accent where they wouldn't normally occur. In other words, a syncopated rhythm places stress on a weak beat, or creates a strong impulse on a subdivision of a beat, an in-between beat. Weak beats and in-between beats are also known collectively as "offbeats," and syncopated rhythm may be thought of as "offbeat rhythm."

**Continual syncopation creates a hypnotic influence on the frontal lobe.**

There is nothing inherently wrong with intermittent, occasional syncopation. It has been an important element in musical compositions for centuries, and remains as one of the most versatile tools that composers can employ to create rhythmic interest and variety. From the masters of the Middle Ages to Bach to Mozart to Beethoven to Tchaikovsky, it's difficult to find a composer who has not occasionally utilized syncopation. Depending on the tempo of the music and the type of syncopation, a syncopated rhythm can result in music that sounds jaunty, jazzy, unsteady, surprising, uncertain, exciting, or just plain interesting.

Some forms of music emphasize syncopation virtually all of the time. Ragtime, for example, would not be ragtime without the jaunty syncopations in the melody set against the steady un-syncopated bass. The swing rhythm in big-band jazz and the "back-beat" of many types of rock are the most common types of syncopated rhythm today. While infrequent syncopation for a measure or two may add a refreshing variety to a musical selection, problems arise with continual syncopation, which produces the hypnotic, frontal lobe declining effect. Offbeat and continual overemphasis on syncopation, which goes against the natural rhythm of the body (and of nature), is particularly detrimental to the goal of achieving peak mental performance for reasons discussed in the following paragraphs.

## THE POWER OF ENTRAINMENT

One of the most powerful aspects of music involves the physics phenomenon of resonance, which results in something scientists know as "entrainment." Entrainment is defined as the tendency for two oscillating bodies to lock into phase and vibrate in harmony, or the synchronization of two or more rhythmic cycles. The principle of entrainment is universal, appearing in chemistry, pharmacology, biology, medicine, psychology, sociology, astronomy, architecture, and more. In a classic example, two pulsing heart muscle cells, when brought close together, begin pulsing in synchrony.

Entrainment was first discovered in 1665 by a Dutch scientist, Christian Huygens. While working on the design of a pendulum clock, Huygens found that when he placed two clocks on a wall near each other and swung the pendulums at different rates, they eventually ended up swinging at the same rate due to their mutual influence on each other.[926]

In the musical realm, entrainment occurs when the rhythm of music enters the body and the physiological functions begin to match the rhythm of the music. When the rhythm of the music is highly syncopated (e.g. contains unnatural accents which do not match rhythms in the body or nature), the body rhythms synchronize with the unnatural rhythms, producing a negative effect on the emotional and physical health of the individual involved.[927]

Everything in nature, including the human body, functions in a natural rhythm. The heartbeat, respiration, speech, and even the brain all follow a rhythmic pattern. The human heart, and many other organs, function in a steady, unsyncopated rhythm.[928] Music that goes against the natural rhythms of the body has an exciting, unnatural effect, which is made even more prominent by another musical element that deserves our attention: the volume of music.

## THE EFFECT OF VOLUME

The level of volume at which music is played emphasizes whatever emotion is being expressed. More often than not, amplified music played in major chords involves splendor, courage, and confidence while soft music focused on major chords results in a subdued charm. Loud minor music, on the other hand, often invokes solemn feelings or even tragedy.[929]

The power of thunderous rhythm to invoke a physical and emotional response has long been understood by military leaders. Throughout the history of organized warfare, drummers have attempted to enrage soldiers as they sallied forth into battle by beating out rhythms first softly and slowly (consistent with the heart beat), and then more intensely as combat begins. By awakening the "fight or flight" response, the drummers, in the words of one sage, "play music designed to make your feet take you where your head never would..."[930]

By invoking the survival response, such music causes the blood pressure to increase and the heart to beat faster. The body's perceived goal is to pump blood (and with it, oxygen) to the muscles so the body can fight the "attack." The blood thickens, so that if injured in the battle, you won't bleed to death. Blood cholesterol increases. We experience hyper brain wave activity designed to make us more vigilant. The palms of our hands get sticky, so we can grip the club to fight off the beast. There is no beast, of course, but the body doesn't know that.

High volume levels not only amplify the sound, but also the negative effects of rhythms that are unnatural to the body.

And therein lies the problem. All of these physiological responses kick into gear as we lounge in the living room recliner. And some of us like the "rush," so we artificially create this response over and over again, for hours on end.

Video game producers understand this, which is why their most popular games rely not so much on incredible graphics as on music that starts at a low frequency pulse, near the heartbeat rate.[931] That pulse, which accelerates as the game progresses and is played more often, grips the body and mind of the player. The speed of the game picks up, the volume escalates, the soundtrack plays louder, and the player's body beats to the time of the music. Adrenaline rushes through the veins, feel-good endorphins kick in, and the player is "hyped." He wants more. The same riveting physical effects are achieved through the rhythm and volume of music in action or adventure movies.

*"Music can make the difference between withdrawal and awareness, between isolation and interaction, between chronic pain and comfort -- between demoralization and dignity."*

—Barbara Crowe (past president of the National Association for Music Therapy)

Research has shown that the high decibel sounds invoked in these entertainment venues, or any type of noise for that matter, is not conducive to optimal mental performance. Studies by Dr. Castelo Branco, of the Center for Human Performance in Lisbon, Portugal, revealed that long-term exposure to High Intensity/Low Frequency (HI/LF) noise created a number of health problems including visual problems, epilepsy, stroke-type neurological deficiencies and psychic disturbances such as anxiety, depression and hostility. Exposure to whole body vibration and sound is particularly egregious, triggering homeostatic imbalance and disease, as well as interfering with human behavior and performance.[932]

## LOUD MUSIC AND SAFETY

In another study, researchers Helen Beh and Richard Hirst at the University of Sidney found that loud music interferes with driving ability. Study participants subjected to 85-decibel rock music were around a tenth of a second slower in their response time to road hazards emerging from the periphery than other drivers. Peripheral road hazards are quite common, so drivers listening to loud music are less safe behind the wheel.[933]

Research performed by Otolaryngologist R. W. Cantrell also indicated elevations in cortisol (a stress hormone) and cholesterol when participants were exposed to thirty days of short bursts of sound at 80 to 90 db levels. Although the release of cortisol is helpful for individuals in danger, the artificially stimulated release of this substance can alter appetite, cripple the immune system, shut down processes that repair tissue, block sleep, and even contribute to osteoporosis.[934]

Exposure to High Intensity / Low Frequency (HI/LF) noise such as is featured at many ball games and music concerts can also result in poor judgment and confusion. In an article entitled "Feeling the Music Can Be Dangerous to Your Health," Dr. Bart Billings, a military acoustic expert, reports compelling evidence that HI/LF sound is not only dangerous, but addictive.

Billings reports that sailors who work on the flight deck of aircraft carriers sometimes become disoriented and walk off the edge of the deck for no apparent reason. Billings reasoned that the long exposure of the sailors to HI/LF noise from jet engines could be the cause of the confusion and disorientation. Despite the presence of protective headgear, the immense vibration of the jet engines enters and envelops the entire body, creating not only the potential for confusion, but also the possibility for incredible and potentially addictive release of endorphins with an adrenaline rush.

Interviews with military personnel appeared to confirm Billing's suspicions. One crew member described how the noise and pressure from a jet taking off from the aircraft carrier was so strong, it felt like a large vibrator was placed on his chest. Flight deck crews, who had learned to enjoy the adrenaline/endorphin release, would purposely stand as close to the catapults as they could to feel the power of the planes. Crew members went on to tell Billings that most of the accidents that happened resulted from personnel being distracted by the intense vibration coursing through them as the engines revved up.

"Working the flight deck was the most exciting thing I've ever done," a crew chief told Billings," but I also hated every second of it. Once the planes left the flight deck on flight operations, there was always a let-down, kind of like coming down from a drug high. Once the planes returned, your energy level quickly increased."

Dr. Billings noted that the reaction of the crew members to the intense noise and vibration of the engines was consistent with addictive behavior. As a result of his experience and the things he had learned, Billings warned against listening to sound or music that "hurts, enrages and triggers fight or flight brain reactions, resulting in physiological changes that can be harmful."

Studies have shown that music which combines HI/LF sound with a focus on the backbeat is particularly powerful. Researchers from Louisiana State University in Shreveport concluded that listening to slow easy-listening music lowered the heart rates and allowed for longer physical training sessions in a group of 24 young adults.

Listening to hard-driving rock music had the opposite effect; heart rates increased and workouts were shorter. The study's author, B. Don Franks, Ph.D., professor in the university's Department of Kinesiology, says the soft music may make the exercise seem less difficult and allow people to work out longer.[935]

While we can be thankful for military personnel who are exposed to various sound hazards in the line of duty, those interested in attaining optimal mental performance should seriously question the necessity of voluntary exposure to HI/LF noise in a rock concert, ballgame, or other entertainment setting.

Optimizing your musical diet leads to health, just as optimizing your dietary habits does.

## OPTIMIZING YOUR MUSICAL DIET

The key to selecting brain-enhancing music is really to keep things in balance. When one element (such as the rhythm or volume) becomes so strong that it dominates or even obliterates other important elements (such as melody and harmony) that music needs to be questioned. Even the sweetness of music can tilt out of balance through over-emphasis. This is demonstrated in the gushingly sentimental music that is common in the entertainment industry and sometimes referred to as "schmaltzy."[936]

Just as food can be divided into four basic categories - Clearly Bad, Somewhat Bad, Somewhat Good, and Optimal - music could also be divided into similar categories. Some music is obviously bad for your brain, in the same way deep fried lard chips would be clearly bad for the health of your body. The lyrics are degrading, the lives of the performers and composers are twisted, and the elements of the music itself fight against the natural rhythms of the body. Other music is not so easily classified, however, falling into the middle. Some (like eating a piece of birthday cake) is clearly not good for you, but not as bad as the worst. Other music is like cooked vegetables: good, but not necessarily ideal. And some music (like fresh vegetables and fresh fruit for the body) are optimal nourishment for the brain.

*"Music washes away from the soul the dust of everyday life."*

—Berthold Auerbach (German novelist, 1812-1882)

Two figures follow that will aid you in selecting the healthiest music for your mood. **Figure 19.7** is provided to help you choose good music by assessing it with a few standard questions. The reasons behind the questions provided are found throughout this chapter, so if you don't understand why one or more of these questions is important, please read this chapter again. In addition, in **Figure 19.8** you'll find some of the compositions recommended by Dr. Juanita McElwain, a music therapist who is known as the "mother of music therapy."

The question I would ask is this: If you wish to achieve optimal mental performance, why not provide your brain with the very best music there is? Why edge as close as possible to the line dividing good and bad songs, when an abundance of superior music options not only exist, but can be yours to hear at the click of a button? Choose uplifting, balanced, harmonious music that works with your body's natural rhythms, and you will be pleased at how your thinking ability and mental health are enhanced.

## QUESTIONS TO ASK WHEN SELECTING MUSIC

- Is there a healthy balance between the melody, harmony, and rhythm of this music? Or is one element (such as rhythm) overshadowing all the rest?
- Does this music feature a storyline-type melody with a beginning, climax, and ending? Or does it create a hypnotic effect by focusing on one or two notes? (hint: New Age music generally lacks an ending, and some of the praise music in use today is so repetitive as to be hypnotic).
- Does this music use syncopation only occasionally to add interest, or is most (if not the entire piece) built around syncopation or an "offbeat," hypnotic rhythm?
- Are the words to this music ennobling or uplifting, or is it focused on the dark side of life?
- What is the intended and frequently achieved affect of this type of music? War or peace? Hate or love? Tranquility or agitation? Fidelity or sexual looseness?
- Is this music being played so loudly that I fear for my hearing, or that I experience the confusion and disorientation that frequently accompanies HI/LF sound?
- Was the composer of this music in a drugged, demented, or mentally unstable state when they wrote it? If music affects emotions, and the composers or performers were in a psychotic state, what can I expect as a listener?
- Is this music primarily harmonious, or clashing and discordant?
- Does it move along without being hysterically fast or laboriously draggy?
- Is there some sense of order and organization to the music that leaves me with a sense of order and peace, or is it jerky and unpredictable?

*Figure 19.7*

## RECOMMENDATIONS FROM A MUSIC THERAPIST EXPERT

### Music for Physical Energy
- Sousa, Stars & Strips Forever
- Beethoven, Turkish March
- Anderson, Bugler's Holiday
- Clarke, Trumpet Voluntary

### Music for Strength and Courage
- Steffe, Battle Hymn of the Republic
- Elgar, Pomp & Circumstance, March No. 1
- Brahms, Symphony No. 2, Final Movement
- Key, Star Spangled Banner

### Music for a Quiet Home
- Pachelbel, Canon in D
- Grainger, Blithe Bells
- Grieg, Lyric Suite
- Debussy, Clair de Lune

### Music for Relaxation
- Bruch, Scottish Fantasy
- Kreisler, Humoresque
- Copeland, Appalachian Spring
- Mantovani, Strings

### Music for Clear Thinking
- Bach, Brandenburg Concertos
- Soundtrack, Born Free
- Telemann, Concerto for Three Violins & Orchestra
- Brahms, Violin Concerto

### Music for Learning
- Handel, Concerto No. 1 in F
- Vivaldi, Winter from The Four Seasons
- Bach, Harpsichord Concerto in F Minor
- Telemann, Double Fantasia in G Minor for Flute & Strings

### Music for Meditation & Prayer
- Williams, Fantasia on a Theme of Thomas Tallis
- Handel, Largo (from Xerxes)
- Bach, Come Sweet Death
- Bruckner, Symphony No. 8 Third Movement

### Music to Relieve Boredom
- Liszt, Hungarian Rhapsodies
- Haydn, Trumpet Concerto
- Rimsky-Korsakov, Scheherazade
- Respighi, Ancient Dances and Airs, Pines of Rome

*Figure 19.8*

# References

890. 1 Samuel 18:10-11, 1 Samuel 19:9-10, 1 Samuel 20:30-32. *The Holy Bible.* Authorized King James Version.
891. 1 Samuel 16:14-19. *The Holy Bible.* Authorized King James Version.
892. 1 Samuel 16:23. *The Holy Bible.* Authorized King James Version.
893. Burney C. *A general history of music, volume 1.* New York: Harcourt, Brace & Co. 1937. 1499-163.
894. Meinecke B. "Music and medicine in classical antiquity." Dorothy Schullian and Max Schoe, eds., *Music and Medicine.* New York: Henry Schuman., Inc. 1938.
895. Cholden L. "Psychiatric concepts of music therapy." *Music Therapy*, 1952. Lawrence, Kansas: Allen Press, 1953, 27-31.
896. Boonshaft PL. "Teaching music with passion: conducting, rehearsing and inspiring." Galesville, MD: *Meredith Music.* Publications, 2002. p. 167.
897. "The Road from Eden: Studies in Christianity and Culture." Palo Alto, CA: Academica Press, p. 148, page 228.
898. Clark AV. "Psychology Of Moods." September 16, 2005, *Nova Science Publishers.*148.
899. Sheikh A. "Healing Images: The Role of Imagination in Health." Amityville, NY: Baywood Publishing Company (2003). 126.
900. Kerkvliet GJ. "Music Therapy May Help Control Cancer Pain," *J Natl Cancer Inst*, Mar 1990; 82: 350 - 352.
901. Van de Winckel A, Feys F, De Weerdt W, Dorn R. "Cognitive and behavioural effects of music-based exercises in patients with dementia." *Clin Rehabil* March 2004 18: 253-260.
902. Johnson JD, et al. "Violent Attitudes and Deferred Academic Aspirations: Deleterious Effects of Exposure to Rap Music." *Basic and Applied Social Psychology* 16: 1/2 (February): 27-41. 1995.
903. Helmes E, Wiancko DC. "Effects of Music in Reducing Disruptive Behavior in a General Hospital." *Journal of the American Psychiatric Nurses Association* February 2006 12: 37-44.
904. Särkämö T., et al. "Music listening enhances cognitive recovery and mood after middle cerebral artery stroke." *Brain* (2008) 131(3): 866-876.
905. McKinney CH, et al. "Effects of guided imagery and music (GIM) therapy on mood and cortisol in healthy adults." *Health Psychology.* Vol 16(4), Jul 1997, 390-400.
906. Allen K, Golden LH, Izzo JL, et al. "Normalization of hypertensive responses during ambulatory surgical stress by perioperative music." *Psychomatic Medicine* 2001:63(3),487-492.
907. Carson B, Lewis G. *The Big Picture: Getting Perspective on What's Really Important.* 2000. 35.
908. Allen K. Blascovich J. "Effects of Music on Cardiovascular Reactivity Among Surgeons." *JAMA*, 21 September 1994, 272:11,882-884
909. Hill L, Levitin DJ. "This Is Your Brain on Music: The Science of a Human Obsession." Atlantic Books. 2007. 84.
910. McElwain J. *Personal Communication.* Retired Chair of Music Therapy Department, Phillips University. Enid, OK.
911. Torres CA, Torres LR. "Notes on music." St. Maries, ID: LMN Publishing International.
912. Scheel KR. "Heavy metal music and adolescent suicidality: an empirical investigation." *Adolescence* - 01-JUL-1999; 34(134): 253-73.
913. "1999 College-Bound Seniors National Report: Profile of SAT Program Test Takers," *The College Entrance Examination Board*, Princeton, New Jersey.
914. Sergent J, Zuck E, Tenial S, MacDonnall B. "Distributed neural network underlying musical sight reading and keybpard performance." *Science*, 257, 106-109.
915. Schlaug G, Jancke L, Huang Y, Steinmetz H. "In vivo morphometry of interhemispheric asymmetry and connectivity in musicians." In I. Deliege (Ed.), Proceedings of the 3rd international conference for music perception and cognition. 1994. Liege, Belgium. 417-418.
916. 1994 Texas School Survey of Substance Abuse Among Students: Grades 7-12.
917. Gardiner M, Fox A, Knowles F, Jeffrey D. "Learning Improved by Arts Training" *Nature*, May 23, 1996.
918. American Psychological Society. (18 August 2004). "New Research Provides the First Solid Evidence that the Study of Music Promotes Intellectual Development." Psychologicalscience.org.
919. A Little Music With Exercise Boosts Brain Power, Study Suggests. *ScienceDaily* (Mar. 24, 2004).
920. Caine J. "The effects of music on the selected stress behaviors, weight, caloric and formula intake, and length of hospital stay of premature and low birth weight neonates in a newborn intensive care unit." *J Music Ther.* 1991 Winter;28(4):180-92.

921. White EG. *Testimonies Volume 6*, "Singing That is to God's Glory."
922. McElwain J. *The Story of Music.* Juanita McElwain, Kerens, West Virginia. January 1, 2007. 22.
923. McElwain J. *The Story of Music.* Juanita McElwain, Kerens, West Virginia. January 1, 2007. 22.
924. McElwain J. *The Story of Music.* Juanita McElwain, Kerens, West Virginia. January 1, 2007. 22.
925. McElwain J. *The Story of Music.* Juanita McElwain, Kerens, West Virginia. January 1, 2007. 23.
926. Clemens JK, Dalyrymple S. "Time Mastery: How Temporal Intelligence Will Make You a Stronger, More Effective Leader." *AMACOM*, 2005. 99.
927. Wigram T, Saperston B, West R. "The Art and Science of Music Therapy: A Handbook." London: Harwood Academic. 65.
928. "Rhythms of life: the biological clocks that control the daily lives of every living thing." New Haven, Conn: Yale University Press. 11.
929. McElwain J. *The Story of Music.* Juanita McElwain, Kerens, West Virginia. January 1, 2007. 22.
930. Billings B."Feeling the Music Can Be Dangerous to Your Health." http://www.omnisonic.com/bbillings.html.
931. Orr J. "Rhythm and intimacy in VR. Internet communication." *Computer Graphic World.* 1996.
932. Branco C, Rodriguez E. "The vibroacoustic disease-an emerging pathology." *Aviation, Space, And Environmental Medicine;* (1999) 70(3,Suppl.):A1-6. Alexandria, VA.
933. Spinney L. "Pump down the Volume." *New Scientist,* New Science. Publications, Holborn Publishing Group, London, Vol.155, No.2091, July 19, 1997. 22.
934. Cantrell R. "Prolonged exposure to intermittent noise: Audiometric, biochemical, motor, psychological and sleep effects." *Laryngoscope*, 84. 4-55. Fearn, R. (1972). "Noise levels in youth clubs (correspondence)." *Journal of Sound and Vibration*, 22, 127-1228.
935. Gottlieb B. *New Choices in Natural Healing: Over 1,800 of the Best Self-Help Remedies from the World of Alternative Medicine.* Rodale Press, 1997. Page 127.
936. McElwain J. *The Story of Music.* Juanita McElwain, Kerens, West Virginia. January 1, 2007. 21.

# THE LOST ART OF THINKING

*How to Improve Emotional Intelligence and Achieve Peak Mental Performance*

## Section 3:

# *PULLING IT ALL TOGETHER*

Chapter 20

EVEN PEOPLE WHO HAVE NEVER BEEN DEPRESSED BEFORE STRUGGLE WITH SITUATIONAL DEPRESSION WHEN FACED WITH A SIGNIFICANT LOSS.

# Living After Loss

## *Optimal thinking can help you overcome loss.*

Jane had not felt depressed for even one day in her life. Not that life didn't throw her any curves—she had just been able to handle them. Then came the fateful phone call, the start of an agonizing day that Jane will never forget. Her only child, a much loved son who Jane was very close to, had been killed in a tragic car accident. Jane was crushed. She'd been through a few trials in life, but nothing approaching the intensity of this pain. A normally social individual, Jane now found it easy to cut off her friends. She wanted to grieve alone.

As the weeks after the funeral slipped by, Jane stayed home more and more. Activities that used to bring pleasure seemed dull and meaningless now. Soon Jane—the typically happy one who had always encouraged everyone else with her cheerful and buoyant spirit, was mired in a deep depression.

Like Jane, many people begin their struggle with depression as a result of a surprising and often devastating loss. This loss-induced sadness is often accompanied by situational depression. The trigger may be a pink slip, a debilitating injury, or the death of a loved one. No one wants to face bereavement, and we would all like to think that it won't happen to us. But studies have shown that by age seventy, 99% of Americans will suffer from situational depression due to a significant loss in their lives. With the passing of enough time, the loss of parents, a spouse, siblings, or children is unavoidable. The longer you live, the likelihood that you will experience bereavement is extremely high. There are many types of loss, aside from the loss of a loved one (see **Figure 20.1**). Because it has a great impact on both future success and mental health, the manner in which you process loss is especially critical.

In my book *Depression: the Way Out*, I described ten categories of "hits" that significantly contribute to depression. When four of those ten factors are operative, the individual will most likely suffer from depression, anxiety, or another mental illness. Complicated grief is actually one of those "hits."

For just about any disease, there are appropriate steps that lead to health and healing. The same is true of grief. Unfortunately, when grief is not handled in the appropriate way, the individual's mental performance often suffers.

## DEALING WITH OVERWHELMING LOSS

We had the humble experience of assisting the grieving victims of both the Oklahoma City bombing and the September 11 terrorist attacks in New York. While there were similarities between these two tragic events, I also noticed some major differences. There was tremendous loss of life in the Oklahoma City bombing, but none of the survivors lost their jobs. There was loss of a workplace, but those individuals were quickly transferred to another facility. And there wasn't really a loss of homes.

September 11 was a different story. Loved ones were lost on a rather grand scale. In many cases the bodies of the deceased were unrecoverable.

### COMMON TYPES OF LOSSES

Although there are many varieties of loss, losing the things listed below can cause considerable grief.

- a spouse through death or divorce
- a child, parent, or sibling
- wealth or social status
- a job or career
- a home or significant property
- a body part
- the ability to maintain a physical
- function (particularly with aging)
- a goal or vision (where an individual had definite plans set, and then for some reason those plans did not go through)

*Figure 20.1*

In addition to the greater number of casualties, many lost their jobs and social status. Many individuals who were able to continue working for the same employer were transferred into different capacities after the disaster. Additionally, there was tremendous loss of homes. People who had lived in apartment complexes for years could no longer return.

As I was studying how best to help these people, I turned to scientific medical literature to learn how others had dealt with these types of situations. The psychological process of going through a war was the closest thing I could find, and the last time the United States had anything approaching the ferocity of these attacks within its borders was the Civil War. The things I learned from studying how people dealt with war-related losses were a springboard for some of the concepts in this chapter.

**Grief is an emotional reaction that follows the loss of someone or something of great value. Mourning is the psychological process that occurs when you experience loss.**

## THOUGHTS ARE A KEY TO HEALING

One of the most important processes that needs to happen during times of loss is for the grieving individual to step back and analyze his or her own thinking. I was reminded of that fact while presenting a seminar about lifestyle diseases in Texas. One of the attendees had just become a centenarian, and in spite of her age, she could walk on her own and enjoyed good mental clarity. She had a great sense of humor, and her memory of both past and recent events was very clear. She could tell us when the first car pulled into town, who was there to see it, and even what they said about it.

After singing "Happy Birthday," we had her blow out 100 candles. A news anchor covering the event then put a microphone under her chin.

"Tell us ma'am," she questioned, "what's so special about being 100 years old?"

"No peer pressure," was the centenarian's instant reply. Everyone had a good laugh, including myself. Later, however, I thought about the layers of loss this lady must have endured. While visiting with her, she shared that she had outlived every single person who was important to her during her life. She had lost her spouse. She had lost children to diseases of old age. She lost every close friend she'd had in her 20s, 30s, 40s, 50s, and 60s. She had to develop new friends—yet she still had a wit about her. She was able to carry on.

Today, studies are showing that your lifespan is dependent on more than how you treat your body and what you put into it. While those two factors are very important, your manner of processing loss is also critical to your longevity. The centenarian from Texas is a wonderful testimony to that fact. She had sustained many losses, but processed them in an appropriate way. Despite the setbacks, she continued living a happy life.

## HAPPY THOUGHTS VERSUS ACCURATE THOUGHTS

Motivational speakers place great emphasis on positive thinking, and rightfully so. But while thinking happy and positive thoughts is certainly important, our real goal should be to think accurate thoughts. Accurate thinking is especially important in times of bereavement. Escaping to a fantasy land as a means of coping can actually be harmful in the long run, because those aren't accurate thoughts. By living in "another world," you are actually telling yourself a lie.

To think "I'm losing an important part of my life" is an accurate, appropriate way of stating loss. In contrast, to say "my world has ended" is actually a cognitive distortion. The world is going on. The very fact that you can state that your world is ending is proof that it still exists!

"I can't live without her" is another distorted thought. In order to even think that thought, the grieving individual must be alive.

"I will miss the companionship and love that we shared" is a much more realistic and desirable way of thinking about loss. While helping the grieving person to process the loss, it also adds deeper meaning to life.

Some people, when faced with this kind of grief, tell themselves that they'll never be happy again because someone they loved died. That thought, which is based on distorted thoughts, triggers feelings of hopelessness and

## SOCIAL TIES ARE IMPORTANT

Unfortunately, many human beings were subjected to torture in World War II and a number of other wars. The torture was prolonged and repetitive, which has dire consequences for the mental health of the individuals involved.

Studies done on victims of torture have shown that those with poor social support had a much greater risk of depression later in life. In contrast, individuals with strong social support went on to make strong recoveries and lead happy, normal lives.

If you have gone through a significant loss and allowed yourself to become socially isolated, then, you're actually going to do worse than a survivor of torture who stays socially connected after their release. Maintaining social ties is very important after suffering from loss.

***Figure 20.2***

self-pity. The end result is a complicated grief which leads to defeat, especially if the individual repeatedly thinks those thoughts. Maintaining social ties after suffering a loss is important, as explained in **Figure 20.2.** [937]

## DEALING WITH LOSS: A PRIMER

When a bone is broken, the steps taken to mend the bone affect the success of the healing process. If not set properly in a cast, that bone could end up causing us pain, discomfort, and even permanent disability. However, if we have the bone set properly and go through the healing process, however, that bone will eventually be almost completely normal.

The same principle holds true with regard to emotional loss. While appropriate ways of handling such losses lead to eventual healing, an inappropriate response can lead to ongoing cycles of pain. In fact, major depression is often simply a manifestation of unhealed and prolonged grief.

If 12-18 months have passed since a significant loss and you are still suffering from a profound sense of emptiness, apathy, fatigue, or sadness—you have slipped beyond grief into a major depression.

## STAGES OF GRIEF RECOVERY

Proper handling of grief involves going through several stages.[938]

### Stage 1: Shock and Disbelief

This first stage occurs at the time of the loss, when events seem very unreal. Many people who were at the scene during the September 11 tragedy say it seemed "surreal." They had to keep reminding themselves of the reality of it all, because it seemed more like a scary movie than anything else.

Typical reactions during "Stage 1" of the grieving process include weeping, extreme anger, or screaming. This intense reaction to a significant loss should last anywhere from a few seconds to 24 hours. It is actually healthy for it to last up to several hours. If 24 hours have passed and you are still in denial, make a special effort to come to grips with reality. Otherwise, you won't be able to handle the loss appropriately, and the other stages in the grieving process will be delayed as well.

**The first stage of grief is shock and disbelief.**

It's true that feelings such as "this can't be real" are typical responses during the first stage of a loss. But while we may feel numb or even be in denial that the loss has actually happened, it is critical that we accept reality early on.

I witnessed the downside of continued denial firsthand in the life of one graduate of the *Nedley Depression Recovery Program*. Although this woman had been severely depressed and on medication for years, her depression had completely cleared as a result of the program. By putting the principles of the program into practice, she was able to get off medication and live a highly effective life.

About three years after her recovery, this woman suffered a devastating loss. Her only biological son, a 19-year old with whom she was very close, died in his apartment one day. When she found him, his body was cold and stiff. As she touched him, she should have realized that he had been dead for hours. However, she called 911 and did CPR anyway.

Though deep in her mind she knew he was dead, she kept telling herself that he wasn't. His body was transferred to Oklahoma City for an autopsy, and she was so distressed that they ended up taking her to the emergency room. There she continued telling others that the EMTs were doing CPR on her son.

"He's being taken to Oklahoma City for medical help," she kept saying. "But he's going to be all right." In the case of this grieving mother, "Stage 1" of the grief process was quite prolonged. By repeating inaccurate statements over and over again, she definitely began the grieving process on the wrong foot. Her level of denial was not only incredible, but detrimental to the long-term healing process.

Fortunately, one of the instructors in the *Nedley Depression Recovery Program* met her in the emergency room. In the midst of the woman's hysteria, the instructor was able to help her face what had happened and get her on the track to appropriate grieving.

### Stage 2: Developing Awareness

The second stage in recovery, which usually lasts from 3-12 months, involves a preoccupation with the loss. When we are in this stage, just about everything we do reminds us of what we used to have that is no longer "ours." Other common experiences during this stage of loss are included in **Figure 20.3**.

The preoccupation with loss that happens during "Stage 2" of the grieving process is really quite normal and actually healthy. During this stage it is especially important that we keep our circadian rhythms on track with healthy sleeping patterns. We also need to analyze our feelings of guilt to determine if they are appropriate.

**STAGE 2 REACTIONS**

- restlessness
- anxiety
- difficulty sleeping
- loss of appetite
- digestive problems
- fatigue
- anger
- guilt

***Figure 20.3***

One individual I know of was driving a car that hit and killed a young girl. He was not speeding, but she darted out in front of him and there was really nothing he could do to avoid the accident. Even though he had virtually no chance to avoid the mishap, he was plagued by guilt.

"If I would have just stayed longer at the grocery store," he would tell himself, or "If only I had stayed home." Despite the fact that he could not possibly have foreseen or averted the accident, he beat himself over the head with "what-ifs" over and over again.

This inappropriate guilt can be especially daunting where death is involved and the surviving party did not right any wrongs before the loss. That is why it is so important to learn from the ancient proverb not to let the sun "go down upon your wrath."[939] It's a terrible thing to wish you could say you're sorry after it's too late.

Identification with the lost loved one is another common characteristic of the second stage of the grieving process. In contrast to the denial that is so common in the first stage, we are now very aware both of the loss and it's consequences. If the loss involved death, we may feel like we hear the voice of the deceased when really we don't.

We may also sink into depression when the anniversary of the loss rolls around. Significant mood swings are common as well in this stage.

During this phase of the recovery process, many people inappropriately expect that they should be feeling better day by day or, at the very minimum, week by week. A better way to analyze progress, however, would be month-by-month. At the end of each month, ask yourself the questions in **Figure 20.4**.

If you find yourself regressing in the recovery process, actually doing worse in month four than you were in month three, for example, you will need additional help. At the very least, you should read some recommended materials on depression recovery or dealing with loss. Completing an interactive program in earnest would offer greater benefits. The *Depression Recovery Program DVD and Workbook Series* offered on my website (www.drnedley.com) is a good place to start.

## MONTHLY RECOVERY CHECKUP

- Am I doing better?
- Am I thinking more clearly?
- Is my mood more stable now than it was last month?

***Figure 20.4***

### Stage 3: Resolution

This stage usually begins within 3-12 months after the loss. Ideally it would begin within 3 months, but it is not uncommon for it to take a full year. This stage of "resolution" cannot begin until Stage 2 (Awareness) has been completed.

During this phase of recovery, the grieving individual is involved in lifestyle changes and the formation of new habits in response to the loss. Depending on the nature of the loss, some of the lifestyle changes may have actually taken place earlier. (For example, in the case of an individual who lost their job and went on unemployment).

Making wise plans for the future is one of the important tasks to be accomplished during this phase, where the individual actually begins to take charge of their life again through activity, readjustment, and education. It is best to stay active during this phase, learning as much about the healing process as possible while adjusting to the loss.

Grief over the loss of a loved one is often followed by periods of introspection or a personal reaffirmation of life's worth and meaning. This is a healthy process, much healthier than saying "well, we just need to move on and try to forget about it." **Figure 20.5** discusses a study of 40 men recovering from loss, and the impact of how the handling of loss affected their future health.[940]

The ability to appropriately process loss is a major reason that some individuals are able to live for 100 years or more, and do so enjoyably. They are able to retain their wit and even give advice while avoiding the self-pity and hopelessness that entraps so many others.

## A PERSONAL LOSS

In 2002, I experienced a significant loss in my own life with the passing of my dad. I had an excellent father who was a great role model. I wouldn't be doing the things I am doing today if it weren't for his guiding influence.

My father was a sharp and objective thinker. As such, he was a great person to go to for advice, and often available by phone. Whenever I had an important decision to make, I could pick up the phone and get good advice from Dad. He also helped me a great deal in the publishing work. Instead of telling me what to do, he would help me think through whatever situation I was facing. He was a real blessing to me, and I was privileged to have him as part of my life. (Please see **Appendix IV** for more about my father.)

The first two books I published would not have been written so well if it hadn't been for my father. He was an engineer by profession, but had a great way of making things easy for people to understand. So when my father passed away suddenly, it was a huge loss for me.

This is in contrast to some fathers I have heard about who were not very available to their children because of alcoholism. work priorities, or

## A CASE STUDY IN GRIEF RECOVERY

**Participants**: 40 men whose immune systems had been compromised prior to experiencing a tragic loss.

**Observation**: The men were studied 4-9 years after the loss. The researchers recorded the correlation between cognitive processing of the loss and mental and physical health.

**Results**: 65% of the men had thoughtfully considered the meaning of their loved one's death (they had reflected upon the loss and attempted to mentally process the experience). 35% of the men did not attempt cognitive processing (an unhealthy choice that can lead to mental health issues).

The men who tried to process the loss were then divided into three groups:

Group 1: These men considered the loss, but determined that their loved one's death only emphasized the negative aspects of life. This group did not do very well mentally or physically.

Group 2: This group, after processing the loss, simply accepted the death and moved on. They fared no better health-wise than Group 1.

Group 3: The loss of a loved one led these men to a commitment to improve their personal lives, and also a new-found respect for life in general. These men went through the stages of grief and cognitive processing and decided to become better men because of what they'd been through. In contrast to the other subjects of the study, these men showed a significant improvement in immune function. This group displayed a healthier mental state and also outdistanced the other groups in long-term survival.

***Figure 20.5***

other reasons. I've met people who hardly knew their fathers. The only advantage they have is that when the father dies, the loss isn't felt as intensely. But when you have experienced a relationship with someone who is very helpful and close to you, the loss of that person is very significant and can hit you hard for years to come. The healthy way to process such a loss is to honor that person for who he or she was. You can also pay tribute to their life, by developing a newfound respect for life and commitment to self-improvement as a result of the loss.

I had to go through this process after the loss of my father. At first, I couldn't see how life could possibly be good or even better without my dad around. My mother was going through this same process. It was difficult for us to understand why this happened to a person of such magnitude, who was so helpful not only to his family, but also to his fellow man.

As I contemplated these things, I came to realize that the greatest historical individuals this world has ever known still died. John the Revelator died, and John the Baptist died, and many others like them. It seems we would all be better off if John the Baptist or John the Revelator were alive, active. The world is simply not as good because they are gone. Their influence can continue, however, if we honor these individuals by living out their principles and making a commitment to significantly improve our own lives and the lives of others around us.

As I thought about my father, I recognized two reasons for the wisdom he had so freely shared and which I valued so highly. He was very good at analyzing things, but more importantly, he was very close to God. When I called him on the phone, it was almost as if I could hear the voice of God, the voice of truth and love. As I considered these things, I realized that if I were going to continue to be the type of son he wanted me to be, I needed to forge a closer relationship with the God of Truth and Love myself. I wanted to hear God's voice more clearly, just as my father had done. It took some cognitive processing, however, for me to move past the heartache, analyze the situation, and be inspired toward a stronger commitment.

## CLOSE THE FILE

It's beneficial to your mental and physical health to diligently work to put the trauma of loss behind you. When you linger on the sorrow of painful situations too long, you impair your ability to lead a healthy, successful life. Open memories continue to play a role in a person's life, and when that memory is distressing, it negatively impacts physical, emotional, and mental wellness. Closed memories, in contrast, have been resolved and no longer torment or burden the person. While a natural grieving period is healthy and necessary, it's very important to work toward finding closure.

At times the circumstances surrounding a tragedy cause those mourning to continually question and doubt the actions that led up to the loss. This is a distinct barrier to bringing closure to the unfortunate event. For example, I know a woman who struggled with guilt after the death of her father, repeatedly recalling possible signs she might have missed that would have alerted her of his dire condition. She had convinced herself that she would have seen and acted on the minor symptoms had she not been preoccupied with telling him of her own exciting plans. In reality, her father was not displaying any physical indications that should have caused her great concern, and her enthusiasm about sharing her news did not cause her to neglect the father she loved. However, it took awhile before she was able to overcome the persistent thoughts of what she could have done differently.

This woman was engaged in what Aldo Pucci calls "nonsense arguments" (mentioned briefly in chapter 8 of this book). Nonsense arguments often begin with "if" or "if only." For example, "If only I had noticed that his breathing was a bit labored, I could've rushed him to the hospital and the doctors would have saved him." Or, "If only I hadn't gone hiking that day, I wouldn't have fallen and broken my leg, and I wouldn't have this limp." Life can be filled with nonsense arguments if we allow it. "If only my parents hadn't gotten a divorce," "if only my grandfather hadn't gone bankrupt," or "if only I hadn't married this man..."

Nonsense arguments may be totally accurate, totally inaccurate, or partially accurate. The accuracy of nonsense arguments is not the important issue: the issue is that such arguments about the past distract the person from what they should be doing in the present. Events in the past cannot be changed, and so the problem with these nonsense arguments is that they are largely irrelevant. The only reason to consider past mistakes is to learn from them. Beyond that, nonsense arguments only serve as an obstacle to closure and emotional healing. Instead of dwelling on what could have been, it is better to ask, "what can I do about my situation now?"

Research suggests that people who bring closure to negative past experiences enjoy a better self-image and physical health. "It's important to get closure on things that happen to you," says Denise Beike, an assistant professor of psychology at the University of Arkansas in Fayetteville. "If you fail to do this, you run the risk of decreasing your sense of self-worth, and perhaps your physical health as well."[941]

Another way that people often dwell on irrelevant thoughts that hinder the healing process is by trying to assign blame. They point fingers at other people, entities, and ultimately, God. While a spiritual relationship with God can be extremely helpful during difficult times, problems sometimes arise in this area when people blame God for their loss. Blaming and questioning God is just as detrimental to finding closure as blaming yourself or questioning your past actions. I witnessed an example of this in two patients of mine. The dear couple lost their son in a tragic car accident. He was coming home from work and apparently fell asleep at the wheel. The parents blamed God for the accident and became very preoccupied in asking how He could have allowed this to happen. Unfortunately, their persistence in harboring such thoughts resulted in adverse effects to both their spiritual and physical health.

Nonsense arguments and blame delay gaining closure on the traumatic event, and prevent you from moving forward. Because our brains don't have an automatic filter to detect nonsense thoughts, we need to build a protective filter. The key is to recognize nonsense thoughts they moment they enter your brain and quickly discard them.

There's an expression, "There's no point shoveling last year's snow!"

In other words, what's done is done. Though it is important to learn from the past, your energy should be focused on resolving current concerns and creating a happy tomorrow —not on nonsense thoughts or blame.

This does not mean that you should try to immediately forget the loss and pretend as if it didn't happen. There is a healthy way to grieve that allows you to find closure and maintain emotional wellness and mental performance.

## HEALTHY GRIEVING

**Writing or journaling about loss can help the recovery process.**

Handling grief in a healthy way is not something that comes naturally to humans. We are not born with an innate knowledge about how to process loss. We may learn from watching others, but there is work—hard work—and a process involved. Setting a broken bone can be a difficult process. It may require a lot of work to get that bone lined up. A tremendous amount of pain could also be involved.

The process of healing from grief can be very empowering to the mourner, even those who feel very helpless. Many people don't realize there are things they can do to help them through the process. Some people say that if given time, things have got to get better. However, the old adage that "time is a healer" is not 100% true. Time does not always heal wounds, but working through wounds over time can indeed bring healing.

The time needed for full and complete healing depends on the loss. In most cases, healing can occur in 18 months or less. For the loss of a loving spouse, complete emotional recovery can take up to eight years.[942]

J. William Worden, the author of several books on grief counseling and therapy, describes five tasks that we need to work through in our efforts to overcome loss in an appropriate manner.[943]

### Task #1: Accept the reality of the loss

Communicating about the loss to others can be helpful in this regard. It is also important to have a mourning ritual, such as a funeral service, to help move the grieving and healing processes forward. I've had friends who didn't want to go to a loved one's funeral because they didn't want to face the loss. Some people turn to drugs to escape the reality of a loss. I'm frequently asked to prescribe Xanax, which gives a bit of a buzz and makes the individual feel as though the loss didn't really happen.

Avoidance and prescription drugs both deter the grieving process. The individual must eventually come to grips with the loss, and the sooner that happens, the better.

### Task #2: Work through the pain

Pain is an inevitable part of loss that simply has to be worked through. Be honest about your feelings during the process, but do not avoid the pain, as it will only prolong your emotional healing.

## EMOTIONAL PAIN MANAGEMENT TIPS

- Eat a balanced diet.
- Exercise regularly.
- Maintain social ties.
- Get adequate rest.
- Keep a schedule.

***Figure 20.6***

Writing or journaling about the loss can help in this regard. In this process, it's best to write like a journalist, documenting the events of the loss. The lady I mentioned earlier in this chapter, who suffered the loss of her 19-year-old son, found healing through this exercise. She was struggling with achieving closure, partially because she didn't know the cause of his death for a long time. It took a while for the autopsy results to come back, and there were suspicions of murder. There was no suicide weapon around, and there were no drugs nearby, deepening the mystery.

Mentally, the grieving mother kept going over and over how she had found him, what he was like, the expression on his face, and all the details surrounding the loss. Every time she came to my office I would hear more minutia about the loss. Finally I realized that she needed to write things down and save her record in a safe place so if need be, she could refer to it again. It was her fear of forgetting some details about the loss that kept her preoccupied with it for weeks on end.

When she actually sat down to write out the details, it took her less than a day. It wasn't until this very important task was completed that she began to obtain some relief. Because things were written down, she somehow felt she could mentally file them. She could put it away, and no longer needed to be preoccupied with the loss.

People were asked to journal about their loss after the Oklahoma City bombing as part of the healing process. The value of journaling is supported by scientific research, which has verified that the act of writing about bereavement lessens grief.[944] Some other factors that are very important when working through the pain are documented in **Figure 20.6**.

It is also important to get adequate sleep, nutrition, and exercise. While these lifestyle factors are important at any time, they are especially critical during a period of loss. If you get off your regular schedule with regard to rest, meals, or fitness, it will catch up with you much more quickly during a time of grief.

If appropriately handled, difficult experiences in life should not burden us, so much as they soften and refine us, as illustrated in **Figure 20.7**.[945]

### Task 3. Adjust to the changed environment

In the weeks and months following a loss, it's important not to make major, life-changing decisions that can be avoided. Individuals who have just lost a spouse through death or divorce need time to sort things out. Our minds aren't usually as sharp while we are processing grief, making it harder to objectively weigh the pros and cons of any decision.

During this phase, you'll need to identify the roles that the individual or job that you lost played in your life. You'll also need to find out how these functions can be met now. Often they can't be completely met, and if that is the case, that fact needs to be recognized.

### Task 4: Emotionally relocate the loss

"Relocating" a loss doesn't mean that you have to forget about it. Whatever you lost was an important part of your life, one that you will want to reminisce about from time to time. As you move forward, however, it is important to find new interests even as you continue the old ones that were good. You'll also want to develop new routines and build on current or new relationships during this phase of recovery.

### Task 5: Grow from the loss

As difficult as loss can be, there are still ways to find roses amid the thorns. Many people who have survived cancer or suffered through a difficult divorce look back on those losses as times of great personal or spiritual growth.

As you process your loss don't settle for a mere survival mode existence. Honor the lost person, vision, or thing by growing through your bereavement. Reflect on what you have learned or gained through the loss and let life become more meaningful. The Bible says "We know that in all things God works for the good of those who love him."[946] Many times from our own human perspective, it's hard to see how anything good can come from what we are going through. But, though our vision is limited, we can still take comfort in the fact that loss was not meant to be. It was not part of God's original plan. He didn't want sin to enter in. It only entered because voluntary love and freedom was so important, and because others besides God made choices that led to loss.

## FREEDOM TO LOVE VOLUNTARILY

Many people wonder why an all-powerful God can allow such evil, pain, and suffering to take place. God is not the reason why sin exists. He permitted sin to happen because he honors our freedom of choice and freedom of conscience, but He did not cause it.

## WHEN THE CAGED BIRD SINGS

"In the full light of day and in the hearing of the music of other voices, the caged bird will not sing the song that his master seeks to teach him. He learns a snatch of this, a trill of that, but never a separate and entire melody.

But the master covers the cage and places it where the bird will listen to the one song he is to sing. In the dark he tries and tries again to sing that song until it is learned, and he breaks forth in perfect melody. Then the bird is brought forth and ever after he can sing that song in the light. Thus God deals with his children. He has a song to teach us, and when we have learned it amid the shadows of affliction, we can sing it ever afterward." - E.G. White in *The Ministry of Healing*

***Figure 20.7***

Freedom of conscience is one of those supreme principles which is greatly valued by God. Although God really loves us and desires our love in return, He wanted our affection to be voluntary, rather than programmed or forced. This gift of freedom, which is so beautiful when rightly used, is also what made it possible for sin to enter this world. While the effect of sin has been horrible to say the least, the "era of sin" is really a short experiment in the context of universal time. As we work through our grief, we need to realize that even though God is not the author of sin and suffering, He has power to help us through it.

John the Baptist was the cousin of Jesus, someone He felt a special kinship to because of their callings. Jesus even called John "the greatest prophet who ever lived. Yet He "allowed" John to suffer the horror of decapitation.[947]

We can't blame God for what happened to John the Baptist. Herodius, working under the influence of Satan, was actually behind this evil deed. It was a horrible sin that affected a noble and innocent person. But the beheading of John, like many other tragedies, was not caused by God. This understanding is critical to us as we work our way through the process of grief recovery. As we acknowledge these things, it will be easier for us to embrace the foundational principles of God's government. These supreme principles, which (as keys to peak mental performance) are discussed in later chapters, are truth, freedom, and love.

The process of working our way through pain is actually a great opportunity for us to develop another positive mental health attribute, the virtue of patience. Patience has been defined as the capacity to endure hardship, difficulty, or inconvenience without complaint. Another definition, from the *American Heritage Dictionary*, calls patience "the power of suffering with fortitude, or uncomplaining endurance of evils or wrongs as toil, pain, poverty, insult, oppression, or calamity."[948]

The virtue of patience has been recognized since ancient times. One particularly famous admonition, by the apostle Paul, tells us to "run with patience the race that is set before us."[949] While the process can be exceptionally painful, suffering loss is one of the best ways to develop this important characteristic.

## THE OTHER SIDE OF LOSS

We don't often think of loss in this manner, but loss is really the other side of love. Those who love, risk loss, and the greater the love, the greater the risk of loss. Because my father was so loving, I miss him terribly. The other option would be an unloving father whose loss leaves less of an impact. Which would I have rather had? Of course, the loving father. True love cannot be experienced without freedom. Freedom cannot be experienced without the potential for lack of love and its ultimate result of losses. What would you rather have? I would rather have love in the world, than no love, and no loss.

The good news is, there is a God who has a long-term plan that we should never experience loss, sadness, or death again. If we let Him into our lives He can recreate us during times of loss. Then, no matter how painful the road, we can "run with patience the race that is set before us."

# References

937. Carlsson JM, Mortensen EL, Kastrup M. "Predictors of mental health and quality of life in male tortured refugees." *Nord J. Psychiatry* 60 (2006).
938. Townsend MC. "Loss and Bereavement." *Psychiatric Mental Health Nursing:Concepts of Care.* 4th ed. Philadelphia: F.A. Davis Company, 2002.
939. Ephesians 4:26. *The Holy Bible.* Authorized King James Version.
940. Bower JE, et al. "Cognitive processing, discovery of meaning, CD4 decline, and AIDS-related mortality among bereaved HIV-seropositive men." *Journal of Consulting and Clinical Psychology.* 66.6 (1998): 979+.
941. NEW YORK, Dec 08 (Reuters Health) Copyright @ 2000 Reuters Limited. All Rights Reserved (article by Merritt McKinney.
942. Lucas RE, et al. "Reexamining adaptation and the set point model of happiness: reactions to changes in marital status." *Journal of Personality and Social Psychology* 84.3 (2003).
943. Worden JW. "Understanding The Mourning Process." *Grief Counseling and Grief Therapy: A Handbook for The Mental Health Practitioner.* 3rd ed. New York: Springer Pub., 2002. 25+.
944. Honos-Webb L, Hart S, Scalise JT. "How to Help After National Catastrophes: Findings Following 9/11." *The Humanistic Psychologist* 34.1 (2006).
945. White EG. "Help in Daily Living." *The Ministry of Healing.* Mountain View, Calif.: Pacific Press Publishing Association, 1909. 472.
946. John 6:64. *The Holy Bible.* Authorized King James Version.
947. Luke 1:13, 36, Luke 7:28, and Mark 6:27. *The Holy Bible.* Authorized King James Version.
948. The American Heritage® Dictionary of the English Language, Fourth Edition.Houghton Mifflin Company, 2004. 10 Mar. 2008. <Dictionary.com http://dictionary.reference.com/browse/patience>.
949. Hebrews 12:1. *The Holy Bible.* Authorized King James Version.

Chapter 21

THE DECISION TO ALLOW GERMAN SUBMARINES TO SINK AMERICAN PASSENGER SHIPS DURING WORLD WAR I WAS AN UNWISE CHOICE .

# Make Smarter Choices

***Making wise decisions can lower long-term stress in your life. Learn one of the most effective models for this from Ben Franklin.***

The year was 1917. Germany was embroiled in war with England, with the highly-effective German submarines making life especially difficult for British passenger and cargo ships. There was only one hold-up for the German subs: American citizens were aboard some British ships.

At the outset of World War I, the German army made an effort not to shoot or sink any ships with uninvolved Americans on board. This suited the United States just fine, since the country as a whole preferred the "isolationist" strategy.

Then somewhere, in the war rooms of Germany, a fateful decision was made.

"Wouldn't life be much easier if our subs didn't have to worry about who was aboard?" someone likely suggested. The German command liked the idea, and soon German subs were sinking British ships with abandon.

This turned out to be a pivotal—and very poor—decision for the Germans. So many Americans lost their lives due to this change in protocol that popular opinion in the U.S. quickly turned. The United States decided to enter the war, helping to turn the tide and defeat the Germans. Perhaps the Germans would have lost the war anyway, but their defeat was at least hastened by this military miscalculation.[950]

## BUYER'S REMORSE

Unfortunately, humans as individuals and as a race don't always make good choices. We may move through the decision-making process too hastily, rely on bad information, reason from emotion, or act on a fleeting impulse. In the real estate industry, the sense of regret felt after a poor decision is known as "buyer's remorse."

Many bad decisions could be avoided if the decision-makers involved did nothing more than allow more time to consider their options. Since "gut reactions" are quite frequently wrong, and intuition (even a woman's) can be unreliable, important decisions should never be rushed.

While there are times when snap decisions must be made (such as dangerous situations), as a rule, allowing adequate time to consider the matters at hand generally pays off handsomely in the long run. As Thomas Jefferson said, "Delay is preferred to error."

The road of life is filled with decisions, some of which are mundane and some of which will alter our lives forever.

## BEN FRANKLIN ON MAKING DECISIONS

One of the more popular and effective methods for making choices today implements a weighted decision-making model. If you have not heard of this method, you might think it was a cutting-edge, recently developed methodology. Like so many other smart strategies, however, the weighted method of decision-making has its roots far before the modern era. For an overview written in colonial days, we need to look no further than the pen of the great American inventor and philosopher Ben Franklin, who had it down to a science. In a letter addressed to Joseph Priestly, Franklin explained how he analyzed his decisions. You may read Ben Franklin's letter, with his explanation of the decision-making model, in **Figure 21.1**.[951]

Franklin's insights were certainly ahead of his time. He recommended against rash decisions, allowing several days to develop a list of pros and cons for each of the available options. Franklin's system is far superior to the decision-making model used by many today, who fool themselves into thinking they can make good choices after a few hours of unstructured discussion and "hard" thought.

Even group decisions for businesses, churches, and other organizations are frequently made in a haphazard way. Meetings which are hastily scheduled tend to jump from topic to topic. While relevant points may be subject to discussion, some equally important considerations may receive no contemplation at all. Stronger, more vocal personalities in the group may dominate the discussion, often to a degree far beyond the level justified by their knowledge or experience. Meanwhile other less forward members of the group, who may have valuable input but can't get a word in edgewise, remain painfully silent. In such a setting, a decision is finally "made" because it appears that everything has been considered, or the group is running out of time.

What a contrast it would be if Ben Franklin's method could be utilized, even in a group setting. If each member in the group were asked to consider

## BEN FRANKLIN ON MAKING DECISIONS

Dear Sir:

In the affair of so much importance to you, where in you ask my advice, I cannot, for want of sufficient premises, advise you what to determine, but if you please I will tell you how.

When those difficult cases occur, they are difficult, chiefly because while we have them under consideration, all the reasons pro and con are not present to the mind at the same time; but sometimes one set present themselves, and at other times another, the first being out of sight. Hence the various purposes or information that alternatively prevail, and the uncertainty that perplexes us.

To get over this, my way is to divide a sheet of paper by a line into two columns; writing over the one Pro, and over the other Con. Then, during three or four days consideration, I put down under the different heads short hints of the different motives, that at different times occur to me, for or against the measure.

When I have thus got them all together in one view, I endeavor to estimate their respective weights; and when I find two, one on each side, that seem equal, I strike them both out. If I find a reason pro equal to some two reasons con, I strike out the three.

If I judge some two reasons con, equal to three reasons pro, I strike out the five; and thus proceeding I find at length where the balance lies; and if, after a day or two of farther consideration, nothing new that is of importance occurs on either side, I come to a determination accordingly.

And, though the weight of the reasons cannot be taken with the precision of algebraic quantities, yet when each is thus considered, separately and comparatively, and the whole lies before me, I think I can judge better, and am less liable to make a rash step, and in fact I have found great advantage from this kind of equation, in what may be called moral or prudential algebra.

Wishing sincerely that you may determine for the best, I am ever, my dear friend, yours most affectionately,

**Figure 21.1**

the matter, writing out the pros and cons as they see them, the discussion might take an entirely different turn. The pros and cons could even be weighted, as a measure of determining which are most important to the group. At the end of the process, a combined list of pros and cons could once again be privately weighted by each individual in the group. The resulting tally would be not only enlightening, but improve the quality of decisions made in many cases.

The same type of decision-making model could be used in a family setting. By going through this process, the views of all family members would at least be recognized and heard.

## A LIFE-LONG TASK

Whether we wish to accept it or not, life is filled with decisions. Some daily decisions, such as which socks to wear or in which hand to hold the toothbrush, are so mundane we usually make them out of habit. Other choices require a little more thought, such as what we will eat for dinner, how to organize our days, and where to spend our vacation. Though these choices often seem small and insignificant, when woven together, they form the tapestry of our daily lives.

**Realizing that you are in peril is the first step toward preventing it. Even the recognition that you are lacking in judgment can be a positive sign if it helps you avoid a "slip-up."**

Then there are the life-altering decisions, those mind-boggling choices with major implications for months and frequently years into the future. Deciding on a career path, job change, relocation, marriage, divorce, parenting, or church to join all fall into this often difficult category. Thus far, this book is focused primarily on decisions about "what to think." Since some scientists estimate that humans think as many as 60,000 thoughts in one day, there are a tremendous number of decisions to make in this area alone.

Many of the principles of cognitive behavioral therapy outlined in this book can help you make better decisions. Clear-headed thinking, setting aside cognitive distortions (such as magnification, minimization, mental filters, and emotional reasoning), plays a vital role in making the best choices for your future. In addition to thinking clearly, there are a number of intelligent strategies that can assist in the decision-making process. This chapter will detail some of those important strategies which, if implemented, can vastly improve the quality of your life by helping you make better decisions.

## GOOD INFORMATION NEEDED

Of course, the weighted decision-making model described in this chapter is only as good as the information it is based upon. Basing your decision on factors that include hearsay, gut instinct, or illusory correlations (connecting bits that are not actually related) can lead to a bad decision.

While technology has made it relatively easy to accumulate vast amounts of data, the key is to determine which pieces of information are relevant to the decision at hand. Computers are great at formatting and printing out reports, but a human mind still needs to analyze and think through the data.

This task requires an attribute known as "judgment," which was defined by Webster as "the process of forming an opinion or evaluation by discerning and comparing; an opinion or estimate so formed; the capacity for judging; discernment; the exercise of this capacity; a proposition stating something believed or asserted."[952]

If you feel you are lacking in judgment, that may be a positive sign. The very fact that you recognize your lack places you miles ahead of others who are not only lacking in judgment, but also unaware of their dearth. If you are young, inexperienced, unsure of yourself, or simply venturing into previously uncharted territory, there is good news. There is much you can learn from the wisdom—and mistakes—of others. You may have heard the saying, "those who do not study history are bound to repeat it." If you do not wish to repeat the history of those who have previously failed at what you are now trying to do, study their examples—both good and bad.

The more important the matter, the more beneficial it will be to seek counsel from others who are experienced and have a history of making wise decisions on difficult issues. If possible, surround yourself with individuals who are further along on life's journey than yourself. By taking their counsel and learning from their successes and mistakes, you may ensure that your own learning curve won't be nearly as steep.

A wise mentor can often offer questions not previously thought of, contribute important insights, confirm inclinations, and remove doubts. Choose a mentor who will take the time to think things through and offer sound "big picture" or biblical advice, rather than just saying what you want to hear. In the words of the wisest man who ever lived, "plans fail for lack of counsel, but with many advisers they succeed.[953]

King Solomon's wisdom is an amazement even to many today. Some of his wise sayings are found in the book of Proverbs. While Proverbs isn't a decision-making textbook, it can provide tremendous help as we navigate through life.

The book of Proverbs promises that the counsel contained in its pages will help the reader develop the mental sharpness needed to process complex information. The book of Proverbs is a powerful tool for promoting peak mental performance and clarity. Reading, contemplating, and understanding a chapter a day can strengthen the frontal lobe of the brain and give you greater mental performance.

## PHYSICAL EFFECTS ON DECISION-MAKING

Your level of physical comfort can affect your ability to make smart choices. Some important factors that have been found to influence the high-stakes decision-making of physicians include temperature, humidity, and ambient noise. When a physician is exhausted, or uncomfortable due to heat, cold, hunger, thirst, pain, or illness, decision-making is generally less efficient.[954]

Physicans are not alone in being influenced by these factors. It doesn't take a rocket scientist to know that decision-making skills are likely to be greater when an individual is comfortable than when they are soaked in sweat, freezing cold, or physically exhausted. While there are situations where decisions need to be made under such unhappy circumstances, we can enhance our ability to make good decisions by trying to place ourselves in the best possible scenario when we make them. If you are sleep-deprived and a critical decision is at hand that doesn't have to be made today, why not wait? There is much to be gained in terms of mental clarity with so much at stake.

Research has indicated that sleep-deprived surgeons in training took longer to complete surgical tasks, made more errors, and were more stressed than surgeons who had an undisturbed night of sleep.[955] Research on pilots and other professions have also concluded that lack of sleep affects the ability of an individual to not only process information, but perform complex tasks..[956] Given the commonality of sleep needs for all human beings, the sleep-related studies on surgeons, pilots, and other professions should have serious implications for us as well.

## EMOTIONAL EFFECTS ON DECISION-MAKING

This book has devoted an entire chapter to the cognitive distortion of emotional reasoning and the negative impact it has on the process of thinking (see Chapter 9, "Let Your *Head* Do the Thinking"). Research has indicated that individuals in a good mood tend to be more optimistic in their evaluations during the decision-making process, with just the opposite being true of individuals who are in a bad mood when considering choices.[957]

A depressed individual or a woman in the throes of pre-menstrual syndrome (PMS) may save themselves future grief by recognizing their current emotional state and avoiding major decisions during that time. On the opposite side of the coin, athletes who have just won a major tournament and feel they can conquer the world may wish to regulate their jubilation when facing major decisions the next day, in the interest of achieving peak mental performance.

**Avoid decision-making when you are emotionally or physically exhausted.**

## CIRCUMSTANTIAL EFFECTS ON DECISION-MAKING

In the medical field, doctors are called upon to make many decisions that have long-term (and even life or death) implications for their patients, and often in an environment that demands rapid and accurate judgment.

Although the weighted decision-making model pioneered by Ben Franklin is certainly ideal in most situations, no surgeon or emergency room doctor has time to spend days weighing things out during a procedure. The same is true in our everyday lives, where we are often called upon to make certain important decisions "on the fly." **Figure 21.2** outlines some factors that frequently affect doctors in their split-second decisions—factors that can also play a role in the daily decisions you make.[958] These factors generally cause

## FACTORS AFFECTING DECISIONS

- **Time pressure:** When we are "under the gun," anxiety rises and we are much more likely to ignore relevant evidence and use error-prone cognitive strategies.
- **Importance:** Knowing the decision at hand is extremely important can increase our anxiety and inability to reach timely conclusions. Under that pressure, we are even more likely to ignore the evidence, relying instead on experience and intuition.
- **Fuzziness:** When choices involve a number of options or are not clear-cut, our ability to select the best solution is often impacted.
- **Reversibility:** Anxiety and difficulty reaching conclusions tends to escalate with the irreversibility of a decision. When faced with a difficult, irreversible choice, many tend to fall back on intuition and experience, placing less value on the use of evidence.
- **Incomplete information:** When evidence is incomplete, anxiety and "valleys of indecision" generally increase while reliance on objective evidence tends to decrease. Because the applicability of evidence cannot be guaranteed, judgment plays a larger role.

***Figure 21.2***

the decision-maker to rely more heavily on "gut feelings" rather than hard data, leading to a less informed, more risky decision. By becoming aware of these factors and seeking to minimize any negative impact they may have on our decision-making ability, we can set ourselves up to make better long-term choices.

### DECISION-MAKING EXAMPLES IN THE BIBLE

The Bible is filled with examples of decision-making, both good and bad. Eve made a bad choice when she wandered from Adam's side in the Garden of Eden, an even worse choice when she decided to talk to the serpent, a more damaging choice when she reached out to touch the fruit, and the most damaging choice ever when she decided to believe the serpent over God's word and ate the fruit. And that was just the beginning of sorrows—or bad decisions—for the human race.[959]

The Children of Israel made a particularly bad decision when they decided to attack the city of Ai without asking God's counsel first. There was sin in their camp, and God would have told them if they had sought His counsel. But exuberant with the confidence of victory, they decided to march on the city without His guidance.[960]

The resulting military defeat was widely reported to their other enemies, many of whom quickly marshaled their forces in hopes they could defeat what had previously seemed like an unconquerable foe, together.

There are also many examples of solid, courage-based decision-making in the Bible. One of the best would be the story of Nehemiah. While working as the cupbearer in the palace of a foreign king, Nehemiah received some very bad news from his homeland. Many of his country's exiles who had been allowed to return home were living in trouble and disgrace, and the gates of the city of Jerusalem had been burned with fire.

As a faithful member of the Israelite nation and one with strong feelings for his homeland, Nehemiah took this news pretty hard. The Bible tells that when Nehemiah heard these things, he sat down and wept. He also mourned and fasted over the situation for a number of days—and then he prayed. Nehemiah's prayer, as recorded in the Bible, was a heartfelt prayer of praise to God and confession for his people. It was also a cry for help.[961]

Nehemiah really wanted to rectify the situation, but he also knew it was quite formidable. The walls of Jerusalem were in disrepair. As for the returned exiles, they were vulnerable and disheartened.

There is much we can learn from Nehemiah's reaction to and handling of this situation. He carefully studied the situation, empathized with those who were hurting, humbled himself before God, and prayed. Nehemiah had learned a lesson that every great leader should learn: all wisdom comes from God.[962] God wants to help us make good decisions, and He is more than willing to help us in this task.

God is the perfect source of good information for our decision-making process. He is sovereign. He knows the end, the beginning, and everything in between. He knows all the options, possible scenarios, and contingency plans. Nothing has ever taken Him by surprise, and nothing ever will. We ourselves obviously don't know everything, but we can know and rely on the God who does. In His great foresight, God even incorporated the foolish, sinful decisions of people into the divine scheme of things.[963] This should be an encouragement to us as we make our decisions in life. There is a master plan to be realized if we will only stop, humble ourselves, recognize our own weakness, and take note of His divine hand at work.

## STEPS TO MAKING SMART CHOICES

Making good decisions is not a matter of skill or luck. Consistently choosing wisely depends on a reliable method of decision making and keeping the right attitude. Making good life choices also means allowing yourself to reconsider situations in which you aren't actively weighing a decision. It is easy at times to ignore areas that require decision-making attention out of complacency, neglect, or resignation that there is no alternative.

Many fall victim to the "sum-cost" effect, believing they must continue on a path simply because they've already invested considerable time, money, or effort into that course. Just because an endeavor has cost much already does not mean you should allow it to further drain energy and resources.

Once you have determined that a decision is at hand, following a predetermined process will put you in the right mind-set and increase the likelihood that you will make the best choice. Following are four steps to assist you in an objective, spiritually-based decision-making process. Refer to **Figure 21.3** for a summary of these steps.

### Step #1: Write out and weigh the pros and cons.

Write the pros and cons related to the decision and possible outcomes, and weigh the importance of each as recommended by Benjamin Franklin. When assigning weights, consider each item in light of your core values. For example, if you believe the happiness, longevity, or eternal life of your spouse or family are more important than money, give heavy consideration to those factors when weighting the pros and cons. If it is a moral decision, hold it up to your personal code of conduct.

**STEPS TO MAKING GOOD, SOUND DECISIONS**

**STEP #1: WRITE OUT AND WEIGH THE PROS AND CONS,** enlisting the counsel of trusted friends or advisors.

**STEP #2: CONSIDER THE DECISION IN LIGHT OF YOUR SPIRITUAL PRIORITIES** while seeking God for guidance.

**STEP #3: WAIT SEVERAL DAYS BEFORE FINALIZING YOUR DECISION** to allow yourself to consider all the factors.

**STEP #4: MAKE THE DECISION** in confidence, knowing you've made an informed, deliberate choice.

*Figure 21.3*

As you compile your weighted list of pros and cons, ask a trusted friend or advisor for their input on the factors in which they might provide some additional insight. Avoid asking friends "what should I do?" Rather, request their thoughtful appraisal of your situation and your list of factors. Depending on the importance and confidentiality of the decision, you may benefit from asking several trusted advisors or family members to help analyze your weighted pros and cons list. This will help to ensure that you have not forgotten key areas or been affected by cognitive bias.

One common cognitive bias is referred to as the "recency effect." This is seen when a person considers only recent events in their decision-making, while disregarding the importance of the long-term history. While recent events are fresh in our memory and may seem to hold more significance, it is prudent to take into account all relevant past experiences. Mental bias is also present when a person is only willing to listen to people and information that confirm their preconceived notions and discount those that disagree with their ideas. This "confirmation bias" is extremely detrimental to arriving at a good decision.

If you take care to prevent cognitive bias and welcome wise counsel, your weighted list of factors will be an effective and important tool in your decision-making process. "Without counsel purposes are disappointed, but in the multitude of counselors they are established."[964]

### Step #2: Consider the decision by your spiritual priorities.

**"A mind troubled by doubt cannot focus on the course to victory."**
*—Arthur Golden*

Write down your spiritual priorities, then ask yourself, "which decision best satisfies these priorities?" Reflect on the spiritual impact for you, your family, and your circle of influence. If you are confused about what your spiritual priorities should be, look for guidance in the Bible, where God has plainly revealed much of His will for our lives. If it is a moral decision, you will find clear direction in God's Word and your response is simply to obey. "We can make our own plans, but the Lord gives the right answer."[965]

As you weigh the spiritual impact of your decision, spend time in prayer. Talk to God about the pros and cons of the decision. Ask for His guidance, and claim the promise "For I know the plans I have for you," declares the Lord, "plans to prosper you and not to harm you, plans to give you hope and a future."[966] As you pray, listen for God's leading. You may find that He reveals critical areas that you have not previously thought of, or urges you to score the weighted list more objectively. Hearing from God may come in the form of a "still small voice" in your heart, or through your circumstances or surroundings. God may also speak to you through other people.

It is difficult, if not impossible, for God to help us if we think we know better than Him. As a result, it is important to seek His guidance and accept His leading, counsel, and advice. "If with all your hearts ye truly seek me, ye shall ever surely find me, thus saith our God."[967] If you truly look for Him wholeheartedly, He has promised that you will find Him. Then, because you are intimately acquainted with Him, you will hear and recognize His voice—a wonderful blessing that will, in the end, make even the most difficult of life's decisions turn out so much better.

### Step #3: Wait several days before finalizing your decision.

The more important and irreversible the decision, the more critical it is to allow adequate time for your thoughts to gel, if at all possible. It is always sensible to ruminate on your listed factors and spiritual priorities for a period before implementing a decision. This will keep you from making a decision based upon emotional reasoning, and also will permit you the time to identify all the pros and cons, request advice, seek counsel, and hear from God.

*"You can observe a lot just by watching."*
—Yogi Berra

This waiting period may also help you avoid another cognitive bias: overconfidence. Often, when a person has been successful in making good decisions in the past, either from luck or a responsible decision-making process, they become convinced that they are naturally a good decision-maker. This may lead them to become less thorough and more impulsive in their decisions, which inevitably leads to an eventual bad decision. Just by determining that you will not make any snap decisions unnecessarily, you can help prevent a poor decision influenced by overconfidence.

### Step #4: Make the decision!

When you have considered all the advice, spiritual counsel, pros and cons, and feel sure you have given yourself the very best opportunity to make an excellent decision, make the decision. Wallowing in the valley of indecision can be an ordeal in itself, so it is merit in bringing matters to a close as promptly as you can. However, if you are really uncertain about making the decision and are under no time pressure to do so, it is generally in the interest of prudence to wait. Often the choices at hand will become more clear with the passing of time, as more information becomes available. Good decisions require adequate information and careful analysis of all of the pertinent facts.

## PROVEN SUCCESS WITH DECISION-MAKING PRINCIPLES

At the age of 15, I began to employ these decision-making principles that have resulted in a far better life, not only for me, but also for many around me. At first, I had the help of my father as a trusted counselor (please see a portion of my father's eulogy in **Appendix IV**). He never told me what decision to make, he just gave me principles that helped in the decision making process. One of the first major decisions I made was in regards to marriage at an early age. My affections were set on one young woman at age 17. I just knew I wanted to marry her and spend my entire life with her. But my desire was overruled by an important principle my father had taught me years earlier: education first. The pros, including a more successful education while single, becoming a far better husband and provider by having a career first, meeting other eligible women before I made a lifelong decision, far outweighed the con of putting off my emotional desire.

Since I'd decided (using Dad's reliable principles) that the best place to obtain my needed education was at a college hours away from my home town, I thought it best to break up with my lovely girlfriend. This was not because I had developed less affection for her, but because weighing the pros and cons of staying in a young relationship while living hours apart convinced me that the wise decision was to split up. If we ended up marrying each other down the road, it would be a clearer sign that we were actually meant for each other. Although I enjoyed the company of college girls, I never allowed myself to pair off and develop affections for another girl. Without any particular girl in mind, I wrote an English composition piece entitled "The Woman Neil Nedley Will Marry." It was just a one-page summary, but it had seven character/personality attributes that this woman must have, another nine attributes of which she should have the majority, and another seven physical or personality traits that would be bonus if she had any. I took my essay home during a break and showed it to my parents. As they were smiling, my older sisters wanted to read it. My sisters then pronounced me single for life, as they did not believe such a girl existed. I told them I was happily single, and would remain so until such a woman was found.

One year later, I actually met a girl that had all seven attributes of category 1, all nine in category 2, and the majority of category 3. There were two problems. First, I did not realize she had those attributes, and second, I was still not even close to completing my education. It took me five years to become fully cognizant of this girl's attributes (which is a long interesting story, in and of itself). Just before medical school graduation, I married Erica, a decision I have never regretted. Although it seems impossible, Erica and I are actually more in love now than when we married, and our marriage has never had a downward phase. I believe our thriving marriage is a result of not only love and emotional affection, but also our determination not to compromise our priorities and stick to a rational method of decision-making.

Objective, comprehensive pro-con lists, combined with spiritual resources have also helped me make the right decisions in regards to my career, my medical specialty, where to practice medicine, what house to buy, and even where each of our boys should be educated. In regards to where to set up practice, neither Erica nor myself emotionally wanted to come to Oklahoma. We were both disappointed when Ardmore, Oklahoma came up on top of the weighted pro-con scoring system, but after the move, there has been no doubt that this was the best place for us and the raising of our four boys. In addition, it seems clear that my interest and practice of lifestyle medicine would not have flourished in the other considered locations. Although many opportunities to move have come our way, applying the objective comprehensive approach in making decisions has served us well. We both realize that if we utilize emotional reasoning in our decision making process, it will result in inevitable emotional suffering. We also realize that although we have made good decisions in the past, we must resist the temptation to become overconfident and must consistently apply the principles in this book and in this chapter in order to continue to enjoy the effects of making smart choices.

## References

950. American Entry into World War I, 1917. Ed. U.S. Department of State. Bureau of Public Affairs. 5 June 2008 <http://www.state.gov>.
951. *Mr. Franklin: A Selection From His Personal Letters*. Ed. Whitfield J. Bell Jr. and Leonard W. Labaree. New Haven, CT.: Yale University Press, 1956.
952. "judgment." Merriam-Webster Online Dictionary. 2008 Merriam-Webster Online. 5 June 2008 http://www.merriam-webster.com/dictionary/judgment
953. Proverbs 15:22. *The Holy Bible*. New International Version.
954. Samkoff JS, Jacques CH. "A review of studies concerning effects of sleep deprivation and fatigue on residents' performance." *Academic Medicine*. November 1991 - Volume 66 - Issue 11.
955. Samkoff JS, Jacques CH. "A review of studies concerning effects of sleep deprivation and fatigue on residents' performance." *Academic Medicine*. November 1991 - Volume 66 - Issue 11.
956. Samkoff JS, Jacques CH. "A review of studies concerning effects of sleep deprivation and fatigue on residents' performance." *Academic Medicine*. November 1991 - Volume 66 - Issue 11.
957. Papenhausen C. "Half full or half empty: The effects of top managers' dispositional optimism on strategic decision-making and firm performance." *Journal of Behavioral and Applied Management* (2006).
958. Sevdalis N, McCulloch P. "Teaching Evidence-based Decision-making." *Surgical Clinics Of North America* 86.1 (2006).
959. Genesis 3. *The Holy Bible*. Authorized King James Version.
960. Joshua 7. *The Holy Bible*. Authorized King James Version.
961. Nehemiah 1. *The Holy Bible*. Authorized King James Version.
962. James 1:5. *The Holy Bible*. Authorized King James Version.
963. Titus 3. *The Holy Bible*. Authorized King James Version.
964. Proverbs 15:22. *The Holy Bible*. Authorized King James Version.
965. Proverbs 16:1. *The Holy Bible*. New Living Translation.
966. Jeremiah 29:11. *The Holy Bible*. New International Version.
967. Jeremiah 29:13. *The Holy Bible*. Authorized King James Version.

Chapter 22

"JESUS SAITH UNTO THEM, I AM THE WAY, THE TRUTH AND THE LIFE..."
—*JOHN 14:6*

# Truth Matters

***Truth is the concept underpinning one of the most effective psychiatric treatments ever developed, cognitive behavioral therapy.***

Julie was devastated. She had just received notification of a mandatory meeting with her boss and the head of HR the following week. She felt certain she could predict what this meeting was about, because a rumor had been circulating around the office about layoffs, and her coworker thought he heard the boss refer to their department as unprofitable. She convinced herself that she was going to lose her job.

Over the following week, Julie became more and more upset, sleeping and eating poorly, avoiding friends and family, and performing half-heartedly at work. By the time she walked in to her appointment, she was an emotional and physical wreck. When the meeting resulted in a promotion for Julie—managing new employees that were needed to keep up with her department's soaring production—she could hardly smile because she had worked herself into such a distressed state.

Julie's reaction was based on misinformation, or untruths. Because she believed the rumors and hearsay as if they were truth, she was affected just as if the misinformation were true. Untruths are capable of causing significant angst, and sometimes lasting detriment to your health, even though they are unfounded.

## THE CBT-TRUTH CONNECTION

Truth is defined as conformity to undistorted facts or reality. Truth is in exact accordance with what is, or has been, or shall be. Truth is not just an opinion, it is the correct opinion. There is a constancy and exactness about it. And, it does matter.

The opposite of truth is not just a lie. It is a lie that is believed; a deception. Deception is usually mixed with some truth to make it more believable. That is why a deception is often called a "distortion of the truth." If correcting cognitive distortions is a large part of Cognitive Behavioral Therapy (CBT), then truth is what we seek to achieve peak mental performance.

Distortions of the truth actually cause a great deal of pain and suffering in the world, mentally and physically. Since I do many gastroenterology endoscopic procedures, I am often confronted with a common medical myth. Many people believe that those with a bowel condition called diverticulosis (out-pockets in the colon caused by lack of fiber in the diet) must avoid seeds, popcorn, nuts, tomatoes and corn. This myth was perpetuated by a surgeon who, many years ago, was operating on a patient with ruptured diverticulosis (now called diverticulitis) and found a seed caught in the diverticulum (an out-pocket). He concluded that these foods presented a danger to the patient, yet medical science has conclusively revealed that these foods actually prevent diverticulitis.[968]

*"Be transformed by the renewing of your mind."*
—Romans 12:2

High fiber foods, including seeds and nuts, actually decrease the internal colon pressure and thus can prevent the diverticulum from forming, or if it is already there, from rupturing.[969] The consequence of this myth is that many more people have undergone significant pain and suffering from diverticulitis because they were on a diet that excluded the very foods that would have helped their condition.

In the future, I have a desire to write a book about medical and health myths that have been proven as false, yet are still believed by the majority of lay people and the majority of doctors. The example above is just one of over one hundred myths that I could write about that have caused people undue pain. These health myths illustrate the point that lies that are believed can hurt you and others significantly.

Believed lies not only result in physical consequences. They often result in emotional pain and instability as well. Just as medical myths can cost us our health or even our life, other non-truths can adversely effect our emotions, our relationships, and critically affect our future success. Negative thoughts that cause emotional turmoil nearly always contain distortions, as in the example of Julie. The thoughts on the surface appear valid, but when examined more closely are irrational and wrong. Such twisted thoughts are a major cause of suffering.

Another key to achieving peak mental or physical performance is to recognize that there are a lot of truths that you don't know yet. I recently spoke at a physician assistant (P.A.) graduation ceremony. I spoke to them about two principles that were worthy of great sacrifice, one of which was truth. I reminded them that even though they learned enough to graduate, the number of truths they don't know far exceeds the number of truths they do know. In fact, even the greatest expert in a particular area often is not yet acquainted with innumerable truths about his particular area of expertise. An admission of this fact produces humility, which is the key to being teachable so that you can learn more truths.

Truth is critically connected with Cognitive Behavioral Therapy. Truth is a powerful motivator for positive lifestyle change. In fact, people only change for the better when they first come across knowledge that they are convinced is accurate.

Developing emotional intelligence also relies on truth, since non-distorted thoughts are the hallmark of a high level of emotional intelligence.

It has been said that knowledge is power. In the long run, accurate knowledge, or truth, is more potent than the most potent military force. As Abraham Lincoln said, "Force is all conquering, but it's victories are short-lived."[970] In contrast, truth's victories can be sustained for eternity. In the words of George Washington, "Truth will ultimately prevail where there is pains taken to bring it to light."[971]

As a very wise man said, "Be willing to pay any price for truth and never sell it."[972]

*"Men occasionally stumble over the truth, but most of them pick themselves up and hurry off as if nothing happened."*
—Winston Churchill

## THE COGNITIVE DISTORTIONS

The ten cognitive distortions that CBT seeks to correct are not the only untruths we tell ourselves, nor is simply identifying misbeliefs or "untruths" the only desired result. The real goal goes beyond clearing up distortions, to acknowledging and telling ourselves the truth.

So how can we know whether our thoughts are true or false? First we must listen to our thoughts, identify them, and analyze them for distortions, by using our reasoning powers. We must also pose the age-old question posed by Pontius Pilate at the trial of Jesus: "What is truth?" but unlike Pilate, we must stop and think and patiently wait for the answer.[973]

**TRUTH IS:**

- a powerful motivator for change.
- imperative in developing emotional intelligence.
- critically connected with CBT.

***Figure 22.1***

| THE DISTORTION / DECEPTION | |
|---|---|
| Incorrect All or Nothing Thinking | Everything is seen in black or white absolutes. |
| Overgeneralization | Hypothesis is held as fact, generalizations are made from too few instances. |
| Mental Filters | Focus is directed so much on one side of the issue that the other side is ignored. |
| Mind Reading | The individual is convinced he or she "knows" what other people are thinking. |
| Fortune Telling | Belief is held that one can predict certainly how situations will end. |
| Magnification or Minimization | Thoughts are out of proportion to how things actually are. |
| Personalization | Belief is held of personal control in a situation, instead of influence. |
| Emotional Reasoning | Moods and feelings are equated with the reality of actual events. |
| Mis-labeling | Incorrect definitions or distorted labels are applied. |
| Discounting the Positives | Positive aspects are acknowledged, but discounted. |

***Figure 22.2***

Some people turn to the opinions of others to assist them in clearing up distortions. Such advice is not always a reliable guide since others, and even the majority, can be very wrong. Cognitive behavioral therapists generally agree on the common untruths, which are the listed in **Figure 22.2** [974]

Despite their agreement about these distortions, many cognitive behavioral therapists do not have the answer to the question "what is truth?" Outside of reasoning, they can't tell you how to find it.

While there is truth to be found in literature, I would submit to you that the only reliable source of truth in this world—and thus the best tool for clarifying untruths in our thinking—is the Bible. This is why this book includes examples and principles found in the Bible.

## AN AGE OF MORAL RELATIVISM

We live in an age of moral relativism, where truth often seems quite elusive. In centuries past, ethical crises that arose usually centered around the violation of certain moral principles. The principles themselves (such as honesty, fair dealing, and marital fidelity) were not in dispute. Rather, scandals erupted because the principles of truth had been transgressed.

Today, however, many people are not so much concerned about principles of truth being violated as they are about the debate as to whether absolute moral principle even exist. The very idea that there is a moral right and wrong, or a group of moral absolutes, is under attack.[975] This is the essence of moral relativism and the springboard of situational ethics. These prevalent concepts center around the notion that the very determination of right and wrong, if there is such a determination at all, is relative.[976]

*"Be more concerned with your character than with your reputation. Your character is what you really are while your reputation is merely what others think you are."*
—John Wooden

It may be that this whole difficulty we have in finding the "truth" today is enhanced by the fact that modern life is filled with illusion. Thanks to the wonders of modern technology, we can immerse ourselves in "virtual realities" that seem incredibly lifelike. Although these technological wonders stimulate our senses and attempt to trick our mind into believing the fabrication, these experiences are in no way "reality." We can "Photoshop" people in and out of pictures and even video with the greatest of technological ease. Optical illusions are the stuff great Superbowl ads are made of, with High Definition TV (HDTV) making things all the more gripping.

The road to this unreal world actually started many years ago, with movie scenes where people who were not really married acted like they were, victims who were not really dead faked horrible deaths, surgeons who were not really doctors wielded the knife, and murderers who were not really killers pulled the trigger.

Is it any wonder that the truth has become a blur, when our lives are so filled with fictional entertainment? As we seek to uncover our cognitive distortions and discover what really is the truth, we would do well to distance ourselves from the illusions that characterize our day. Simplicity is not only a virtue; it is also a powerful aid to help us uncover the truth.

## QUESTIONS TO ASK IN YOUR SEARCH FOR TRUTH

- On what facts do I base this notion?
- What are the most effective arguments I can come up with to contest this notion?
- What is the evidence that this thought is true or false?
- Have I had any experiences that show me that this thought is not true all the time?
- If my best friend said this, what would I think?
- When I'm not feeling this way, would I think this?
- What has God said in His Word?

*Figure 22.3*

### TRUTH IS SOMETIMES ELUSIVE

Truth doesn't always drop conveniently into your lap. Indeed, the search for truth may be long and the end result can be difficult to discover. In some emotionally-charged situations, you may have to take minutes, hours, or even days to calm down before continuing the search for truth. When you are seeking the truth, ask yourself the helpful questions listed in **Figure 22.3** to evaluate your thoughts for accuracy and truth. It may also be necessary to request outside help in finding the truth.

When you know your thoughts are distorted and can't think of any rational (truth-filled) response to those thoughts, it may be worthwhile to write them down and try to forget about them for a few days. Then, when you are emotionally calmer and can approach the matter with a fresh perspective, you will be able to find the truth more easily. The key is to identify distorted thoughts and reconstruct them, no matter how long it takes. Then we must believe our reconstructed accurate thoughts. In time, our changed thinking will become more habitual.

This will take time, and we may feel worse before we feel better. During these times, it is important to understand that there is often a difference between feeling better and getting better. While feelings can come and go spontaneously, getting better comes with applying and reapplying the methods of accurate thinking.

## A BIBLICAL VIEW OF TRUTH

As humans, each of us is under some level of authority. Whether it is parents, teachers, a boss, a husband, our church, or the government, we can all relate to this concept. Many Christians consider God to be the ultimate authority in the universe. After all, He has the power and knowledge and to do as He pleases. However, there is another authority that, though intrinsic to the very nature of God, is also something He reckons with Himself. That authority is truth.

The Psalmist calls God "the Lord God of truth," and Jesus Himself said "I am the Way, the Truth and the Life."[977,978] The Bible calls the Holy Spirit "The Spirit of Truth," and the Bible tells us that "God does not lie."[979,980]

God cannot lie because He is the embodiment of truth and without Him, truth would not exist.[981] It exists because He exists. Some people have a problem with equating God with truth because they don't understand absolute truth. They think that if truth is intimately connected with a being, that truth will change along with the being, and thus truth is not fixed. But the Bible not only says God cannot lie; it also says that God is the same yesterday, today, and forever.[982] So God, and therefore absolute truth, does not change. Many of the world's great thinkers discover and say truthful things, but they are only (perhaps unwittingly) reflecting rays from the Author of truth.

*"Ye shall know the truth, and the truth shall make you free."*
—John 8:32

Jesus told Pilate that His whole purpose in coming into the world was to "bear witness unto the truth," and also stated that "every one that is of the truth hears my voice."[983] Christ is the truth personified. He valued truth over life itself. This fact is particularly enlightening when we reflect that one of the core tenets of Cognitive Behavioral Therapy is finding and telling ourselves the truth.

The good news is that while CBT has been around for some years now, God, through the Bible, has been advocating truth since ancient times! Paul states "whatsoever things are true, whatsoever things are honest, whatsoever things are just…if there be any virtue, and if there be any praise, think on these things."[984] David said, "I have chosen the way of truth."[985]

## THE ULTIMATE TEACHER OF TRUTH

The apostle John stated in his gospel that, during His life on this planet, Jesus shared a vast amount of truth with His disciples. These truths were difficult for them to comprehend, because the disciples had been thoroughly immersed in the half-truths and traditions of the scribes and Pharisees. Their thoughts were so filled with earthly things, so steeped in one way of thinking, that they didn't grasp many of the great truths Jesus had to share with them. Their minds had become confused. As a result, many of His lessons seemed almost lost to them.

Jesus had a strong desire to tell them more truth, but He knew that their minds would not grasp it and would actually misunderstand. In His great compassion, He promised that the Holy Spirit would come to guide them into all truth.[986] The Holy Spirit is referred to as the Spirit of truth because it is His job to define and maintain the truth. The Holy Spirit is also known as the "Comforter" because there is comfort and peace in the truth.[987]

In contrast, no real comfort or peace can be found in falsehood. Lies are the chief weapon in the arsenal of the arch enemy, as through false theories and traditions he gains power over human minds and misshapes their characters.

The Holy Spirit is God's messenger against lies.[988] When we read the Scriptures with an open mind, He impresses truth upon our heart. He then exposes error, expelling it from our very souls.

The Holy Spirit is a gift from God.[989] Just as surely as God gave His Son to die for us, He also gave the gift of the Comforter to be our continual guide and teacher. Pretty amazing, wouldn't you say? Thousands of years before psychology recognized the great value of and comfort in knowing the truth, God sent us an expert teacher to help us in this regard. Some spiritual promises for truth seekers are detailed in **Figure 22.4**.

## JESUS EMPLOYS CBT

One of the most touching stories in the Bible is told in Luke 24 of two grieving disciples traveling on the road to Emmaus shortly after the death and resurrection of Jesus. I am indebted to R.N. and pastor, Don Mackintosh, for pointing out to me that Jesus employed CBT in this interaction (summarized in **Figure 22.5**). The disciples were discussing the great events that had recently taken place, including the crucifixion. The Bible tells us that their faces were very downcast. As they were talking, Jesus Himself came and walked with them. However, they were kept from recognizing Him.

"What are you discussing together as you walk along?" Jesus asked them.

"Are you only a visitor to Jerusalem and do not know the things that have happened there in these days?" came back the reply.

| SPIRITUAL PROMISES FOR TRUTH SEEKERS |
| --- |
| "LORD, who shall abide in thy tabernacle? who shall dwell in thy holy hill? He that walketh uprightly, and worketh righteousness, and speaketh the truth in his heart." Psalms 15:1,2 |
| "Sanctify them through they truth. Thy word is truth." John 17:17 |

*Figure 22.4*

## CBT ON THE ROAD TO EMMAUS

- The falsehoods or cognitive distortions were diagnosed, disputed, and uprooted.
- The truth was told that Christ's sacrificial death was a fulfillment of prophecy and necessary for Him to be a Redeemer.
- The disciples were re-energized and reoriented to the source of all truth, the Scriptures.
- They were then able and motivated to share the truth and comfort they had received with others.

***Figure 22.5***

"What things?" Jesus asked, not because He didn't know, but because He wanted to hear it from them. Sadly the two disciples recounted the events of the crucifixion, even mentioning that the body of Jesus was now missing and some women claimed He had been resurrected. They actually revealed their own distortions when they said, "We had hoped that he was the one who was going to redeem Israel." They had believed that Christ was to be a conquering king and there was no way He could lose. They also thought they would share in His rule. Because of Christ's death, they no longer believed that He was the Redeemer.

Jesus began by addressing this major "cognitive distortion." He must have spoken very kindly, because He managed to tell them they were foolish and should have known better, yet they didn't take offense. Jesus not only addressed the distortion or misbelief, He went on to reason with them and share the truth. Jesus' source of truth was not pulled out of the air, it was scripture. Then "beginning with Moses and all the Prophets, He explained to them what was said in all the scriptures concerning himself."

Though fascinated with the truths they were hearing, the disciples still did not recognize Jesus. When they reached their destination, Jesus acted as if He were traveling on. He stayed to eat with them, however, after they urged Him strongly. It was then, as He broke the bread and gave thanks, that their eyes were finally opened and they recognized Him, and He immediately vanished from their sight. What a story!

"Were not our hearts burning within us while He talked with us on the road and opened the Scriptures to us?" they asked each other. They had been depressed, but now they were filled with new hope. Instead of turning in for the night, they retraced their steps back to Jerusalem (a full seven miles) to tell the other disciples.

In the story of the disciples on the road to Emmaus, the ABCs of cognitive behavioral therapy can be expanded to the "A through Gs:"

**A**ctivating event: Christ had died after a cruel, unfair trial.

**B**elief: They now understand that Christ's death on the cross was an important fulfillment of Bible prophecy. As a result of their newfound belief about the activating event, they now also had a new…

**C**onsequence: Though still sorrowful, they were now rejoicing! They had undergone this great positive change (behavioral and emotional) because they had…

**D**isputed: Their faulty beliefs had been disputed and uprooted! Furthermore, they had…

**E**valuated: And through that evaluation, realized that what had seemed like a great disappointment was really an appointment. As a result, they now saw an incredible…

**F**uture: Because of their irrational beliefs, the disciples had actually become unbelievers. After receiving CBT, they were not only believers, but bold and blessed. Because of this new understanding and hope, they now had…

**G**oals: Their first goal, which was to clear up the thinking of the eleven remaining disciples of Jesus, was quickly expanded to include the city of Jerusalem, then Samaria. Soon they were taking the message "to the uttermost parts of the earth!"

*"The truth is found when men are free to pursue it."*
—Franklin Roosevelt

Many Christians accurately believe that Christianity would be nothing without the resurrection. But it wasn't just the resurrection alone that expanded Christianity after the cross. It was the resurrection plus cognitive behavioral therapy, using the Scriptures as the source of truth, which propelled Christianity into a greatly expanded movement, a movement that would circle the globe.

This story of the disciples on the road to Emmaus provides an ancient example of how CBT positively affects motivation and goals. Another excellent tool, and one which I highly recommend, is featured in **Figure 22.6**. When CBT is properly applied, E.Q. is improved, motivation spirals upward, and goals are set and eventually met. When the mind is thus cleared, it opens the way for the Holy Spirit to work in a mighty way, such as it did at Pentecost. This is why, when people utilize Scripture (truth) to correct their distorted thoughts, it can have a long lasting positive effect on them, and this can spread the affect to the entire world.

## AN EXCELLENT TOOL FOR R.E.S.T.

One of the more helpful tools in discovering truth, and combining it with spiritual therapy, is studying the book of Daniel.

Daniel is a classic, non-sectarian book. The Jews, Muslims, and Christians all revere Daniel.

Each chapter in the book of Daniel starts out with a disappointment and ends with an appointment. Going from disappointment to appointment does not happen without a cause, however.

In each chapter, there is at least one spiritual key that turned the disappointment to an appointment. These spiritual keys are applicable to your life as well.

I recommend a thoughtful, thorough study of the book of Daniel to assist you in obtaining peak mental performance through Rational Emotive Spiritual Therapy (REST).

***Figure 22.6***

This was just one of many instances where Jesus met error with truth and corrected crooked thinking. Jesus was the Master of both CBT and another term used to describe it: REST (Rational Emotive Spiritual Therapy). His truth claims were not pulled out of the air, but were biblical and spiritual in nature. "It is written" was His watchword, the Scriptures were His safeguard.[990] Because of this, He was, and still is, "the Way, the Truth and the Life."[991] It is no coincidence that He is also called the Prince of Peace—for only in finding the truth do we find real peace.[992] May we all be changed by the truth that God so wants to transform the world with.

## References

968. Strate LL. *Journal of the American Medical Association*, July 27, 2008.
969. Aldoori WH, et al. "A prospective study of diet and the risk of symptomatic diverticular disease in men."*Am J Clin Nutr* 1994 60: 757-764.
970. Churchill JW, Harris J. *The Andover review: a religious and theological monthly, Volume 10.* Houghton Mifflin & Company, Cambridge, MA. 1885. 24.
971. Washington G. *Writings of George Washington.* Russell, Odiorne, and Metcalf, and Hilliard, Gray & Company. Cambridge, MA. 1834. 450.
972. Proverbs 23:23. *Clear Word Bible.* Review and Herald Publishing. Silver Spring, MD. 1994.
973. John 18:37-38. *The Holy Bible.* Authorized King James Version.
974. Burns DD. *Feeling Good: The New Mood Therapy.* New York: Avon-HarperCollins, 1999. 8-11.
975. Singhapakdi A, Vitell SJ, Leelakulthanit O. "A Cross-cultural Study of Moral Philosophies, Ethical Perceptions and Judgements: A Comparison of American and Thai Marketers", *International Marketing Review*, Vol. 11 Iss: 6, pp.65 – 78. 1994.
976. Beckwith FJ, Koukl G. *Relativism: Feet Firmly Planted in Mid-air.* Grand Rapids, Mich. : Baker Books, c1998.
977. Psalms 31:5. *The Holy Bible.* Authorized King James Version.
978. John 14:6. *The Holy Bible.* Authorized King James Version.
979. John 16:13. *The Holy Bible.* Authorized King James Version.
980. Titus 1:2. *The Holy Bible.* Authorized King James Version.
981. Titus 1:2. *The Holy Bible.* Authorized King James Version.
982. Hebrews 13:1. *The Holy Bible.* Authorized King James Version.
983. John 18:37. *The Holy Bible.* Authorized King James Version.
984. Philippians 4:8. *The Holy Bible.* Authorized King James Version.
985. Psalms 119:30. *The Holy Bible.* Authorized King James Version.
986. John 16:13. *The Holy Bible.* Authorized King James Version.
987. Psalms 119:30. *The Holy Bible.* Authorized King James Version.
988. John 16:13. *The Holy Bible.* Authorized King James Version.
989. Acts 2:38. *The Holy Bible.* Authorized King James Version.
990. Acts 44:7. *The Holy Bible.* Authorized King James Version.
991. John 14:6. *The Holy Bible.* Authorized King James Version.
992. Isaiah 96. *The Holy Bible.* Authorized King James Version.

# Chapter 23

THE VOLUNTEER "BOYS OF POINTE DU HOC" TOOK ON THE "MOST DANGEROUS MISSION OF D-DAY."

# Love to Live

***A growing body of research shows altruism and unselfish love promote sound mental health, and life itself, in the giver.***

Turbulent waves in the English Channel buffeted the column of tiny, cramped landing boats carrying Lt. Col. Rudder and his 225 U.S. Army Rangers on June 6, 1944. The men, who had volunteered for the "most dangerous mission of D-Day," peered across the heaving seas at their objective: the looming cliff at Pointe du Hoc, France.

The success of the entire D-Day invasion hinged largely on the action of this highly trained force. Their task: to scale the 100-foot cliffs at Point du Hoc, destroy six powerful artillery guns, cut German communications, set-up roadblocks, and hinder enemy reinforcements from reaching the beaches.

The massive guns at the top of Pointe du Hoc's 100-foot cliffs, with their 15-mile range and position overlooking two beaches, posed a major threat to the D-Day invasion. If the mission wasn't successful, those guns would decimate Allied troops as they stormed the beaches of Normandy below. It seemed like an impossible job, but those guns had to be destroyed—and it was the ranger's job to do it.

Against all odds, and with courage that defied self-preservation, the rangers braved raging seas, heavy bombing, towering cliffs, expert snipers, and a savage defense by the Germans to successfully complete their mission.

After waiting three days for rescue with little food or ammunition, only 50 of Rudder's Rangers remained standing, but they stood tall.[993]

40 years after that fateful day, President Ronald Reagan paid tribute to the men who conquered the cliff. Twenty-two of the surviving rangers, who traveled to France for the memorial service, were seated in Reagan's audience for the now famous speech that would be compared to Lincoln's Gettysburg Address.

*"Do not let what you cannot do interfere with what you can do."*
—John Wooden

"These are the boys of Pointe du Hoc," said the President. "These are the men who took the cliffs. These are the champions who helped free a continent. These are the heroes who helped end a war."[994] Then he turned to the row of rangers sitting beneath his podium, asking them questions that still echo off the cliffs of Pointe du Hoc.

"You were young the day you took these cliffs; some of you were hardly more than boys, with the deepest joys of life before you. Yet, you risked everything here. Why? Why did you do it? What impelled you to put aside the instinct for self-preservation and risk your lives to take these cliffs?"[995]

Why indeed? Why would anyone volunteer for the most dangerous mission of D-Day? Why would anyone looking at a 100-foot cliff, with grenades exploding around him, comrades drowning or falling with machine gun wounds, be so filled with courage, so steeled against fear, so intent on their goal that they would choose the death-defying act rather than escape the entire deadly scenario?

While there are multiple answers to the above questions, one thing seems certain: the men who scaled the cliffs of Pointe du Hoc were willing to sacrifice their comfort, safety, and even their lives for a cause they saw as greater than themselves. There was nothing for them to gain personally by scaling those cliffs. They did what they did in the service of their country, with an altruistic spirit that reached far beyond themselves.

## ALTRUISM UNDER ATTACK

Good deeds done for selfish reasons don't really qualify as altruistic, since by definition altruism involves selflessly giving without a hope for reward.[820] Even so, truly altruistic acts occur all the time by genuine people. While they do exist, the values of self-sacrifice and altruism have come under attack in our society today. Some have even argued that true altruism, the unselfish act of doing good for someone else without expecting a reward, doesn't really exist.

This was the case with Erik Roby, who once made that very argument in a University of Kentucky philosophy class. Roby knows differently now, after a complete stranger donated a kidney that saved his life.[996] The altruistic stranger, a regional restaurant manager, was passing through town when he overheard someone discussing Erik's need for an organ donor with O-positive blood. After giving the matter some thought and talking it over with family and friends, Larry Smiley contacted Erik, who could hardly believe his ears.

"I told my dad not to get too excited," he said later. "This is some random guy off the street we don't even know who only overheard the conversation. I was just so skeptical about the whole thing."[997] But Larry was serious about the offer, and his unselfish organ donation for a complete stranger not only saved, but transformed Erik Roby's life.

"It really did change my mind on the whole altruism debate," Erik told his local newspaper, adding that words couldn't describe what Larry had done for him.[946] As father of a 4-month-old child, he wanted to be around to raise his little girl, yet didn't see how that could happen. Erik found Larry's attitude, as well as his generosity, to be truly amazing.

"He expects nothing from me in return, not even a thank you," Erik said. "It brings tears to my eyes thinking about what type of person he is. If more people were like Larry, the world would be a completely different place."[998]

Larry doesn't think what he did was all that special, commenting that he is an average person who simply did what he needed to do. "It's about Erik getting a kidney, feeling better, growing up healthy as a son and father with someone he loves. It's about him getting better." But Larry did receive something, unknowingly, in exchange for his selfless act. In helping Erik, he actually helped himself to improved mental wellness.

## BENEFITS OF ALTRUISM

There is mounting evidence that altruism is definitely beneficial to the health of the giver—even more health-giving than family ties or social relationships. Some of these benefits are listed in **Figure 23.1**.[849,850] While having close relationships with family and friends is good, bringing the selfless focus

### HEALTH BENEFITS OF ALTRUISM

- greater sense of well-being
- better physical and mental health
- higher levels of happiness and enjoyment in life
- increased ability to handle the death of a spouse
- longer lifespan
- more involvement and better social life
- higher self-esteem
- more self-confidence and faith in the future
- lower stress levels
- increased likelihood of healthy lifestyle choices

***Figure 23.1***

of helping others into those relationships is even better. Studies have shown that, as long as the altruistic individuals are not overwhelmed by "helping tasks," unselfish emotions and behaviors are associated with greater well-being, health, happiness, and longevity.[999,1000] Scientific research by a Stanford University professor on thousands of subjects also made a strong case for the health benefits of altruistic behaviors such as volunteering one's time.

In this study, the older Americans (greater than 70 years old) who volunteered most had a significantly lower risk of death than those who never volunteered.[1001] Depending on the subgroup studied, this decrease in mortality rate reached 60 percent or more.

## HAPPY AND HEALTHY

In addition to the health benefits attributed to altruism by this growing body of research, evidence is mounting about the "happiness index" of altruistic individuals. Altruistic behavior increases more than the lifespan of those who practice the principle of "giving while living;" it increases the likelihood that they will be happier throughout their lives as well.[1002]

**Volunteerism is often motivated by the concept of altrusism.**

For example, a recent German study found that altruism and health were the two most significant factors providing meaning in life for individuals in their 60s.[1003] Another compelling study which used a "prosociality scale" to measure altruistic behavior found that those scoring higher on the scale were more happy, active, sociable, involved, and had a greater level of enjoyment than those with low scores.[1004] The same study also shed light on the intersection between faith and altruism, as investigators found that individuals who were religious and scored high on the prosociality scale "reported higher self esteem, self-confidence, and faith in the future" than those who scored equally well on the scale but were "non-religious."[1005]

Yunqing Li, PhD, reviewed the research literature on the subject of volunteerism and health and found that volunteer participation reduced stress and increased the likelihood that one would make healthful lifestyle choices.[957] Dr. Li's own research on volunteerism in the context of widowhood yielded similar conclusions. She found that, following the loss of a spouse, volunteer activities decreased the risk of depression and increased one's sense of control in life.

Of course, not all volunteers are motivated by altruism. Up-and-coming professionals frequently volunteer on non-profit boards as a means of developing leadership skills, networking, and building a public image.

Interestingly enough, one research study suggested that the level of one's commitment to the volunteering venture may be critical to obtaining optimum quality-of-life benefits. The study, conducted by Dr. Van Willigen of East Carolina University, found that volunteers 60 years old or older appeared to reap greater benefits from volunteerism than younger volunteers.[1006]

After reviewing the evidence, Dr. Van Willigen suggested that "the context in which older and younger adults volunteer and the meaning of their volunteerism" were likely explanations for the differential in benefit received.[1007] In other words, a young person who volunteers primarily for job experience (i.e., to further their personal career aspirations) may not get the same benefits that come to a senior who volunteers from true altruistic motives.

In an unrelated study of 2000 Presbyterian Church members, a researcher at the University of Massachusetts Medical School found that providing help to others "was a more important predictor of better reported mental health than receiving help."[961] This provides scientific evidence for the biblical statement, "It is more blessed to give than to receive."

These and other data present a clear picture that focusing on the needs of others is critical to our own health and well-being. As the wise man said centuries ago: "Cast thy bread upon the waters, for thou shalt find it after many days."[1008] Indeed, by helping others we help ourselves.

## ALTRUISM IN NATURE

The benefits of altruism are not exclusive to humans. Some of the altruistic cycles of nature are described in **Figure 23.2.** There are also many examples of altruistic behavior in the animal world that are associated with positive health effects. For example, it is believed that about 10 percent of bird species show "cooperative breeding" behavior in which one or more mated pairs produce chicks that are fed not only by the parents, but by other birds sharing

### THE WATERFALL TAKES TO GIVE...

There is nothing, except the selfish heart of man, that lives only to please itself. There is no bird that graces the skies, no animal that moves upon the ground, that doesn't contribute to the well-being of some other form of life. Every tree and leaf and shrub pours forth that essential element, without which neither man nor animal could live. In turn, both men and animals minister to the life of tree, shrub and leaf. The fragrance of flowers blesses the world, while the ocean receives the streams from every land, but takes to give. The mists ascending from the ocean fall in showers to water the earth, that even more flowers may grow...

God wants us to give cheerfully, willingly, and gladly. It is impossible to keep His law of love without ministering to or giving to others. Only when we work for the good of others, will we be truly happy.

***Figure 23.2***

the territory as well.[1009] Scientists researching the Australian superb fairy-wren found that female birds who were breeding cooperatively had an 80% chance of surviving the next year, compared to a 67% chance for females raising their young without "helpers." In this study, as well as in an unrelated study of African starlings, researchers found that cooperative, altruistic breeding enabled the birds to produce more eggs, thereby improving the survival rate for the species.[1010]

Researchers studying the Common Guillemot found that "allopreening," where the birds removed parasites and helped to maintain the plumage of other birds, resulted in less stress, fewer fights, higher breeding success, and long-term benefits for the survival of the offspring.[1011] Female ants and wasps devote their long and complex lives to the service of their queen and her young, while amoebas (a form of pond organism) give up their lives so that other amoebas can survive and later multiply.[1012,1013,1014]

In each of these examples, altruistic behavior has been tied to the greater good of the recipient, offspring, or species. Despite the cruelty that often takes place in nature, altruism is alive and well in the animal kingdom.

## EVOLUTION'S DILEMMA

Although examples of altruism in nature, animals, and humans are abundant, the macro evolutionary theory has had a difficult time deciding whether altruism is as "primal" an impulse as ferocity, lust, and greed.[1015] Evolution, with its focus on natural selection, doesn't do much to explain acts of extreme self-sacrifice such as when a bee dies to defend a hive or an animal spends its whole life helping others rear their children instead of having its own.

According to evolution, extreme altruists have no descendants, since they either sacrifice themselves for others or are too busy being helpers to raise their own young.

**Evolution, with it's emphasis on primal instincts, has a hard time explaining the presence of altruistic love.**

In an effort to ease the evolutionary predicament of trying to explain how altruism could "evolve" in a worldview that seems more dog-eat-dog than anything else, evolutionist William Hamilton speculated about the existence of an "altruistic gene" which could actually be passed between generations. "Hamilton's rule" proposes that genes which promote altruistic actions will spread if the benefit of the act is high enough, and the relationship between the altruist and beneficiary is close enough to outweigh the cost of the self-sacrificing deed to the altruist.[1016] Hamilton divided altruistic animal behaviors into two categories: "cheap" ones, which don't have much cost to the giver (such as when a dog barks to warn others of danger), and "expensive" behaviors, such as when a bird spends its entire life raising the offspring of others. Although he went to great lengths to rationalize the altruistic behaviors he observed, even Hamilton couldn't deny the existence of genuine altruism. The truth is, unselfish love is not only alive and well among animals and humans alike, it is a fundamental characteristic of how we were designed.

## WHAT'S LOVE GOT TO DO WITH IT?

Many scientists besides Hamilton are perplexed by the rapidly accumulating body of evidence revealing that humans are engineered for love rather than merely existing as biological survival machines. Without love, our bodies fail to thrive.

*"Try not to become a man of success but rather try to become a man of value."*
—Albert Einstein

In one study, researchers measured social support by posing several questions that inquired if the participants felt they had friends or family that they could count on to care for them in times of need. Their answers indicated whether they felt they had someone who loved and cared for them. Those that replied "no" were three to five times more at risk for premature death and disease from all causes than those that offered one or more close relationships they could rely on. The increased risk includes everything from allergies and alcoholism to autoimmune diseases and cancer. The same degree of risk increase was found in both people who were healthy and those who were unhealthy at the beginning of the study.[1017,1018,1019] In addition, the people that answered "yes" to having loving support were more likely to choose life-enhancing behaviors than self-destructive ones.[1020,1021,1022]

In another study, scientists at Yale documented the effect of love on the health of 119 men and 40 women who were undergoing coronary angiography. Those who felt the most loved and supported had substantially less coronary artery blockage. The researchers found that the emotional factors were significant predictors of the severity of artery blockage, and this remained true even when controlling for age, diet, exercise, cholesterol, diabetes, and other influential factors. In other words, the availability of deep emotional relationships was associated with less coronary stress, independent of standard risk factors.[1023,1024]

While the data on love and health is just recently gaining more attention, the findings are not new. Even in the thirteenth century, studies showed the importance of intimacy to human survival. In a cruel but telling experiment, the German king Frederick II conducted an observation intended to determine what language children would grow to speak if they were never spoken to. Babies were placed in the care of nurses who were forbidden to touch or speak to the infants. The shocking result was that the babies spoke no language at all—because they all died. They could not live without the sense of love and connection that is communicated through human contact.[1025,1026]

The famed Dr. Dean Ornish studied the effects of love on human well-being and presents his findings in his book *Love and Survival.* Ornish cites numerous studies that demonstrate how love is the main factor in determining mental, emotional, and physical health. He concludes that "anything that promotes feelings of love and intimacy is healing; anything that promotes isolation, separation, loneliness, loss, hostility, anger, cynicism, depression, alienation, and related feelings often leads to suffering, disease, and premature death from all causes."[1027,1028]

The research shows that it is not simply affection, heroic gestures, or volunteerism that humans need to thrive, but genuine love. The love that is active in the examples above—the kind of love that is life-giving—is not the same sort of "love" referred to so prolifically in pop culture. It is not romantic love, or brotherly love, or even the kind of "love" one professes for a favorite food or fashion or sports team. The love that sustains life is unconditional love that expects no reward and requires nothing from the recipient. This selfless principle is exemplified in the following story.

At 2 a.m. on February 26, 1852, the Royal Navy troopship Birkenhead struck a rock two miles off the coast of South Africa. Besides the troops, who were nearly all young recruits, there were about twenty women and children. When the ship hit Danger Point while rounding the Cape, the water rushed in and drowned many soldiers in their hammocks. The remainder fell-in on deck under their officers, manned the pumps, and got the few lifeboats safely away with the women and children.

When the ship broke up, the commander called on his men to stand fast, lest they should endanger the nearby lifeboats by jumping overboard. Though facing certain death by obeying, the men bravely kept rank and went down with the ship. Of the 643 on board, only 193 survived; but all the women and children were saved.

The unselfish bravery of these troops fired the world's imagination, and their story was read aloud to every regiment in the Prussian Army as an example of supreme discipline, courage, and self-sacrifice.[1029]

There was nothing reciprocal about the sacrifice of these troops, or of many others who have made similarly gallant choices. And such heroics, while admirable, are not all that rare. Humans, such as the firemen going into the collapsing World Trade Center, often risk their lives for total strangers.[1030] True unrestricted love gives even when there is no hope of an equal return for the giver.

If the evolutionary theory were true then the logical conclusion would be that we should be impersonal creatures governed only by our survival instinct. But the evidence indicates that humans are psychologically and biologically dependent on giving and receiving love.

**September 11, tsunamis, hurricanes, and other disasters provide many anecdotal examples of altruism in action.**

There is one universal desire that pulses through all of humanity that is not explained by science. Each and every person has a longing, and the need, to love and be loved. The common thread that unites us all is the need to experience the exchange of unreserved commitment, absolute trust, and substantial, deep, unalterable love. And it is the exchange that is pivotal—the desire to be trustworthy, loyal, devoted, and true is just as vital as the desire to be perfectly valued and cared for.

Because science shows that we operate optimally with the life-sustaining principle of love, could it be that the only real explanation is a personal God who created human beings to love? Our insatiable desire for unfailing love exists because we were originally made in the "image of God," and "God is love."[1031,1032] The inner workings of the human psyche was crafted after the pattern of a divine God whose essential character is love. Could it be that the only complete way to find the answer to our longing, to fulfill our desire by expressing altruistic love, is to seek the God that is the source of this love?

Author Ty Gibson states the results of his own research in this way: "The deepest rational sense of our hearts is speaking to us of the ultimate "Other," but we're trying hard not to listen. We're expecting the data to end up pointing to ourselves as the highest reality, except it's not pointing that way. What's happening on the frontiers of knowledge is that the more we know, the more obvious it's becoming that there is more to reality than the observable, material universe."[1033]

## TAKING LOVE A STEP FURTHER

One of the best definitions of altruistic love is actually in the Bible. This well-known passage has been considered so pivotal on the topic, that it is commonly called the "Love Chapter." As helpful as 1 Corinthians 13 can be, however, it barely scratches the surface of what unselfish or altruistic love truly is. To get an even deeper understanding, we must not only read about it, but see it with flesh and bones on it, so to speak.

*"What a man desires is unfailing love."*

—Proverbs 19:22, NIV

One way to see altruistic love in action is in the lives of other people, as there are many in this world who value and practice the principle of agape (the biblical Greek word for altruism) love. When parents put the interests of their children above their own, they are practicing altruistic love. When a teacher tirelessly gives extra time to a struggling, handicapped student, she is practicing altruistic love. And when a hero or heroine knowingly makes the ultimate sacrifice, giving up their own life to save the life of another, they are practicing the ultimate form of altruistic love.

No doubt this is what makes the story of Jesus Christ and the phenomenal sacrifice He made on the cross so very compelling. To think of someone so incredibly wealthy, gifted, loved, and blessed giving up all of that to be born to an impoverished couple, under the stigma of illegitimacy, defies comprehension. To give up exuberant life and happiness, for a life of shouldering the burdens of ailing humans, boggles the naturally selfish mind. To be deserted by one's very best friends, denied and betrayed in a critical hour of need, is more than most people could fathom.

Add to that being scourged, dragged, slapped, and strung up, publicly naked on one of earth's cruelest inventions, and the burden seems truly unbearable.

But there was more. Add a heaping dose of watching one's aging, anguished mother suffering through it all. Add the taunts of a crowd, the silence of supporters, and worst of all, the lack of His Father's presence as black clouds encircled the cross. What creed, what motivation, what incentive could there be to go through this incredible physical and emotional flagellation—all for lowly rabble who apparently didn't even appreciate it?

## THE CBT-ALTRUISM CONNECTION

The following chart demonstrates how the biblical "Love chapter" (1 Corinthians 13) effectively corrects the ten cognitive distortions central to CBT.

| | | |
|---|---|---|
| **1.** | All-or-nothing thinking | *You* look at things in absolute categories and insist on your own way. *Love* is not self-seeking. (v. 5) |
| **2.** | Overgeneralization | *You* view a few trials as a never-ending pattern of defeat. *Love* always perseveres. (v. 7) |
| **3.** | Mental filter | *You* view your circumstances in a negative light. *Love* always protects. *Love* rejoices in the truth. (v. 6) |
| **4.** | Mind reading | *You* assume that people are reacting negatively to you when there's no definite evidence for this. *Love* always trusts. (v. 7) |
| **5.** | Fortune telling | *You* arbitrarily predict that things will turn out badly. *Love* never gives up hope. (v. 7) |
| **6.** | Magnification or minimization | *You* inappropriately magnify yourself and minimize the value of others. *Love* is not boastful or proud. (v. 4) |
| **7.** | Personalization and blame | *You* blame yourself for something you weren't entirely responsible for, or blame others and overlook your own contribution to a problem. *Love* keeps no record of wrongs. Love does not dishonor others. (v. 5) |
| **8.** | Emotional reasoning | *You* reason from how you feel: "I feel like an idiot, so I must be one." Or "I don't feel like doing this, so I shouldn't do it." *Love* does not delight in evil, but rejoices in the truth. (v. 6) |
| **9.** | Labeling | *You* identify with your shortcomings, telling yourself, "I'm a loser," or you classify someone else as a jerk for their mistakes. *Love* is very patient and very kind. *Love* is not easily angered. (v. 4, 5) |
| **10.** | Discounting the positives | *You* claim that your accomplishments or positive qualities "don't count." *Love* does not envy. *Love* rejoices in the truth. (v. 5, 6) |

***Figure 23.3***

Especially if one had the power to come down off the cross at any moment, or call fire down from heaven? The answer is found in two words: agape love.

Is it any wonder that one author who recommended we read the Love Chapter (1 Corinthians 13) through each day, also wrote that we would all be much benefited if we spent a thoughtful hour each day contemplating what happened at the cross?[92] We may read hundreds of self-help books and undergo months of therapy, and these may be helpful and good. But there is nothing quite so powerful, so transforming, so life-changing as time spent thinking on the ultimate, earth-shattering demonstration of all-out agape love. A brief summary of some major points in this famous Biblical description of altruistic love, and how they relate to cognitive behavioral therapy, is detailed in **Figure 23.3**.[858]

**Christians see the sacrifice of Jesus on the cross as the best demonstration of altruistic love—ever.**

It's true that some people exemplify agape love outside of the Christian realm. Admiring the virtue of unselfishness, they have chosen to practice it in their lives. But the ultimate passion for others, the epitome of agape love, is found at the foot of the cross. Amazing, isn't it? The life-changing principle so foundational to Cognitive Behavioral Therapy was exemplified in its highest form over two thousand years ago. How intriguing it is that, after decades of Freudian and similar "thought innovations," the secular world of psychology is now scientifically promoting a therapeutic model that really has roots in the Bible.

The Bible has a lot to say about agape love. One of the claims it makes is that all such love comes from God. In other words, naturally selfish human beings cannot possess agape love apart from God. So whether a person realizes it or not, such unselfish love in action comes as a result of His divine influence.

## THE CBT CONNECTION

Given the overwhelming data showing the mental and physical benefits of altruism, the concept of unselfish "love" has become an integral, irreplaceable element of Cognitive Behavioral Therapy.

There are some fascinating correlations between the principles of altruism and CBT—principles that have been known since ancient times. CBT is all about telling ourselves, and others, the truth. Many of the cognitive distortions have to do with thinking inaccurate negative thoughts about ourselves or others. Pride (magnification of self), one of the ten cognitive distortions to be avoided, is the exact opposite of altruistic love.

Selfless, unconditional love drives out cognitive distortions, and brings emotional, mental, and spiritual health. This one principle effectively and comprehensively addresses the frontal lobe of the brain, and therefore supports emotional wellness and excellent mental performance.

## References

993. Brinkley D. *The Boys of Pointe Du Hoc: Ronald Reagan, D-Day, and The U.S. Army 2nd Ranger Battalion*. New York: W. Morrow, 2005.
994. Brinkley D. *The Boys of Pointe Du Hoc: Ronald Reagan, D-Day, and The U.S. Army 2nd Ranger Battalion*. New York: W. Morrow, 2005.
995. Brinkley D. *The Boys of Pointe Du Hoc: Ronald Reagan, D-Day, and The U.S. Army 2nd Ranger Battalion*. New York: W. Morrow, 2005.
996. Shafa D. "Altruistic gift: Stranger donates kidney to Owensboro native." Owensboro Messenger-inquirer 28 Oct 2007. 29 Feb. 2008 <http://www.courierpress.com/news/2007/oct/28/altruistic-gift-stranger-donates-kidney-to/>.
997. Shafa D. "Altruistic gift: Stranger donates kidney to Owensboro native." Owensboro Messenger-inquirer 28 Oct 2007. 29 Feb. 2008 <http://www.courierpress.com/news/2007/oct/28/altruistic-gift-stranger-donates-kidney-to/>.
998. Shafa D. "Altruistic gift: Stranger donates kidney to Owensboro native." Owensboro Messenger-inquirer 28 Oct 2007. 29 Feb. 2008 <http://www.courierpress.com/news/2007/oct/28/altruistic-gift-stranger-donates-kidney-to/>.
999. Schwartz C, Meisenhelder JB, Ma Y, Reed G. "Altruistic Social Interest Behaviors Are Associated With Better Mental Health." *Psychosom Med* 2003 65: 778-78.
1000. Wilson J. "Volunteering." *Annual Review of Sociology*. Vol. 26: 215-240 (Volume publication date August 2000).
1001. Harris AHS, Thoresen CE. "Volunteering is Associated with Delayed Mortality in Older People: Analysis of the Longitudinal Study of Aging." Journal of Health Psychology 10.6 (2005). 5 Mar. 2008 <http://hpq.sagepub.com/cgi/content/abstract/10/6/739>.
1002. Post S. "Altruism, Happiness and Health: It's Good to be Good." *International Journal of Behavioral Medicine*. 2005. 12: 66-77.
1003. Fegg MJ, et al. "Meaning in life in the Federal Republic of Germany: Results of a representative survey with the Schedule for Meaning in Life Evaluation [SMiLE]." Health and Quality of Life Outcomes 5.59 (2007).
1004. Post, SG (editor). "Health and The Ecology of Altruism." Altruism and Health: Perspectives From Empirical Research. New York: Oxford University Press, 2007.
1005. Post, SG (editor). "Health and The Ecology of Altruism." Altruism and Health: Perspectives From Empirical Research. New York: Oxford University Press, 2007.
1006. Van Willigen M. "Differential Benefits of Volunteering across the Life Course." Journal of Gerontology: Social Sciences (2000).
1007. Van Willigen M. "Differential Benefits of Volunteering across the Life Course." Journal of Gerontology: Social Sciences (2000).
1008. Ecclesiastes 11:1. *The Holy Bible*. Authorized King James Version.
1009. Russell AF, et al. "Maternal investment tactics in superb fairy-wrens." Proc Biol Sci. 275.1630 (2008): 29+.
1010. Rubenstein DR, Lovette IJ. "Temporal Environmental Variability Drives the Evolution of Cooperative Breeding in Birds." Current Biology 17 (2007): 1414+. 15 May 2008 <http://www.current-biology.com/content/article/fulltext?uid=PIIS0960982207017113>.
1011. Lewis S, et al. "Fitness increases with partner and neighbor allopreening." Biology Letters 3 (2007).
1012. Capinera J. *Encyclopedia of Entomology*, Volume 3. Springer Publishing Company. 2nd ed., 2008, LXIII. 2152.
1013. Strassmann JE, Queller DC. "Colloquium Papers: Insect societies as divided organisms: The complexities of purpose and cross-purpose." *PNAS* 2007 104 (Suppl 1) 8619-8626.
1014. Strassmann JE, Queller DC. "Altruism Among Amoebas." *Natural History*. 2007. 24.
1015. Nowak MA, May RM. "The spatial dilemmas of evolution." *Int. J. Bifurc*. Chaos 3 (1993) 35-78.
1016. Judson O. "The Selfless Gene." Atlantic Monthly Oct 2007. <http://www.theatlantic.com/doc/200710/generosity-and-evolution>.
1017. House JS, Landis KR, Umberson D. "Social relationships and health." *Science*. 1988; 241(4865):540-5.
1018. Ornish D. *Love & Survival: The Scientific Basis for the Healing Power of Intimacy*. New York: HarperCollins, 1998.
1019. Ornish, D. "Can atherosclerosis regress?" *Cardiovascular Risk Factors1992*, 2 (4) :276-81.
1020. Ornish D. *Love & Survival: The Scientific Basis for the Healing Power of Intimacy*. New York: HarperCollins, 1998.
1021. Schulz U, Pischke C, Weidner G, Daubenmier J, Elliot-Eller M, Scherwitz L, Bullinger G, Ornish D. (2008). "Social

support group attendance is related to blood pressure, health behaviours, and quality of life in the Multicenter Lifestyle Demonstration Project." *Psychology, Health & Medicine*, 13(4), 423-437.
1022. Dienstfrey, H. "What makes the heart healthy? A talk with Dean Ornish." *Advances*, 1992, 8 (2) :25-45.
1023. Ornish D. *Love & Survival: The Scientific Basis for the Healing Power of Intimacy.* New York: HarperCollins, 1998.
1024. Ornish D. M., L. W. Scherwitz, R.S. Doody, et al. "Effects of stress management training and dietary changes in treating ischemic heart disease." *Journal of the American Medical Association*, 1993, 328 (4) :282-83.
1025. Egerton FN. "A History of the Ecological Sciences, Part 8. Frederick II of Hohenstaufen: Amateur Avian Ecologist and Behaviorist" *Bulletin of the Ecological Society of America.* 2003 84:1, 40-44.
1026. Einstein DG. Emperor Frederick II. *Philosophical Library,* 1949. 207.
1027. Ornish D. *Love & Survival: The Scientific Basis for the Healing Power of Intimacy.* New York: HarperCollins, 1998.
1028. Ornish D. *Love & Survival: The Scientific Basis for the Healing Power of Intimacy.* New York: HarperCollins, 1998. 29.
1029. *The Headington (Parish) Magazine.* St. Andrew's Church, Headington, Parish Magazine, Volume 4. 1872. 16.
1030. Judson O. "The Selfless Gene." Atlantic Monthly Oct 2007. <http://www.theatlantic.com/doc/200710/generosity-and-evolution>.
1031. Genesis 1:26. *The Holy Bible.* Authorized King James Version.
1032. 1 John 4:8. *The Holy Bible.* Authorized King James Version.
1033. Gibson T. *A God Named Desire.* Pacific Press. 2010. 14.

Chapter 24

A WORLD WITHOUT RULES, LIKE A ROAD WITH NO SPEED LIMITS, IS NOT REALLY FREE.

# Freedom to Change

***Understanding true freedom of choice and extending that freedom to others can have a transforming impact on your life.***

"I am so glad to be here!" Mitch smiled over at Megan, his wife. "All my life I've dreamed of driving a road with no speed limits, no stop signs, no traffic lights, and best of all, not one single cop on the road."

"Eeeeek!" Megan interrupted Mitch's philosophizing with a blood-curdling scream. "What's that semi truck doing barreling the wrong way on our side of the road."

"There's no wrong way on this highway," Mitch played chicken with the truck for a moment, before swinging onto the shoulder just in time.

"Take me home!" Megan, who already had an iron grip on Mitch's leg, dug in even more.

"Hey, we've only just begun," Mitch stomped on the accelerator and the Porsche roared in response, streaking and weaving through slower and opposing traffic as if there were no tomorrow. Stop lights and freeway entry ramps were especially exciting. Since the signals had been turned off and there were no traffic laws, Mitch could never be sure what other drivers would do.

It was a wild ride while it lasted. The freeway was soon littered with serious accidents and angry drivers engaged in heated arguments. It was like high speed bumper cars, with a heavy dose of road rage, and Mitch and Megan were trapped in the middle of it all. Within a matter of minutes, Mitch's pride and joy, the beautiful Porsche he had dreamed of for so long, had slammed into a concrete wall, mangled beyond repair. As for Mitch and Megan, they were critically injured, and there was no one to help…

*"There are two freedoms—the false, where a man is free to do what he likes; the true, where he is free to do what he ought."*
—Charles Kingsley

A hush fell over the concert hall as the lights in the chamber dimmed. Finely dressed gentlemen and ladies in evening gowns settled into their seats, as tuxedoed members of the world-renowned orchestra filed silently onto the stage. A ripple of applause spread through the crowd as the maestro took the stand. The eyes of a hundred musicians were on him. A quiet motion of his hand, and the orchestra quietly sat down. Another gesture, and instruments raised to the ready. The maestro looked from face to face in the orchestra, giving whispered reminders and assurance with eye contact. As the audience waited in eager silence, he raised his baton and counted to set the pace of the music. Then with a giant sweep of his arm, the symphonic evening began.

An outsider looking in might have noticed that there was something quite orderly about the occasion. The orchestra members wore starched and pressed matching uniforms, and the audience was dressed to the nines. The concert hall was spotless, and instruments were polished to perfection. And the music—the beautiful, majestic music—rose and fell with the move of the maestro's hand. When he became animated, the orchestra played faster and louder. When he moved softly, the orchestra also played softly. Whole sections of musicians played in unison, then in harmony, always in time with the music, always under direction.

The result was an evening of perfection. The hearts of the people were moved by the music, their emotions rose and fell with the symbol crashes and quieter passages, and at the end of the concert, the entire audience stood to their feet to deliver the ultimate musical compliment, a standing ovation.

The first illustration involved a scene where there were virtually no rules; a situation many might think would be the "ultimate freedom." In the second story, the world-renowned maestro, his orchestra, and even the people in the audience were all operating by a very stringent (some would say rigid) set of rules. Which leads us to the first of several questions about freedom that we will consider in this chapter: which of the scenarios above displays real freedom?

If one defines freedom as the complete absence of rules, Mitch and Megan had the greatest freedom. They were driving on a road with no traffic rules or law enforcement. But were Mitch and Megan really free? They couldn't zoom through intersections without high risk, as it was impossible to know when it was safe to zoom. The fact that people were driving whichever direction they wanted, on either side of the road, at vastly varying rates of speed, all added up to a level of disaster that most would rather avoid. There may have been no rules on the road they were driving, but freedom to move about without impediment was quite noticeably absent.

If freedom is defined as being able to do exactly what we want to do, when and how we want to do it, the maestro and his orchestra were the ones who had perfect freedom. They were thrilled to be part of a "magical" musical evening and weren't burdened by the rules they followed. Under the maestro's direction, they achieved a harmonious sound not possible had they each played however they chose. Although they moved in an orderly way, they were free from the discordant clash that results from a lack of rules.

But wait a minute, you might say. They had to dress up. They had to be there on time. They had to play by the music and follow the maestro's hand with careful precision. Could that really be called "freedom?"

Let us go back to our definition of freedom once more. Freedom is being able to do what we want, when and where we want to do it. The musicians loved to be in the orchestra. They practiced for hours to learn their parts. Performances were the high points of their musical lives. Though they were acting in an ordered, predictable way, they were doing exactly what they wanted to do, when, where, and how they wanted to do it. It is true they had musical and cultural rules to follow, but they weren't restrictive because the musicians loved to perform. They had rules, but they also had perfect freedom!

> *"Freedom is not merely the opportunity to do as one pleases; neither is it merely the opportunity to choose between set alternatives. Freedom is, first of all, the chance to formulate the available choices, to argue over them—and then, the opportunity to choose."*
>
> —C. Wright Mills

## FREEDOM AND CBT

As you've learned about Cognitive Behavioral Therapy, there may have been moments when the techniques used for overcoming the ten cognitive distortions seemed like "a bunch of rules." Most people don't naturally like being told what to do, and the principles of unselfishness and humility called for in addressing the ten cognitive distortions go against our natural grain.

For U.S. citizens, the idea of freedom or liberty is part of the natural culture. The words of Patrick Henry at the start of the Revolutionary War are still ringing in our collective ears: "Give me liberty or give me death."[1034]

But while most of us value liberty and understand the importance of freedom, we have also unwittingly adopted some common fallacies about freedom itself. The very idea that true freedom means the absence of rules couldn't be more untrue. As our traffic anecdote illustrated, the absence of rules results in very painful consequences, which is not freedom.

Another common fallacy is the idea that rules are by nature a burden. Readers familiar with the Bible may remember that Jesus admonished the Jewish scribes and Pharisees for making life a burden with long lists of senseless man-made rules.[1035] Many people are so turned off by such displays of "legalism" that they go to the other extreme and throw out rules altogether.

## THE URGE TO "BE FREE"

Sometimes it's easy to think that if we had no boss at work, no parents at home, no teachers or school or government, we would be "free at last!" Everyone could do as they pleased; we would have total freedom! Then again,

Self-discipline must be practiced. An ordinary mind, well disciplined, will accomplish more work, of superior quality than will the most highly educated, eloquent, or talented individual, without self-control.

if someone wanted your car, they could steal it without any worry of being caught by the law. If someone didn't like you, they could kill you without fear of punishment. Society would be reduced to chaos because everyone could do their own thing without regard for others. Whatever freedom you had could be taken, trampled on, and destroyed by others. This sounds more like slavery and chaos than freedom!

The whole idea that rules are not necessary, and we could have freedom without them, has already been tested in our world on a rather grand scale. The Bible teaches that God has a law, called the "law of liberty," but Lucifer wanted to live outside it.[1036] The vast amount of trouble in our world today is a testimony to the law-breaking experiment of Lucifer (now called the devil).[1037]

## LOVE AND THE LAW OF LIBERTY

There are two core concepts behind God's law or rules. One is love for God, and the other is agape or unselfish love for our fellow man. Jesus explained this in Matthew 22:37-40, when He said "thou shalt love the Lord thy God with all thy heart, and with all thy soul, and with all thy mind; this is the first and great commandment. And the second is like unto it: Thou shalt love thy neighbour as thyself. On these two commandments hang all the law and the prophets."[1038]

In other words, the reason for God's law is to teach us how to love. When we do what is right and good for the right reasons, such as practicing unselfish love for God and fellow man, we will be truly happy. A few of the many scriptures supporting these statements are found in **Figure 24.1**.

## TRUE FREEDOM

True freedom is only found in doing what is right for the right reasons. When we understand the reasons behind the rules, agree with the rules, and love to do what is right, rules don't even seem like rules. The rules are still there, but they don't feel like a burden at all. When we do right, we are really only doing what we want to do anyway. This is true freedom.

Many people misunderstand God and the set of rules, or law of liberty, He has for the universe. Because they don't understand the rules, they assume they are petty, legalistic, arbitrary, or worse. But though many people view God's law as a burden, it doesn't have to be that way. Like the members in the orchestra who so happily followed the maestro's lead, we may actually love to do the will of our heavenly commander. This is what the Psalmist was talking about when he wrote, "I delight to do thy will, O my God: yea, thy law is within my heart."[1039] It can be our experience as well.

## GOD GIVEN FREEDOM TO CHOOSE

Once upon a time, thousands of years ago, there was a Supreme Being who was very intelligent and incredibly creative. Although He occupied His time in a number of different ways, designing and making new things was one of His favorite things to do. The "things" He made were really quite extraordinary. It is one thing to paint a picture or sculpt a snowman, quite another to breathe life into a lake or ocean or planet. But that is exactly what this Supreme Being, the Ultimate Creator, did.[1040]

You would think that Someone of this magnitude, with this level of power, would have everything He could ever desire. And in many ways, He did. He had companionship, a beautiful place to live, and a growing portfolio of vibrantly living places and creatures to show for all of His efforts. But there was something missing.

You see, the vast degree of intelligence enjoyed by this Supreme Being was matched by an equally vast capacity to love.[1041] He gave all His creatures the gift of intelligence, plus the wonderful capacity to love. Of course, in order to experience true love, a mutual exchange of feelings had to take place. That is, the Creator not only loved His creatures immensely, but yearned to receive their love in return.[1042]

This is a delicate matter, for true love cannot be forced. It cannot take place where there are "conditions" attached. For the moment love is demanded, it ceases to be true love. Forced love produces feelings of bitterness, disappointment, and even deceit.[1043]

The Supreme Being understood that in order to give and receive the highest level of love from His created beings, He had to bequeath to them the

## THE BIBLE SAYS GOD'S LAW IS NOT A BURDEN

"And I will delight myself in thy commandments, which I have loved." (Psalms 119:47)

"I will delight myself in thy statutes: I will not forget thy word." (Psalms 119:16)

"Oh how I love thy law! It is my meditation all the day." (Psalms 119:97)

The Bible refers to God's law as the "law of liberty". (James 1:25, James 2:12)

Jesus said "if ye love me, keep my commandments". (John 14:15)

"For this is the love of God, that we keep his commandments: and his commandments are not grievous." (1 John 5:3)

Those who are saved at last will be those who keep the commandments of God "Here are they that keep the commandments of God, and the faith of Jesus." (Revelation 14:12)

***Figure 24.1***

freedom of choice. But with that freedom came the ability to reject the Creator whose love had been given so freely. God understood full well the terrible risk He was taking in creating beings with the capacity for the highest level of intelligence, love, and rebellion. The entire universe revolves around a cohesive, organized, and well-thought-out plan—a plan built on the foundational principles of truth, love, and freedom. One act of rebellion by a created being could influence others and throw the whole plan out of balance.

But He was willing to risk it all to create a people who could both appreciate and return His love. God never forces love.[1044,1045] He does not want robots. Because He highly values the foundational principles that order the universe, God is willing to step back and let humans decide for themselves. These sacred principles, also known as the law, are as sacred as God Himself. So sacred, in fact, that He'd rather die than break them. Which is exactly what He did to preserve truth, love, and freedom (see **Figure 24.2**).

## FREEDOM IN RELATIONSHIPS

*"Force is all conquering, but its victories are short lived!"*
—Abraham Lincoln

There are two aspects to freedom. The first is refusing to be a slave to anyone or anything. The second is to be sure and extend freedom to others. May we use the power of persuasion to help others live a better life and have a better future? Absolutely. But we must remember that God never forces His way on us, and if He doesn't do this to us, why should we do this to others? We must remember that although "force is all conquering, it's victories are short-lived."[1046] The Revolutionary War and many other historical conflicts attest to the fact that when freedom is trampled on, rebellion and the absence of love are sure to result. Persuasive truth, taught in a setting of empathy and love, is far more lasting and powerful.

An example that comes to mind on this point was a lady who came to one of our *Depression Recovery* programs. She was having a lot of trouble with her children, but through the principles of the program, she realized that to God, truth and unselfish love were even more important principles than personal salvation. When she recognized that preserving the truth and exercising unselfish love towards her children was even more important than trying to "save them," it changed her whole manner of parenting. Not surprisingly, her children noticed this and, in time, ceased their rebellious behavior. What she wanted so badly had been accomplished, not through her own Herculean efforts, but by upholding the principles that God Himself held to be dearer even than the life of His Son.

Children whose parents rule with an iron hand may march to the family drum while they have no other option, but the seeds of rebellion sown early on will grow up sooner or later. While children need guidance until their brains are fully developed and they have an understanding of truth (which takes up to 25 years), they need to be given freedom as they become mature enough to manage it. There are times in life when a child is racing unknowingly towards a dangerous "cliff," and swift force is the only thing that will save them from ruin. But a gentle touch and sound counsel, rather than force, is the best mode of operation.

*"Him that I love, I wish to be free—even from me."*
—Anne Morrow Lindbergh

As we've discussed, true love cannot exist where there is force. A controlling relationship stifles freedom, and therefore love. Take, for example, Connie and John. When they first met, he was the man of her dreams. But alcohol, and a good degree of mind control, were wrecking the shambled remains of their marriage. John seemed to enjoy "getting inside Connie's head." He wanted to know where she was at all times, deriving a strange sense of satisfaction from ordering her around. He wanted back rubs, foot rubs, maid service, and complete submission, and he wanted it NOW! He also had a list of favorite home-cooked meals that were time-consuming to prepare, which he demanded on a regular basis regardless of what other stresses Connie had in her life.

John also had complete control of the finances, including Connie's paycheck. Her name wasn't on the house, she wasn't a signer on "their" checking account, and John required a strict accounting of the meager allowance he gave her each week. John didn't like Connie to have outside friends, and he really didn't care for her family, either.

Not surprisingly, the love Connie once had for John had long since left the relationship. She gave various reasons for staying with him: financial support, the children, pride. Love, however, was no longer part of the equation. Although Connie's love for John had faltered for many reasons, the flame was stamped out when she lost her freedom. John had really been a gentleman during their courtship, but now he might as well have been a bandit, waving a pistol in Connie's face. Love—true agape love—is a choice. It simply cannot be forced, and neither can it thrive where force is the primary factor in a relationship.

## GOD'S POWER OF CHOICE

God made the ultimate demonstration of agape (unselfish) love when He was willing to sacrifice the life of His own Son in order to preserve the Law.

He valued these principles over the life of His Son:

- the principle of unselfish or agape love toward wayward humans
- the principle of human freedom of choice
- the principle of preserving truth

***Figure 24.2***

*"We who lived in concentration camps can remember the men who walked through the huts comforting others, giving away their last piece of bread. They may have been few in number, but they offer sufficient proof that everything can be taken from a man but one thing: the last of the human freedoms—to choose one's attitude in any given set of circumstances, to choose one's own way."* —Viktor Frankl

## EXERCISING OUR FREEDOM OF CHOICE

God's choices are all about freedom. God's choices are not addictive or enslaving. In contrast, the devil's choices all lead to lack of freedom. His system of persuasion is really one of enslavement.

Those who are addicted to a bad habit or substance are really like voluntary slaves. Because the addiction seems to help them to feel better when they are under it's influence, they reason that they are being helped by it. An example of this is what many consider to be a harmless addiction – caffeine.

Eighty percent of Americans consume caffeine regularly, and although there are certainly more harmful addictions, there is no doubt that caffeine is addictive.[1047] A study from John Hopkins showed that if you drink just 2 cups of coffee a day and quit, you will not only likely get severe withdrawal headaches, but you will feel as wiped out as someone undergoing chemotherapy for 2-3 days. (see **Figure 24.3**).[1048]

Most people, however, feel that the stimulant effect of caffeine is of greater benefit to them than the problem with its addictiveness. Bristol University researchers found that caffeine beverage drinkers develop a tolerance to both the anxiety-producing and the stimulating effects of caffeine, meaning that it only brings them back to baseline levels of alertness, not above them.

The study was performed on 379 people and controlled by placebo. "Although frequent consumers feel alerted by caffeine, especially by their morning tea, coffee, or other caffeine-containing drink, this evidence demonstrates that this is actually merely the reversal of the fatiguing effects of acute caffeine withdrawal," wrote the scientists, led by Peter Rogers of Bristol's department of experimental psychology. The measurements showed that the caffeine users post-caffeine levels of alertness were actually no higher than the non caffeine consumers who received a placebo, suggesting caffeine only brings coffee drinkers back up to "normal." Simply put, all the reported benefits of caffeine are present virtually all day in those who don't consume it.[1049]

If this is true with a relatively mild addiction (caffeine) it is even more profoundly true with other addictions. The point is that voluntary slavery is far worse than freedom, even though there may be a temporary price to pay for freedom (such as headaches and fatigue for 2-3 days in the case of caffeine).

For those under slavery, the long-term benefits of fighting for complete freedom are so profound they actually cannot be measured. Until you experience that complete freedom from imposed or voluntary slavery, you cannot even imagine the lasting joyfulness that results. To experience an improved mood while also improving your emotional intelligence is a life bonus that is worth any struggle, including the temporary unpleasant withdrawal symptoms.

If you are addicted to anything, you are not free. To fully embrace the principles of freedom in your life, why not take a moment and see if there is anything you are doing habitually that is threatening your future? From correcting inaccurate thoughts to giving up foods or substances that lead to harm, you can make the decision to stand for freedom, even though it may seem like a sacrifice at first.

*"I have always thought that all men should be free; but if any should be slaves, it should be first those that desire it for themselves, and secondly those who desire it for others."*
—Abraham Lincoln

## CHOOSE TRUTH, LOVE, AND FREEDOM

The principles of God's Law are intricately connected. Yes, freedom is risky, but love and truth cannot exist without it. And positive change and true happiness cannot be realized without all three. This is why the cost of freedom is priceless, and why men have fought for and willingly given up their lives for it. Freedom is life-changing and life-giving.

### CAFFEINE WITHDRAWAL

According to a study done by John Hopkins University, caffeine is addictive. Individuals who drink as little as two cups of caffeinated beverages a day usually experience a few headachy days complete with that "zombie-like" feeling when trying to quit. The effects of caffeine withdrawal, even at this level, have been compared to undergoing chemotherapy.

**Figure 24.3**

You are free to choose. Choose to accept God's love and freely return it. Choose to offer freedom in your relationships. Choose to turn away from addictions that enslave you. Uplift freedom in your life. As one unknown author stated, "He who has lost freedom has nothing left to lose." Nothing, that is except life itself. So while you still have life, exemplify, practice, honor, and prize freedom.

## References

1034. Henry P. "Give me liberty or give me death: oration delivered to the Second Revolutionary Convention at Richmond," Virginia on March 23, 1775. Fleuron Press. 1956.
1035. Luke 11:46. *The Holy Bible*. Authorized King James Version.
1036. James 1:25. *The Holy Bible*. Authorized King James Version.
1037. 1 John 3:8. *The Holy Bible*. Authorized King James Version.
1038. Matthew 22:37-40. *The Holy Bible*. Authorized King James Version.
1039. Psalm 40:8. *The Holy Bible*. Authorized King James Version.
1040. Genesis 1:1-31. *The Holy Bible*. Authorized King James Version.
1041. Ephesians 3:17-18. *The Holy Bible*. Authorized King James Version.
1042. Jeremiah 31:3. *The Holy Bible*. Authorized King James Version.
1043. Goode WJ. "Force and Violence in the Family." Journal of Marriage and Family Vol. 33, No. 4, Special Double Issue: Violence and the Family and Sexism in Family Studies, Part 2 (Nov., 1971), pp. 624-636.
1044. Revelation 3:20. *The Holy Bible*. Authorized King James Version.
1045. 1 John 4:8. *The Holy Bible*. Authorized King James Version.
1046. Churchill JW, Harris G. The Andover review: a religious and theological monthly. Volume X, July, 1888. 24.
1047. National Coffee Association Coffee Drinking Trends Survey, 2010.
1048. Silverman K, Evans SM, Strain EC, Griffiths RC. "Withdrawal Syndrome after the Double-Blind Cessation of Caffeine Consumption." N Engl J Med 1992; 327:1109-1114. October 15, 1992.
1049. Rogers PJ, et al. "Association of the Anxiogenic and Alerting Effects of Caffeine with ADORA2A and ADORA1 Polymorphisms and Habitual Level of Caffeine Consumption." *Neuropsychopharmacology* 35, 1973-1983 (August 2010)

Chapter 25

REAL CHANGE IS A MARATHON, NOT A SPRINT. BUT IF YOU'RE WILLING TO APPLY THE PRINCIPLES IN THIS BOOK, YOU CAN WIN THE RACE.

# Making Changes Stick

## *The overarching principles of truth, love, and freedom help you stick with positive changes.*

Although many people recognize the need to make changes in their lives, few are able to make lifestyle changes that "stick." The vast majority of smokers recognize that cigarettes are injurious to their health, yet they still smoke. They recognize the danger, and even wish to make a change, yet they haven't been able to quit. The same principle holds true for gambling, alcoholism, drug use, overeating and many other addictions. In addition, even habits that are not really addictive, such as distorted thoughts, can be hard to change, even when the need to change is recognized. All the information in this book, although fascinating, will not bring you lasting benefit unless you apply the information—and then change.

Simply put, change isn't easy. The word itself can produce a fearful reaction. Somehow, we feel more secure when things stay the same. I've often heard people complain over policy changes at work, or the fact that they got a new boss. Yet if you ask them how they feel four months later, they often tell you the changes were good!

There is something unsettling about change when it first happens, even when everyone involved agrees that things turned out positively in the end. Perhaps that is why we humans are such creatures of habit. Good habits contribute to a certain familiarity in our lives, reducing the number of choices we have to make and simplifying daily living.

## STAGES OF CHANGE

| Prochaska's Phases | The Individual... | Stage | Peter's Ladder |
|---|---|---|---|
| Pre-contemplation | is not even thinking about change, though they would benefit from it. | Unconsciously Incompetent | Faith |
| Contemplation | realizes the need for change, and is thinking about it, but hasn't put any plan into action. | Consciously Incompetent | Virtue |
| Preparation | is making timetabled, actionable plans to accomplish the change. | Consciously Incompetent | Knowledge |
| Action | has begun the process of change. | Consciously Competent | Temperance |
| Maintenance | is sticking with the change that has been made. | Consciously Competent | Patience (Endurance) |
| Termination | no longer has to work on the change. | Unconsciously Competent | Godliness<br>Brotherly kindness<br>Charity (Agape Love) |

*Figure 25.1*

They also strengthen with time, becoming harder and harder to break. Unfortunately, the same principles holds true with bad habits. The longer we engage in a bad habit, the harder it is to change.

## STAGES OF CHANGE

When seeking to change behavior or a way of thinking, it can be especially helpful to understand what to expect during the various stages of change.

*"A tiny change today brings us to a dramatically different tomorrow."*
—Richard Bach

### Stage #1: Unconsciously incompetent

This is the pre-contemplation stage, where the individual is "unconsciously incompetent." Even though they need to make a change, they are totally unconscious of their need.[1050]

Most people realize that there is some level of responsibility attached to an increase in knowledge. Some even make intentional efforts to stay in darkness on certain subjects. No doubt there are people who would rather not read this book, for fear they might learn about something which they need to do but don't want to. They are buying in to the old (but very untrue) adage, "ignorance is bliss." The problem is that ignorance is only full of bliss for a limited time. Eventually the effects of the ignorance catch up with the person lacking knowledge and suffering occurs in ways that the person in stage one has no control over.

### Stage #2: Consciously Incompetent

As a result of understanding sound and accurate information, the individual becomes contemplative, or "consciously incompetent." In addition to needing to make a change, they now realize their own need to make a change.[1051]

The Bible points out how important knowledge actually is, with God stating, "My people are destroyed for lack of knowledge."[1052]

Don't underemphasize the importance of truth and accurate knowledge in facilitating change. Without it, positive change is virtually impossible.

### Stage #3: Consciously Competent

Knowledge alone is not enough to produce change, however. As mentioned earlier, 90% of cigarette smokers know that smoking isn't good for them, yet continue to smoke.[1053] They haven't moved up the "ladder of change" to conscious competence. Arriving at this stage means that the individual has actively instituted the change in their life.[1054]

### Stage #4: Unconsciously Competent

If the change is maintained, the individual eventually becomes unconsciously competent. The new habit has been developed, the individual is experiencing the benefits of that new habit, and it is no longer an effort in their mind. It comes naturally; they don't have to work at it anymore.[1055]

These stages of change tie very nicely into what I call the "Ladder of Change" described by the Apostle Peter. Peter's levels in the ladder of change, which can also be found in II Peter 1:5-7, are shown in the fourth column of **Figure 25.1**.[1056] Dr. Prochaska, a psychiatrist who has studied and published about change, developed his own levels of change, which are listed in the first column.

*"If you do these things you shall never fail."*
—II Peter 1:10

## PETER'S LADDER: BIBLICAL LEVELS OF CHANGE

### Faith

The Bible tells us that to every person is given a measure of faith.[1057] This is unique to humans, for humans are the only mammals with the intelligence, and frontal lobe size, to worship. There is a seed of faith in the heart, which must be watered if it is to blossom. Every human being worships. The difference is who or what the particular individual is worshipping. But the ability to believe and change is there in everyone, even in stage one, the pre-contemplative stage of unconscious incompetence.

### Virtue

Virtue, or the desire to do what is right, is necessary in the process of change. Unless you have a willing heart, all the accurate knowledge in the world will not bring about change. You must first be ready to learn; then you are ready to let accurate and helpful knowledge bring about change.

### Knowledge

During stage two the individual realizes the need for change, or becomes conscious of their incompetence. This fits the third rung in Peter's ladder, which is knowledge. Positive change in your thoughts or behaviors is only possible with good knowledge. In this preparation phase, the individual actively plans for the change, but it still is not seen in their life.

### Temperance

Dr. Prochaska's phase four, action, represents the rung of temperance on Peter's ladder of change. Temperance is abstaining from the harmful and using the healthful in moderation. During this stage the individual takes action to become temperate. Sometimes there is a waffling back and forth between conscious incompetence and conscious competence.

### Patience

It takes a lot of endurance, or patience, to maintain a victory over difficult habits. Generally, 14-21 days are necessary for changes in thinking to be almost effortless and habitual. During these rungs on Peter's ladder, the individual remains competent, but still consciously so. That means they have to put forth an effort, and watch out lest they stumble or fall.

## Godliness:

This stage is where happy, abundant, and productive living occurs. As the individual becomes temperate and develops patience, the trait of godliness is eventually developed. This is a state of unconscious competence, meaning the individual no longer has cravings or desire for the previously harmful habit. They naturally desire to do what is best for them and are experiencing the benefit and natural dopamine elevations that unconscious competence brings. The psalmist was speaking about this state when he wrote:

"I delight to do thy will, O my God: yea, thy law is within my heart."[1058]

"In Thy presence is fullness of joy, at Thy right hand are pleasures forevermore."[1059]

## Brotherly Love / Charity:

Prochaska's last phase of change is termination, which corresponds with achieving unconscious competence. In this phase the individual no longer has to focus so intently on the changed behavior.[1060]

Peter's final rung on the ladder of change takes this a step further, recognizing that change is not just about oneself. True change in one individual will also benefit others. First, family and the ones we love, but then even those that are not naturally lovable can experience self-sacrificing love from those who have reached the top rung of Peter's ladder.

Peter implies there is not complete victory until you get to the top of the ladder. Here is the reward—a state of unconscious competence. At this point, the individual is making right choices naturally, enjoying life to its fullest, experiencing love daily, and being free from the bad habits that formerly ruled the life. It is also the stage where we will be most able to extend a helping hand to others.

This doesn't mean that individuals in the beginning stages of change cannot show love to each other. It just means that there is a natural progression to improvement. It would be difficult, for example, for an individual who is lacking in knowledge to develop the trait of temperance. It is especially challenging for an intemperate individual to be patient. A person should develop patience before they can be considered godly, and so it goes.

Once the top rung of the ladder is reached it can then be a catalyst for others to change. Those with charitable love for others have empathy, a critical ingredient in helping others to make positive lifestyle changes.[1061] With a live example of positive change, combined with the feeling of love extended to the person in need of change, more positive change can result in a person in need. The cycle can then be repeated in others, and the world becomes a better place!

## STORY OF CHANGE

### Unconscious Incompetence

Kathy had the bad habit of amplifying her negative emotions to an unrealistic degree. When she was slightly annoyed by the traffic, she would exclaim, "This traffic is ruining my whole day!" When she was frustrated by a co-worker's mistake, she would fume, "I can't stand his uselessness anymore!" Although, in reality, the backed-up highway only affected a small portion of her day, and she could easily tolerate her colleague's imperfections, Kathy's reactions were excessive.

### Conscious Incompetence

Kathy began to notice the disapproving glances from those around her when she responded to a small irritation or disappointment with an extreme statement, and realized that her outbursts were unwarranted. She learned that her pessimistic attitude was negatively affecting the people in her office, and several employees had threatened to quit. Her family and friends were also avoiding spending time with her. Then Kathy attended a seminar on emotional intelligence and learned about magnification, "I-can't-stand-it-itis," and low frustration tolerance (described in chapter 6). Kathy knew that she needed to change.

### Conscious Competence

Kathy decided to stop using such severe phrases to describe her circumstances. She made a deliberate and conscious effort to replace those over-the-top outbursts with accurate thoughts. When she was tempted to describe something as "totally awful," she would instead think to herself, "this is a nuisance, but I can handle it." If she faced a setback, she would express her disappointment then try again rather than proclaim that the project was "completely ruined." At this stage, she did not always have the right attitude immediately when faced with a frustration. Over and over again she had to tell herself, "No, I'm not going to react emotionally. I'm going to look at this objectively and realistically." It took Kathy 21 full days to work her way through this stage of change.

### Unconscious Competence

Finally the day came when Kathy encountered a situation that seemed horrible, but her first thoughts naturally turned to an accurate description of the situation. She admitted her irritation but knew she could stand it, and she wasn't tempted to make outrageous statements about how intolerable it was. No longer did she have to remind herself to view the circumstances truthfully. She had become unconsciously competent!

The levels of change we have to work through may involve painful withdrawal, and even temporary suffering.[1062] Many people aren't willing to suffer, which is why they don't overcome. But there is power to be gained as we climb Peter's ladder of change, adding positive character traits to the faith that God has planted in each of our hearts. It is a journey, and it doesn't happen overnight. But whether you call it unconscious competence, agape love, or some other name, there is peace, fulfillment, and joy at the top of the ladder.

## SET UP FOR SUCCESS

According to Dr. Prochaska, a key factor in whether or not lifestyle changes will be successful is whether the person making the change receives empathy from those who are trying to help him or her.[1063] If you have reached the final stage of change and enjoy unconscious competence, you may find it difficult to conceive how someone in the early stages of change could possibly make poor lifestyle choices. However, at this point they likely feel just as puzzled at how you maintain your healthy lifestyle. Your empathy toward those struggling up the ladder will play an important role in their success.

*"Failure is only the opportunity to begin again more intelligently."*
—Henry Ford

It is also critical that we plan for success (rather than temptation). If we are really serious about quitting smoking, we will not carry cigarettes around in our pocket or even have them in the house. If we are serious about not overeating, we will steer clear of the foods and situations that lead us to binge. There may be certain people in your life whose company hinders your progress. If Kathy, from the story above, had a friend who joined in her undue tirades or instigated a poor attitude by using magnifying words around Kathy, then it would be wise for Kathy to avoid interaction with that friend while she is trying to cure her own "I-can't-stand-it-itis." Like Kathy, you may have to give up some familiar faces or places that could sabotage your success, but the alternative is a sure road to failure.

In setting yourself up for success, you should focus not only on eliminating bad influences, but also seeking out positive ones. If you really want to kick a habit, you'll replace the detrimental thoughts or behaviors with desirable habits. Likewise, you should replace negative relationships or activities with more constructive ones. You can even go a step further and ask someone who is a positive influence (a trusted friend or family member) to gently correct your inaccurate statements and keep you accountable. Changing your surroundings goes a long way in paving the road to success.

## CHOOSING OUR PLEASURES

We humans have the wonderful ability to choose our own pleasures. When I first learned that tahini is good for me because of its high tryptophan ratio, I didn't care for tahini at all. But after trying it on bread several times, I began to like it, and now I actually enjoy it. Conversely, there was a time when I enjoyed cheese pizza, even though that was not the most healthful choice for my body. When I chose to avoid cheese pizza,

I found that it did not appeal to me anymore. How encouraging to know that you have the ability to choose your likes and dislikes!

This concept applies to lifestyle choices as well as food preferences. If you expose yourself to a habit long enough, you will come to enjoy it. How many people enjoyed smoking the first time they puffed on a cigarette? I would presume not very many. They had to develop the bad habit. In the same way, it is necessary to develop good habits. You'll have to acquire a taste for true thought, healthy behaviors, and the good things in life. It may take time to cultivate a liking for healthier things, but once you do you will be pleased to see that you can actually choose your own pleasures.

## THE BIG THREE

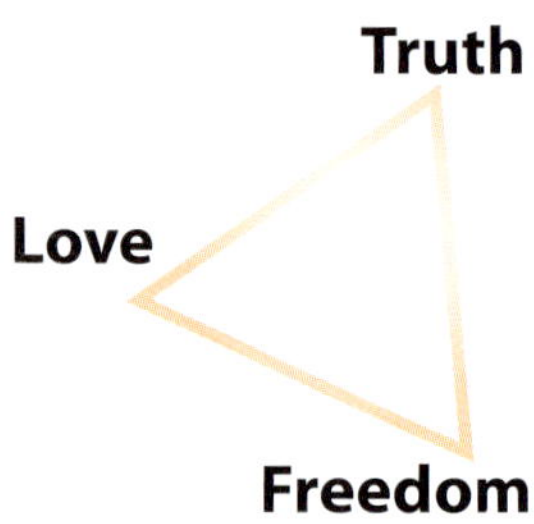


It's interesting that within the stages of change are seen the overarching principles of freedom, truth, and love. Each individual has the freedom to make changes for the better. Without a sense of freedom to choose, a person will not make any positive changes. Truth (accurate knowledge) is also essential to move an individual to contemplate and activate positive change. Undistorted truthful thoughts, absent emotional reasoning, minimization, and mental filters are also necessary in producing lifelong lasting changes. Rounding out the top of the change paradigm is the highest form of love: self-sacrificing, empathetic, altruistic love. This love cannot exist without freedom. Possessing such love is not only health giving to the individual who has it, but it produces the very real possibility for others who are in contact with such an individual to change for the better.

As I close this book on improving your emotional intelligence and mental performance, I want to make one final appeal to you, the reader. Hunger and thirst after truth. Desire it, honor it, respect it, and sacrifice for it. Search for it in an objective, unbiased way. Once you understand it, think consistently truthful thoughts and apply truth to your daily lifestyle. Then get ready to enter the largest room in the world—the room for improvement.

Such truth needs to be balanced by an equally important principle, empathetic love. My final appeal to you is: hunger and thirst after true love. Desire it, honor it, respect it, and sacrifice for it. Truth that is only self-centered is actually distorted, since it leads to emotional reasoning and filtering out the big picture. Truth without love is no longer the whole truth. In a similar way, love without truth is not absolute love. It becomes a self-centered love (pride, the magnification of self), which is actually the opposite of the self-sacrificing, altruistic love that you, I, and the world are so much in need of. Love without truth ceases to be true love.

This conclusion seems irrational to those who live deceptive, self-centered lives: place truth and love above your self. Don't ever let your own selfish interests get in the way of your pursuit and application of truth and true love. Then get ready for the effects of a sky-high emotional intelligence and mental performance, happiness and success in ways you never thought possible, healthy loving relationships, and true freedom. You will be a powerful and persuasive element for good, without coercion, since you believe in true freedom, the foundational element for true love's occurrence. You will finally obtain the fulfillment the rest of humanity yearns and searches for, but never is able to obtain by putting self ahead of truth or love. You won't be disappointed in the slightest.

## References

1050. Coombs RH, Howatt WC. *The Addiction Counselor's Desk Reference.* Wiley. 2005. 53-54.
1051. Cutliffe JR, Butterworth T, Proctor B. *Fundamental themes in clinical supervision.* Routledge. 2001. 44.
1052. Hosea 4:6. *The Holy Bible.* English Standard Version.
1053. Mullins R, Borland R. "Do Smokers Want to Quit?" *Australian and New Zealand Journal of Public Health.* Vol. 20 Is 4. Blackwell Publishing Ltd. 1996.
1054. Cutliffe JR, Butterworth T, Proctor B. *Fundamental themes in clinical supervision.* Routledge. 2001. 44.
1055. Cutliffe JR, Butterworth T, Proctor B. *Fundamental themes in clinical supervision.* Routledge. 2001. 44.
1056. Prochaska JO, Norcross J, DiClemente C. *Changing for Good: A Revolutionary Six-Stage Program for Overcoming Bad Habits and Moving Your Life Positively Forward.* Harper Paperbacks. 1995. 36-39.
1057. Romans 12:3. *The Holy Bible.* Authorized King James Version.
1058. Psalm 40:8. *The Holy Bible.* Authorized King James Version.
1059. Psalms 16:11. *The Holy Bible.* Authorized King James Version.
1060. Prochaska JO, Norcross J, DiClemente C. *Changing for Good: A Revolutionary Six-Stage Program for Overcoming Bad Habits and Moving Your Life Positively Forward.* Harper Paperbacks. 1995.274.
1061. Kathol RG, Perez R, Cohen JS. *The Integrated Case Management Manual: Assisting Complex Patients Regain Physical and Mental Health.* Springer Publishing Company. 2010. 52.
1062. Prochaska JO, Norcross J, DiClemente C. *Changing for Good: A Revolutionary Six-Stage Program for Overcoming Bad Habits and Moving Your Life Positively Forward.* Harper Paperbacks. 1995.253-254.
1063. Prochaska JO, Norcross JC. *Systems of Psychotherapy: A Transtheoretical Analysis.* Brooks Cole. 2009. 44.

# Appendix I

## *Assessing Toxin Exposures*

Use the following tables as a guide to identify symptoms of toxicity and possible sources of exposure, as well as find the necessary testing to determine if your own levels are dangerously high.

| TOXIN | COMMON SOURCES OF EXPOSURE |
|---|---|
| Arsenic (a heavy metal) | • ingesting small amounts present in your food and water or breathing air containing arsenic<br>• breathing sawdust or burning smoke from wood treated with arsenic<br>• living in areas with unusually high levels of naturally-occurring arsenic in rock<br>• working in a job that involves arsenic production or use, such as copper or lead smelting, wood treating, or pesticide application |
| Benzene (an industrial solvent) | • breathing outdoor air that contains low levels of benzene from tobacco smoke, automobile service stations, exhaust from motor vehicles, and industrial emissions<br>• inhaling vapors (or gasses) from products that contain benzene, such as glues, paints, furniture wax, and detergents<br>• air around hazardous waste sites or gas stations that contain higher levels of benzene<br>• working in industries that make or use benzene |
| Cadmium (a heavy metal) | • eating foods containing cadmium (low levels are found in all foods; highest levels are in shellfish, liver, and kidney meats)<br>• smoking cigarettes or breathing cigarette smoke<br>• breathing contaminated workplace air<br>• drinking contaminated water<br>• living near industrial facilities that release cadmium into the air |

| POSSIBLE SYMPTOMS | TESTING FOR TOXICITY |
|---|---|
| Ingesting toxic levels can cause nausea and vomiting, decreased production of red and white blood cells, abnormal heart rhythm, damage to blood vessels, and a sensation of "pins and needles" in hands and feet. | The urine test is the most reliable test for arsenic exposure within the last few days. Tests on hair and fingernails can measure exposure to high levels of arsenic over the past 6-12 months. |
| Breathing high levels can cause drowsiness, dizziness, rapid heart rate, headaches, tremors, confusion, and unconsciousness. Eating or drinking foods containing high levels of benzene can cause vomiting, irritation of the stomach, dizziness, sleepiness, convulsions, rapid heart rate, and death. | Benzene can be measured in the breath or blood if assessed shortly after exposure. In the body, benzene is converted to products called metabolites which can be measured in the urine. The metabolite S-phenylmercapturic acid in urine is a sensitive indicator of benzene exposure. |
| Long-term exposure to lower levels of cadmium in air, food, or water leads to a buildup of cadmium in the kidneys and possible kidney disease. Kidney disease in turn, can cause significant mental health compromise. | The amount of cadmium in your blood shows your recent exposure to cadmium. The amount of cadmium in your urine shows both your recent and past exposure. |

| TOXIN | COMMON SOURCES OF EXPOSURE |
|---|---|
| DDT, DDE, DDD (persistent organic compounds related to pesticide use) | • eating contaminated foods, such as root and leafy vegetables, fatty meat, fish, and poultry (levels are generally very low)<br>• eating contaminated imported foods from countries that still allow the use of DDT<br>• breathing contaminated air or drinking contaminated water near waste sites and landfills that contain higher levels of these chemicals<br>• breathing or swallowing soil particles near waste sites or landfills that contain these chemicals<br>• infants fed on breast milk from mothers who have been exposed |
| Lead (a heavy metal) | • consuming food or water that contain lead (pipes in older homes may contain lead solder that can leach into the water)<br>• spending time in areas where lead-based paints have been used (deteriorating paint contributes to lead dust)<br>• working in a job or engaging in certain hobbies in which lead is used, such as making stained glass<br>• using health-care products or folk remedies that contain lead |
| Mercury (a heavy metal) | • eating fish or shellfish contaminated with methylmercury<br>• breathing vapors in air from spills, incinerators, and industries that burn mercury-containing fuels<br>• release of mercury from dental work and medical treatments<br>• breathing contaminated workplace air or skin contact during use in the workplace (common in dental, health services, chemical, and other industries that use mercury)<br>• practicing rituals that include mercury |

| POSSIBLE SYMPTOMS | TESTING FOR TOXICITY |
|---|---|
| DDT affects the nervous system. People who accidentally swallowed large amounts of DDT became excitable and had tremors and seizures. These effects went away after the exposure stopped. No effects were seen in people who took small daily doses of DDT by capsule for 18 months. | Laboratory tests can detect DDT, DDE, and DDD in fat, blood, urine, semen, and breast milk. They may show low, moderate, or excessive exposure to these compounds, but cannot tell the exact amount of exposure, or whether you will experience adverse effects. These tests are not routinely available at the doctor's office because they require special equipment. |
| Lead poisoning can affect almost every organ in the body. The main target for lead toxicity is the nervous system. Long-term exposure can result in decreased nervous system performance, weakness in fingers, wrists, or ankles, severe brain and kidney damage, and ultimately death. | A blood test is available to measure the amount of lead in your blood and to estimate the amount of your recent exposure to lead. |
| The nervous system is very sensitive to all forms of mercury. Methylmercury and metallic mercury vapors are more harmful than other forms, because more mercury in these forms reaches the brain. Exposure to high levels of metallic, inorganic, or organic mercury can permanently damage the brain, kidneys, and developing fetus. Effects on brain functioning may result in irritability, shyness, tremors, changes in vision, or hearing and memory problems. | Blood or urine samples are used to test for exposure to metallic mercury and to inorganic forms of mercury. Mercury in whole blood or in scalp hair is measured to determine exposure to methylmercury. |

| TOXIN | COMMON SOURCES OF EXPOSURE |
|---|---|
| Polychlorinated Biphenyls (PCBs, persistent organic contaminants) | • using old fluorescent lighting fixtures and electrical devices and appliances, such as television sets and refrigerators that were made 30 or more years ago (these items may leak small amounts of PCBs into the air when they get hot during operation)<br>• eating contaminated food (mainly meat, dairy products, and sportfish caught in contaminated lakes or rivers)<br>• breathing air near hazardous waste sites and drinking contaminated well water<br>• during repair and maintenance of PCB transformers<br>• accidents, fires, or spills involving transformers, fluorescent lights, and other old electrical devices<br>• disposal of PCB materials |

| POSSIBLE SYMPTOMS | TESTING FOR TOXICITY |
|---|---|
| Studies in exposed workers have shown changes in blood and urine that may indicate liver damage. Liver damage if significant may affect brain functioning. Other effects of PCBs in animals include behavioral alterations. | Tests exist to measure levels of PCBs in your blood, body fat, and breast milk, but these are not routinely conducted. Most people normally have low levels of PCBs in their body because nearly everyone has been environmentally exposed to PCBs. |

# Appendix II

## United States Water Quality Information and Testing Services*

| RESOURCE | INFORMATION AVAILABLE | CONTACT INFORMATION |
|---|---|---|
| The Environmental Quality Institute (EQI) of the University of North Carolina at Asheville (UNCA) | EQI provides reasonable testing of water sources for lead and arsenic for a nominal fee. | Clean Water Lead Testing, Inc., UNCA<br>One University Heights<br>Asheville, NC 28804-3099<br>828-251-6800<br>info@leadtesting.org<br>http://www.unca.edu/eqi/ |
| The United States Environmental Protection Agency | Municipal and private suppliers are required to prepare annual public water quality reports. | Safe Drinking Water Hotline:<br>800-426-4791<br>Contact your water supplier for their annual Consumer Confidence Report.<br>http://www.epa.gov/safewater/ccr1.html |
| NSF International | NSF provides free consumer information as well as certifying bottled water providers and water purification systems. | Consumer Affairs Office<br>1-877-8-NSF-HELP (1-877-867-3435).<br>http://www.nsfconsumer.org/index.asp |
| South Dakota State University | SDSU offers a broad range of water testing services including pesticides, minerals, alkalinity and hardness. | SDSU<br>ASC 133 Box 2170<br>Brookings, South Dakota 57007<br>605-688-4910<br>http://wri.sdstate.edu/samples.htm<br>Nancy_Stuefen@sdstate.edu |

** These contact sources are provided to serve as a starting point if you want to have a water analysis performed. They all appear to be reputable sources, but I have not performed or accessed any independent reviews. I therefore cannot endorse any particular provider.*

## *International Water Quality Information and Testing Services**

| RESOURCE | INFORMATION AVAILABLE | CONTACT INFORMATION |
|---|---|---|
| **EUROPE**<br>The British Geological Survey (BGS) | The BGS operates a Water Chemistry Laboratory which specializes in detailed water analyses using small volume water samples. | British Geological Survey,<br>Maclean Building,<br>Crowmarsh Gifford,<br>Wallingford,<br>Oxfordshire OX10 8BB.<br>+44 (0)1491 838800<br>http://www.bgs.ac.uk |
| **CANADA**<br>Grotek™ Analytical Lab | Grotek offers a wide variety of tests to assess the quality of drinking water, as well as water for agricultural and industrial uses.<br><br>Testing includes: Acidity (pH), dissolved solids, hardness, chloride, nitrates, ammonium, sulfates, aluminum, cadmium, copper, iron, lead, sodium, and zinc. | Grotek Analytical Lab<br>9850 - 201st Street<br>Langley, B.C. V1M 4A3<br>http://www.grotek.net/contact/<br>lab@grotek.net<br>+1 604-881-7244 |
| **AUSTRALIA**<br>The Australian Water Quality Centre (AWQC) | The Centre has expertise in water quality research, monitoring and testing. It offers a wide range of international products and services including water quality analysis. | Private Mail Bag 3<br>Salisbury,<br>South Australia 5110<br>+61 1 300 65 33 66 or<br>+61 (0) 8 8259 0215<br>awqc@sawater.com.au<br>www.awqc.com.au<br>www.sawater.com.au |

** These contact sources are provided to serve as a starting point if you want to have a water analysis performed. From my limited research, these appear to be reputable sources, but I have not performed or accessed any independent reviews. Furthermore, it is difficult to evaluate international sources. I therefore cannot endorse any particular provider.*

| RESOURCE | INFORMATION AVAILABLE | CONTACT INFORMATION |
|---|---|---|
| **AUSTRALIA**<br>National Association of Testing Authorities (NATA) | NATA is the national authority for accreditation of laboratories conducting tests, calibrations and measurements in a wide variety of technical fields including drinking water testing. They have a directory of approved water testing facilities throughout Australia. | Head Office:<br>Dom Cerneaz, Manager<br>7 Leeds Street,<br>Rhodes, NSW 2138<br>+61 2 9736 8222<br><br>NATA's directories are accessible at: http://www.nata.asn.au/fs_directory.htm<br>Access water testing facilities by looking under Chemical Testing, then specifying potable water. |
| **ASIA**<br>Pakistan Council of Research in Water Resources (PCRWR) | Water analysis services are provided. However, realize that most water samples in the developing world are microbiologically contaminated. This necessitates that sampling be done using pre-sterilized containers and refrigerated shipping to the lab in a short time. Those arrangements should be worked out in connection with the laboratory. | PCRWR<br>Ministry of Science and Technology, Government of Pakistan<br>H # 3, Street # 17,<br>F-6/2, Islamabad<br>Mr. M. Aslam Tahir, Director<br>+92-51-9218992<br>matahir2k@hotmail.com |

| RESOURCE | INFORMATION AVAILABLE | CONTACT INFORMATION |
|---|---|---|
| **ASIA**<br>Pak EPA Quality Laboratory<br>Pakistan Environmental Protection Agency | Another Pakistani source for water analysis. Please note previous comments regarding collecting and shipping samples for analysis. | Pak EPA Quality Laboratory<br>Ministry of Environment and Local Bodies, Government of Pakistan<br>Blue Area<br>Islamabad<br>+92-51-9204498<br>pakepa@isb.compol.com |
| **ASIA**<br>ALS Technichem (Malaysia) | ALS provides drinking water testing and other environmental monitoring and testing services. | ALS Technichem (M) Sdn Bhd<br>9 Jalan Astaka U8/84<br>Bukit Jelutong Science Park<br>40150 Shah Alam, Selangor<br>+60-3-7845-8257<br>info@ALSMalaysia.com<br>http://www.alsmalaysia.com/HomePage/services.php |

# Appendix III

## What Do You Hear?

To gain the most benefit from uplifting music, close your eyes and picture in your mind what the composer and performers are trying to communicate. The following thoughts were imagined by one person who listened intently to two CDs I recommend (available on www.drnedley.com).

***Selections from Pefection of Panflute by Pan Bogdan***

**The Swan from "Carnival of the Animals:"** I see a hawk gliding on the soft updrafts coming off the side of a mountain. The bird takes in the dramatic panorama all around him, while keeping a sharp lookout for the prospects of a meal. As the music becomes more dramatic, the hawk makes a steep dive toward its prey.

**Minuet:** Children are frolicking and playing in a lush green backyard nearby. They are chasing butterflies, chasing each other, and playing hide and seek. None have a care in the world.

**Gaiement:** I am on vacation, in a carefree mood, and driving down the highway through a very picturesque landscape. I am especially enjoying the sights that I don't often see in the part of the country where I live.

**Sicilienne:** I am walking through a flower garden noticing all the scents, sights and sounds. Bees and butterflies and birds flutter around. The wonderful smells of the roses and other flowers take my breath away.

**Hungarian Dance:** I am doing my exercise workout, interval training. The program starts out with lots of energy, but just as my heartrate rises, the music slows down. Then I repeat the pattern, all in time to the music.

**Humoresca/Dvorak:** A small child is skipping down a country lane, pausing occasionally to take in interesting things that they come across: a bird's nest, a hopping toad, or a caterpillar. They look at the things they are seeing and marvel at creation – then they move on.

**Allegro/Loeillet:** A very busy person is in the office typing, answering e-mail and multitasking. Though hit from every side with requests and tasks that need to be done, they remain professional, handling the busy-ness in a professional way.

***Selections from Uplifting Worship by Mantovani***

**Beautiful Isle of Somewhere:** Sitting in a church in a reflective mood. The last few notes of the melody are very uplifting, changing the mood from somber to hopeful.

**Jesu, Joy of Man's Desiring:** I feel myself in a very calm and peaceful place in the early morning. The sky is slowly brightening, causing me to feel happy and contented.

**All People That On Earth Do Dwell:** I am high up standing on an outcropping of rock with a view of the sun setting on the multi-colored walls of the Grand Canyon. It is very quiet but for the occasional noise of a bird or rustling animal. The sights, sounds and smells of creation are filling my senses as if nature is producing a symphony.

**A Mighty Fortress Is Our God:** Nestled in the spectacular mountainous scenery of the French Alps, I sit by a mountain stream with peaks soaring high overhead. It took a day's hike to get here, and somehow with the strength of the ledges around me and the sound of a soft rushing stream, I feel very secure and that God is near and I am protected and safe.

**Whispering Hope:** Sitting under a tree, I think about my goals and how nice it will be to achieve them. Now I am taken away in a dream and my goals have become reality and it is truly wonderful. Better than what I had imagined, which turns my thoughts toward heaven.

**The Lord's My Shepherd:** A peaceful scene out in the countryside comes to mind. Perhaps a gentle brook babbling nearby, the wind blowing gently through the leaves of a nearby tree, the fragrance of wildflowers flooding my senses, and birds chirping happily in the warm sunshine.

**Abide With Me:** I bolt upright in the middle of the night, awakened by a terrible dream. As my mind clears and the fogginess lifts from my brain, the promises of God's presence bring calmness again, and peace settles in on my soul.

**The Holy City:** I am in a kayak paddling down a great river out west. As the pace of the music rises and falls I pass through slower and faster sections of the river. With the final crescendos I rush through the wildest stretch of all, then am thrown out into a calm pool as my journey ends.

# Appendix IV

## *The Life of Lloyd "Bud" Nedley*

A. Lloyd Nedley Jr. was born August 23, 1924 in Denbo, Pennsylvania to A. Lloyd Nedley, Sr. and Fern Smith Nedley. His family called him "Bud" and his associates later called him Lloyd. He died a tragic death on Thursday, September 19, 2002 at Mercy Memorial Hospital, in Ardmore, Oklahoma from Legionnaire's disease, a terrible lung infection (usually contracted from water) that destroyed his lungs. He practiced a very healthy lifestyle and enjoyed medication-free vibrant health until just before his death.

Lloyd's father was an accountant for the J & L Steel Corporation, and his mother, a homemaker. Raised a Methodist, he was the fourth of five children. He graduated from Centerville High School in Pennsylvania as valedictorian at the age of 16. Lloyd's older brother, Chuck Nedley, was his mathematics teacher in high school. Like Chuck, Lloyd enjoyed teaching and enrolled to become a teacher at Penn State. Later he transferred to California State Teacher's College in California, Pennsylvania.

Shortly after the Japanese bombed Pearl Harbor, Lloyd joined the Navy and went to officer training school. Before he joined the Pacific Fleet in 1942, his mother had a serious conversation with him in which she requested that he promise never to drink alcohol. Lloyd had a great love for his mother, and gave her his promise. Under tremendous ridicule for his stance, he was one of only two people on his ship who refused any alcohol. While on leave during the war, Lloyd married his high school sweetheart, Orvetta Charlton. The wedding took place on June 29, 1944 in Centerville, Pennsylvania.

Lloyd served as an officer in the U.S. Navy from 1942 to 1946. When he was leaving the ship for the last time, he heard his name being paged overhead to come to ship headquarters. His commanding officer, who was the most vicious in his attempts to get Lloyd to drink alcohol, stated, "Lloyd, before you leave, I just want you to know how much I respect you for the unpopular stance you took regarding alcohol. I made it hard on you, because I knew I should be standing for the same convictions. I was wrong and you were right. I now want to encourage you to keep up the good work, and always live by your convictions."

Despite his love for teaching, Lloyd next enrolled in pre-engineering at Washington and Jefferson College in Washington, PA. He later graduated with a Bachelor of Science in Mechanical Engineering from Carnegie Tech in Pittsburgh, PA. While attending school, Lloyd earned income as a pianist and composer-arranger for Johnnie Jay's Jazz Orchestra and performed in many nightclubs in Western Pennsylvania. Though he had little formal musical training, his ability to arrange and write music for all instruments and vocalists was absolutely amazing.

Lloyd and Orvetta began their family in Pennsylvania. Their first two children, Donna and Wayne, were born in Brownsville, PA. After becoming a father, Lloyd recognized that playing in nightclubs was not good for him--or the people who enjoyed his music. He felt his need for an improved spiritual life. Desiring to understand the Bible, he sought out those that might help him. He became frustrated when some religious leaders cautioned him not to get "too close" to the Bible, and refused to heed their warnings.

After obtaining his engineering degree, Lloyd and his family moved to Santa Monica, California, where he went to work for Douglas Aircraft (later McDonell-Douglas Corp.) as a designer draftsman. Every Sunday, Lloyd visited a new church, seeking a group who respected and studied the Bible. He also began to seriously study the Bible on his own and was convicted to follow its teachings. He finally found a group that not only deeply revered the Bible, but studied it in an analytical and logical manner that appealed to his objective thought processes. He felt the power of the Holy Spirit moving in his life, as he changed his life, step by step, in accordance with Biblical teachings.

After a year in Southern California, Lloyd went back to school and obtained his Masters in Mechanical Engineering from Lehigh University in Bethlehem, PA. During this time, more Bible study led him to change his musical tastes and performances to uplifting hymn arrangements. Lloyd and Orvetta looked for and found a group whose beliefs were based on the Bible alone and joined the Seventh-day Adventist Church in 1953.

After graduating with his Masters, Lloyd worked for General Motors Research in Detroit, Michigan and later worked for General Motors as a Chevrolet Design Engineer. He was most often assigned "cutting edge" engineering tasks. He pioneered research in many design areas, obtained multiple patents for G.M. on his designed products, and authored several published engineering studies for the Society of Automobile Engineers. He often would comment on how much he loved his job. His family frequently heard him say, "It doesn't seem right that I get paid for a job that I thoroughly enjoy doing. Even if I did not get paid, I would want to do exactly what I do, just for the fun of it." Three more children were born to Lloyd and Orvetta in Michigan: Diane, Janice, and Neil.

Lloyd continued to love teaching, and taught engineering and thermodynamics at Wayne State University in Detroit, Michigan as part of the evening school faculty for 17 years. He was voted engineering "Teacher of the Year" many times by his students. He had more of a working knowledge of history, science, math, music, agriculture, and the Bible than most people who are professionals in each of these areas their entire lives. Yet, he never made anyone feel dumb and never talked down to anyone. He was the type of person who never met a stranger and enjoyed talking to anyone, regardless of their rank or status in life. Children always enjoyed being around Lloyd. He not only played with children of all ages, but enjoyed educating them in ways that were truly fun—especially in areas of music, science, and the Bible. He had a special knack for making the complex simple and enjoyable. He taught a well-attended and popular weekly Bible study class for over 40 years. The discovery of raw and basic truth was a thrill to him.

Lloyd continued to share his unique musical talent over the years. After hearing a song on the radio that he had never heard before, he would play the exact melody—only with better harmonies than the original. His ability to change keys and bring out or modulate melodies was effortless and uniquely Lloyd. His favorite instrument was the piano, but he also loved to play the pipe organ. In addition, he could play several brass instruments including the tuba, baritone, and euphonium. A favorite for his children were the times when Lloyd would get out his "sweet potato" (a flute-like instrument) and play folk songs. He could play all styles of music, and would love to demonstrate the different styles and effects they have on the body and mind. He could aptly demonstrate why popular music is not always the best music for the mind. A yearly highlight for the family was going to the University of Michigan on the first Sunday every December to hear Handel's Messiah performed with full orchestra and a 350-voice choir.

Lloyd also served as organist and pianist for many Sabbath and Sunday churches and played for countless weddings and funerals. He composed his son Neil's bride's wedding march for three trumpets and pipe organ and designed it so the march would end precisely when the bride was at the altar.

Lloyd arranged countless numbers for the Flying Four male quartet that would emphasize the strengths (while minimizing the weaknesses) of each voice. As a pilot he would fly these four males to perform religious music in many churches surrounding the Great Lakes. His flying stories could keep kids spellbound for an entire afternoon. For as much flying as he did in a four-seater Cessna in Michigan weather, Lloyd was very fortunate to have lived as long as he did!

Lloyd's last assignment for General Motors was during the fuel crunch era of the early 1980s. He was assigned the position as chief engineer for an automobile that would be jointly designed by G.M. and Suzuki of Japan, but built by Suzuki. The purpose was to achieve high fuel economy. Lloyd had been to Japan as a soldier in his youth—now he was going as a team player-leader. The car that he designed then, the Chevrolet Sprint, and now the Geo Metro, got better gas mileage than any car on the road for many years. After 35 years of service to G.M., Lloyd retired and started his own engineering consulting firm, Nedley Associates.

During his "retirement" years, Lloyd served as architect and builder of two homes in Tennessee: one for his daughter Janice Crawford's family, and the other in Gallatin, Tennessee, which became a "dream home" for he and Orvetta. There are many unique features in these homes that would soon become "the standard" if they were advertised.

Lloyd also served on the board of directors of a private Christian high school (Ouachita Hills Academy) that trains students in high academic standards, uplifting spiritual music, and soul winning through the study of the Bible.

He translated scientific and health information into an enjoyable and easily understood illustrative format. Lloyd edited two sizeable books authored by his son, Dr. Neil Nedley: Proof Positive, which has become a world-wide bestseller, and *Depression: the Way Out*. He was at the large printing house in Massachusetts as printing began for Depression on September 10, 2001. Under Lloyd's cheering and encouragement, the weary and short-handed staff continued to work through the night and finished the task at 8 a.m. on September 11. Because of what happened at 9 a.m. he had to drive the many miles back to Nashville rather than fly, but the printing of the book was just in time to help the grieving in New York City and the rest of the country. *Depression: the Way Out* was used during the first public "Grief and Depression Recovery Seminar" to be held in NYC after the 9-11 attack.

Lloyd's life was one of compassion; he always thought of others before himself. If there was anything he could do to help others experience less pain, he would do it—with no thought of himself. Lloyd always gave others the benefit of the doubt and frequently complimented others in a genuine manner. Those who disagreed with him philosophically found him very enjoyable to be around. Even those who thought they were his enemies became his friends.

His enjoyment of the simple pleasures in life was a sight to behold and one that was often commented on by others. Bringing produce in from the garden would produce a smile and glee like a kid with a brand new toy. He would often exclaim, while viewing nature or eating tasty, natural food, "Isn't it great to be alive!" And he truly meant it.

Lloyd was a man who always followed his convictions, even when that meant personal inconvenience, hardship, or the sacrifice of pleasure. He has been missed in many ways since his passing, but perhaps in no greater way than his sound counsel and advice. He could reason through the most complex situation or problem in a completely objective and logical manner. He would look at all the evidence and come out on the side of right. In a way, we were spoiled, since truth and love were always so accessible. Though he unfortunately was not here to edit "The Lost Art of Thinking," (thus significantly delaying the release of the book) the principles of honesty, self-sacrificing love, and clear thinking that undergird this book would be no stranger to Lloyd, for they were the principles he so often demonstrated in his life.

# Index

**C**

H

## P



## Q

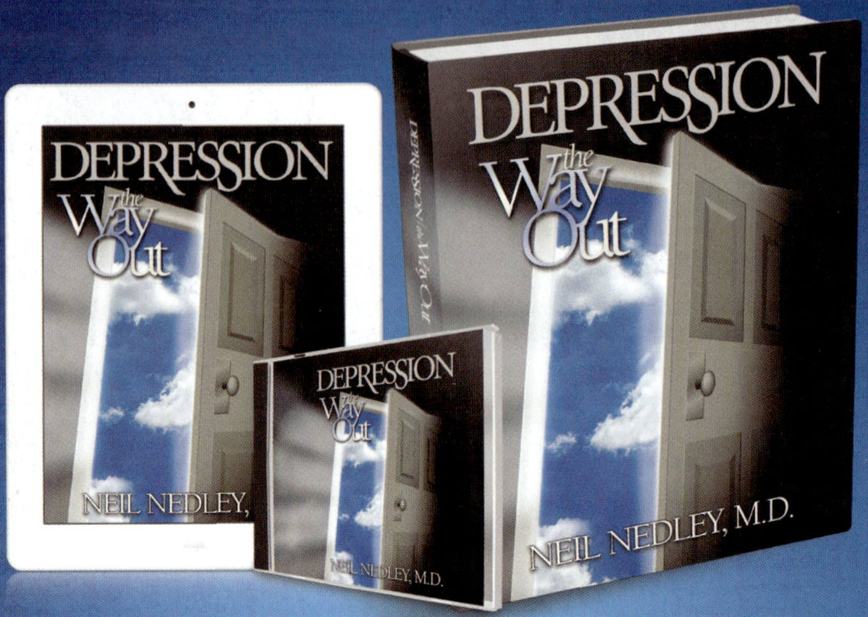


In this comprehensive book on depression, learn the signs, symptoms and lasting treatments for depression recovery. Dr. Nedley's scientific approach unveils the important role that nutrition and lifestyle play avoiding and treating depression and anxiety. *Depression the Way Out* can help you or loved one find the road to complete renewal and wellness.

Join Dr. Nedley in this eight-part series recorded in front of a live audience. Hear from people who have suffered and reclaimed their lives as they tell which aspects benefited them most.

Learn all the keys of his 20-week turnaround as you walk step-by-step through this comprehensive program.

A nine-part DVD series that reveals the keys to achieving peace of mind and restoring energy, joy and satisfaction to your life.